# Ideas and Economic Crises in Britain from Attlee to Blair (1945–2005)

T0330568

Faced with a crisis, a politician will either turn to established rules of the game for direction or engage in radical reform. In economic policymaking, this choice between continuity and change is fundamental, and yet also highly uncertain. This book argues that to understand continuity and change in economic policymaking, we need to analyze both the impact and – crucially – the narration of economic crises in the shaping of a government's economic policy.

During the period from 1945 to 2005, Britain underwent two deep-seated institutional transformations when political elites successfully challenged the prevailing wisdom on how to govern the economy. Attlee and Thatcher were able to effectively implement most of their political platforms. During this period there were also two opportunities to challenge existing institutional arrangements. Heath's "U-turn" in 1972 signaled his failure to implement the radical agenda promised upon election in 1970, whilst Tony Blair's New Labour similarly failed to instigate a major break with the "Thatcherite" settlement.

Rather than simply retell the story of British economic policymaking since World War II, this book offers a theoretically informed version of events, which draws upon the literatures on institutional path dependence, economic constructivism and political economy to explain this puzzle. The book is able to unite "long-durée" path dependent accounts of political stasis with "critical juncture" path-shaping moments of political change in one single theoretical framework. It will be of great interest to both researchers and postgraduates with an interest in British economic history and the fields of political economy and economic crisis more widely.

**Matthias Matthijs** is Assistant Professor of International Politics at the School of International Service at the American University in Washington.

# Routledge explorations in economic history
Edited by Lars Magnusson
*Uppsala University, Sweden*

# Ideas and Economic Crises in Britain from Attlee to Blair (1945–2005)

Matthias Matthijs

Routledge
Taylor & Francis Group

LONDON AND NEW YORK

First published 2011
by Routledge
2 Park Square, Milton Park, Abingdon, Oxon OX14 4RN

Simultaneously published in the USA and Canada
by Routledge
711 Third Avenue, New York, NY 10017

*Routledge is an imprint of the Taylor & Francis Group, an informa business*

First issued in paperback 2012

© 2011 Matthias Matthijs

Typeset in Times New Roman by Wearset Ltd, Boldon, Tyne and Wear

*British Library Cataloguing in Publication Data*
A catalogue record for this book is available from the British Library

*Library of Congress Cataloging in Publication Data*
A catalog record for this book has been requested

ISBN: 978-0-415-57944-5 (hbk)
ISBN: 978-0-203-84274-4 (ebk)
ISBN: 978-0-415-53343-0 (pbk)

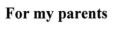

# Contents

# Illustrations

## Figures

## Tables

# Acknowledgments

This book took much longer to finish than I originally expected in 2008. Since it is adapted from my doctoral dissertation, the genesis of the main argument harks back to 2004 in Washington, DC. Consequently many people were involved in the writing process, and there are many that I would like to mention here. First and foremost, I want to thank my PhD advisor at Johns Hopkins University's School of Advanced International Studies (SAIS), David Calleo, for teaching me his interdisciplinary approach to the study of Europe – combining history, economic theory, politics, philosophy, and the history of economic ideas. He encouraged me to go to Britain and spend enough time there to get a real feel for the history and politics of the country, and the book gained tremendously from my stay in London during the autumn of 2006. Professor Calleo has always shown particular interest in my research, and I can only hope that he finds the end result measuring up to his standards.

Mark Blyth at Brown University no doubt deserves a paragraph of his own. He helped to refine the thesis, suggested the expansion of the historical case studies from two to four, and overall made the whole argument much stronger. He read all the chapters very critically and usually got back to me within a couple of weeks' time with multiple pages of detailed comments. He always pushed me to improve my writing and the book greatly benefited from his constant encouragement. He has been involved in this project from the very beginning until the very end and it would be an understatement to say that it has been an immense pleasure to work with him. I simply cannot thank him enough. It is true when I say that I stand on the shoulders of an intellectual giant.

I would also like to thank my three other doctoral dissertation committee members. Erik Jones at SAIS' Bologna Center in Italy was instrumental in the early stages of formulating the original thesis and developing the prospectus in 2005. Kendall Myers' knowledge of Britain is endless and what he taught me about British history and politics greatly informed and enriched the dissertation. He has been very generous with his time by reading drafts of all the chapters. Finally, Kathleen McNamara at Georgetown was so kind to agree to serve as my outside examiner. She carefully read the first full draft in 2007, and her comments were invaluable in making the theoretical framework stronger and more fully positioned within the existing ideas literature.

A couple of other academics also deserve a special mention since they all showed interest in the dissertation and taught me a lot about Britain and political economy. First, I want to thank Robert Skidelsky for reading the Thatcher and Blair chapters very closely and sharing his knowledge on the topic with me during his stay in Washington in the spring of 2007. Second, many academics in England have given me comments on written chapters and have answered specific questions. All were very helpful in refining many of the arguments, especially Colin Hay, Andrew Gamble, Helen Thompson, Richard Heffernan, Peter Hennessy, Mark Wickham-Jones, Fiona Ross, and Hugh Pemberton.

I also have to thank all the people that agreed to be interviewed during the autumn of 2006, especially the former Chancellors of the Exchequer of the United Kingdom: Denis Healey, Geoffrey Howe, Nigel Lawson, Norman Lamont, and Kenneth Clarke. Others, whose insights were particularly useful for this study include Tony Benn, Samuel Brittan, Terence Burns, John Eatwell, Eddie George, Anthony Giddens, Ralph Harris, Michael Heseltine, Jeremy Heywood, Eric Hobsbawm, Will Hutton, Neil Kinnock, Robin Leigh-Pemberton, Anatol Lieven, Cecil Parkinson, Peter Riddell, Anthony Seldon, Dennis Skinner, Andrew Smith, Norman Tebbit, and Geoffrey Wheatcroft.

Furthermore, I want to thank many friends and colleagues in Washington and Bologna for the many long and lively discussions that helped me structure my thoughts and make my arguments much stronger. In no particular order, I want to thank Timo Behr, Frederick Hood, Gabriel Goodliffe, Andy Wolff, Marco Cesa, Tom Row, Stephen Szabo, Dorothee Heisenberg, Adrian Lyttelton, Charles Gati, Pravin Krishna, Riordan Roett, Wendy Takacs, Bruce Parrott, Pablo Pardo, David Ellwood, Scott Featherston, David Beffert, Arturo Porzecanski, Randall Henning, Michelle Egan, Steve Silvia, Tamar Gutner, Mack Moore, Kevin Croke, Joost Gorter, Jim Gale, Domenec Rumenec-Devesa, Gregg Johnson, and Roman Didenko. Saverio Grazioli-Venier and Caitlin Hughes deserve a special mention for their generosity and hospitality while letting me stay in their beautiful apartment in Primrose Hill in London during my research visit to England in the autumn of 2006.

SAIS and American University's School of International Service (SIS) have been my institutional homes during the writing process, and I want to thank the deans Jessica Einhorn and Louis Goodman as well as academic deans John Harrington and Maria Green Cowles at both institutions for all their support. Also, I want to thank those schools' exceptional graduate students for their constant stimulus in the classroom. The book manuscript further benefited from the outstanding research assistance I received from my graduate research assistants, both at SAIS and SIS, over the past two years. I would like to thank Jessica Stahl, Natalie Weinstein, Neil Shenai, and in particular Lara Loewenstein for all their hard work and dedication.

I want to specially thank Alysson Oakley, who proved to be an indefatigable and immaculate editor. She read the manuscript closely and with a critical eye while working full-time in Jakarta, Indonesia. She suggested numerous ways to better formulate my thoughts and, without any doubt, the book is much better thanks to her. Finally, I would like to thank Tom Sutton and Simon Holt, my editors at Routledge, for their advice and for ably steering the manuscript through the publication process. Of course, the usual disclaimer applies: all errors and omissions remain solely my own.

Last but not least, I want to thank my family, and my parents, Erik and Eliane, in particular. I think they are as happy as I am to see the book in print. I owe them a huge intellectual debt and this book is dedicated to them.

Bologna, Italy
March 2010

# 1 Continuity and change in British economic policymaking

Let's go forward into this fight in the spirit of William Blake: "I will not cease from mental fight, nor shall the sword sleep in my hand, until we have built Jerusalem in England's green and pleasant land."

Clement Attlee (1951)[1]

We will have to embark on a change so radical, a revolution so quiet and yet so total that it will go far beyond the programme for one parliament, far beyond the decade, and way into the 1980s.

Edward Heath (1970)[2]

I prefer to believe that certain lessons have been learnt from experience, that we are coming, slowly, painfully, to an autumn of understanding. And I hope that it will be followed by a winter of common sense. If it is not, we shall not be diverted from our course. To those waiting with bated breath for that favourite media catchphrase, the "U" turn, I have only one thing to say: "You turn if you want to. The lady's not for turning."

Margaret Thatcher (1980)[3]

You create a settlement that your political opponents have to come to an accommodation with, and at the moment the Conservative Party is not in that position. What we want to create is a situation where the great postwar settlement for welfare, for public services, for the type of country we are, is renewed and modernized thoroughly for today's world.

Tony Blair (2005)[4]

## Introduction

Faced with a crisis, a politician will either turn to established rules of the game for direction or engage in radical reform. When it comes to economic policymaking this choice between continuity and change is fundamental, and yet fundamentally uncertain. While continuity entails using longstanding mechanisms such as existing institutions, ideas, and routines to address current economic problems, change introduces innovative ideas that establish new norms of economic policymaking that subsequent governments are compelled to follow. This book examines continuity and change when the fundamentals of policymaking, and indeed policy purpose, are uncertain. It argues that to understand continuity and change in economic policymaking, we need to analyze both the impact and – crucially – the narration of economic crises in the shaping of a government's economic policy. As we shall see, in some cases, how the fact is explained is more important than the objective fact itself.

One salient example of the importance of crisis narration occurred in the late 1990s in Great Britain. After almost two decades in opposition, Tony Blair and Gordon Brown resurrected the Labour Party in May 1997 through a decisive election victory that swept them to political power and banished the Conservative Party to the opposition benches for years to come. Blair would go on to lead his party twice more to electoral success in 2001 and 2005, each time with comfortable majorities, giving substance to New Labour's claim to have replaced the Conservatives as the "natural party of government."[5] In an attempt to counter prevailing disillusionment with statist social democracy and unfettered market capitalism, Blair's so-called "Third Way" promised to achieve the traditional social democratic objectives of social justice and national solidarity, while concurrently ensuring high economic efficiency and market flexibility.[6]

This strong mandate should have given Blair, Brown and New Labour the capacity to accomplish the radical reform of government institutions necessary to fulfill such an ambitious vision. However, while their policy platform had intellectual underpinnings in Third Way thinking,[7] after more than ten years in power, the New Labour governments could not claim to have lived up to their promise to create a "New Britain."[8] Blair's version of the Third Way established no new norms of economic policymaking that broke with the neoliberal consensus policies of the mid-1990s. Instead, New Labour's economic policy built directly on the legacies of Conservatives Margaret Thatcher and John Major, whose policies Blair's party should have reformed were they to accomplish the social democratic objectives of the Third Way. As this book will argue, Blair did not successfully construct or narrate a crisis that would have given him the political capital to implement more radical reforms.

As a result, while some reforms in health care, education, and social welfare were instituted, Blair and Brown did not change the overall terms of the economic debate, let alone reach a new settlement for Britain.[9] The general feeling that Blair's governments wasted opportunities for reform endures, especially amongst the Labour Party faithful, as does the belief that Blair was not radical enough in the pursuit of his public services agenda, opting for continuity rather than change from the Conservatives' policies of the 1980s and 1990s.[10]

Blair was unable to institute more radical reform in the late 1990s despite the fact that, in many ways, New Labour had a unique opportunity to correct some of Britain's long-standing economic problems. Politically, Blair was in a strong position to take decisive action. First, New Labour enjoyed a formidable popular mandate that was backed by a large majority in the House of Commons.[11] Second, Britain had, and still has, one of the most centralized political systems in Western Europe, with the prime minister possessing comparatively far-reaching powers. Last, after 18 years of often divisive Tory rule – especially given the corruption, infighting and so-called "sleaze" of the final years of the Major government – the general mood of the British electorate was adamant: it was high time for a change.[12] In addition, there were serious economic problems under Thatcher and Major that had become part of the prevailing British economic landscape: the miserable state of public services, the untenable short-term housing and consumer booms, and the chronic underinvestment in the real economy. The recession of 1990–1992 was the most prolonged since the Great Depression, and had revealed deep, structural problems, most of which persisted under Major's government in the mid-1990s. For these reasons, Blair and Brown had the potential as well as the political strength to make radical reforms. Once in power, they opted nevertheless to continue the policies of their Conservative predecessors. Even more surprising, they ended up formally institutionalizing some of those policies in Britain's economic paradigm.

Why did Blair turn to already-established mechanisms, rather than to reforming existing economic policies and institutions? Ironically, Blair has often compared his New Labour governments with Britain's two reforming center-left administrations of the twentieth century – the Liberal governments of 1905–1915 and the Labour governments of 1945–1951 – and also with the drive, impact and determination of the Conservative governments of 1979–1990.[13] Those three governments, of Herbert Asquith, Clement Attlee, and Margaret Thatcher respectively, all had one thing in common: they challenged the received economic wisdom of the time and created a new economic settlement by redefining the role of the state in the British economy. All three also changed the consensus of what the main goals of economic policy ought to be.

Asquith, inspired by the economic ideas of Alfred Marshall and Arthur Pigou, was the first prime minister to accept state responsibility for assisting the poor through redistributive taxation, contrary to prevailing economic theory at the time. His Liberal governments enacted policies such as old age pensions, a national insurance scheme for the sick, disabled and unemployed, and a (modest) minimum wage for certain industries.[14] Attlee, following the wartime proposals of John Maynard Keynes and William Beveridge, introduced full employment as the main goal of economic policy and made the welfare state universal. Through a program of nationalization of the "commanding heights" of the economy, the creation of a National Health Service and eventually through Keynesian macroeconomic demand management,[15] he fundamentally shifted the boundaries between the public and private sectors and the consensus on how to run a modern economy.[16] Thatcher was influenced by the ideas of Friedrich von Hayek and Milton Friedman, and changed the terms of the political debate in the late 1970s and early 1980s, often by dogmatically following monetarist macroeconomic policy prescriptions in the pursuit of price stability, significantly reducing the relative power of the trade unions in the decision making process, instituting a process of far-reaching deregulation and liberalization, and all but reversing the nationalizations performed under the Attlee governments.[17]

The New Labour legacy cannot be favorably compared to any of those three innovating twentieth century governments Blair himself professed to admire and emulate. In some respects, Tory leader Edward Heath offers a closer analogy to Blair than either Attlee or Thatcher. Just as Blair could have challenged the Thatcherite consensus in Britain in the late 1990s, Heath could have changed the existing postwar settlement when he came to power in 1970. In 1965, Heath had been elected the youngest leader of the Conservative Party, defying the odds against the party favorite Reginald Maudling, and went on to win a surprising general election victory five years later. In an effort to address postwar Britain's relative economic decline, Heath had campaigned on a platform that embraced fairly radical monetarist and free market policies.[18] As prime minister, Heath initially steered his government on a – for the time – rather radical free market path, but reversed course after less than two years in the face of a national miners' strike and unemployment nearing the psychologically important one million mark. In 1972, in order to revive the British economy, Heath retreated to the familiar Keynesian policies of old. Many of Thatcher's later supporters, not least Thatcher herself, would never forgive him for this U-turn, blaming Heath personally for wasting four valuable Conservative years in power due to a lack of courage and conviction.[19]

Why were Attlee and Thatcher capable of translating many of their ideas and electoral promises into lasting government policies? And why did Heath and Blair merely consolidate and prolong existing institutional arrangements?

Where did Thatcher and Attlee succeed; and where did Blair and Heath fail?

## Ideas and crises in postwar British economic policymaking

The purpose of this book is to outline theoretically informed answers as to why Attlee and Thatcher, once elected, proved to be so successful at drawing up new institutional "rules of the game" that subsequent governments felt so compelled to follow when concerned with the proper conduct of economic policy. In so doing, this book also explains why Heath and Blair avoided or failed to achieve more radical change even though they had the opportunity to do so at the time they came to power.

Of particular interest to political scientists are broader questions about the causes of continuity and change in a country's political economy. In this regard, this book addresses the following: are there certain structural factors that create the conditions for radical reform of government institutions? How do new ideas rise to political prominence? When do ideas matter in explaining economic policy change, as opposed to mere political expediency? How do ideas become embedded in organizations and patterns of discourse? When existing institutions lose their legitimacy during periods of crisis, what factors determine the future path of institutional development? And, which factors explain the often long periods of institutional stability over time?

To focus on those particular moments in time when radical change is more likely to occur, and the conditions under which institutional transformations become most likely, it is necessary to reexamine the concept of economic "crisis." The key argument of this book is that, in order to understand continuity and change in economic policymaking, we need to comprehend and clearly define the impact of economic crises in shaping a government's economic policy.[20] When moments of financial turmoil or severe economic downturns are perceived both by the political establishment and the general electorate as a real "crisis," new ideas will suddenly matter since they give a clear, though often simplified, explanation of "what went wrong, and how to fix it."[21] Perception is critical.

This book argues that a crisis is not a self-evident state of affairs, but a perception – shared by elites – of a situation that requires action and needs to be explained in a convincing narrative to the public at large.[22] During a crisis, ideas function as a roadmap for any emerging institutional structure. If there is, on the other hand, no real perception of crisis, because of a lack of a convincing crisis narrative, then there is limited incentive to radically change the state's institutional setup. As a result, at most there will be incremental change. In the latter case, new ideas only play a marginal role and are only implemented insofar as they fit within the existing institutional framework. This leads to future institutional development that is largely path dependent with the old ideas.[23] Instead of changing the status quo, these marginal changes in fact end up strengthening existing institutions by correcting their minor weaknesses. This makes future radical reform all the more difficult.[24]

Great Britain provides an able case for the examination of ideas, crises, and economic policymaking. The state of the economy has preoccupied and constrained the British political class with a regularity and potency unmatched by any other issue throughout the entire postwar period.[25] That there has been quite significant social and political change in postwar Britain is merely stating the obvious. Yet whether such change is interpreted primarily in terms of continuity or discontinuity is dependent upon the context and timeframe under which that change is assessed.[26] This book emphasizes the discontinuities in British economic policy over time, treating 1945, 1970, 1979 and 1997 in particular, as key moments of *potential* policy realignment. Each date marks the point at which a new generation of politicians took office by challenging the dominant understanding of how best to revive the British economy's flagging fortunes. During all four of these moments, strong and, maybe with the exception of Attlee, very charismatic opposition leaders were in a position to provide a credible alternative on how to run the economy.[27] These governments are those of Attlee (1945–1951), Heath (1970–1974), Thatcher (1979–1990) and Blair (1997–2005).

In order to gain a better understanding of the decisions made by these four governments, we avoid a pure agency-based approach, and also take into account the many structural and institutional constraints of the British economy, the international economic pressures from an integrating Europe and "globalization" in general, as well as the ideas that have informed policymakers' decisions over the postwar years. The analysis that follows is anchored by a strong historical institutionalist perspective and works within a theoretical framework that combines the study of ideas with the study of existing institutions.

Of course, across those four governments there were powerful strands of policy continuity that we cannot disregard so easily.[28] It would therefore be wrong to adopt an overly static "punctuated equilibrium" framework of "institutional equilibrium → punctuation → new institutional equilibrium," where stable periods of policymaking characterized by hardly any change are the norm and are only occasionally interrupted by periods of crisis, which then in turn lead to a new "normal" period.[29] Rather, this book favors a "punctuated evolution" model, which builds on the concept of "evolutionary change" with certain "critical junctures" showing much more rapid institutional change than others.[30] Change is episodic and marked by brief periods of crisis or critical intervention (or non-intervention) followed by longer periods of relative stability and path dependent evolutionary change.[31]

Not only is Britain a theoretically compelling case study for the reasons mentioned above, Britain is also a particularly interesting case study. As the world's first industrial nation, it has perhaps more to teach us about economic policy than any other country. Britain is also the only country in Western Europe that underwent a radical and full-blown neoliberal experiment. Ever since Adam Smith laid the foundation for modern economics in the late eighteenth century, Britain has been the home to a myriad of some of the world's most influential economic thinkers.[32] New economic ideas in Britain were never lacking; what changed was the political will and political opportunity.

One of the important themes in recent research in comparative political economy is the idea of "varieties of capitalism." Despite growing trade and capital flows and increasing economic interdependence between countries, which presumably generates significant pressures towards convergence in economic policies, the advanced industrial societies continue to exhibit fundamental differences in their core institutional structures. In this scholarly tradition, Germany is identified as a coordinated market economy (CME), while Britain together with the United States is a good example of a liberal market economy (LME).[33] To date, as Paul Pierson has rightly observed, "this literature has done a better job of identifying and describing this diversity than it has of explaining what generates and sustains it."[34] In order to understand the differences in institutional infrastructure between the advanced industrial countries, a more historical institutionalist perspective that takes into account the role of competing ideas during periods of crises would help fill that gap.

In short, this book aims to make both a theoretical and an empirical contribution to the existing academic literature. It will amount to an original and useful addition to the ongoing debate on path dependency theory, still largely underdeveloped theories about crises, and strengthen the existing constructivist scholarship that is mainly concerned with the role of economic ideas. Postwar Britain provides a most suitable case study to juxtapose these historical and ideational research traditions, although it is clear from my synthesis in the next chapter that they are not to be seen as mutually exclusive, but as broadly complementary and reciprocally enriching. The empirical contribution will come from the analysis of the economic records of the Attlee, Heath, Thatcher, and Blair governments.

The book will combine empirical economic data with critical political analysis, putting the Attlee, Heath, Thatcher, and Blair years in their national party and historical economic contexts. It will show the key factors that allowed Attlee and Thatcher to emerge as the "innovators" in postwar Britain, while Heath and Blair – without denying their substantial economic achievements[35] – will be remembered as the "consolidators," forced to work within the broad economic settlements forged by their respective predecessors.[36]

## Methodology

The theoretical synthesis proposes six hypotheses. These hypotheses consist of inductively derived analytic propositions that explain the four qualitative case studies. Social scientists have long considered case studies the weakest of all research methods for two basic reasons.[37] First, some argue that case studies provide the least opportunity to control for the effect of perturbing third variables. Second, it is often asserted that case study results can rarely be generalized or applied to other cases.[38]

These criticisms are unfair. As to the first criticism, the fact that all four cases are in the same country presents us with fairly uniform conditions, and all cases allow for a number of general observations about the independent variables (ideas, existing institutions, and economic downturns or shocks) and dependent variables (the overall institutional framework). The second criticism can only really apply to single-case studies. According to Stephen Van Evera, the case method has two significant strengths. First, tests performed with case studies are often strong, given that the predictions tested are quite unique and not made by other known theories. Second, the case study method allows us to "process trace," or examine the "process whereby initial case conditions are translated into case outcomes."[39] According to Sheri Berman, process tracing is most suited for ideational analyses: it allows us to gain significant insights into economic decision making since it involves the reconstruction of actors' motivations as well as their definitions and evaluations of particular situations.[40]

The specific case study method that I apply in this book is that of "qualitative structured and focused comparison." According to George and Bennett, the method is "structured" in that the researcher writes general questions that reflect the research objective. These questions are asked of each case under study to guide and standardize data collection, which then makes systematic comparison and accumulation of the findings of the cases possible. The method is "focused" in that it deals only with certain aspects of the historical cases that are examined.[41] I will focus purely on the continuities and changes in economic policymaking in Britain. Furthermore, I have opted for a largely qualitative approach – although I make extensive use of descriptive economic statistics – instead of a quantitative approach, given that I am mostly dealing with the role played by economic ideas and the largely subjective perceptions as well as narratives of economic crises, which are by their nature very difficult to quantify. For obvious reasons, it is not because one cannot quantify certain social phenomena that they did not actually happen. Also, a quantitative time series approach treats all points in time in the same manner, disregarding the fact that in the social world, certain points are much more important than others. This is especially true for critical junctures: these are moments that have a multitude of information, without which the researcher would find it impossible to explain the points that follow.[42]

The selection of the four cases (Attlee, Heath, Thatcher and Blair) follows a combination of John Stuart Mill's "method of difference" and "method of agreement."[43] In the method of difference, the researcher chooses cases with similar general characteristics and different values on the variable whose causes he seeks to establish; in our case, institutional continuity or change. In the method of agreement, the researcher chooses cases with different general characteristics and similar values on the study variable.[44]

In doing the four historical case studies, there are inherent dangers in attaching particular significance to an item that supports the researcher's "preexisting or favored interpretation." This usually results in downplaying the significance of items that would challenge the researcher's prejudices. George and Bennett point out that cognitive dissonance theory teaches us that "most people operate with a double standard in weighing evidence." Indeed, we more readily accept new information that is consistent with our existing mindset just like we tend to employ higher thresholds for giving serious consideration to information challenging our existing preferences.[45] It is thus useful to remind ourselves that "all good historians are revisionist historians," and that we must be prepared to revise all existing interpretations when new compelling evidence emerges. Obviously, new information about a case must be properly evaluated, and requires academic distance, especially when the subject matter is highly politicized, as is certainly the case for this book.[46]

Apart from a large volume of secondary literature, a significant amount of primary sources were consulted such as official government documents, official political party documents, election manifestos, transcripts of conferences, declassified closed door cabinet and shadow cabinet meetings, main actors' political diaries, and autobiographies. Furthermore, close to 40 "elite" interviews were conducted in London with leading politicians and civil servants from the Prime Minister's Office, HM Treasury, the Bank of England, as well as some of the leading analysts in the various economic think tanks and British academics who have studied the subject for over 40 years.[47] The methodological problems in empirical research that select the individual as the unit of analysis in an attempt to understand the workings of a larger political system will be addressed by focusing on the links between individual members of the bureaucracy and their influences on the economic policy structure.[48]

## Organization of the book

This book continues in Chapter 2 with a more detailed explanation of a new theoretical framework characterized by "punctuated evolution," which explains the importance of crisis opportunities to the reform of economic institutions and the central significance of crisis narration therein. Chapter 2 also reviews relevant literature, and discusses how this thesis juxtaposes two important schools of thought, the institutionalist and the ideational, filling a gap in, and adding to, their line of thinking. The chapter concludes with an overview of the evolution of postwar Britain's political economy which provides the historical, political and economic background to the case studies of the book.

The next four chapters comprise case studies that utilize the new theoretical model to explain continuity and change through a look at the impact of economic crises and crisis narration on economic policymaking.

Chapter 3 looks at the years of postwar consensus (1945–1970). It studies the conditions under which Clement Attlee's Labour came to power after the 1945 general election, the subsequent creation of the universal welfare state, and the adoption of a Keynesian macroeconomic policy with full employment as its overarching goal. Chapter 3 pays special attention to the inherent virtues of the postwar settlement, which prompted an "age of affluence" in the 1950s and 1960s.

Chapter 4 looks at the economic faults of the postwar consensus (1959–1979), focusing on the political elite's fixation on Britain's "relative decline" and the various attempts in the 1960s to reverse it. In this chapter, we will focus on the conditions under which Edward Heath came to power in 1970, examine the logic of his economic ideas and political platform, and assess why he was forced to make a U-turn in 1972, to eventually lose the general election of 1974 by failing to convince the electorate of the need for a decisive economic intervention.

Chapter 5 examines the birth of Thatcherism out of the crises of the 1970s, the unraveling of Attlee's postwar consensus, Thatcher's triumphant overhaul of the leading policies and institutions of that postwar consensus, her establishment of new neoliberal economic institutions, and the strengths of her new settlement (1975–1990).

Chapter 6 studies the flaws of the Thatcherite settlement, the significance of Labour's loss in the 1992 election, the creation of and ideas behind New Labour, and Blair and Brown's missed opportunity to break with the economic policies of their Tory predecessors, as well as their eventual consolidation of Thatcher's legacy (1987–2005).

Chapter 7 offers the conclusion of the book and suggests avenues for future research. Finally, in the postscript, I reflect on the significance of the global financial crisis that started in September 2008, the future of neoliberal economic ideas, and the applicability of my punctuated evolution model to Britain's general election of 2010.

# 2 Crisis, ideas, and path dependence

## Theoretical framework and postwar Britain's changing political economy

There is enormous inertia, a tyranny of the status quo, in private and especially governmental arrangements. Only a crisis – actual or perceived – produces real change. When that crisis occurs, the actions that are taken depend on the ideas that are lying around. That, I believe, is our basic function: to develop alternatives to existing policies, to keep them alive and available until the politically impossible becomes politically inevitable.

Milton Friedman, *Capitalism and Freedom* (1962)[1]

Contemporary state regimes are not inherently disposed to spontaneous or unconstrained structural transformation. Their evolution as complex systems thus tends to be both path-dependent and conditional upon path-shaping moments of perceived crisis. [...] Thus, state institutions do not respond directly to systematic contradictions, but rather to the constructions and narratives placed upon such contradictions.

Colin Hay, "Crisis and the Structural Transformation of the State" (1999)[2]

Economic ideas provide agents with both a "scientific" and a "normative" account of the existing economy and polity, and a vision that specifies how these elements should be constructed. [...] Ideas allow agents to reduce uncertainty, propose a particular solution to a moment of crisis, and empower agents to resolve that crisis by constructing new institutions in line with these new ideas.

Mark Blyth, *Great Transformations* (2002)[3]

Once established, patterns of political mobilization, the institutional "rules of the game," and even citizens' basic ways of thinking about the political world will often generate self-reinforcing dynamics. Once actors have ventured far down a particular path, they may find it very difficult to reverse course. Political alternatives that were once quite plausible may become irretrievably lost.

Paul Pierson, *Politics in Time* (2004)[4]

## Introduction

Much has been written about ideas, institutions, and postwar British economic policymaking. Nevertheless, as we will see, current literature – both theoretical and historical – has not entirely reconciled major debates and important points of contention, which have dogged successive attempts to provide a comprehensive framework that brings theory and history together to explain continuity and change in Britain's postwar economic policy.[5]

This chapter begins with a review of existing historical analysis of postwar Britain, and explains how a different approach is useful. We proceed with existing, or "standard" political science explanations for institutional continuity and change. We then delve into the theoretical underpinnings of a new model described as "punctuated evolution" that considers ideas, crises, and institutions together to explain both continuity and change in economic policymaking. This leads us to our synthesis which puts forward six inductively derived analytic propositions that inform our four case studies. Finally, the chapter explains why Britain, in many ways, is an ideal case study.

## Postwar British economic policymaking: a new approach

The legacies of Clement Attlee, Edward Heath, Margaret Thatcher and Tony Blair have been widely debated and are probably among the most studied topics in British politics. Not only is there a vast academic literature, there are also numerous accounts by politicians and civil servants who were directly involved in the decision making process over the years. Furthermore, the story has been told over and over by many British journalists and pundits on both sides of the political spectrum.

Nevertheless, there are many remaining debates and points of contention in the literature. First, there are ongoing disagreements about the political significance of the power transfers in Britain from Labour to the Conservatives and back, especially in the area of economic policymaking. On the one hand, there are scholars who underline the areas of cross-party agreement and broad policy continuity (e.g. Peter Kerr, David Marsh, Paul Addison, Ben Pimlott and Paul Pierson). On the other hand, there are those who emphasize the path-breaking decisions and innovating policies of the different incoming governments (e.g. Dennis Kavanagh, Colin Hay, Andrew Gamble, and Peter Hennessy).

Of particular interest for this book are the transfers of power in Britain in 1945 (from Churchill to Attlee), 1970 (from Wilson to Heath), 1979 (from Callaghan to Thatcher) and 1997 (from Major to Blair). These transfers of power are still not fully understood and will receive detailed attention in the case studies. For example, regarding the first transfer of power there is still debate concerning the radicalism of the Attlee government. Paul Addison claims that the postwar consensus was forged during the shared experience of total war, especially during the severe German bombings of the Battle of Britain, and sees broad continuity with regards to economic policy between the Attlee government and the wartime coalition government led by Winston Churchill.[6] Peter Hennessy, however, rightly argues that "it [would be] misleading to suggest that Labour's social programme after 1945 was merely a continuation of coalition policies with a red tinge." Hennessy stresses Attlee's audacity in almost fully implementing Labour's 1945 manifesto *Let Us Face the Future*, especially given the severe financial constraints after the abrupt ending of Lend-Lease and the persistent sterling and balance of payments crises occurring at the time.[7] This book will further strengthen Hennessy's argument by emphasizing the often severe differences between the views of Attlee and Churchill concerning the need for economic planning, the extent of nationalization, the universalism of the welfare state, and the role of the government in managing a modern economy.

The second area of debate in the literature of modern British politics is the existence of what has come to be known as the "postwar consensus" – defined by Colin Hay as a "shared belief in continuity, stability and the replication of long-enduring [British] traditions."[8] Scholars who believe that consensus existed contend that after 1945 both the Labour and the Conservative Parties accepted as given a set of policies that encompassed full employment, the relative power of the trade unions, public ownership of basic and monopoly utilities and indus-tries, state provision of social welfare, and an active role for government in steer-ing the economy towards those goals.[9] Other scholars question whether there was any consensus at all, suggesting that this was merely a "mirage" and largely "the product of retrospective wisdom."[10] Still others suggest that the theory of the postwar consensus relies too much upon a static and oversimplified account of political change and fails to address the complex and multilayered factors which continually converge to generate that change.[11]

This book concurs there was indeed a broad bipartisan agreement on the postwar "settlement" from the early 1950s onwards and shows how successive Labour and Conservative governments reinforced the institutional mechanisms set in motion by the Attlee government. However, "consensus" is perhaps a mis-leading term. Postwar economic history shows that there were many disagree-ments about which *tools* to use to achieve certain economic outcomes both within the major political parties and between them. Our analysis nevertheless will show that there was an unusual degree of agreement on the main *goals* of economic policy during this time, such as full employment as the economic basis for a universal welfare state, especially when compared to, for example, the 1920s, 1930s or 1970s, when the overall goals of economic policy were very much in contention.[12] We note, however, how governments from 1945 to 1970 had significant conflicts about various aspects of economic policy, even though the main goal of full employment was never in doubt.

The third important debate about postwar Britain focuses on the merits and legacy of the Heath government in the early 1970s. In their "reappraisal" of the Heath government, Stuart Ball and Anthony Seldon distinguish four rival inter-pretations.[13] First, the "Heath loyalist" view believes that the government was a success given that it implemented most of its electoral promises and showed flexibility in the face of grave economic problems. Second, the Thatcherite view sees Heath's government as an unqualified disappointment, as it abandoned its initial free market policies after the first minor economic crisis. Third, there is the pessimistic view, arguing that the government had some initial successes, but nothing of those successes lasted in the long run. Fourth, the contingencies view argues that Heath failed ultimately to fully achieve his objectives because of circumstances well beyond his control.[14]

The view I put forward in this book is probably a combination of the second and third interpretations as identified by Ball and Seldon. In my analysis of Heath's ideas and policies in the early 1970s, I do see a clear shift away from the consensus ideas of the postwar settlement towards a more openly free market approach – leaving aside the question whether Heath was a "true believer" or not. I also argue that his failure to convincingly narrate the crises of 1972 and 1973–1974 – clear moments when decisive interventions by his government were needed – meant that he had to abandon many of his earlier free market policies, and as a result he would ultimately lose power in the general election of February 1974.

The fourth area of disagreement in the literature is over the impact, radicalism, and legacy of the Thatcher governments of the 1980s. Building on the existence of a bipartisan postwar consensus, Kavanagh and Gamble see the advent of Thatcher as a radical rejection of the postwar consensus and as the birth of a new settlement, upon which New Labour would later build.[15] Thatcher's new governing philosophy, with its emphasis on strong but limited government, mass privatization, weak trade unions and a rule-based, monetarist macroeconomic policy, did challenge the prevailing wisdom on how to run the British economy.[16] On the other hand, many have questioned the extent of Thatcher's radicalism, instead emphasizing the areas of significant policy continuity, especially in welfare provision – an area which has proved remarkably resistant to far-reaching reform.[17] Others have cast doubt on many of the ambitious claims made about the Thatcher record, claiming that the Thatcherite revolution is more a product of rhetoric than of any tangible political reality.[18]

In this book, I argue that the Thatcher government did manage to forge a real paradigm shift in economic policy from 1979 onwards.[19] It is beyond doubt that there was a pragmatic shift towards monetarism in 1976 under Callaghan, *prima facie* changing the main priority of economic policymaking from full employment to low inflation. However, Nigel Lawson was correct to point out that this was merely "unbelieving monetarism."[20] After the IMF loan was approved and its basic conditions were met (colloquially referred to as "sod-off day"), Labour Chancellor Denis Healey went back to revive the British economy through Keynesian fiscal policy and another round of income policies.[21] The real paradigm shift would come in May 1979 when Thatcher seized on the so-called "Winter of Discontent" – a period marked by multiple public sector union strikes during the winter of 1978–1979, which seemingly brought the country to a standstill – as a theatrically illustrative example of all of Britain's economic problems.[22] The "British Disease" – as it was referred to in the 1970s – comprised several features including slow growth, fractious industrial relations, an inflexible labor market, and a highly defensive attitude towards change.[23] Thatcher was successful in recruiting enough adherents to her vision of the necessary response to the crisis of an overextended state. The initial victory of Thatcherism lay in the

Conservatives' ability to mould perceptions of the nature of the crisis of the 1970s, creating the dominant narrative of what needed to be done. In so doing, they imposed the rigorous free market remedies they thought were required on a reluctant British electorate.[24]

A fifth area of ongoing debate lies in the process of gradual modernization of the Labour Party that started in the mid-1980s under Neil Kinnock and the significance, once Blair was elected party leader, of the ideas of Anthony Giddens' *Third Way* and Will Hutton's *Stakeholder Society*. Most analysts see the Third Way as nothing more than a clever electoral strategy to move the Labour Party to the right or "center ground" of British politics, accepting the new realities of the Thatcherite settlement.[25] But to think of the Third Way simply as an electoral strategy would do it injustice, as it also tried to encompass a new type of politics and a new policy agenda.[26] The intellectual foundation of the Third Way was laid by Giddens, supported by thinkers such as Will Hutton, Geoff Mulgan and Charles Leadbeater, as well as the left-of-center think tank Institute for Public Policy Research (IPPR).[27]

Giddens tried to counter prevailing disillusionment with statist social democracy and free market neoliberalism. The Third Way, he argues, should be seen as a "renewal of social democracy," concerned with the revision and modernization of social democratic regimes to respond to the new challenges of globalization and the knowledge economy. Giddens insists that this is a genuine "third" way and not some compromise between Keynesian social democracy as practiced in Britain during the postwar consensus years and Hayekian free market neoliberalism as practiced during most of the 1980s and 1990s.[28] In this sense, Giddens argues, it is quite different from the course Harold Macmillan had suggested in the late 1930s when he wrote *The Middle Way*.[29] For Macmillan, the "middle way" was a compromise between Soviet communism and Western-style capitalism. By contrast, New Labour's approach would achieve the traditional social democratic objectives of social justice and solidarity while ensuring high economic efficiency and labor, capital, and product market flexibility.[30] Will Hutton, for his part, sees a distinction between successful and unsuccessful forms of capitalism, which for him revolve around the rate of investment.[31] For Hutton, investment is directly linked to the financial system, "which in Britain should be reformed in order to lower the cost of capital and lengthen the payback period required of investment projects."[32] Unfortunately, the Third Way never developed sufficiently tangible arguments to provide a comprehensive alternative theory of the economy like monetarism, active demand management, or industrial policy.[33]

In this book, I will argue that, in many ways, New Labour could have tackled the British economy's long-standing structural problems, not least in industry and manufacturing (or at least what remained of it), if it had had the intention and political will to do so. Giddens' and Hutton's main contributions to Third Way thinking, however, never made it into Labour's election manifesto. Reluctant to attack the Thatcherite settlement head on, both Blair and Brown significantly watered down Third Way ideas by trying to make them fit within the existing Conservative framework. New Labour's policies would stress the important continuities with Thatcher's economic approach, while only promoting some incremental changes within that approach.

A sixth and last issue of contention in the ongoing academic debate about Britain's political economy surrounds the role of ideology and ideas. Michael Freeden called ideology the "Stranger at the Feast" in his article for the inaugural issue of *Twentieth Century British History* in 1990.[34] Freeden argued that it was not uncommon to encounter skepticism among modern historians about the role of ideas and ideologies in British politics, and wrote that there is a clear need to distinguish between the traditional history of ideas and the study of the interrelationship between ideology and public policy. Freeden sees great difficulty in analyzing ideas, given that the "isms" (liberalism, conservatism, socialism) are constantly in flux, incapable of being reduced to a simple list of characteristics, while the question of formal doctrine evidence is often tenuous. Hence, he believes the reverse process, of working backwards from acts of public policy to ideological assumptions implicit in their formulation, may often be more promising.[35] The reason for that is obvious for Freeden: "the evidence for political thinking is unobservable and hence its reflection must be sought in acts – of expression, of writing, of doing."[36]

This book puts the question of ideas and ideology at the heart of the analysis of the evolution of economic policymaking. Building on the existing constructivist literature in political economy, I take ideas seriously by looking at the circumstances under which they are most likely to play a decisive role in the policymaking process. As we will see, moments of crisis will play a crucial role in creating the conditions for new ideas to come to the fore, and set in motion the mechanisms for them to flourish and eventually function as blueprints for the creation of new institutions.

What is still missing in the existing literature is a systematic attempt to view the economic decisions and policies from Attlee to Blair in light of the socio-economic ideas of both parties, as well as the existing institutions and ideas that were already in place once they assumed power. David Marsh rightly argues that there is a need for a "multidimensional approach" in understanding postwar British politics: "taking a strong historical perspective that is theoretically informed, but empirically grounded."[37] This book aims to bring together the ideas, political institutions, and structural constraints of the British economy into one coherent framework. While a challenging task, anything less inclusive, I fear, is bound to be seriously distorting.[38]

## Existing theoretical explanations for institutional continuity and change

There are several important lines of analysis that have been developed to explain continuity and change in national economic policies. The key claims of three competing approaches suffice to give an overview: structural or "materialist" approaches, coalition and interest group approaches, and the institutionalist or "state-centric" approach. This book adapts aspects of this latter school in a new model characterized as "punctuated evolution." Understanding existing theoretical explanations for institutional continuity and change ably places us to then explore a synthesis of ideational and historical institutionalist models in constructing our new model.

The structural or "materialist" approach is a particularly influential strand in the literature. This approach looks at the impact of an integrating world economy on national economic policymaking. According to these structural explanations, it is "globalization" – the increased intensity of international trade, capital, and information flows – that drives a government's economic policy decisions. Helen Milner and Robert Keohane spell out three pathways by which changes in the world economy have altered domestic politics over time: by creating new policy preferences and coalitions, by triggering domestic economic crises, and by undermining government control over macroeconomic policy.[39] Jeffry Frieden and Ronald Rogowski argue that the sheer magnitude of international exchange flows have affected policies in virtually every country, as evidenced in the "widespread repudiation of tax, regulatory and macroeconomic policies that inhibit international competitiveness."[40]

This literature emphasizes the importance of exogenous international shocks, such as the oil shocks in the 1970s or the liberalization of capital markets in the 1980s. One of the problems with this line of thinking is that the effect of the policy under discussion often precedes the supposed cause. For example, the liberalization of financial markets in Britain (or so-called "big bang") did not trigger the Thatcherite experiment: it only happened in 1986, when Thatcher's neoliberal policies were already well under way. Also, if one were to take materialist theories at face value they would point the way towards a convergence in national economic policies and institutions. Of course, one only needs to take a quick look to see the vast diversity in political economic arrangements all over Western Europe and North America.

The second approach, that of coalition and interest group theories, seeks to explain how political alliances are formed and uses these alliances to explain the occurrence of continuity or change. In this view, political actors are driven by a desire to maximize their income share of the national economy, and coalitions emerge as a result of the tendency of socioeconomic groups to pursue their economic interests. Politicians are seen as the translators of societal pressures into policy choices. These politicians, however, do not play any major independent role in the process.[41] The alliance choices of political actors are instead seen as predetermined by their respective positions in the international and domestic political economies. Therefore, the coalitions that eventually emerge in each country are the result of the particular economic logic in that country at the time. For example, Gourevitch and Rogowski argue that the political alliances formed during the Great Depression of the 1930s were held together by shared economic goals and interests.[42] In this domestic interest view, collective ideas are simply those notions put forward by the most powerful groups or individuals. If you push this to the extreme, ideas have, in Jeffrey Legro's words, "no power to constrain groups, let alone constitute their interests."[43] In other words, according to this theory, understanding radical change in a country's economic policy framework is a matter of understanding first how the relative power and interests of smaller groups within the state either shift or endure. New ideas are brought to the forefront by the rise and fall of these interest groups.

Interest group theory explanations can be summarized in the framework developed by Frieden. Frieden's framework aims to identify the distributional consequences of increased international capital mobility, arguing that the intensified pace of capital flows across national borders has produced new sources of harmony and friction over how national economic policy is shaped. Tension arises between internationally oriented investors and firms on the one hand and domestically oriented ones on the other.[44] These cleavages eventually play out in the policy arena, and the winning coalition is eventually able to convince the national government to pursue a specific economic policy agenda.[45] This type of argument attributes the adoption of certain economic models and policies to the pressures of powerful economic interests, which can alter due to the changing nature of the global economy.[46]

The problem with coalition and interest group theories, as I argue later in this chapter, is that economic and political interests are not directly perceived by political actors. Rather, these interests are perceived through the lens of the existing ideologies in different historical settings. What coalition and interest group theories cannot explain is what brings about the development let alone the change in interest perceptions in the first place.

The third approach, institutionalist or "state-centric" theories, tends to focus on the policymaking process rather than on structural pressures, exogenous shocks, or alliance formation. Most institutionalist analyses argue that the kinds of policies political actors will choose to pursue can be predicted by examining the specific characteristics of the state and the domestic institutional context.[47] Institutional analysis highlights both formal and informal institutional relationships "that bind the components of the state together and structure its relations with society."[48] For Peter Hall, institutional factors play two fundamental roles: first, the organization of policymaking affects the degree of power that any one set of actors has over policy outcomes; and second, organizational position also influences an actor's definition of his own interests, by establishing his institutional responsibilities and relationship to other actors.[49] For example, for Margaret Weir and Theda Skocpol, countries' acceptance or rejection of Keynesian ideas in the 1930s crucially depended on the type of preexisting national unemployment programs and the nature of the countries' economics profession.[50]

Although I use aspects of institutionalist analysis in my own theoretical framework, one of the main problems with this approach as it is generally conceived is that it does not do a very good job of explaining "paradigmatic" change in a country's institutional setup. Institutionalists are able to provide the context in which most "normal" politics is conducted, explaining the incremental nature of economic policymaking over time. But where they are on shakier ground is in explaining those moments of much more radical change and what brings about critical junctures in the normal path of a country's institutional framework.

These three approaches explain established ways of describing the process of economic policymaking and define interests in different ways. All three place very little or marginal emphasis on the role of ideas. In the next section I explain how deepening the institutionalist school of thought, bringing ideational models in, and adding the importance of crisis narration leads us to a fuller understanding of the divergent political economic outcomes in postwar Britain.

## Towards a new model: crisis, ideas, and path dependence

In order to fully understand the reasons for the diverging political economic outcomes in Britain that eventually arose from the general elections of 1945, 1970, 1979, and 1997, we must move beyond traditional theoretical explanations of continuity and change by first synthesizing two bodies of literature within the institutionalist school of political economy. The first school, the historical institutionalist school, is led by, among many others, Peter Hall, Paul Pierson, Kathleen Thelen, Sven Steinmo, Wolfgang Streeck and Theda Skocpol. This school emphasizes the role of history in social science analysis, explaining socioeconomic outcomes largely through such concepts as institutional stickiness, recurrent mechanisms of positive feedback, and historical path dependence.[51] The second school of thought, that of the ideational institutionalist, is mainly associated with Kathryn Sikkink, Kathleen McNamara, Mark Blyth, Sheri Berman, Jeffrey Legro, Rawi Abdelal, Craig Parsons, Nicolas Jabko, and Colin Hay. The ideational school stresses the importance of economic ideas during periods in history characterized by relatively high uncertainty.[52]

In this book, I bring the first school's persistent path dependence accounts of political stasis together with the critical juncture path-shaping moments of ideational political change of the second school into a single coherent theoretical synthesis.

### Institutional path dependence

For most historical institutionalists, the key mechanism that explains institutional stability over time is path dependence, defined as

> a process whereby contingent events or decisions result in the establishment of institutions that persist over long periods of time and constrain the range of actors' future options, including those that may be more efficient or effective in the long run.[53]

Centering on this mechanism of path dependence, Paul Pierson argues that there are indeed strong grounds for believing that "self-reinforcing processes will be prevalent in political life."[54] Once established, patterns of political mobilization, the institutional rules of the game, and even citizens' ways of thinking about the political and economic world generate self-reinforcing dynamics. In other words, onwards from the moment actors have chosen a particular path, they may find it very difficult to reverse course, and real political alternatives – that were once quite plausible – may become lost.[55]

The concept of path dependence was at the center of Douglass North's comprehensive reinterpretation of economic history. Trying to answer the question of why there has been such limited convergence of economic performance across countries over time, North concluded that the persistence of institutional traditions explains the anomaly of continued divergence. Once in place, institutions are hard to change, and they have a tremendous lag effect on the possibilities for generating sustained economic growth. Since individuals and organizations tend to adapt to existing institutions, economic development therefore shows strong path dependent tendencies.[56]

In *Politics in Time*, Pierson looks at issues of institutional origin as well as those of change, shifting the debate from institutional selection to the problem of institutional development.[57] Pierson rejects purely functionalist explanations of institutional arrangements, where institutions take the form they do because skillful actors engaged in rational, strategic behavior intended to generate the observed outcomes. Instead, Pierson, like North, stresses the sizeable time lag between actors' actions, which tend to be more concerned with short-term outcomes, and the long-term consequences of their actions. It is those long-term effects of institutional choice that are often the most salient ones, Pierson notes, and should be seen as by-products of social processes rather than actually embodying the rational goals of social actors. In order to understand how institutional arrangements can become deeply embedded over time, Pierson suggests the need to focus on the processes of institutional development unfolding over significant periods of time, rather than taking a snapshot view of political life.[58]

Deepening this idea, historical institutionalists like John Campbell claim that political actors are embedded in institutions in ways that both constrain and enable them.[59] Institutions constrain actors insofar as they limit the range of innovations they can envision or create, but also enable actors by providing them with the principles and resources with which to craft solutions to their problems. From this idea, it follows that political entrepreneurs have to demonstrate that their solutions fit within the prevailing institutional framework in order to be successful. Because their solutions, however innovative, still fit within the permissible range of solutions, institutional change is more likely to be evolutionary rather than revolutionary.[60]

One crucial aspect of path dependent institutional development is the existence of certain "critical junctures" that prompt the process of positive feedback that reinforces the current setup. Simply, a critical juncture forces policymakers to evaluate existing institutions and to make small improvements. These small improvements inevitably make the institutions even stronger, and thereby more resistant to change.

Critics have argued that path dependent models can be "too contingent and too deterministic."[61] In other words, path dependence does not explain what actually brings about a critical juncture, what shapes new institutions during that seemingly brief moment of punctuation when policy evaluation takes place, or how real radical change happens at all.[62] Pierson does recognize that nothing in path dependent analyses necessarily implies that a particular alternative is permanently locked in following the move onto a self-reinforcing path. This locked-in presumption is no doubt the weakest element in historical institutionalist analysis.

Pierson rightly sees the long periods of continued institutional stability as a remarkable feature of the social world, stressing that most of the time we can explain observed outcomes through institutional path dependence.[63] However, significant though those long periods of stability are, they are evidently not always the norm, and path dependence crucially fails to convincingly explain institutional crises and periods of more revolutionary change. The most insightful historical periods to study are those where established institutions completely collapse and are replaced by fundamentally new ones. Path dependence fails to explain what brings about these "critical junctures" and which shape new institutions will eventually take. Hence, while identifying self-reinforcing processes can help us understand why institutional practices are often so extremely persistent, they cannot give a coherent explanation as to the causes of abrupt and radical changes.

In an effort to resolve this deficiency, Douglass North stresses that at every step of the way there are "important political and economic choices to be made, which provide real alternatives."[64] For North, path dependence is a technique to conceptually narrow the choice set and to tie decision making through time. It is not a story of inevitability in which the past neatly predicts the future.[65] While certainly a relevant point, this does seem to be an attempt to have it both ways. In the end, path dependence theory does not sufficiently explain how critical junctures arise, how they are dealt with, or what comes after. As Peters, Pierre, and King have argued, "[the] retrospective feature of historical institutionalism leads scholars to investigate only the persistence of the victorious policy option, instead of bringing out the complexity and uncertainty that characterize formative moments in the creation of policies."[66] Historical institutionalists fail to recognize that real choices are available at critical times and hence that the process is not as inevitable as it may later appear. Path dependence is not necessarily so dependent. The fundamental question then becomes whether historical institutionalism can stand alone as an approach to understanding continuity as well as change in economic policymaking.[67] The answer is: not really. What is missing?

### *Ideas*

It is ironic how many economists and political scientists, who spend most of their scholarly lives arguing and debating political and economic ideas, have neglected to study the role and impact of those ideas on major social events until the early 1990s, with the publication of Kathryn Sikkink's first book, *Ideas and Institutions*.[68] Even then, it would take almost another decade until a broader range of scholars would start treating ideas as genuine independent variables in their treatment of political and economic change.[69]

*Early "ideational" approaches to the study of politics*

Let us examine early ideational approaches to the study of politics, for their failings inform our efforts at a new approach to the study of economic policymaking. In *The Political Power of Economic Ideas*, Peter Hall identifies several ideational approaches that have provided significant contributions to our overall understanding of the relationship between ideas and politics.[70] We focus on two of the approaches, "state-centered" and "coalition-centered," both of which focus on a distinct set of factors that are intimately involved at different stages of the policy process.[71]

The state-centered approach[72] looks primarily at the effects of bureaucratic influences on economic policymaking and suggests that "the reception accorded new ideas will be influenced by the institutional configuration of the state and its prior experience with related policies."[73] Hall points out that the weakness of the state-centered approach is that it posits its main actors at the center, relegating other important factors to the sidelines. In this case, the state-centered approach tends to overplay the role of public officials and bureaucrats and exaggerates the resiliency of institutions, while downplaying the contribution of elected politicians and their advisers in shaping policy objectives and outcomes.[74]

The coalition-centered approach[75] brings both politicians and social groups into a paradigm that explains policy outcomes, recognizing that "policies must mobilize support among broad coalitions of economic groups on whose votes and goodwill elected politicians ultimately depend."[76] The problem with this last approach is that it leaves open the question of how these groups come to define their interests in the way that they do.[77] What is required is a mechanism through which we can trace how groups come to believe what exactly their interests are.

Mark Blyth has criticized this ideational turn as an attempt to patch up the limitations of the existing historical institutionalist school and sees this renewed interest in ideas neither as a progressive extension of institutionalist thought, nor as a serious effort to study the role of ideas in political economy.[78] More to the point, Hall's approach still fails to treat ideas as explanatory variables in their own right. Hall does consider ideas as an important factor in his approach, but ultimately, ideas themselves do not decide the actual institutional outcome. For Hall, it is the wider theoretical framework in which ideas are entrenched that finally performs this function.[79] By continuing to give priority to institutions over ideas, the historical institutionalist school fails to elucidate the mechanism by which new ideas batting around the isolated sphere of academic debate are translated and enter into the sphere of genuine popular awareness.[80]

In order to overcome these historical institutionalist limitations, Blyth suggests two possible ways in which ideas could be examined.[81] First, ideas should be seen as providing the basic conditions for successful collective action among actors interested in reforming distributional relationships. In moments of uncertainty, when it is almost impossible to even define what one's interest in fact is, ideas help to redefine them, opening a path for the creation of new coalitions based on these newly defined interests. By doing so, "ideas can build bridges across class and consumption categories by redefining actors' perceived interests."[82] As we discuss later in this chapter, narrators or ideational entrepreneurs are essential to this process. Second, ideas should be seen not just as the catalyst of radical policy change, but as an actual precondition for it. Although it is probably true that most policy changes in advanced economies tend to be implemented incrementally, during periods of rapid institutional transformation this is not the case. As Blyth points out, "incrementalism is not the norm when economic ideas advocate the dismantling or reform of existing institutions."[83] Ideas therefore have real institutional effects, without necessarily reducing them directly to institutions as is the wont of these traditional approaches.

### *Defining ideas*

The surge in ideational scholarship in the late 1990s was born partly out of a general dissatisfaction with the prevailing structural accounts of institutional continuity and change. As we have seen, these latter accounts explained the evolution of a country's institutional framework mainly as the logical and rational response to material phenomena such as globalization, regional economic integration, and major economic shocks such as the quadrupling of oil prices in 1973 or the growing liberalization of international capital markets in the 1980s.[84] Since these structural explanations logically expected national convergence in economic policies, and tended to leave little role for agency and political entrepreneurship, they seemed rather deficient in accounting for the very different forms of capitalism that emerged all over the industrialized world in the 1990s.

We have also seen how limitations in traditional approaches to ideational politics prevents them from satisfyingly explaining interest definition while simultaneously overplaying the role of certain actors and not others, as well as the resiliency of institutions. What is needed is an approach that values ideas as variables in their own right.

To treat ideas in their proper, more developed context, I adopt the definition of ideas enunciated by Sheri Berman, who defines ideas as "programmatic beliefs."[85] Ideas are programmatic beliefs in the sense that they are cognitive and outcome oriented, and because they provide political actors with prescriptions which enable them to chart a clear and specific course of action.[86] For Berman, programmatic beliefs are somewhere in between policy positions and ideologies. She suggests that ideologies, defined as "total visions of the world", are too broad to be useful, while policy positions are too narrow to be relevant for the study of how actors make decisions. Emphasizing the role of "ideational carriers" – usually politicians that act as intellectual entrepreneurs by bringing ideas into the political system – Berman argues in *The Social Democratic Moment* not only that "a particular actor will make similar choices over time, even as the environment changes," but also that "actors with different ideas will make different decisions, even when placed in very similar environments."[87] In other words, political outcomes may vary quite significantly and are by no means predetermined by structural factors.

One crucial distinction ideational scholars make is between *interests* and *ideas*. Interests are objectively given by virtue of an individual's concern with improving his or her well-being, while ideas are subjective social constructions.[88] Blyth contends that social scientists need to reassess the relationship between ideas and interests, especially during periods of uncertainty, so that ideas are not presumed as something anterior or external to interests.[89] We thus have to think of ideas as central elements in the determination of how actors perceive their actual interests. For example, interests should be defined in terms of the ideas that actors hold about the risks and insecurities they are facing. Invoking the theories of Alexander Wendt, Blyth reminds us that in order to specify the content of certain interests, one must have previously specified those beliefs that an agent holds about what is desirable in the first place. Therefore, in the real world, "we want what we want because of how we think about it," not because of the innate properties of the object desired.[90] If this position is accepted, then specifying interests becomes less about structural determination and more about the role of ideas in shaping those interests.

### Ideas, institutional stability, and change

How do ideas account for institutional stability over time? It is certainly true that moments of paradigm shifts and radical institutional transformations, which we discuss at length in this book, are the most interesting episodes to study, but they are also rare. Most of the time, the political world is characterized by institutional stability, standard operating procedures, and the day-to-day dealings and decisions of the state bureaucracy. Although periods of economic crisis and rapid institutional change are attractive to examine, we cannot possibly build a comprehensive theory of institutional development based on that alone. Thus to account for those factors that provide institutional stability over time is just as important as explaining which factors bring about radical change.

Historical institutionalists have usually argued that ideas, once they are successfully embedded in new institutions, inform subsequent policy making.[91] New ideas will advance stability over time by spawning rules and beliefs that make the institutional coordination of agents' expectations possible. In other words, ideas manage probabilities and give political actors a predictive framework of what institutional future to anticipate.[92] As a consequence, Blyth theorizes that economic ideas make stability possible through the generation of conventions. By establishing a new orthodoxy, ideas that are permanently locked in will be difficult to exit from and will encourage "intellectual path dependence."[93]

There are many examples of this phenomenon. A good example is the socialist ideas of Tony Benn in England, which were seen as quite legitimate in the 1960s and 1970s, but have somehow been pushed to the sidelines by the neoliberal ascendancy in Britain and much of the rest of the world in the 1980s and 1990s. Ideas that once formed a plausible alternative have been marginalized by the proselytizing activity of the right-wing press and the Tory machine and are now still referred to as the dangerous teachings of the "loony left."

Let us turn to how ideas matter in explaining radical institutional change. Three explanations are illustrative. In *The Currency of Ideas*, Kathleen McNamara stresses the importance of the neoliberal ideational consensus[94] that emerged during the economic crises of the late 1970s in bringing about European monetary unification.[95] Although McNamara sees the neoliberal ideas as a crucial variable in the eventual success of Economic and Monetary Union (EMU), she carefully weighs their impact against other material and structural factors that in her view also affected the behavior of Europe's statesmen.[96] She concludes that EMU would have never been possible if it had not been for Europe's main political actors during the 1980s sharing the idea that price stability, and not full employment, should be the main goal of a country's monetary policy. For McNamara, ideas therefore deserve to be treated as variables in their own right.

In *Rethinking the World*, Jeffrey Legro shows how power relationships, unfiltered by prior collectively held ideas about cause and effect in international relations, can tell us very little about major power behavior.[97] For Legro, it is the weight of inherently attractive ideas that explains the direction of major shifts in a country's grand strategy during periods of crisis, moments marked by a collapse of the prevailing international system such as major wars or economic depressions. However, like John Stuart Mill,[98] Legro is cautious to point out that ideas have to interact with other factors, such as a state's relative power position and domestic politics.[99]

The role of ideas in institutional change was most developed by Mark Blyth in *Great Transformations*.[100] Blyth argues that in periods of economic crisis, ideas – not institutions – reduce uncertainty. Simply, ideas allow agents to resolve a crisis by crafting a blueprint for new institutions. By clarifying interests, ideas provide political actors with both a logical and a normative account of the existing economy and polity, enabling them to suggest specific solutions at a moment of crisis. Once those ideas have inspired the birth of new institutions, they become the conventions that underpin these institutions and will help to foster a period of relative institutional stability.[101] In essence, in addition to promoting change in times of increased insecurity, ideas provide stability over time by generating the conventions that make the institutional coordination of various agents' expectations possible.[102] Ideas become embedded in organizations, patterns of discourse, and collective identities. Ideas thereby take on a fuller life of their own – separate from the original conditions that gave rise to their prominence.[103] In the long term, the implementation of programmatic beliefs by political actors may lead to long lasting decision making processes and institutional legacies that have more subtle indirect and self-reinforcing or path dependent effects that eventually constrain change.[104] According to Blyth, ideas will thus act as "cognitive locks"[105] that restrict decision makers to certain intellectual paths.[106]

For Blyth, ideas have different causal effects at different points in time. Periods of rapid institutional change follow a specific temporal sequence. During periods of economic crisis, ideas have five different causal effects at different time points. These five effects are: uncertainty reduction, coalition building, institutional contestation, institutional construction, and expectational coordination. By seeing ideas as having different causal effects in different time periods as part of a sequence of change, Blyth formulates a dynamic theory that explains both continuity and change within the same intellectual framework.[107] However, Blyth does not fully develop the framework through which crisis and crisis narration can be analyzed, even though crises are central for Blyth, and he does suggest that the discursive construction or narration of crisis is important. In the next section, we will lay out a crisis typology that we will use to develop our own theoretical model.

### Crises, failures, and unsustainable equilibria

By uniting the causal theories of both ideational and historical institutionalist schools, one can argue that economic ideas play a crucial role during "critical junctures," since they will reduce uncertainty and provide guidance for future policymaking. The key question that remains unanswered, however, is when and how a sharp economic downturn or major social event, such as a world war or a natural disaster, will actually lead to a "critical juncture" in institutional development. It is obvious that not every single crisis will lead to radical change, let alone to a new institutional framework. In the social world, critical junctures are exceptional phenomena, and we often see them as "critical" only after the fact.[108]

The central question is when an economic crisis will result in an actual "critical juncture" that will open the door to new ideas, which can then function as a blueprint for new institutions. We first need a clear definition of "crisis." For Legro, crises are mainly structural events caused by exogenous shocks, which involve the collapse of the reigning orthodoxy accompanied by widespread agitation to replace it.[109] Blyth, on the other hand, defines crises as moments of "Knightian uncertainty."[110] In contrast to ordinary risk situations, actors in moments of such Knightian uncertainty find it impossible during a crisis to assign probabilities to future states of the world or imagine what these states of the world might look like. During such moments, conventional practices often prove self-defeating or are rendered so illegitimate that they can no longer be contemplated.[111]

In order to answer the crucial question of when a crisis will lead to a "critical juncture" and cause more revolutionary change, I adapt the crisis typology that was originally developed by Colin Hay (see Table 2.1).[112] This typology makes a distinction between a crisis, an unsustainable or fragile equilibrium, and a failure. A crisis here is understood as a moment of decisive intervention in the process of institutional change when contradictions in the system are generally acknowledged; an unsustainable equilibrium occurs when the symptoms of state failure are readily apparent and widely perceived, yet no sense of crisis is mobilized and no decisive intervention takes place; and failure takes place when contradictions, though present, are not identified as such.[113]

*Table 2.1* Hay's crisis typology

|  | Decisive intervention | Incremental or no change |
| --- | --- | --- |
| Contradictions perceived | Crisis | Unsustainable/Fragile Equilibrium |
| Contradictions not acknowledged | Tipping point | Failure |

Source: Adapted from C. Hay, "Crisis and the structural transformation of the state: interrogating the process of change," *British Journal of Politics and International Relations* 1 (3), October 1999, p. 325.

Hay's typology is useful as it recognizes that crises are by no means objective material events. Crises need to be socially constructed into a view capable of explaining what went wrong and how it can be resolved by a radical change to the current institutional setup. A sharp economic downturn will only result in a real "crisis" if it has been successfully constructed as such and a decisive intervention is called for. Ideas are central to this social construction. I add to this typology the importance of crisis narration which explains how a crisis, subjectively defined, becomes perceived as such by the public and can then be acted upon.

### Ideas and crisis narration

Now that we have identified what a crisis entails, we turn to the importance of its narration. Any moment of economic crisis and prolonged state failure will call into question the received economic wisdom of the day. In such a climate of uncertainty, the reigning paradigm no longer predicts or accounts for the glitches within the system. However, before political actors can even begin to work out ways to solve an abrupt economic downturn, the "crisis" itself must be clarified.[114] Certain actors wield unique influence in determining the dimensions of the crisis, which groups are directly or indirectly affected by it, what its main sources are, as well as setting the range of possible alternatives for dealing with its consequences. To do so actors need to have the tools for evaluating a crisis in order to mobilize the necessary political and economic resources for coping with imminent problems that are associated with it. This is important because "a crisis diagnosis makes a strong explanatory claim"[115] about the appropriateness of selecting a certain set of means to attain desired ends.[116] Additionally, crises often open the policy dialogue to various new participants with different points of view.[117] The tools actors need to evaluate a crisis and then to mobilize the necessary political and economic resources for coping with the problem are therefore their ideas.

Particular coalitions that expound new economic ideas that are able to explain the anomalies in the system by constructing a convincing crisis narrative will vie for the right to transform institutions according to their new paradigm. In this political battle, ideas – defined earlier by Berman as "programmatic beliefs"[118] – can be considered as effective weapons to invalidate the current institutions by contesting the old economic ideas that underlie them.[119] By openly defying the conventional view of how the economy functions, new ideas not only delegitimize existing institutions, but also alter actors' conceptions of what their own interests might be.[120]

But what will define which ideas will eventually prevail during moments of crisis? Many scholars have suggested that new ideas replace old ones simply because they are better at explaining the rules of a continuously changing political economic system than the old ideas.[121] In other words, certain ideas gain in ascendancy because they are intrinsically "better." I take issue with this argument, which embodies the notion of progress in ideational change. As Berman has pointed out,

> despite the hopes of many intellectuals, the intrinsic attractiveness of ideas plays only a limited role in their chances of gaining wide political resonance. Ideas can indeed make history, but not just as they please, and only under circumstances found, given and transmitted.[122]

Some ideas, I will argue in this book, prevail because they can give a convincing and simplified solution to perceived problems, not necessarily because they are inherently superior at explaining how the economy works.

Ultimately, the question of who will convince the policy elite and the electorate at large that an accumulation of economic contradictions constitutes a real crisis that requires a decisive intervention will depend on the ability to construct a coherent narrative of the ongoing crisis. In general, this will involve "the discursive recruitment of policy failures as symptoms of a crisis of the state."[123] At every critical juncture, competing political actors will offer fundamentally different solutions. Which solution will eventually prevail will depend on the ability of political actors to bring a great variety of independent policy failures together in a unified crisis discourse. As Hay observes, "the mobilization of perceptions of crisis thus involves the formulation and triumph of a simplifying ideology which must find and construct points of resonance with a multitude of individuated experiences of state and economic failure."[124] Attlee was able to do this during the 1945 general election campaign, where he linked the hardships of the Depression with the hardships of the war while concurrently warning not to repeat the mistake of returning to the status quo ante as had happened after World War I. Playing on the popular feeling of "never again," Attlee convinced an idealistic electorate of the virtues of economic planning and "fair shares," pointing out that if planning had won the war, planning could win the peace. He painted Churchill's alternative as going back in time, to the "class system" and dole queues of the interwar years. Also Margaret Thatcher did this to an astonishing extent during the "Winter of Discontent" in 1978–1979, when she was able not only to convince the electorate of the validity of her description of Britain as "a monolithic state held to ransom by the trade unions,"[125] but also of the necessity of following her specific policy prescription to solve the crisis. As Hay has argued, this was arguably the only real hegemonic moment of Thatcherism.[126]

After the delegitimation of existing institutions, the political "carriers" of the new body of ideas that have won the power struggle (e.g. by winning a general election or by forming a dominant coalition in government) inform the architecture of the nascent institutional settlement. Thus, new ideas not only act as sticks in the fight over existing institutions, they will also act as a blueprint for those new institutions. After having reduced the risks and uncertainty of a crisis and successfully dethroning the ideas behind the earlier coalition's institutional settlement, the new coalition's ideas will also define the outline and content of the new institutions. As Blyth states, "radical institutional changes make little sense without reference to the ideas that agents were able to use to form the authoritative diagnosis of the crisis at specific historical moments."[127]

### *Punctuated institutional evolution*

Having laid out the existing literature on institutional path dependence, ideas, and crisis, I will now put forward my own "punctuated evolution" model that will explain both continuity and change in a country's institutional framework. This model will function as the theoretical foundation of the book and inform the case studies. The synthesis that follows includes six propositions that will be illustrated in the next four chapters, each containing one of the four cases of British governments that I will examine more closely.

The synthesis aims to be a comprehensive model for continuity and change by including the following theoretical concepts discussed in this chapter: the four different typologies of "crisis," the path shaping and path dependent power of economic ideas, and the positive feedback mechanisms of institutions. What follows is the main theoretical contribution of the book.

#### Proposition One

An abrupt economic downturn or systemic collapse is a necessary though not sufficient condition for paradigmatic change.

On the face of it, this first proposition is the most intuitive, since it seems almost impossible to overhaul an existing institutional framework in the absence of a catalyzing mechanism that sets in motion the process which justifies radical change. As explained above, there are two conditions for an economic downturn to be a genuine crisis and cause an actual paradigm shift: first, the contradictions in the current system have to be widely perceived; and second, a decisive intervention has to take place. In all other cases (fragile equilibrium, tipping point, or failure), there will be no lasting paradigm shift, but merely a prolonged period of muddling through. More often than not, however, moments of systemic breakdown are not seen as critical junctures at the time they occur, but only later – and with the benefit of hindsight – recognized as such. As a consequence, during moments of perceived crisis there is a rare opportunity for political leaders to exploit the escalating anomalies in the system and frame it in a way that promotes their economic ideas.

**Proposition Two**

Crises are by no means self-apparent phenomena, but need to be constructed
and explained in a coherent narrative, which find resonance with the public
at large and can convince a majority of the need for a radical intervention.

This is a crucial insight from Colin Hay. There is no doubt that there are cases
when economic downturns are widely experienced by the whole population, such
as the beginning of the Great Depression in 1929–1931, or the runaway inflation
accelerated by the oil shocks in 1973–1974 that were accompanied by power cuts,
industrial strife and a three-day work week in Britain. The point is, however, that
these moments are not necessarily followed by interventions that break with the
governing institutions. In order to make that happen successfully, political leaders
need to explain the crisis in a simplified and coherent narrative, however constructed, that will convince the required majority of the electorate of the need for
policy intervention. In other words, they need to convince us we are in a deep crisis
and how it happened. During such moments, there are a myriad of competing narratives available to explain the causes of the systemic breakdown that occurred and
give different policy options for setting the system on a new and better path.

**Proposition Three**

During a moment of "crisis," economic ideas will play a decisive role by
explaining what went wrong and how to fix it, and by providing a blueprint for new institutions.

This point has been comprehensively discussed by Mark Blyth in his examination of the "double movement" from market to state and back in Sweden and
the United States during the 1930s and 1970s.[128] As Milton Friedman pointed
out in the opening quote of this chapter, when crises – real or perceived – occur,
the choice of policy response depends on what ideas are available, or "lying
around."[129] Some ideas promote a response within the existing institutional
framework, whereas other ideas promote a change in the institutions themselves.
In this sense, there is a battle between ideas that define whether or not a crisis
will also be a critical juncture in the institutional development of the state. If the
old ideas can no longer explain what is happening with the economic system, a
crisis will be the fertile ground for new ideas to flourish. Which ideas eventually
prevail depends on the ability of political leaders to construct the most convincing narrative of what went wrong with the system, and how their ideas provide
the answers to those contradictions. Once one set of ideas triumphs, usually
through an election victory of their political promoters, the new ideas will
provide the blueprint for the new institutional setup of the state.

**Proposition Four**

Economic ideas are selectively used by political parties insofar as they can
be reconciled with or promote the party's guiding ideology.

Although there are notable exceptions, politicians are rarely themselves professional economists. They have certain beliefs about what is fair in a society, a political intuition on what is expedient, and a certain idea about which platform will bring their parties to power. Politicians rarely incorporate a comprehensive economic theory into their party policy platform. They pick and choose certain elements of economic theories that they find particularly attractive and feel comfortable with given the often long-standing traditions of their parties. Also, politicians might use the ideas of economists that go seemingly against the party's current ideology by claiming that they take the party back to its real ideological roots. In short, politicians use selective parts of certain ideas in economic theory that can promote their personal or political party agendas.

### Proposition Five

In the absence of a crisis, ideas will at most bring about incremental change and only matter insofar as they "fit" within the existing institutional paradigm.

If political leaders and their parties come to power without having created a mandate for radical change – in our framework only possible through the construction of a convincing crisis narrative – their new ideas will not bring about a paradigm shift. There are two possibilities. First, if a government tries to engineer a radical overhaul of the system without a crisis, and thus without their new ideas explaining what went wrong and how it could be fixed, these ideas will not stand on firm enough footing and will lack real legitimacy. When certain anomalies then start building up within this new provisional arrangement, the reaction will often be to reach back to the old ideas since the new solutions did not prove to be lasting ones. Second, if a government comes to power without the aim of changing the dominant institutions of the state, their new ideas will only be applied as long as they can be reconciled with the existing institutions and fit within the governing ideas that underpin those institutions. In short, without a crisis that justifies the urgent need to implement a party's new ideational framework, only incremental change to the existing system will be achieved.

### Proposition Six

Ideas, just as much as institutions, show strongly path dependent tendencies, and will give continuing legitimacy to the existing paradigm. There will be relative systemic stability until a new crisis calls into question the legitimacy of the existing institutional arrangement.

The path dependent logic of existing institutions is a crucial insight from Paul Pierson. Taking it further, it needs to be complemented with the path dependent power of existing economic ideas in order to understand institutional stability over time. As already mentioned in this chapter, critical junctures are the most interesting moments in institutional development for social scientists to study since the whole system then is in flux and everything we thought we knew is being called into question. But those moments are atypical. Most of the time, there is relative institutional stability and an absence of real crisis. Stability is then made possible by the perceived legitimacy of the existing institutions, just as much as the economic ideas that form their foundation.

"Punctuated evolution" thus describes continuity and change by using crises, crisis narration, and ideas to explain path dependence as well as times of radical change. It is a dynamic model that synthesizes the explanatory variables of path dependent accounts of political stasis as well as critical juncture path shaping moments of ideational political change, and yet corrects for their limitations. As we will see below, it is a model that can explain how certain British governments were able to institute radical change in the country's governing economic institutions, while others tried and failed.

## Application to the case of Britain

The six propositions outlined in the previous section explain both continuity and change in a country's institutional framework. A practical way to see how they fit into our case studies is to understand how they explain different categories of political circumstances that do or do not lead to change. These categories are framed in the typological setup described by Stephen Skowronek in *The Politics Presidents Make*. Skowronek demonstrates that American presidents are persistent agents of change because they continually disrupt and transform the political landscape.[130] But since each president also inherits a particular type of political and economic context – a regime shaped by his predecessors that he either seeks to reject or affirm – presidential leadership needs to be understood in "political time."[131]

For Skowronek, three factors are important to political time: who the new president is replacing; what previous program he or she is rejecting or extending; and whether there exists strong resistance to the new agenda. In his book, Skowronek constructs a typology of four recurrent structures of presidential authority, which is presented in Table 2.2. For our purposes, it is highly instructive to apply his typology to the case of postwar Britain by replacing American presidents

*Table 2.2* Skowronek's typology applied to Britain

| *Previously established policy commitments* | *Prime Minister's political and economic ideas* | |
| --- | --- | --- |
| | *Opposed* | *Affiliated* |
| Vulnerable | Politics of reconstruction *Attlee/Thatcher* | Politics of disjunction *Heath after U-turn/Callaghan* |
| Resilient | Politics of preemption *Heath before U-turn* | Politics of articulation *Macmillan/Major/Blair* |

Source: Adapted from S. Skowronek, *The Politics Presidents Make: Leadership from John Adams to George Bush*, Cambridge: Harvard University Press, 1993, p. 36.

with British prime ministers. What is remarkable about Skowronek's typology, explicitly constructed for US presidential politics, is how well it fits the different postwar British prime ministers.

In the first cell of the typology, the *politics of reconstruction*, the prime minister heralds from the opposition party, and the existing institutional arrangements have become vulnerable to direct repudiation as "failed or irrelevant responses to the problems of the day."[132] This is the most promising of all situations for the exercise of political leadership. These conditions applied to both Attlee and Thatcher when they came to power, making it possible for them to become the great "innovators."[133]

The second cell, the *politics of disjunction*, represents a situation where the incoming prime minister comes to power as affiliated to his predecessor or, for our purposes, to the broad ideas of his predecessor. While the environment proves vulnerable, they do not manage a real transformation of the existing system. The best example of this situation is Callaghan in 1976, but we could also apply it to Heath after he made his U-turn in 1972 when he essentially realigned himself with the politics of postwar consensus.[134]

The third cell, the *politics of preemption*, paints a situation where the new prime minister comes from the opposition, and aims to change the current institutional setup, but fails given the resilience of the existing system. Heath, when he came to power in 1970, challenged the consensus with free market ideas but eventually failed to implement radical changes. He is the prime example of the politics of preemption.[135]

Finally, the fourth cell, the *politics of articulation*, is probably the most common of all in politics. Here we have a new leader coming to power being affiliated with the current regime and under rather durable systemic conditions. The best examples are Macmillan and Major, but it applies in many ways also to Blair, who sought to align himself with the bulk of the Thatcherite settlement during his three years as opposition leader, and thus ended up articulating the existing institutional arrangements.[136]

A typology, which is exhaustive by definition, is not a theory, just a useful framework for our analysis. The six propositions we have discussed in the previous section bring together new and old ideas, existing institutions, and the social construction of economic crisis, and blend them into a new synthesis that explains how actors in the Skowronek typology end up in the categories that they do.

This punctuated evolution model that has been laid out in this chapter is also appropriate for the case of Britain for the following reasons.

First, looking at the evolution of Britain's postwar political economy, one cannot help but discern a history that is rife with drama, economic crises, diverging responses, and ensuing results.[137] Financial and balance of payments crises had to be overcome in 1949, 1956, 1967, 1976, and 1992, and there were a series of accompanying political and foreign policy crises. Furthermore, since Britain's political system is extremely centralized, with a powerful prime minister at the helm of a machine that tends to deliver disproportionately large majorities to the victorious party, governments actually have far-reaching powers to implement their economic platforms.

Second, starting with Adam Smith in the late eighteenth century, Britain has been at the vanguard of new economic ideas. In the case of a crisis, ideas are readily available for economic policymakers. Not only have ideas that originated in Britain reverberated around the world, they have also been very influential in British economic policymaking. David Ricardo and Richard Cobden, preaching the virtues of international free trade, were instrumental in the repeal of the Corn Laws in 1846, and Alfred Marshall's writings heavily influenced the Liberal Government of 1908–1916 to accept state responsibility for the poor through redistributive taxation.[138] But nowhere would economic thinking affect British policies more than in the twentieth century. Sometimes referred to as the century defined by the "battle of ideas,"[139] the two main antagonists of the twentieth century debate over the world economy – Keynes and Hayek – both had a decisive influence on economic policy making in Britain. Keynes' advice and analysis of the Great Depression in his *General Theory* were instrumental in forging Attlee's postwar "settlement," while Hayek's *Road to Serfdom* and *The Constitution of Liberty* provided the intellectual inspiration for the minds of Churchill and Thatcher, respectively.

Third, Britain's postwar political system also shows numerous instances of institutional and ideational path dependence. "Butskellism" in the 1950s was a reference to the policy continuity between Labour's Hugh Gaitskell and the Tories' Richard ("Rab") Butler, despite their different party platforms. Edward Heath's infamous U-turn in 1972 showed his government's difficulty in breaking with the existing Keynesian institutions. And Blair's New Labour policies and ideas have shown striking similarities to the Thatcher–Major era.

Uniting the three previous arguments together, the case of Great Britain offers the researcher a multitude of political and economic events against which to test the theoretical synthesis that was developed above.

## Postwar Britain's changing political economy

In order to understand political decision making in Britain, it is indispensable to keep in mind the colorful historic backdrop against which these decisions were taken over the last half century.

Once greatly admired as the "workshop of the world" and the dominant power in international politics reigning over a global *Pax Britannica* during much of the nineteenth century, Great Britain has gradually been reduced to a medium-sized regional economic and military power with an uncertain role in the world. In the economic realm, this status was confirmed when Britain, under Heath, formally joined the European Economic Community in 1973, leading many to believe that Britain could no longer forge ahead alone as it once did.[140]

As in all other advanced economies, immense structural and geographic changes have taken place in the British economy since 1945. There are four issues in particular that have affected Britain: the changing employment structure of the British economy; its increasing "Europeanization;" the ongoing debate on relative economic decline; and the role of the pound sterling in upholding London's status as a leading financial center in the world.

### *The economy's shifting structure*

The most striking change in the British postwar economy is the radical shift from industry to services, as illustrated in Table 2.3. While 45 percent of the labor force was still employed in the industrial sector in the 1960s, only 22 percent remained there by the beginning of the twenty-first century. David Coates has observed that so many people worked in banking and retailing by the year 2000 that Britain had genuinely become, by then, what Napoleon had disparagingly called it 200 years earlier: "a nation of shopkeepers."[141]

This process of deindustrialization manifested itself most dramatically in the manufacturing sector, where employment fell from 35 percent of the total labor force in 1960 to just below 12 percent in 2005.[142] Many academics have pointed out that especially in the 1980s, British manufacturing shed employment – especially full-time employment – at an unprecedented rate. In the 1980–1982 recession in particular, manufacturing employment fell from 7.4 million to 5.4 million – a reduction of 2 million jobs or 27 percent of the 1979 manufacturing labor force.[143] But it is important to stress that this process continued under New Labour, with just over 3 million jobs left in the sector by 2005. Although many analysts on the center-left have blamed the intensified range and depth of international competition, this is only part of the story. International competition from the four Asian Tigers in 1989, for example, only constituted 4 percent of world trade.[144]

Most economists explain the decline in manufacturing in terms of technical change (capital no longer needed as much labor), productivity growth differentials (with higher productivity growth in manufacturing reducing the need for labor in that sector), higher levels of income that drove increased service consumption, and inflexible labor markets.[145] It should therefore be no surprise that the recessions of the early 1980s and early 1990s hit those industrial sectors that were most labor intensive the hardest.

*Table 2.3* Structure of employment in Britain[1] (1960–2005)

|  | *Agriculture (%)* | *Industry (%)* | *Services (%)* |
| --- | --- | --- | --- |
| 1960–1973 | 3.8 | 45.5 | 50.7 |
| 1974–1979 | 2.8 | 39.9 | 57.3 |
| 1980–1989 | 2.5 | 34.4 | 63.1 |
| 1990–2000 | 1.9 | 28.2 | 69.9 |
| 2000–2005 | 1.3 | 22.3 | 76.4 |

Sources: OECD, *Historical Statistics*, Paris, 1999 and 2001; OECD, *Labour Force Statistics*, Paris, 2005.

Note
1 Measured as a percentage of civilian employment.

*Table 2.4* Annualized income growth (1997–2005) and average income levels (2005)

|  | Growth (%) | 2005 Level (weekly) (£) | Relative to London |
|---|---|---|---|
| North | 1.50 | 359 | 0.67 |
| Wales | 2.00 | 366 | 0.68 |
| Yorkshire | 1.70 | 368 | 0.68 |
| West Midlands | 1.80 | 377 | 0.70 |
| East Midlands | 2.20 | 388 | 0.72 |
| North-West | 2.40 | 391 | 0.73 |
| Scotland | 2.50 | 397 | 0.74 |
| South-West | 2.90 | 424 | 0.79 |
| East Anglia | 2.50 | 444 | 0.82 |
| South-East | 1.90 | 483 | 0.90 |
| London | 3.70 | 539 | 1.00 |

Source: M. Brewer, A. Goodman, J. Shaw, and L. Sibieta, "Poverty and Inequality in Britain: 2006," *Commentary no. 101*, London: Institute for Fiscal Studies, 2006.

The fall in employment in industry went together with a rise in service sector employment from about 50 percent of the total labor force in the 1960s to almost 78 percent in 2005.[146] This structural shift between economic sectors over the postwar period led to a sweeping geographical rearrangement of the British economy as well. Britain in the 1940s was still an economy based primarily on coalfields, located in river valleys alongside major ports in the North of England. By the 1960s, the economic center of gravity had moved southwards, to the British Midlands, and was primarily electricity powered. By the end of the century, the main areas driving British prosperity were in greater London and the South-East of England. The new distribution of leading sectors left Britain as a whole regionally unbalanced, with the bulk of prosperity heavily concentrated in greater London and the South, as shown in Table 2.4.[147]

Not only was there a geographical movement from north to south in Britain during the postwar period, the economy also saw a continuous shift in ownership from the private to the public sector, and then back again. This was especially striking for the steel and road haulage sector, both of which were nationalized after World War II under the Attlee governments, only to be privatized again under Churchill in the early 1950s. In 1967, Wilson's Labour government brought steel back under public ownership, a decision that was eventually reversed yet again by Thatcher's program of privatization in the 1980s.[148]

### Europeanization versus globalization

An important element of change in the British economy is the extent to which its external sector has become "Europeanized" over the postwar period. Looking at Figure 2.1, the trend becomes clear immediately: while only around 20 percent of British exports went to the EU-12 countries in 1960, this share has risen to 60 percent by 2004.[149] However, one has to note that since the completion of the Common Market in 1992, there has been a relatively modest rise in Britain's export share to the European Union, partly caused by the slower pace of economic growth on the European continent.

This "Europeanization" trend is particularly striking in Britain when we compare it to other European countries (Table 2.5). The European Union has not only become the chief export market for British goods and services, it also has a considerable and growing impact on public policymaking in Britain. By definition, membership of the European Economic Community (EEC) required the incorporation of the body of European Community law – the *acquis communautaire* – into UK law. As Jim Buller has argued, Europeanization manifests itself in the growth of European legislation as a core element of the business of Westminster and Whitehall. According to Buller, British politicians – whether they like it or not – have increasingly concluded that the only response to the challenges of globalization was to "seek solace in the supra-national institutions of the European Union."[150]

### *The issue of relative decline*

It is hard to overestimate the influence of relative economic decline on British economic policymaking in the postwar period.[151] Ever since the reelection of Harold Macmillan in 1959, when the idea of relative decline started to dominate academic and public debate on the British economy, successive British governments have been trying to reverse the trend of decline with differing economic policies: from French-style state planning to German-style corporatism and American-style market liberalism.[152] It is therefore imperative to see the evolution of economic policymaking – especially in the 1960s, 1970s, and 1980s – against the backdrop of the British elite's obsession with relative decline, which captured their political imagination.[153]

In fact, it is hard to think of a more intensely debated topic in the ongoing story of Britain's postwar political development than the issue of decline.[154] There is a vast literature on the subject of Britain's decline and for decades it has been at the heart of party political debate. There are two distinct senses in which

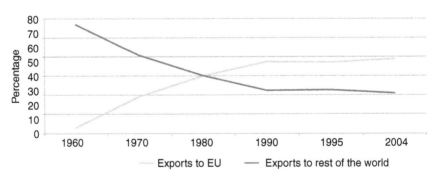

*Figure 2.1* British exports to the European Union[1] (source: Eurostat, 2006; and own calculations).

Note
1  As a percentage of total British exports.

*Table 2.5* Exports to EU countries as a percentage of overall exports[1]

|  | *1960* (%) | *1970* (%) | *1980* (%) | *1990* (%) | *1995* (%) | *2004* (%) |
|---|---|---|---|---|---|---|
| Denmark | 57.1 | 64.4 | 66.8 | 64.7 | 58.5 | 70.7 |
| (West) Germany | 40.3 | 59.5 | 60.6 | 64.0 | 56.7 | 63.9 |
| France | 38.4 | 60.5 | 58.1 | 65.1 | 63.4 | 65.3 |
| Italy | 40.2 | 57.6 | 55.8 | 62.3 | 56.1 | 59.3 |
| Netherlands | 61.2 | 76.6 | 76.9 | 75.3 | 71.9 | 79. |
| Sweden | 61.9 | 60.4 | 59.0 | 62.2 | 58.2 | 58.8 |
| United Kingdom | **23.1** | 39.1 | 49.8 | 57.3 | 57.1 | **58.9** |

Source: Eurostat, *External and Intra-EU Trade, Brussels:* European Commission, 2005; and own calculations.

Note
1 This table does take into account the changing composition of the European Union. In other words, it treats the EU-15, which only came into being in 1995, as already being a customs union from 1960 onwards.

the word "decline" is applied to the British experience.[155] First, in the military-political sense, Britain has seen an absolute decline in world influence with the gradual dismantling of the British Empire and the gradual transfer of hegemony to the United States at the end of the interwar period. Second, and more relevant for this book, is decline in the economic sense. This may seem suspect from a purely national British perspective, since standards of living have steadily risen since 1945 and unemployment rates were at historic lows during much of the 1950s and 1960s. Indeed, Macmillan won the 1959 election for the Conservative Party traveling around the country proclaiming that the people of Britain had "never had it so good."[156] Britain's economic decline only emerges when its performance is compared to its major industrial competitors in Western Europe and Japan. The paradox of an absolute rise in output combined with relative decline led to "Britain winning a smaller slice of a much larger cake."[157]

Especially over the period 1950–1973, Britain was outperformed in almost all of the main economic indicators (Table 2.6). Though Britain's economy grew at a very respectable annual rate of 3 percent during that period, France at 5.1 percent, Germany at 6 percent, Japan at 9.7 percent, and even the United States at 3.7 percent, all did much better. Economists usually point to the relatively low increases in productivity in Britain over that period as the main cause of the slower growth. British unemployment was also at historic lows during the same period, but again not as impressive as in Japan, Germany, or France.[158]

One of the most notable consequences of Britain's relatively slow productivity growth has been a loss of international competitiveness that has manifested itself especially in the manufacturing sector. Britain's share in world trade of manufactures dropped from 25 percent in 1950 to just over 6 percent in 1990, while over that same period, Japan and Germany saw their shares increase from 3.4 percent and 7.3 percent to 11.5 percent and 15.1 percent respectively.[159] This apparent failure to keep pace with its major industrial competitors has fostered a myriad of explanations in academia and across the political spectrum from a

*Table 2.6* Main economic indicators for six OECD countries (1950–1973)

|               | Growth (%) | Productivity (%) | Unemployment (%) | Inflation (%) |
|---------------|------------|------------------|------------------|---------------|
| United States | 3.7        | 2.4              | 4.8              | 2.7           |
| Japan         | 9.7        | 7.6              | 1.6              | 5.2           |
| Germany       | 6.0        | 6.0              | 1.8              | 2.7           |
| France        | 5.1        | 5.0              | 2.1              | 5.0           |
| Italy         | 5.5        | 5.5              | 4.7              | 3.9           |
| Britain       | 3.0        | 3.2              | 2.9              | 4.6           |

Source: A. Cox, S. Lee, and J. Sanderson, *The Political Economy of Modern Britain*, pp. 48–53.

divisive class system, an anti-industrial culture, and an adversarial party system to the domination of industry and government by the interests of the financial triumvirate of the Treasury, the Bank of England, and the City of London.[160]

In *Governing the Economy*, Peter Hall sees a partial consensus emerging around three factors seen as the major causes of Britain's relatively poor economic performance after 1945: low rates of investment, a slow rate of industrial adaptation, and inefficient organization of the workplace. The problem, according to Hall, is that these are more symptoms than causes, which in and of themselves need to be explained. The most popular explanations of those symptoms are the growth of state intervention, misguided macroeconomic policies ("stop–go"), and the peculiarities of British culture. Rejecting all three, Hall suggests that Britain's economic decline may be related to the institutional structure of its markets. It would be unfair to blame British entrepreneurs or trade unions, when, from a market-incentive point of view, their actions were perfectly rational.[161] Hall agrees with Alexander Gerschenkron on the apparent paradox that Britain's success in being the first country to industrialize also sowed the seeds of its industrial decline.[162]

### The restraining role of sterling

The relative strength or weakness of the pound sterling and the uncertain exchange rate regime under which it operates has been a continuing and resurgent worry for British governments from the end of World War I until Black Wednesday in September 1992.[163] Various critical episodes have been continually debated over the years: Churchill's decision to return to prewar gold parity in 1925, the move off gold in 1931, the Imperial Economic Conference in Ottawa in 1932 that established "imperial preference," the creation of the sterling area in 1933, the convertibility crisis of 1947, the devaluation in 1949, the aborted "Operation Robot" in 1952 where the Bank of England suggested a freely floating pound, and the recurring balance of payments crises. These balance of payments crises triggered a run on the pound in 1956, 1967, 1976, and 1992, and were blamed for Britain's "stop-go" cycles of macroeconomic management.[164] Hall, among others, has argued that the British government's persistent defense of the pound drew attention and resources away from the structural problems in the domestic economy.[165]

This obsession with maintaining a strong pound meant that most postwar governments were severely constrained in what they could do and de facto could not use monetary policy to manage domestic economic demand.[166] There are three main reasons for this "strong pound policy," all of which are mainly political and make little economic sense. First, there is the cross-party political commitment to maintain Britain's role as a world power with global reach combined with the prestige of having London as a world financial center.[167] Second, since most of the overseas sterling balances were held in the official reserves of nations who once belonged to the old sterling area, a drop in the currency's value was seen as diplomatically unacceptable, with major potential repercussions across the Commonwealth countries.[168] Third, the experience of empire left Britain with financial institutions heavily oriented towards overseas lending instead of linked to domestic industry; it is therefore no surprise that the City became such a powerful lobby against devaluation.[169] One reason that does make some economic sense – at least to the City of London – was the existence of sterling as a "denominative asset" and a "hedge currency" against the dollar, the yen, or any other major European currency. Without a strong pound, the rest of the world would be reluctant to hold sterling assets.

## Conclusion

This chapter has presented the book's theoretical framework that will be used to analyze Britain's economic policy making since the 1940s. Following Hay and Blyth, I argued that the transformation of the state is neither simply evolutionary, nor simply step by step. Looking at postwar Britain, it takes the form of a "punctuated evolution" process, iterative yet cumulative change animated and informed by particular political-economic paradigms.[170] During moments of sharp economic downturn these paradigms may be challenged and replaced to alter the trajectory, if not necessarily the pace, of institutional change. Existing regimes are not intrinsically disposed to spontaneous or unconstrained structural transformation: their evolution as complex systems thus tends to be both path dependent and conditional upon path shaping moments of perceived "crisis."[171]

Thus at the center of my analysis is the concept of economic crisis, and how it is experienced, narrated, and explained by the different parts of the political elite to the society at large. I have argued that the ability of political actors to construct a convincing narrative of the causes of a crisis is of critical significance and ultimately shapes their capacity to radically change prevailing popular and elite views of the political and economic context. If political entrepreneurs prove successful in doing exactly that – i.e. persuade a sufficient majority of the merits of their solutions out of an economic or political impasse – they will create the necessary conditions for a radical transformation of the preexisting institutional arrangement.

Let us now turn to the first of our case studies.

# 3 Clement Attlee's postwar "settlement" (1945–1970)

## Depression, war, Keynes, Beveridge, and a new consensus

There is no "compact" conferring perpetual rights on those who Have or on those who Acquire. The world is not so governed from above that private and social interests always coincide. It is *not* so managed here below that in practice they coincide. It is *not* a correct deduction from the Principles of Economics that enlightened self-interest generally is enlightened; more often individuals acting separately to promote their own ends are too ignorant or too weak to attain even these. Experience does *not* show that individuals, when they make up a social unit, are always less clear-sighted than when they act separately.

> John Maynard Keynes, "The End of Laissez-Faire,"
> *Essays in Persuasion* (1926)[1]

Now, when the war is abolishing landmarks of every kind, is the opportunity for using experience in a clear field. A revolutionary moment in the world's history is a time for revolutions, not for patching. [...] Organisation of social insurance should be treated as one part only of a comprehensive policy of social progress. Social insurance fully developed may provide income security; it is an attack upon Want. But Want is one only of five giants on the road to reconstruction; the others are Disease, Ignorance, Squalor and Idleness.

> William Beveridge, *Social Insurance and Allied Services* (1942)[2]

Does freedom for the profiteer mean freedom for the ordinary man and woman, whether they be wage-earners or small business or professional men or house-wives? Just think back over the depressions of the twenty years between the wars, when there were precious few public controls of any kind and the Big Interests had things all their own way. Never was so much injury done to so many by so few. Freedom is not an abstract thing. To be real it must be won, it must be worked for. [...] Britain's coming Election will be the greatest test in our history of the judgement and common sense of our people.

> "Let Us Face the Future," *Labour Party Manifesto* (1945)[3]

Driving the British New Deal was a fusion of philosophies of social justice and national efficiency. And the heart of the 'deal' was this: there would be an end to avoidable injustices, inequalities and privations in return for a mitigation of old, deep-rooted class, social and industrial antagonisms which both pulled down Britain's economic performance and weakened the fibre of its society. This was a great prize in itself, but the British New Deal would also create an indispensable base for underpinning the new settlement and a platform for further advance.

Peter Hennessy, *Having It So Good* (2006)[4]

## Introduction

The summer of 1945 was a turning point in British history. On May 8, 1945, the Allied forces finally brought Hitler's *Third Reich* to its knees and forced Nazi Germany into unconditional surrender. Victory in Europe (VE) Day marked the ultimate victory for Great Britain, which had pulled together as one during the Battle of Britain (1940–1941) when the island nation and its dominions stood alone in their defense against the Axis powers. Not since the Napoleonic wars of 1806, or even the threat of King Philip II and Spain's "Invincible Armada"[5] in 1588, had Britain's national survival been so severely at stake.

One person in particular embodied Britain's victory over the forces of fascism: Winston Churchill. During the war, Churchill's approval ratings never fell below 78 percent, and despite a wealth of German propaganda picturing him as a cigar-smoking, brandy-guzzling folk hero, the British people had found comfort and resolve in the rhetoric of his many wartime speeches and radio broadcasts.[6]

Although the spirit of that 1945 summer was one of triumph, solidarity, and hope, there was also an overwhelming feeling of "never again" – the general understanding that Britain could not go back to politics as usual as was widely believed to have happened after World War I.[7] The drudgery of the interwar years, marked by mass unemployment and economic crisis during the Great Depression of the 1930s, was not forgotten, and the hardships endured during the war were still fresh in memory.[8] The overall sentiment of Britain's population was that things would have to be done completely differently in Whitehall once victory against Germany was secured.[9]

Just as the troops began to return from the European front in June and July 1945, the country was gearing up for a general election. Churchill wanted the wartime coalition that had been governing the country to stay on until the Japanese surrender, but this was unacceptable to the Labour Party. Labour was clearly ahead in the polls and eager to ask the electorate for a mandate to implement its vision of a socialist Britain.[10] Churchill was forced to form a caretaker government, which he was confident would be back in power after the next general election. Such expectations were widely held, as many people vividly remembered Lloyd George's triumph in 1918.[11] Yet, what should have been an easy election victory for Churchill's Conservatives would turn out to be a landslide for Clement Attlee's Labour Party. The election outcome was sensational: Labour swept to power with almost 400 seats, while the Conservatives trailed far behind with just over 200 seats. Although the seat distribution result was somewhat exaggerated by Britain's "first past the post" electoral system, there is no doubt that the election marked a major shift in the country towards the left.[12]

What went wrong for Churchill and the Conservatives? Although widely admired as a wartime leader, the majority of voters did not seem to trust the "grand old man" and his party to "win the peace."[13] Furthermore, the Conservatives were blamed for their incompetence in dealing with the economic hardships of the Great Depression, and for failing to rearm and stand up against Hitler during the late 1930s. This latter fact was underlined by the popularity of the polemic book *Guilty Men*, written by three left wing journalists in 1940. *Guilty Men* was nothing less than a complete indictment of Neville Chamberlain as Hitler's "appeaser."[14] Although the book conveniently glossed over the inconsistencies of the left during that period, its analysis summed up what many people at the time believed to be true.[15]

In this chapter I explain how Attlee increased the stakes of the 1945 election by framing it as a "critical choice" in Britain's history that would test the good judgment and common sense of its people. By constructing a persuasive narrative of the Great Depression and World War II in Britain as periods of deep crisis that delegitimated old "Conservative" ideas and institutions, Labour made the case that nothing short of a revolution in the country's institutional framework would avoid similar disasters in the future. Although there was already a significant shift in Britain's political consciousness by 1945, Attlee's Labour Party would successfully recruit enough adherents to its understanding of where things had gone wrong and its vision of how only Labour could be trusted to put Britain on a new and prosperous course. Once in power, the newly elected Labour government would go on to establish a vast array of new institutions and introduce a very different approach to economic policymaking.

The enduring economic difficulties of the Great Depression in the 1930s, together with the subsequent national experience of total war, had created the extreme conditions for new economic ideas to flourish and be tested in political reality. Total war was the ultimate crisis, and the economic ideas that emerged were not only new, they were radically different from existing policy. The first of these ideas was introduced by John Maynard Keynes in 1936 when he delivered a blistering critique of classical economists' assumption that a normally functioning market economy always leads to full employment in his explanation of the Great Slump, *The General Theory of Employment, Interest and Money* (1936).[16] Advocating "enlightened" government intervention in favor of unregulated laissez-faire, Keynes justified an extended role for the state in managing aggregate demand, by fine-tuning the economic system with the goal of achieving full employment. The second idea was propounded by William Beveridge in a widely read report published in 1942, *Social Insurance and Allied Services*, that laid out his vision for a British welfare state that would protect workers from "the cradle to the grave."[17] According to this "Beveridge Report," no British would ever have to suffer again from any of the "Five Giants:" Want, Disease, Ignorance, Squalor or Idleness.[18] Third were the ascending socialist ideas of planning and nationalization that had long been promoted by the Fabian Society, a group that aimed to bring about a socialist society through peaceful means.

The socialist goal of common ownership had been enshrined in Clause IV of the Labour Party constitution for a generation, but the means by which this would be secured had so far received little attention. During the war, the Labour left saw their chance and voted to include a shopping list of industries to be nationalized in the Party's election manifesto. Since the 1945 election was won so convincingly, the left's faith in the popular appeal of public ownership would only be reinforced.[19]

The ideas of Keynes, Beveridge, and the Fabians provided the institutional blueprint for Labour's new society. Over the years 1945–1951, Attlee's two Labour governments radically changed Britain's institutions through a swathe of new legislation and a new approach to economic policy. Once established, Labour's new institutions proved remarkably stable in the two decades to come. Not only did they prove resilient, they also came to enjoy broad bipartisan support and legitimacy in Westminster and Whitehall. Apart from some (in retrospect rather modest) attempts at reform, especially under Harold Macmillan in 1959–1961 and Harold Wilson in 1964–1967, what came to be accepted as the "postwar settlement" – that is, the welfare state, Keynesian demand management, and (apart from iron and steel) the nationalized industries – in Britain did not face any serious challenge until the 1970 election of Edward Heath. Furthermore, during the 25 years after the war, the country experienced a degree of prosperity on a scale that was simply unimaginable for earlier generations. One of the most notable results of the postwar settlement was the stable and high level of employment: During the 20 years between the world wars, unemployment in Britain had never fallen below one million; during the 20 years between 1950 and 1970, it would never rise above it.[20] During those years, Labour's postwar settlement seemed to be delivering on its promise of prosperity and employment for all. Furthermore, given the low levels of unemployment, Keynesian ideas and policies seemed to work and would soon become generally accepted as the economic orthodoxy of the time.

## Britain during the interwar years

> The Victorian economy of Britain crashed in ruins between the two world wars. The sun, which, as every schoolboy knew, never set on British territory and British trade, went down below the horizon. The collapse of all that Britons had taken for granted since the days of Robert Peel was so sudden, so catastrophic and irreversible that it stunned the incredulous contemporaries.[21]

To understand the judgment of the British electorate during the summer of 1945, one must first understand its recent memories of the interwar years, when so many had suffered so much in a time of supposed peace. These memories would feed into the mood that Attlee managed so well, and of which Churchill, the war hero concerned with protecting the British Empire and securing Britain's global role, did not take sufficient notice.

There are lingering debates about the causes of the economic malaise in Britain during the interwar years, the harshness of the slump in 1929–1932, the recovery of the later 1930s, and the importance of policy decisions that were made during that period.[22] Important for our discussion is to understand the severity of the economic crisis during the 1920s and 1930s with respect to how it created the space for new economic ideas to come to the fore. We will see that long held conventional economic doctrines were challenged by new ideas because of their inability to return the economy to equilibrium with a high level of employment. I will briefly review the economic performance of Britain during the interwar period, the geographical divisions that this created between North and South, and the existing economic policies that were used to correct the malaise, before turning to the crisis and the critical juncture that led to Attlee's accession to power.

### Economic performance (1919–1939)

> From 1929 on, unemployment was never less than 9 percent of the work-force; there seemed to be a hard core of one million jobless, good times or bad.[23]

The image of Britain's interwar years as a wasted generation for the British people is enshrined in the enduring popular memory of mass unemployment, long dole queues, and desperate hunger marches. There is no doubt that unemployment was perceived by contemporaries as the dominant social problem of the time. Not only was it the greatest threat to the stability of the state and to the welfare of families and communities, it was also a symbol and a denunciation of Britain's inability to adjust to the demands of a post World War I world "in which the old certainties had suddenly slipped away."[24]

Britain avoided the debt trap which haunted many West European countries after 1918, having financed its war effort largely through foreign asset sales. The country had a net loss of £300 million of foreign investments and, together with the loss of material assets through enemy action, such divestiture reduced British investments abroad by approximately 20 percent. The resulting loss of foreign earnings (or "invisibles") left the country much more dependent upon exports and therefore vulnerable to any sudden economic downturn in world markets. In addition, the war had permanently eroded Britain's international trade position because of major disruptions in trade routes and losses in shipping. Many overseas customers had been lost to international competitors after four years of war and German U-boats cutting off Atlantic trade routes, especially in textiles, steel and coal. In addition, Churchill's decision in 1925 to bring the pound back to prewar parity with the dollar ($4.86 = £1) soon proved to be disastrous for exporters.[25] It would not be until 1934 that Britain again reached the level of national output that was attained in 1918.[26]

Looking at Figure 3.1, which plots real GDP growth and unemployment from 1919 to 1939, it is clear that sustained economic growth only returned in 1934.

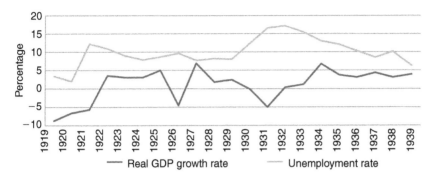

*Figure 3.1* Growth and unemployment in Britain (1919–1939) (source: C.H. Feinstein, *National Income, Expenditure and Output of the United Kingdom, 1855–1965*, Cambridge: Cambridge University Press, 1972, Tables 5, 57 and own calculations).

Average growth over the period 1919–1933 was –0.3 percent, compared to 4.1 percent from 1934 to 1939. However, unemployment remained at historically high levels during the whole period. From 1919 to 1939, unemployment in Britain averaged just over 10 percent (with a peak of 17.2 percent in 1932), which is the approximate equivalent of two million jobless on an annual basis. Another worrying aspect not immediately evident in Figure 3.1 is a radical shift in the duration of unemployment. Looking at Table 3.1, one notices a structural change from short term to longer term inactivity from the 1920s to the 1930s.

The part of the population that was employed, however, saw their standards of living improve, although at a modest rate (Table 3.2). Especially during the

*Table 3.1* Duration of unemployment[1] (1929–1938)

|      | *<3 months (%)* | *>1 year (%)* |
| ---- | --------------- | ------------- |
| 1929 | 43.7            | 7.2           |
| 1932 | 40.8            | 22.0          |
| 1933 | 38.9            | 28.4          |
| 1934 | 41.3            | 29.0          |
| 1935 | 41.6            | 28.5          |
| 1936 | 42.9            | 29.5          |
| 1937 | 46.2            | 28.1          |
| 1938 | 48.3            | 23.2          |

Source: B. Thomas, "Labour Market Structure and the Nature of Unemployment in Interwar Britain," in B. Eichengreen and T. Hatton (eds.) *Interwar Unemployment in International Perspective*, Dordrecht: Kluwer, 1988, p. 112.

Note
1 Percentage unemployed with durations.

*Table 3.2* Rise in real income of wage earners (1920–1938)

|  | Cost-of-living index (1930 = 100) | Net real wages (1930 = 100) |
|---|---|---|
| 1920 | 158 | 95 |
| 1924 | 111 | 92 |
| 1929 | 104 | 97 |
| 1930 | 100 | 100 |
| 1932 | 91 | 106 |
| 1937 | 98 | 105 |
| 1938 | 99 | 107 |

Source: S. Pollard, *The Development of the British Economy, 1914–1980*, third edition, London: Edward Arnold, 1983, p. 187.

late 1930s, real wages per head of employed workers remained relatively constant. If the earnings of the people in work were spread over the whole of the active population, the date at which the high wages of 1913 were once again being earned would be postponed from 1927 to 1930, and would put the postwar peak of 1937 at a scant 5 percent (instead of 13 percent) above the 1913 real wage rate.[27]

### Deep divisions

The effects of the Great Depression were very uneven in Britain (see Table 3.3). Some parts of the country, especially London and the South, fared relatively well, recovering quickly while experiencing relatively high growth rates and lower unemployment. Other areas – the North and Wales stand out – suffered heavily during those years, with continued mass unemployment and poverty until World War II broke out and the British economy transformed from a peacetime to a wartime footing.

   Although unemployment in London and the South East of England was initially as high as 12 percent, the latter end of the 1930s saw growing prosperity in these areas. This prosperity was fuelled by a real estate boom, which took place as a result of low interest rates following the abolition of the gold standard in 1931. The South was also the home of newly developing industries such as the electrical industry, which thrived on the large-scale electrification of housing and industry. Mass production methods brought new products such as electrical cookers, washing machines, and radios into the reach of the middle classes, and the industries which produced them consequently did very well. Another industry that flourished during the 1930s was the motor industry, especially in the cities of Birmingham, Coventry, and Oxford. Manufacturers such as Austin, Morris, and Ford dominated that industry during the 1930s, and the number of cars on British roads doubled within the decade.[28] Also, thanks to the system of imperial preference established at the Ottawa Conference in 1932, the agricultural sector was protected from foreign competition and managed to sustain growth in production levels.[29]

*Table 3.3* Regional unemployment rates in the 1930s

|  | *1929 (%)* | *1932 (%)* | *1936 (%)* |
|---|---|---|---|
| London | 4.7 | 12.6 | 6.4 |
| South-East | 3.3 | 12.0 | 5.0 |
| South-West | 6.0 | 14.8 | 7.1 |
| Midlands | 9.5 | 21.2 | 8.6 |
| North-East | 12.6 | 29.8 | 17.5 |
| North-West | 12.8 | 26.8 | 16.4 |
| Scotland | 10.9 | 25.9 | 15.8 |
| Wales | 18.1 | 37.3 | 29.0 |
| Northern Ireland | 13.7 | 25.9 | 19.6 |

Source: T. Hatton, "Unemployment and the Labour Market," in R. Floud and D. McCloskey, *The Economic History of Britain*, Cambridge: Cambridge University Press, 1994, p. 374.

The North of England was quite a different story. Home to most of Britain's traditional industries such as coal mining, shipbuilding, steel, and textiles, the North bore the brunt of the depression caused by the structural decline in British industry. These industries were outdated, small, less efficient, and overstaffed compared to their continental rivals. This was especially so in the North East around Newcastle, traditionally a major center of the shipbuilding industry. The Great Depression caused a collapse in demand for ships, and between 1929 and 1932 production declined by 90 percent, which in turn affected supply industries such as coal and steel. In some places, unemployment stood as high as 70 percent at one point.[30] Also hit hard was the North West, Manchester and Lancashire, the traditional center of the textile industries, and South Wales, with its many coalmining and steel communities, where queuing at soup kitchens had become a grim, daily fact of life.[31] One government report, published in the mid-1930s, estimated that around 25 percent of Britain's population lived on a subsistence diet.[32]

### Main economic policies

Before focusing on the main policy failures of the interwar period, it is important to point out that the 1930s were relatively successful – economically speaking – in Britain, compared to, for example, France or the United States.[33] The decision to go off the gold standard in 1931, which led to a sharp depreciation of the pound, and Neville Chamberlain's *Import Duties Act* of February 1932 were partly responsible for a relatively strong British recovery, even though Britain could never bring unemployment below the 10 percent mark. Barry Eichengreen, for example, found that the tariff raised output in Britain by 2 to 3 percent.[34] However, there was much direct evidence of Britain's deteriorating competitiveness in world markets from the 1920s onwards. First, Britain made few gains in the rich and expanding markets of North America and Western Europe in the 1920s (exports to Western Europe, for example, fell by 20 percent between 1913 and 1929). Second, Britain was being pushed out of some of her formerly strong markets by alternative suppliers. Third, Britain's share of world trade fell in almost every major industrial category in the interwar period.[35]

Turning to the policy failures of the interwar era, we can single out three major policy decisions that would pave the way for the entree of new economic ideas: Churchill's 1925 decision to return to the gold standard at prewar parity levels, the commitment to balanced budgets in the early 1930s, and the policies enacted in the late 1930s in an effort to spur growth in the North. All decisions would later be seen by a majority of the British establishment as either giant failures or, in the case of growth policy in the North, as "too little too late." All three outcomes would play an important role in rethinking the ideas of Bank of England independence, classical economic orthodoxy, and the promise of nationalization of the commanding heights, given the perceived inherent instability of the capitalist system.

The first decision was the most controversial. In Churchill's defense, the weight of expert advice in favor of the gold standard at the time was formidable. An advisory committee under the successive chairmanships of Austen Chamberlain and Lord Bradbury came down in favor of an early return to gold. For Bradbury, the economic arguments about whether sterling was overvalued against the dollar were clearly secondary to the "quasi-constitutional case for removing monetary policy from political influence."[36] Keynes, speaking as a pamphleteer, referred to this plan as the "Norman Conquest of $4.86," after Montague Norman, the Governor of the Bank of England.[37] Norman was explicit that "the international consideration" should take precedence over the domestic "state of trade," while many Conservatives argued that further social reform, though morally justified, could not be afforded.[38] The return to gold at an overvalued rate (by some ten percent) spelt bad news for British industry and those who directly depended on it for jobs: it depressed exports, led to wage cuts, and introduced deflation.[39] The pressure of unemployment had not brought down wages to the extent required by the gold standard, and British costs remained uncompetitive. On the latter point, Keynes argued that it was simply impossible to attribute unemployment performance to pay cuts or cost reductions.[40] In chapter 2 of the *General Theory*, Keynes explains how workers can bargain over their money wage, not their real wage, during deflation. As such, a policy of wage cuts is individually rational but collectively disastrous since it merely compounds the deflation the wage cut is attempting to get around. This meant that the pressure of unemployment never could have brought the adjustment, since it simultaneously cut the demand that kept investment flowing. In sum, Keynes argued, wages can be perfectly competitive and still not adjust to equilibrium, since there is no equilibrium to which they can adjust.[41]

The second decision goes to the core of economic orthodoxy and the depth of the Great Depression. The minority Labour government of Ramsay MacDonald had appointed a committee to review the state of public finances in 1931. The *May Report* that the committee subsequently produced urged large cuts in public spending to avoid a budget deficit. The issue split the Labour Party, and a new "National" Government under MacDonald's leadership was formed, now with

Conservative Neville Chamberlain as its powerful chancellor. The latter imme-diately issued a draconian round of public spending cuts: public sector wages and unemployment benefits were cut by 10 percent, and the basic rate of income tax was raised from 22.5 percent to 25 percent. These measures further decreased the economy's real purchasing power and made an already bad situation worse. By the end of 1931, unemployment in Britain had reached a total of three million or close to 20 percent of the insured workforce.[42] This is a classic example of the power of economic ideas: the need for balanced budgets was so ingrained in the political elite that it could not anticipate the potentially disastrous effects its pol-icies could have.

The third policy decision was far less controversial than the first two, though its enactment would see a great deal of criticism. In severely depressed areas, or "special areas" as they were called at the time, the government enacted a series of policies to stimulate growth and reduce unemployment. Some of the policies included road building, loans to shipyards in Tyneside and Clydeside up in the North, and tariffs on steel imports. However, it was less clear whether the solu-tion was to move the workers to the jobs by assisting transfers to more prosper-ous parts of the country, or to move the jobs to the workers by encouraging inward investment. In the end, some of the policies helped, but were never on a sufficiently large scale to make a real impact on the historically high levels of unemployment in those areas.[43]

It was only in 1936, when the government embarked on a policy of massive rear-mament to counter the threat from Nazi Germany, that unemployment started to fall substantially. This "accidental" Keynesianism provided the economic stimulus which finally ended the Great Depression in Britain.[44] By 1937, unemployment had fallen to 1.5 million, but it was only completely overcome through the mass enlist-ment of young men after war broke out in Europe during the autumn of 1939. The stark contrast between the huge numbers of unemployed during the 1930s under the free market, and the achievement of full employment during wartime under a de facto planned economy, encouraged the belief of many socialists in the ability of planning and nationalization policies to achieve the same full employment equilib-rium during peacetime. They reasoned that "the state could just as well employ people to build roads, schools, and hospitals as it could soldiers to fight the war. Instead of working for profit, these nationalized industries would work in function of the common good, rather than be at the whim of the unfettered free market."[45]

### The experience of total war

The economic depression of the 1930s, together with the long and dreadful experience of total war with Germany from 1939 to 1945 would make for the ultimate crisis of the British state and lead to our first critical juncture. Two aspects of the war are important for our analysis: the effects it had on transform-ing the national economy, and the damage done by the substantial loss of life and treasure.[46] Both would have a profound influence on the eventual shape of Britain's postwar institutional architecture.

*Effects on the economy*

During World War II, as the country moved from a peacetime footing to one of full-scale war mobilization, Britain was transformed from a predominantly free market economy to a centrally planned one. This is shown in Table 3.4,[47] where one immediately notices the dramatic increase in expenditure on war related activities, from just 7 percent of GDP in 1938 to 56 percent in 1943. This shift was mainly achieved through considerable negative non-war capital formation (or disinvestment) and by severely curbing the growth in the consumption of non-war goods and services. The latter's share of total GDP had fallen by 32 percentage points from 88 percent in 1938, to 56 percent in 1943. The greater involvement of the state in the economy was spectacular: as early as 1940, the share of government accounted for more than half of net national expenditure, almost entirely due to its increased spending on a full-scale war. Another effect of the movement from peace to war was a sharp fall in real personal consumption, which in 1943 dropped as low as 21 percentage points below the 1938 level.[48]

The population as a whole was tied to severe austerity measures and rationing. Figure 3.2 graphs the evolution of the average consumer's expenditure from 1930 to 1945. One can notice that there was a sharp drop in expenditure on food from 1939 onwards. Basic foods were rationed in 1940, and consumption per head of meat, sugar, and tea was cut substantially during the following years. At the end of 1941, there followed a "points system" rationing for other foods, as well as clothes rationing, and in 1942 "personal points" for sweets. Bread was the notable exception; it was not rationed at all during the war.[49] Among other goods, the consumption of tobacco and beer increased most, while consumption of fuel and electricity remained fairly constant.[50]

Interestingly enough, the war also brought about a more equitable distribution of income in Britain. This was not only achieved through progressive taxation

*Table 3.4* The distribution of net national expenditure (1938–1945)[1]

|      | Consumption (%) | War (%) | Non-war investment (%) | Government (%) | Real personal consumption (%) |
|------|------|------|------|------|------|
| 1938 | 88 | 7  | 5   | 17 | 100 |
| 1939 | 83 | 15 | 2   | 25 | 100 |
| 1940 | 72 | 44 | −16 | 52 | 90  |
| 1941 | 63 | 54 | −17 | 61 | 83  |
| 1942 | 60 | 52 | −12 | 60 | 82  |
| 1943 | 56 | 56 | −12 | 63 | 79  |
| 1944 | 58 | 54 | −12 | 61 | 83  |
| 1945 | 61 | 49 | −10 | 56 | 86  |

Source: Combined Committee on Non-Food Consumption, *The Impact of the War on Civilian Consumption in the United Kingdom, the United States and Canada 1945*, p. 144.

Note
1 All measured in percentage changes using 1938 prices.

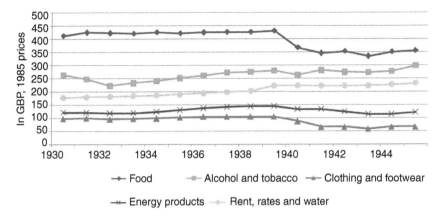

*Figure 3.2* Annual consumer expenditure per capita (1930–1945) (source: T. Liesner, *One Hundred Years of Economic Statistics*, 1900–1987, New York: Facts on File, 1989, Tables UK.7, UK.9; and own calculations).

and subsidies, but also by direct control over goods. Luxuries and non-necessities traditionally consumed by the rich were reduced most drastically, while many non-necessities of the poor – including tobacco, alcohol, and cinema visits – were deliberately maintained, but heavily taxed. The purpose of this policy was to "maintain morale, mopping up spending power and providing a broad tax base."[51] However, as Peter Clarke has argued, the points system provided "a rather sophisticated alternative currency." Those who could afford higher quality goods were better able to manipulate this system; this notwithstanding, the rich actually experienced a bigger fall in their standard of living than the poor, who had always been rationed by price.[52]

### Loss of life and treasure

The war cost Britain about 264,000 casualties in the armed forces, over 60,000 civilian casualties, and more than 30,000 sailors in the merchant navy. Thousands of Indians, Australians, New Zealanders, South Africans, and others died as members of the British Empire armed forces. By comparison, Germany suffered an estimated 3.6 million civilian and 3.25 million service casualties; while US armed forces lost 362,000 lives. Although horrifying by any comparison, the British figures were about half those of the Great War of 1914–1918; and relative to population size, they were much lower than those of most other countries that had participated.[53]

The physical damage of the war and the total loss of treasure were enormous. The financial burden of World War II for Britain was twice that of World War I, destroying 28 percent of the country's total wealth. This left a net deficit in overseas assets: a total debt of £3 billion had been run up with the rest of the sterling area. These came to be known as the "sterling balances." More importantly, the war had reduced the capacity of export industries to a mere fraction of their prewar capacity.[54] By 1941 Britain's foreign exchange reserves had simply vanished, making Britain dependent on American Lend-Lease. By the autumn of 1945, the country was only able to pay for about 40 percent of its overseas expenditure. Furthermore, about two thirds of its merchant fleet was lost and about one third of the housing stock had been either damaged or completely destroyed by enemy action. In addition, many other public buildings such as schools, hospitals, and factories had been hit by Germany's *Luftwaffe* and needed to be rebuilt.[55]

## Revolutionary ideas

The prolonged crisis of the Great Depression and the catastrophe of World War II created the dire conditions for a radical rethinking of how the British political economy should be managed in the future. Three questions in particular were the subject of intense debate during this period and set the stage for new ideas to enter into the minds of the policy elite and eventually also the electorate at large. These three questions were: how to maintain a high level of employment, how to set up a system of universal welfare provision, and how extensive should be the role of the state in the economy.

The traditional or "institutionalized" answers to these questions were widely discredited given their apparent failure during the interwar years. More than ever, the time was ripe for new and imaginative solutions. Indeed, three important intellectual forces would enter the mainstream and provide answers to the question of which shape Britain's institutions should take after 1945. First, on economic policy, Keynes would set the tone in his *General Theory* by accepting full employment as the number one priority. Second, in his famous *Report*, Beveridge would provide a blueprint for the universal welfare state. Third, due to the perceived innate volatility of capitalism, the proselytizing activities of the Fabian Society would eventually result in the public's acceptance of a much greater role of the state in the economy and make nationalization the left-wingers' cherished trophy of Labour's manifesto.

### *The* General Theory *of John Maynard Keynes (1936)*

Given its decisive impact on the discipline's evolution since the 1930s, it is almost impossible to imagine economic theory today without John Maynard Keynes' *General Theory*. First and foremost, Keynes can be seen as the founding father of the separate discipline of "macro-economics," although he would never use the term himself.[56] In the preface to the French edition, Keynes explained why he had termed it a "general theory:"

> I mean by this that I am chiefly concerned with the behaviour of the economic system as a whole – with aggregate incomes, aggregate profits,

aggregate output, aggregate employment, aggregate investment, aggregate saving – rather than with the incomes, profits, output, employment, investment and saving of particular industries, firms or individuals.[57]

One of Keynes' many original contributions to the field was to emphasize the aggregate dimension of the economy, which not only made his work influential for analytical reasons, but also useful as a public policy tool. *The General Theory* was to provide an explanation as well as a policy solution for the empirical puzzles of the Great Depression, i.e. deflation and persistently high unemployment.[58] Keynes also transferred the problem of social justice from micro- to macroeconomics, seeing as "the outstanding faults of the economic society in which we live, the arbitrary and inequitable distribution of wealth and incomes."[59]

Keynes' *General Theory* does not provide an infallible set of tools to put the economy right. Rather, it offers "a pair of economic spectacles through which to look at the world."[60] Full employment, Keynes argued, is not normal but abnormal; there is certainly no self-righting force within the economy that can bring it about. The fundamental problem is that the price mechanism does not always clear the market in a way that leaves all willing buyers and sellers satisfied. The reason for this goes to the core of Keynesian analysis and depends on a few basic ideas. To begin with, the axioms that define individual behavior do not hold for the community as a whole.[61] Keynes liked to point out that one person's expenditure is another person's income, which is something that only becomes clear in the long run. Simply put, each person can decide what to spend and what to save without directly affecting his or her own total income. However, this becomes problematic in the aggregate and in the long run: if everybody saves more money in times of recession, aggregate demand as a whole will fall, thereby lowering total savings in the economy because of a fall in aggregate income. Keynes popularized this notion as the "paradox of thrift."

The point Keynes tried to make was that any single bargainer can beat the system, and many more will accordingly try to do so, but in the aggregate it is impossible for everyone to simultaneously succeed in implementing their incompatible plans. Hence the probability of a self-defeating scramble, either between individuals, firms or nations, is very high. For Keynes, this was essentially a picture of the world in which he lived in the 1930s: a grim place of beggar-thy-neighbor strategies that paved the way for mutually assured impoverishment. Yet, this was a world in equilibrium in the sense that there was no underlying tendency that would change the status quo. For the economy to start shifting towards full employment, something would have to disturb it.[62]

What made Keynes revolutionary is that he shifted the focus of economics from supply to demand. Not so much concerned with supply constraints to growth, Keynes singled out the lack of demand in the economy.[63] His idea that production was limited by effective demand overturned Say's Law that "supply creates its own demand:" a rebuff of the classical view that it was supply, and not demand, which was scarce.[64] For classical economists, unemployment would correct itself through falling wages, eventually bringing the labor market back to equilibrium. Keynes proved this assumption to be wrong. As a result, if the market were left to its own devices, the economy could get "trapped" in equilibrium with mass unemployment. Rejecting the Marshallian tradition in which he himself had been brought up, Keynes insisted that a supposed tendency towards equilibrium was itself a flawed assumption. The solution was for an active government to step in by running deficits during recessions and amassing surpluses during periods of economic boom. In so doing, an active government could "fine tune" the economy by maintaining a level of high employment and smoothing out the business cycle. Quite simply, Keynes enunciated in a theoretic and also practical way why *demand* should be the central concern of economic policy, and how to achieve a level of aggregate demand that was compatible with full employment.

### The Beveridge Report (1942)

Sir William Beveridge's "Report," *Social Insurance and Allied Services*, was a deliberate attempt to provide an all-encompassing blueprint for postwar welfare policy. For Beveridge, a lifelong social administrator in Britain, the report was the culmination of 30 years of experience.[65] The report was published in December 1942, immediately after Montgomery's victory over Rommel at El Alamein. The timing was fortunate since Britain's military success in North Africa significantly relieved the people's anxiety about the further course of the war. What the British people then wanted was "something practical and achievable, consolidating the welfare gains of the war."[66]

The central goal of the report was nothing less than the complete eradication of poverty. The only way to do so, Beveridge imagined, was by attacking its multiplicity of causes – unemployment, disease, old age – from a myriad of angles using a broad array of instruments. Although there were already many separate social security measures in place in the 1930s, the innovation of the Beveridge Report lay in the fact that it "turned a patchwork into a quilt."[67] The report was so popular and widely read (about 600,000 copies were sold in just a few months) that it channeled the force for domestic change behind a plan for remodeling the existing National Insurance scheme, which had been instituted by Asquith's Liberal Government in 1911.

The main points of *Social Insurance and Allied Services* were embodied in its six principles.[68] The first principle was its comprehensiveness: it covered all the known causes of the first of "Five Giants", i.e. *want*. It provided for unemployment benefits, sickness benefits, disability benefits, workmen's compensation, old age pensions, widows' and orphans' benefits, funeral grants, and maternity benefits. In addition to these financial provisions, the Report was based on the assumption that a comprehensive health and rehabilitation service was to be established, and the scheme was to cover the whole population, whether employed or not.

The second principle was that of unification of administrative responsibility, embodied in a single weekly stamp to be paid by the insured person and his employer to cover all insurance provisions. The third principle was that of classification: the whole population was grouped into six main classes, and their contribution rates and benefit rights were laid down accordingly. Those six classes were: wage and salary earners, others gainfully employed, housewives, others of working age, those below working age, and retired persons of above working age. The fourth principle was that of adequate benefits. After careful deliberation, the minimum needs were established and paid as the standard for all types of benefit – in place of the illogical differences of the rates under the existing schemes. The fifth principle, closely tied to the fourth, was that of flat-rate benefits to be distributed according to family size and irrespective of normal earnings or length of benefit. Linked to it was the sixth principle, the flat-rate contribution. To the income of the Insurance Fund, the Treasury and local authorities were to contribute about 50 percent, insured persons (including the self-employed) about 30 percent, and employers about 20 percent. The scheme as a whole would imply a considerable increase in total social security payments.[69]

In order to make his grand vision of social insurance viable, Beveridge needed the country to end mass unemployment once and for all. The crucial assumption of the Report was that full employment would be maintained at all cost. What was required, Beveridge explained, was "not the abolition of all unemployment, but the abolition of mass unemployment and of unemployment prolonged year after year for the same individual."[70]

Beveridge offered five reasons for this argument as evidence. One was that cash payments would have a demoralizing effect in the long run. Another was that it would simply be impossible to test unemployment by an offer of work if there was no work to offer. The third reason was that the availability of work actively drew in people who would otherwise lapse into incapacity. These three reasons were directly concerned with the working of a social insurance scheme, proving its administrative interdependence with an energetic labor market.

Fourth, and most importantly, according to Beveridge's Report, "income security which is all that can be given by social insurance is so inadequate a provision for human happiness that to put it forward by itself as a sole or principal measure of reconstruction hardly seems worth doing."[71] In other words, participation in productive employment was a great end in itself: the ethic of work thus providing a higher compatibility between reforms that slashed the twin-headed hydra of unemployment and poverty. Finally, Beveridge pointed to the heavy cost of his Plan, warning that "if to the necessary cost waste is added, it may become insupportable; for unemployment simultaneously increased claims while depleting available resources."[72]

### The Fabian Society and the idea of socialist planning

The third intellectual force that provided answers to the question of which shape Britain's institutions should take after 1945 were the ideas of socialist planning, which entered the mainstream through concerted efforts of the Fabian Society.[73]

The Fabian Society was founded in 1884 with the aim of bringing about a socialist society by means of intellectual debate, the publication of books and pamphlets, and the infiltration of socialist ideas into universities, the press, political parties, and the government. In contrast to the other means of bringing about socialism that were adopted by most Marxist parties, i.e. the use of violence and revolution to overthrow capitalism, the Fabians wanted to spread socialism through "intellectual guerrilla warfare" against free market societies.[74] Some of the Society's early members included the playwright George Bernard Shaw, the writers Sidney and Beatrice Webb, prominent feminist Emmeline Pankhurst, and the novelist H.G. Wells.[75] The intellectual influence of the Fabians on the Labour Party was, and still is, profound. Many Fabians were present during the founding of the Labour Party in 1900, and Labour's constitution borrowed heavily from the founding documents of the Fabian Society, which were written by George Bernard Shaw. During World War I, Sidney Webb himself was elected to the Labour Party's National Executive, and was instrumental in drafting the party's program *Labour and the New Social Order* as well as the constitution of 1918.[76]

Public ownership was one of the cornerstones of Labour's economic philosophy and was entrenched in Clause IV of its 1918 constitution. According to Clause IV, economic policy should be

> to secure for the workers by hand or by brain the full fruits of their industry and the most equitable distribution thereof that may be possible upon the basis of the common ownership of the means of production, distribution and exchange and the best obtainable system of popular administration and control of each industry or service.[77]

This principle was taken up in the 1930s by the New Fabian Research Bureau, of which Attlee was chairman. The Bureau published 42 research pamphlets; five of these pamphlets concerned nationalization, and were the most influential. The growing frustration with the constant instability and unfairness of the market system in the 1930s greatly increased the significance and attractiveness of these ideas. Many Fabian ideas found their way into the 1945 election manifesto of the Labour Party: public ownership of fuel and power industries, inland transport, iron and steel, and monopolies and cartels.[78] The basic idea was for industries to work in pursuit of the common good, as Tony Benn reasoned: "people thought this to be better than allowing a bunch of gamblers to run the world, where they are not interested in us, but only in profit."[79]

Nationalization would enable the Labour Party to make socialist planning of the economy a reality without replacing the market system through revolutionary means. Friedrich von Hayek, however, argued that central direction of economic activity was incompatible with liberty, and thus incompatible with a real market economy, and that Labour's effort to centrally plan the allocation of resources must either be given up altogether or would lead down "the road to serfdom."[80] As Jim Tomlinson has argued, Keynes was sympathetic to Hayek but rather beside the point in his critique.[81] In a private response to Hayek, Keynes simply answered: "I should say that what we want is not 'no planning,' or even 'less planning,' indeed I should say that we almost certainly want more."[82] Another economist of the period, Arthur Pigou, was both critical and more to the point in his response to Hayek: he explained that the consequences for freedom of only one crucial kind of planning depended on how it was accomplished. If it meant directing specific individuals to specific jobs, then this would clearly be at odds with principles of individual freedom.[83] However, if planning entailed the government providing incentives, such as setting wages to attract or deter workers from particular sectors, then planning did not necessarily result in an erosion of liberty.[84] As we will see next, Hayek's ideas would fail to convince a majority of the political establishment after the 1945 general election.

## The critical juncture: the 1945 general election

The 1945 general election was a critical juncture; it changed the ideas underlying the economic framework of Britain from prewar laissez-faire policies to postwar Keynesian demand management. The pendulum swung from market to state, from private to public, and from capital to labor interests. It is important to frame the circumstances that led to this critical juncture and to stress the significant domestic achievements of the wartime coalition government, led by Winston Churchill but with Clement Attlee largely in charge of the domestic economy. In many ways, that government prepared the ground for a new consensus even though the emerging consensus was fragile and far from set in stone. This is not to say, however, that it would not matter who would win the general election. It will be clear from the following discussion that there were significant differences between the two major parties in their analysis of the causes of the Great Depression and Britain's victory in the war, as well as to what extent a more "radical" shift was needed from the economic consensus that reigned during the interwar period.

It was under Churchill's leadership that the Beveridge Report on social welfare was commissioned in 1942. His government also passed Butler's Education Act in 1944 and published a famous "White Paper on Employment" that same year.[85] The Employment White Paper promised "the maintenance of a high and stable level of employment after the war." Of significance, mass unemployment under Churchill was already beginning to be identified as a macroeconomic problem, a situation where the ideas of Keynes could finally be applied. One passage of the White Paper in particular reveals the thought process behind this and the importance of the entrée of new ideas into policy:

the Government recognizes that they are entering a field where theory can be applied to practical issues with confidence and certainly only as experience accumulates and experiment extends over untried ground. Not long ago, the ideas embodied in the present proposals were unfamiliar to the general public and the subject of controversy among economists. Today, the conception of an expansionist economy and the broad principles governing its growth are widely accepted by men of affairs as well as by technical experts in all the great industrial countries.[86]

In other words, already during the wartime coalition government, there was an emerging bipartisan consensus on the need to maintain full employment and for some kind of comprehensive welfare system. In addition, both parties stressed the need for a comprehensive system of social security that included a comprehensive health service. What still set both major parties apart from each other was the mechanism by which they proposed to achieve these goals and the policy approaches themselves. First, the parties differed on how closely they would adhere to the promises of the Beveridge Report, with Labour being the much more enthusiastic proponent. Second, they differed on the extent to which state planning in the economy would take place, with nationalization being the most partisan issue. These different approaches reveal the parties' conflicting priorities, outlined in their respective election manifestos. The Conservative program, for example, was focused on the personality of Winston Churchill and his individual leadership qualities. In contrast, Labour emphasized collectivity, taking more of a class-based approach by juxtaposing the working class majority with upper class vested interests. The electorate would vote overwhelmingly for only one of these two very different platforms.

The Conservative manifesto, *Mr. Churchill's Declaration of Policy to the Electors*, premised its proposed program with a three page exposition on Britain's role in the world, the safeguarding of the empire, and the need for strong defenses.[87] Only then did the manifesto begin to talk about work (referring to the 1944 White Paper), homes, and food. On national insurance, Churchill promised to "bring into action as soon as we can a nationwide and compulsory scheme of National Insurance based on the plan announced by the government of all Parties in 1944." While promising a comprehensive health service covering the whole range of medical treatment, Churchill emphasized that the success of the service would depend on the individual "skill and initiative of doctors, nurses and other professionals," rather than on the powers of the collective state. Further, the manifesto rejected nationalization on principle and stressed the need to "preserve the incentives of free enterprise and safeguard industry from the dead hand of State ownership or political interference in day-to-day management." The manifesto concluded that:

> Our programme is not based upon unproved theories or fine phrases, but upon principles that have been tested anew in the fires of war and not found wanting. We commend it to the country not as offering an easy road to the nation's goal but because, while safeguarding our ancient liberties, it tackles practical problems in a practical way.[88]

In stark contrast, Labour's manifesto, *Let Us Face the Future*, opened with the proclamation "victory in the war must be followed by a prosperous peace."[89] Labour warned the electorate that the British people had lost the peace after

World War I because they had naïvely taken the "anti-Labour parties' promises" at face value. Social and economic policy after World War II would by necessity be radically different and avoid at all costs a return to the hardships of the depression when "never was so much injury done to so many by so few."[90] In the section "jobs for all," the manifesto promised permanent full employment of national resources, a high and constant purchasing power for all, the creation of a National Investment Board, and the nationalization of the Bank of England. Most importantly, Labour assured that industry from then on would be "in service of the nation," listing those industries that would be taken into public ownership (fuel and power, inland transport, iron and steel). Finally, there was a binding promise to the people that the best health services would be freely available for all through the establishment of a National Health Service.[91]

As one can see, the Conservative manifesto was very much rooted in the past and stressed the glory of Britain's history and the need to preserve its rich heritage and traditions. For Churchill and the Conservatives, the war had been a fight for freedom. Britain had prevailed because it had fought for freedom and that was why the maintenance of freedom needed to come first also after the war. This presupposed that the basic economic mechanisms existing before the war would naturally be sought again in peacetime. The manifesto promised to solve the "practical" problem of unemployment in a "practical way."[92]

The war for Labour meant something quite different. The war had proven that economic planning could indeed deliver and bring about full employment. Britain's victory was thus one for socialism and for a planned economy.[93] For this reason, Labour's manifesto made a clean break with the past and emphasized the great changes the world, and Britain's place within it, had undergone during the war. The only way the peace could now be won was to avoid a return to the malaise of the interwar years, which they blamed on Conservative policies and institutions. Unlike the Conservatives, Labour appealed more directly to the majority working class and vowed to defend the rights of the impoverished and the weak against the rich and privileged.

This perspective on the differences between the parties and their different interpretations of the lessons of the war and the depression that followed is one that is somewhat at odds with much of the academic literature on postwar Britain. Over the years, various authors have stressed a convergence in the platforms of the two political parties and suggest it was a product of the war: that bipartisan consensus was built during Churchill's wartime government in which both parties served. As the argument goes, the fact that Labour won in 1945 was really of minor importance, and Attlee was just lucky that he inherited a legacy where there was already broad agreement on postwar institutions. According to this view, the romantic left has overplayed the significance of Labour's win in 1945, claiming a victory for socialism and the working classes that may not necessarily have been the case.

This view conveniently ignores the realities of the day and the fact that Labour's win meant, and was perceived to mean, a radical change in the governing principles of Britain's political economy. It also ignores the great changes in governing institutions that took place under Attlee, which would not have occurred under Churchill. If one examines the manifestos of both parties, the exposition of the manifestos in the press, the election rhetoric of Churchill and Attlee, and the different opinion polls that were conducted at the time, it is clear that the people of Britain were facing a stark choice between the forces of continuity and the forces of radical change. As it came to be perceived in the campaigns, a vote for Churchill meant Britain would build onto the institutions of the interwar years – principles that had been "tried and tested" – with some adjustments in employment and welfare policy. This would have kept Britain on its established path with small incremental changes along the way, reforming institutions but not truly changing them. By contrast, a vote for Attlee signified a decisive break with the old institutional path. It was Attlee, and not Churchill, who promised a dramatic overhaul of the country's institutions and the creation of new ones.

The point is that it did matter who won the election of 1945. While Churchill would have pragmatically moved Britain into the direction of demand management and gradual expansion of the welfare state, he would have never nationalized the commanding heights of the economy, or established a comprehensive national health service the way Labour did, or expanded labor union rights to the same extent. We know this from his party manifesto and from the steps he took in office preparing his country for peace. Even though one can never know for sure, given the impossibility of a real counterfactual historical experiment, there are enough indications to believe that if Churchill had won in 1945, the postwar path British economic policymaking would have followed would have been significantly different. Moreover, the fact that Attlee's Labour eventually achieved the mandate they did in 1945 meant that they had five years to introduce new institutions, which subsequent governments would feel compelled to build on. Churchill himself was forced to follow these institutions in 1951.

### Crisis narration

Attlee and his Labour Party fought a very effective campaign. Two of their campaign posters reverberated especially strongly with the working classes. One showed a smiling mine worker saying "No more dole queues... so it's Labour for Security. Vote Labour for self-respecting jobs," while the other was aimed specifically at the troops: "Help them finish their job! Give them homes and work! Vote Labour."[94] While a majority of daily newspapers and tabloids supported the Conservatives (52 percent of total circulation), the papers that supported Labour (35 percent of total circulation), especially *The Daily Mirror*, did so with passionate fervor.[95]

Other events would also set the tone and play an important role in the eventual electoral outcome. There was an overall feeling that Churchill, though having been a great leader during the war, was deeply out of touch with the majority of the British people. During one famous radio broadcast he addressed the British people as "you, who are listening to me in your cottages."[96] Little did the "Grand Old Man" seem to know how society had changed and how many people lived in desperate conditions in inner city slums. He was speaking to a population that no longer existed and, for obvious reasons, a population that does not exist cannot listen and cannot vote.

Another famous speech of Churchill was his warning against Attlee's socialist planning. During a political broadcast on June 4, Churchill warned against the dangers of excessive state power:

> No socialist government conducting the entire life and industry of the country could afford to allow free, sharp or violently-worded expression of public discontent. They would have to fall back on some form of Gestapo, no doubt very humanely directed in the first instance.[97]

Comparing Attlee's Labour with Hitler's Gestapo was grossly offensive to the mild mannered Christian-socialist Attlee. As Andrew Marr has written, "Attlee answered him with gentle irony"[98] and replied that it was undoubtedly Churchill's way of demonstrating the gulf between his qualities as a great war leader and those of a mere party leader. Attlee, on the other hand, was quick to exploit Churchill's admiration of Hayek's *Road to Serfdom*. He kept referring to Churchill as being influenced by "this Austrian professor, with the name Friedrich August von Hayek."[99]

The opinion polls during the first half of 1945 were already a clear indication that Labour enjoyed high approval ratings. In February 1945, 47.5 percent of the electorate intended to vote Labour compared to 27.5 percent for the Conservatives. By June 1945, the Churchill effect of "victory in Europe" brought the Tories to 32 percent with Labour still at 45 percent.[100] However, given the scattered and disrupted nature of the electorate after the end of the war, the polls were neither understood nor trusted and their lessons were neither reported nor amplified by the press. Even Gallup lacked confidence in its own surveys and failed to predict a Labour victory. Most of the analysts in government and the media were focused on the war and missed the leftist trend toward Labour. The few that did detect the trend assumed that it was a mere wartime aberration.[101]

The swing of the popular pendulum was unmistakably in Labour's favor. When the election results started to come in, it quickly became clear that Labour had won. With 48 percent of the popular vote for Labour versus 39.6 percent for the Conservatives, the House of Commons was overwhelmed with Labour MPs: 393 versus 210 for the Conservatives. To the world's bewilderment, the great Churchill, freshly decorated with the honors of war, was suddenly, and decisively, out of office. In the summer of 1945, the British people had done the unthinkable: they had voted out the man that had won them the war. Instead, they hoped, they had voted in the man that would help them win the peace.

Attlee won the 1945 election because Labour's narrative of what had gone wrong during the economic depression of the 1930s and how it could be avoided in the future was more convincing than the Conservatives' alternative. The majority of the British people had not forgotten the hardships of the interwar

years and blamed Conservative policies for them. Riding a wave of hope, ideal-
ism, and national solidarity after victory in war, Attlee captured the British
popular imagination by promising economic fairness for all. Labour's analysis
that planning had won the war and now would win the peace persuaded more
voters than Churchill's analysis that the war had been won because of Britain's
ability to harness its forces for freedom and that the postwar period was not the
time for grand socialist experiments. Many people, not least his own Labour colleagues, had underestimated Attlee, but he would go on to become, in Andrew
Marr's words, "one of the two genuinely nation-changing prime ministers of
modern British history."[102]

## Clement Attlee in power: building the new Jerusalem

Labour had it both ways; in addition to being the official opposition party, it also
had credibility from having been part of Churchill's wartime cabinet. For this
reason, Attlee was able to form a cabinet of very intelligent and experienced
ministers, with Ernest Bevin, Herbert Morrison, Hugh Dalton, and Sir Stafford
Cripps being the most decisive and knowledgeable.[103] From the moment Labour
was elected, the Attlee government moved with astonishing speed to implement
the promises of its election manifesto. Not only did the Attlee governments
create the new institutions for Britain's universal welfare state, they also enacted
important trade union reform, changed the boundaries of the public and private
spheres in the economy through a program of nationalization, and by the end of
their first term in office, put into practice the tools for an effective Keynesian
economic policy with the primary goal to maintain full employment. All of this
was accomplished under severe financial constraints and pressure from Britain's
American paymasters who were increasingly worried about the spreading Communist threat and reluctant to finance a socialist welfare state.[104]

This section outlines the major changes introduced under the Attlee governments, changes that were not already a "postwar consensus" at the time, as they
are often conventionally perceived. Rather, what would later come to be known
as the British "postwar consensus" was an effect, not a cause, of new economic
ideas championed by the Attlee governments, which created the new institutions
that were informed by those ideas and would direct the policies of future governments, Conservative and Labour.[105]

### New institutions

#### Social welfare

The impact of the welfare legislation of 1946 was immense. The legislation
included the National Insurance Act, the Industrial Injuries Act, and the National
Health Act. In 1948 the welfare state was completed with the establishment of the
National Assistance Board. Another piece of legislation covering family allowances
had already been enacted in 1945 by Churchill's caretaker administration.[106]

The passing of the National Insurance Act was a historic event: for the first time in Britain's history, the whole population was brought into a comprehensive system "from womb to tomb" that covered maternity, unemployment, sickness, retirement, and death. A Ministry of National Insurance was set up, together with a National Insurance Fund with an initial endowment of £100 million, with guaranteed annual grants from the Treasury. Under the Act, a person was eligible to receive a weekly payment for 180 days after suffering just three days of unemployment. Sickness benefit was given after three days of enforced absence from work and could be received indefinitely until retirement when it was replaced by a pension. The maternity grant was a single payment to the mother on her baby's birth, while fully employed mothers received an allowance for 13 weeks to compensate for lost wages. The death grant was a lump sum to help cover the cost of the funeral, while widows received an allowance. Finally, the Act foresaw retirement pensions to be granted to women at 60, and men at 65.[107]

### Health

To this day, Labour proudly continues to see the establishment of the National Health Service (NHS) as its greatest achievement.[108] Despite the wartime agreement on the need for a health service, it was this part of the postwar welfare legislation that was the most actively contested.[109] The Conservatives voiced substantial opposition to Labour's proposals, but the real hurdle proved to be the vigorous resistance from the British Medical Association. The NHS Act, the brainchild of Labour-left darling Aneurin Bevan, nationalized the country's hospitals and placed them under the supervision of regional boards. The goal was to supply Britain with good enough hospitals to replace the previous system based on local initiative and charity, which had resulted in vastly differing local and regional standards. Bevan wanted "a service which would encompass all the nation's citizens, and provide them all, irrespective of their financial circumstances or where they lived, with completely free and comprehensive medical care."[110]

The act was a personal triumph for Bevan, but it was not free of compromise. First, doctors did not become salaried employees of the state and maintained a considerable degree of autonomy within the system. Second, Bevan was forced to agree to provide private beds in the hospitals in order to encourage specialists to join the new scheme. Third, patients remained free to choose their own general practitioner. In July 1948, when the NHS came into operation, 90 percent of doctors were participating. Bevan was able to transform the NHS from a Labour dream to a respected and enduring British institution. It was to become Labour's greatest electoral asset for the rest of the century.[111]

### Housing and education

Bevan was also the minister responsible for housing, and he inherited a very poor housing situation in Britain after the war: about one third of the housing stock had been damaged or destroyed. During the Attlee governments of 1945–1951, over a million houses were built. Given the shortages of men and materials, this was a significant achievement.[112] Wartime rent controls were extended in an effort to prevent profiteering and to maintain the cost of living at a reasonable level. Attlee's government also passed the Town and Country Planning Act in 1947, obliging local authorities to survey their areas and present comprehensive plans for their development. Previously, local authorities' powers had been merely discretionary.[113]

Although Labour did implement its pledge to raise the school leaving age to 15 in 1947, there was no major reform in education. Since a major Education Act had already been passed in 1944 under the leadership of Conservative "Rab" Butler, the Labour government's hands were tied in many ways.[114] However, it is surprising that, given Attlee's and many Fabians' views of socialism as a process of "leveling-up," there had not been a deliberate attempt to integrate the tuition charging public schools into the state system. Arthur Marwick correctly described the left's disappointment as follows:

> If there ever was a good psychological moment for dealing with the snobbism built into the system, it was in the aftermath of the 1945 election victory. The major public schools were then at a low ebb, and certainly expected little mercy at the hands of a Labour government.[115]

### Trade union reform

As promised in its manifesto, the Labour government in 1946 repealed the reviled 1927 Trades Disputes Act, which was passed into law in 1927 under the Conservatives in response to the *General Strike* of 1926. The Act had restricted the actions of trade unions: prohibiting sympathy strikes, forbidding mass picketing, and barring civil service unions from joining the Trades Union Congress (TUC).[116] Labour gave the unions many of their rights back in a move towards a much more conciliatory approach with respect to industrial relations. "Contracting in" was, once again, replaced by "contracting out" for trade unionists paying the political levy that usually went to the Labour Party. In other words, if a member of a trade union affiliated to the Labour Party did not wish to pay his political levy, he had to contact his branch secretary and sign the appropriate forms.[117] Under the 1927 Act, the burden was on the individual to take the initiative to pay the levy. The importance of this Act for the Labour Party was immense. A good example is the Amalgamated Engineering Union, which tried to get its members to pay the levy during the war. By 1945, fewer than 25 percent did so, while in the first full year after the 1927 Act had been repealed, well over 80 percent paid it.[118] Another consequence of the repeal was that, once again, it became possible for civil service unions to affiliate with the Trades Union Congress (TUC), which further increased the political influence of the Labour Party.

## Nationalization: changing the role of the state in the economy

The program of nationalization was by far the most controversial initiative of the Attlee government's economic policy, and there is no doubt that a Churchill government would not have gone this route. Many socialists had been advocating public ownership to end long term unemployment, significantly redistribute wealth, rationalize the national production process in order to better serve the country's needs, and create better relations in industry. The war years had seen an upsurge in awareness of the principles of public ownership and its potential effect on unemployment. The state played a successful role in mobilizing the nation's resources in preparation for war; a result of this effort was the solving of the tremendous interwar unemployment problem almost overnight.[119] Also, the impressive victories of the Red Army were thought to be largely based on a booming economic system, which was directly controlled by the state.

For most socialists within the Labour Party, the transfer of industry from private to public would alter the rationale of economic life by introducing production for use instead of profit thereby removing the power of the capital owning classes.[120] In so doing, the existing social and political structure of Britain would be transformed, and would bring about a social revolution by peaceful means.[121] During the annual Labour Party conference in Bournemouth in 1946, Attlee explained this as follows:

> These measures of ours are not theoretical trimmings. They are the essential part of a planned economy that we are introducing in this country. ... vital to the efficient working of the industrial and political machinery of this country, the embodiment of our Socialist principle of placing the welfare of the nation before that of any section.[122]

Herbert Morrison steered almost the whole program of nationalization through Parliament.[123] Attlee appointed Morrison to be Lord President of the Council and Deputy Prime Minister with wide-ranging powers in domestic policy. The first three measures proved relatively easy to push through parliament and included the Bank of England Act (1946), the Cable and Wireless

*Table 3.5* Industries taken into public ownership (1945–1951)

| Industry | Date of takeover | Numbers employed |
|---|---|---|
| Bank of England | March 1, 1946 | 6,700 |
| Civil Aviation | August 1, 1946 | 23,300 |
| Cable & Wireless | January 1, 1947 | 9,500 |
| Coal | January 1, 1947 | 765,000 |
| Transport | January 1, 1948 | 888,000 |
| Electricity | April 1, 1948 | 176,000 |
| Gas | April 1, 1949 | 143,500 |
| Iron and Steel | February 15, 1951 | 292,000 |

Source: D. Childs, *Britain Since 1945: A Political History*, London: Routledge, 2006, p. 14.

Act (1946), and the Civil Aviation Act (1946). All three were relatively minor and mere formalities.[124] Soon after, five major acts led to public ownership of five key industries: the Coal Industry Nationalization Act (1946), the Transport Act (1947), the Electricity Act (1947), the Gas Act (1948), and the Iron and Steel Act (1949). The last nationalization was the most disputed as it dealt with the manufacturing industry and not a public utility. The decision to nationalize iron and steel was made in the midst of the 1947 sterling convertibility crisis after which it was held up by the House of Lords. It was not until February 1951 that the necessary legislation was completed.[125]

The financing of these nationalizations was done with considerable ease. The majority occurred through government issuance of public stock as compensation to the shareholders of the companies that were taken into public ownership. Through rather favorable valuations most received a good deal.[126] It must be noted, however, that there was a strong practical case for all nationalizations of the essential public utilities, which was in line with classical economic principles of free competition, i.e. eliminating the deadweight losses of private monopoly power. This did not stop ideological tensions from flaring up between the two main parties, with the Labour left dwelling on "the abolition of the capitalist system through the dispossession of the tsars of big business," and the Conservatives putting up a great deal of opposition in the House of Commons by warning against the dangers to private enterprise of a centrally planned socialist state.[127]

Surprisingly, most academics have played down the economic significance of nationalization, claiming that, although being very important to the left wing of the Labour Party, the measures were far from revolutionary.[128] Instead of being part of some socialist revolution, these critics suggest that the policies would best be seen as lying well within the long tradition of the growth of government responsibility in the economy, as represented by the 1944 Employment White Paper.[129] Again, this conventional view is too simplistic an explanation for what occurred and ignores the perception amongst the public and the policymaking community that nationalization changed the very premise of the state and its relationship with the economy. The Attlee government successfully nationalized a large chunk of Britain's gross domestic product and brought an additional 2.5 million workers into the public sector of the economy. If this were to be done by any government today, it would be considered nothing short of a revolution and a drastic changing of the role of the state in the political economy.[130] Importantly, it was conceived at the time as a revolution. Furthermore, apart from iron and steel, the Attlee nationalizations would rapidly become part of the national consensus and would prove highly resistant to change. It was not until after Thatcher's second election victory in the mid-1980s that "privatization" (or "de-nationalization") would come back in vogue.

### Economic policy

The Attlee government's economic policy tried to marry two objectives: public ownership of the commanding heights and the maintenance of full employment in the economy. In general, the official line of the Labour party was that both objectives would be mutually reinforcing. Since all three Labour chancellors – Dalton, Cripps, and Gaitskell – were against Soviet style planning, nationalization gave them a middle way to directly control the activity of public corporations without openly sacrificing the efficiency of a market economy.[131] During the war, the economy had been mobilized through far-reaching government controls. These were carried into the postwar years and were only gradually loosened until finally being abandoned altogether. The controls were a substitute for the price mechanism in bringing supply and demand into balance and ensured that each consumer had no more than his "fair share."[132] As Alec Cairncross has pointed out, though, the controls could be looked at differently, i.e. instead of an overall shortage of supply, they might signify an excess of demand and a state of "suppressed inflation."[133] Although there seemed nothing wrong with excess demand for a government that was committed to full employment, it was not until Dalton's last budget in 1947 that a serious attempt was made to suppress demand by means of a budget surplus, given already historically low unemployment of around 2 percent.

Eventually, direct controls would be phased out and replaced by Keynesian demand management, which used fiscal and monetary policy to influence aggregate demand. This, however, did not imply that all efforts to control aggregate supply were concurrently abandoned; rather, the budget became recognized as "the most powerful instrument for influencing economic policy which is available to the government."[134] Before Cripps became chancellor, control over economic policy was split between Morrison as Lord President of the Council (economic policy) and Dalton at the Treasury (financial policy). Monetary policy had clearly played a minor role. In 1945, Dalton had tried to enforce "cheaper money" than the already existing low interest rates, relishing Keynes' dictum that a decline in the interest rate, providing that it could be enforced, would bring about the "euthanasia of the rentier."[135] He did realize, however, that because of the failure to issue government bonds in 1946–1947 at the record low level of 2.5 percent, the markets could not always be bullied into buying such stock at such low par. This indicated the limits to which Labour could get its way within the framework of a mixed economy.[136]

It is often forgotten that it was in a climate of severe financial pressure that the array of domestic policy innovations described above were carried out. This makes the achievements of the Attlee government all the more impressive.[137] The de facto financial dependence on the Americans severely curbed Labour's economic maneuvering power. The unexpected cessation of Lend-Lease by Harry Truman after Japan's surrender abruptly cut off Britain's lifeline. Keynes was sent to Washington and negotiated a loan of $3,750 million, topped up by a $1,250 million loan from the Canadians (proportionally much more). The former was conditional upon full convertibility of sterling in the summer of 1947.[138] When that time came and convertibility triggered a run on the pound, the government's pretensions of control over a planned economy were badly shaken. Cripps replaced Dalton at the Treasury and had to embark on a program of fiscal austerity. Only when the Marshall Plan was announced during that same summer would there be some financial breathing space in Britain. Financial Aid from the Marshall Plan, the outcome of America's "enlightened self-interest," however, could not avoid another sterling crisis in 1949, which resulted in a sharp devaluation of the pound from \$4.03 to \$2.80. This finally corrected Britain's chronic dollar deficit.[139]

As already hinted at earlier in the book, an ongoing debate in academia is centered on the radicalism of the Attlee government. It has been argued by many that the first postwar Labour government merely extended the work of social welfare inaugurated by previous administrations, especially of the wartime coalition government under Churchill.[140] I disagree. Churchill definitely accepted the need to focus government policy more on full employment and education, but his means to achieve this were quite different from Labour's. Given his Conservative instincts and past behavior in government in the 1920s, it is certain that he would not have embarked on full-scale nationalization, and would not have expanded labor union rights as much as Attlee did. However, it is certainly true that Churchill's coalition had commissioned the Beveridge Report in 1942, which was used by Labour as a template for its social insurance policy after the war. But Churchill did not seem prepared to implement any legislation incorporating any of the report's proposals during the war.[141]

Public opinion polls taken during the war clearly indicated that the majority of the people were deeply disappointed with the government for not implementing the recommendations from the Beveridge Report and felt that "vested interests had won once again."[142] In February 1943, nearly all Labour backbenchers voted against the government, which entailed a vote against their own leaders who were part of the wartime coalition.[143] Even if the Tories had won the 1945 election, and thus also assuming that a lot more Tory reformers would have been present in the House of Commons, it is still unlikely that a Churchill government would have been as enthusiastic to follow Beveridge's recommendations as Labour proved to be. One good example is the Conservative Party's opposition to the new NHS legislation. J.D. Hoffman pointedly observed about the Tories' time in opposition: "Poor leadership and the absence of a coherent alternative policy allowed the party to drift into a reactionary posture and become the mouthpiece for the vested interests lined up in opposition to the bill."[144]

## The affluent society: Britain's economy in the 1950s and 1960s

The Attlee years established new institutions and brought about significant changes in how Britain chose to – and effectively did – manage its economy and economic policy. These changes, which were based on new economic ideas that emerged from interwar depression introspection, became institutionalized and comprised the new rules of the game for the Conservative governments after Attlee. The very institutionalization of these changes brought about what is now known familiarly as the "postwar consensus."

After the Attlee government was finally brought down in a narrowly lost election in 1951,[145] a period of sustained economic growth ensued in Britain, which combined low unemployment and relatively low inflation.[146] The "twenty glorious years" for Britain (1950–1970) started with the end of rationing and saw a significant consolidation of the new institutions of 1945 under the conservative governments of Churchill, Eden, and Macmillan. Neither of those prime ministers, least of all Churchill himself, had the courage nor felt the need to challenge Labour's postwar settlement. With the notable exception of the denationalization of the iron and steel industry – a clear sop to the right – Attlee's policy innovations and new institutions proved remarkably resilient.

The publication of John Kenneth Galbraith's *The Affluent Society* in 1958 signified a new era of prosperity in Britain, Western Europe, and America.[147] Although Galbraith warned against the growing gap between rich and poor and the dangers of the coming "consumerist" society, he justified the increase in government spending to finance public parks, transportation, education, and other public amenities. In this section, I will briefly look at Britain's economic performance in the 1950s and 1960s and discuss the phenomenon of "Butskellism," which underlined the virtues of what would come to be known as the "postwar consensus" in Britain. This postwar consensus built directly on the changes brought about by the Attlee governments.

### Economic performance

Real annual economic growth averaged just below 3 percent in Britain for the period from 1950 to 1970, and brought about a substantial improvement in living standards. Figure 3.3 shows that growth was very uneven over the years, with periods of boom tempered by periods of relatively modest growth. What figure 3.3 shows us clearly is the infamous "stop-go" cycles the British economy experienced throughout the postwar period.

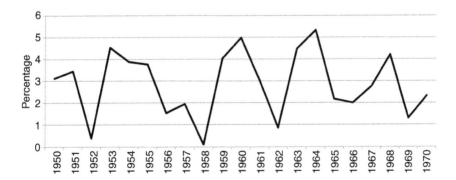

*Figure 3.3* Economic growth in Britain (1950–1970) (source: Liesner, *One Hundred Years of Economic Statistics, 1900–1987*, Table UK.1; and own calculations),

The value of sterling was a constant worry for British governments. Periods of economic boom would lead to a growing deficit on the current account (with imports usually growing much faster than exports), putting pressure on the pound. This was usually followed by a fiscal squeeze to slow down the economy and bring the balance of payments back to equilibrium while maintaining the pound at a stable exchange rate. Since devaluation was regarded as the wrong tool to help increase Britain's competitiveness – an increase of labor productivity was the resolutely preferred answer by the financial and economic establishment – the economy would go through alternating cycles of boom and bust.[148]

Unemployment averaged at an unprecedented low level of 1.6 percent during the 25 years from 1945 to 1970. The foundations of this were laid by the Attlee governments and it is widely seen as the biggest tangible success of the economic policies of postwar Britain. It was only in the late 1960s that unemployment steadily started to rise above 2 percent, never to return to the low levels of the 1950s (see Figure 3.4).

Surprisingly given the low level of unemployment, inflation averaged just under 4 percent during the period from 1950 to 1970 (see Figure 3.5) with one peak of 10 percent in 1951 due to the increased military spending on the Korean War. It was thus no surprise that an ageing Harold Macmillan, upon the appointment of Robin Leigh-Pemberton as governor of the Bank of England in 1983, congratulated him by whispering in his ear: "And, never forget this, old chap: a little bit of inflation has never done anyone any harm."[149] Macmillan, who led two Conservative governments between 1957 and 1963, could not see the inflationary dangers of continuous demand stimulus in the economy because of his own experience of low inflation in the 1950s and 1960s. Macmillan thought the notion that Keynesian demand management could only work in the short run and would only lead to increases in the overall price level in the long run – as would become mainstream thinking in the 1980s – simply absurd.

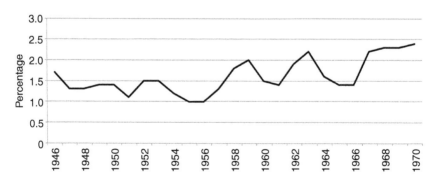

*Figure 3.4* Unemployment in Britain (1946–1970) (source: Liesner, *One Hundred Years of Economic Statistics, 1900–1987*, Tables UK.1, UK.8; and own calculations).

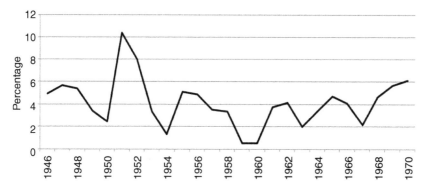

*Figure 3.5* Inflation in Britain (1946–1970) (source: Liesner, *One Hundred Years of Economic Statistics, 1900–1987*, Tables UK.1, UK.8; and own calculations).

### Butskellism and the virtues of the postwar consensus

Although the 1950s and 1960s were not a period of relative calm on the economic front – and there were significant differences between the two major parties at times on how to deal with the economic problems of the day – the central goal of policy, full employment, was never questioned. The debates were mostly about which economic tools to use in order to achieve these objectives, for example monetary versus fiscal policy. Indeed, the policies of Conservative Chancellor Rab Butler (1951–1955) and Labour's Hugh Gaitskell (1950–1951) were so similar that *The Economist* in February 1954 satirically described Britain's economic policy as "Butskellism."[150] The acceptance by the Churchill government in the early 1950s of the broad contours of the Attlee government's new institutions – the welfare state, Keynesian demand management, and (apart from iron and steel) the nationalized industries – proved the path dependent nature of Britain's institutions after the war.[151] It is therefore no wonder that academics and analysts across the political spectrum started referring to this period as the "postwar consensus."[152]

For Peter Hennessy, the postwar consensus in Britain embodied what he calls a "New Deal" between the state and its citizens. In his view, Attlee's postwar government created the conditions for the birth of the "classic welfare state" in Britain, with full employment as the *sine qua non* for the battle against Beveridge's five giants (want, disease, ignorance, squalor, and idleness). The state's answer to these five giants was the universal provision of social security, health care, education, housing, and social services.[153] The impulses which created this New Deal, according to Hennessy, were far deeper in origin than the Liberal reforms of the early twentieth century and went well beyond just making good on the havoc wreaked by the war. Harold Macmillan also instinctively understood that this new thinking went further than simply underpinning the essentials of life, i.e. food, clothing, and shelter. To quote Hennessy again: "[It was] the notion of a collective roof over everyone's head, which bound together the classic welfare model and made it fit for the purpose of slaying Beveridge's 'Five Giants'..."[154] At the heart of this British New Deal were the ideas of Keynes and Beveridge. And although public ownership (which was a Fabian idea very important to the Labour left, but in no way promoted by the "liberals" Keynes and Beveridge) was by far the most hotly debated part of the postwar consensus, the Conservative governments from 1951 to 1964 did very little to dismantle the nationalized industries.

On the surface, the economic policies of the 1950s and 1960s were incredibly successful.[155] A government can only dream of an economy that combines growth with low inflation and incredibly low unemployment. In this sense, Attlee's innovative policies and institutions were a great success. Unfortunately, every success has its price: ostensibly for Britain it was relative decline. Although Britain was doing very well by its own historical standards, it was being systematically outperformed by the continental economies of Western Europe, especially West Germany, France, Italy and the Benelux. From 1959 onwards, when Harold Macmillan was jubilantly reelected on a platform that "the British people have never had it so good," the British establishment became increasingly obsessed with reversing the country's perceived decline. It was not just economic decline. It was also the political adjustment of trying to deal with the loss of an empire that troubled Whitehall. Dean Acheson summed it up best in the early 1960s by observing that "Great Britain has lost an empire and has not yet found a role."[156]

Various formulas were attempted by the Labour and Conservative Parties during the 1960s to reverse relative decline, but these were tried without ever questioning the basic fundamentals that underpinned the postwar consensus. What both Harold Macmillan in the late 1950s and Harold Wilson in the mid-1960s tried to do was merely tweak that consensus and apply some of the lessons from the various successful models from the European continent, be they France or West Germany. It would not be until 1970, with the election of Edward Heath, that the postwar consensus would be openly challenged. The period from 1959 until 1979, when different governments dealt with the emerging economic weaknesses of that postwar consensus and its eventual demise, will be examined in the next chapter.

## Conclusion

This chapter laid out an almost perfect case study for applying the book's theoretical framework developed in Chapter 2. The interwar years of economic depression, along with the austerity and suffering of total war, culminated in what could be called the "ultimate" crisis for the British state. For both the political elite as well as the population at large, it was abundantly clear in 1945 that there was no way the country could go back to the status quo ante. The old ideas and institutions were profoundly discredited by the government's failure to create jobs, maintain economic stability, and deliver rising standards of living for everyone. The experience of total war delivered the final blow to the legitimacy of the old elites and their ideas. In this climate of economic hardship and collapse, neither the existing institutional framework nor the received economic wisdom of the time were able to give convincing answers. The seeds were sown for new economic ideas to emerge and thrive. The electorate had a choice between incremental changes to the existing system or a more radical overhaul of the old institutions, and it chose the latter.

It was during this period that Labour convinced a majority of the electorate of its vision for the future, which was founded on three main lines of thinking, all corresponding to the perceived weaknesses of the preexisting institutional setup. First, given short term price and wage rigidities as well as chronic over-saving, Keynes explained how capitalist economies could get stuck in an equilibrium with high unemployment. Thus he argued that through active demand management, the state would be able to smooth out the business cycle, stimulate growth, and create jobs. Second, Beveridge's blueprint for a social welfare state was the outcome of 30 years of thinking on welfare that imagined a truly comprehensive system of social security to protect people against the perceived injustices of the free market. Third, the Fabians' pamphlets on the inherent instability of capitalism seemed vindicated during the Great Depression, and public ownership of national industry suddenly seemed an attractive alternative to private firms who could go bankrupt at the whim of a capricious market.

The critical juncture came in 1945, when Attlee's Labour Party won the election and received a resounding mandate from the electorate to run the country and transform its ailing institutions. Implementing the ideas of Keynes, Beveridge, and the Fabians, his government achieved a decisive break with the past. The crisis, where the sense of systemic failure justified a decisive intervention, thus became a path shaping moment in Britain's future institutional development. Nationalization, the universal welfare state, and economic policies geared towards managing demand and maintaining full employment all became a political reality in less than six years. Once Attlee was narrowly voted out of power in 1951, the Conservatives felt compelled to broadly accept most of his new institutions and many of the innovations of Keynes and Beveridge as they seemed to be working and there was no clear alternative. In so doing, they made economic policy reversal all the more difficult in the years to come, which is why the idea of a "postwar consensus" seems so appealing. The consensus was an effect of Attlee's policies, not their cause. Radical reforms that Churchill would never have implemented had he won in 1945 were maintained when Churchill himself returned to power in the autumn of 1951. From then onwards, British institutional development proved to be path dependent with only occasional incremental changes to Attlee's original 1945 settlement.

# 4 Relative decline and the unraveling of consensus (1959–1979)

## From "having it so good" to the "winter of discontent"

Let's be frank about it; most of our people have never had it so good. Go around the country, go to the industrial towns, go to the farms, and you will see a state of prosperity such as we have never had in my lifetime – nor indeed ever in the history of this country. What is beginning to worry some of us is, "Is it too good to be true?" or perhaps I should say, "Is it too good to last?"

Harold Macmillan (1957)[1]

In all our plans for the future we are redefining and restating our socialism in terms of the scientific revolution. But that revolution cannot become a reality unless we are prepared to make far-reaching changes in economic and social attitudes which permeate our whole system of society. The Britain that is going to be forged in the white heat of this revolution will be no place for restrictive practices or for outdated methods on either side of industry.

Harold Wilson (1963)[2]

Once a decision is made, once a policy is established, the Prime Minister and his colleagues should have the courage to stick to it. Nothing has done Britain more harm in the world than the endless backing and filling which we have seen in recent years. Whether it be our defence commitments, or our financial policies, or the reform of industrial relations, the story has been the same. At the first sign of difficulty, the Labour government has sounded the retreat, covering its withdrawal with a smokescreen of unlikely excuses.

Edward Heath (1970)[3]

We used to think that you could spend your way out of a recession and increase employment by cutting taxes and boosting government spending. I tell you in all candour that that option no longer exists. […] The cosy world we were told would go on forever, where full employment would be guaranteed by a stroke of the Chancellor's pen, cutting taxes, deficit spending, that cosy world is gone.

James Callaghan (1976)[4]

## Introduction: having it so good?

No figure dominated the British political scene in the late 1950s and early 1960s more so than Harold Macmillan.[5] Appointed prime minister by the Queen on

Churchill's advice in January 1957, after sitting Prime Minister Anthony Eden was forced to resign over the disastrous 1956 Suez campaign, Macmillan would become the embodiment of Britain's newfound prosperity.[6] His personal and vivid memories of the hardships of the Great War in which he served, and the high unemployment that followed during the interwar years – the long dole queues in Stockton, his prewar constituency – made him an ardent believer in Keynesian economics. A lifetime Conservative, Macmillan had even considered joining the Labour Party at one point in the 1930s.[7] In economic terms, he could best be described as a "never again" expansionist, who would always put high employment before low inflation on his list of economic priorities.[8]

Nonetheless, in a move to counter the anxieties of the City of London – Britain's financial center – concerning the accelerating rate of inflation, Macmillan initially appointed the hard-nosed Peter Thorneycroft as Chancellor of the Exchequer along with two apostles of orthodox free market economics, Nigel Birch and Enoch Powell. However, it was not long before Macmillan and Thorneycroft clashed over the government's economic policies during a looming sterling crisis in the summer of 1957.[9] Macmillan feared an unemployment rate rising above 2 percent and was cognizant of impending general elections. In a classic battle of economic prudence (control of inflation) versus political expediency (growth through budgetary expansion), Macmillan and his employment policies prevailed. Thorneycroft, Birch, and Powell duly resigned in January 1958. When asked about the Treasury resignations at Heathrow airport before leaving on a tour of the Commonwealth, Macmillan – in typical fashion – referred to them as "little local difficulties."[10] This episode underscored the government's commitment to full employment and further consolidated the reigning Keynesian postwar consensus.[11]

The budgetary stimuli of the new chancellor, Derick Heathcoat Amory, put the British economy – which had been stagnant in 1958 – on a growth path of 4 percent in real terms in 1959 and 6 percent in 1960. A booming economy thus provided the backdrop for a general election, which Macmillan shrewdly called in the autumn of 1959 when the Treasury's expansionary measures "had found their way into people's pockets."[12] All over the country, the prime minister could boast of widespread prosperity and progress, and a popular myth that he repeated over and over again, "the people of Britain have never had it so good,"[13] would grow. The real slogan of the 1959 general election was equally presumptuous: "Life's better with the Conservatives. Don't let Labour ruin it."[14] The British electorate seemed to agree, and the Conservatives were predictably returned to power with almost half of the popular vote and a majority of 100 seats in the House of Commons. The Conservative landslide was widely recognized as a personal triumph for "Supermac," as Macmillan came to be affectionately known. He would continue to dominate Britain's economic and foreign policies until his resignation in 1963.[15]

Despite this newfound prosperity, 1959 also marked the year in which the underlying troubles of the British economy began to dominate the political debate of London's policy elite. First, there was extensive discussion about the damaging effects of successive governments' stop-go policies on the real economy. This referred to a recurring boom-bust cycle that greatly harmed the British export industry, especially manufacturing, which could have benefited significantly from a weaker pound.[16] Stop-go followed a predictable series of events: an initial economic boom sucked in higher levels of imports, led to a deficit in the current account, put pressure on the pound, and forced governments – which were always under the powerful pressure of City financial interests not to devalue – to choose to deflate the economy instead of permitting a sterling devaluation.[17] Second, from the late 1950s onwards, it started to become clear that the British economy, although doing very well by its own historical standards, was consistently being outperformed by its direct industrial competitors.[18] Due to improvements in statistics and measurement methods of national income accounts, it was now possible to compare the performance of all major economies.[19] Not only were economic miracle Japan and *Wirtschaftswunder* West Germany growing much faster, but also France, Italy, the Benelux, and even the United States were doing much better than Britain. In short, there was perceived to be a significant side effect of the otherwise virtuous postwar consensus – relative decline – even though the decline had little to do with the consensus itself.

Ongoing attempts in the 1960s to reverse Britain's relative decline, by both Tory and Labour governments, saw neither apparent nor immediate success. There were various attempts to address Britain's decline using different economic formulas in the period 1959 to 1979. Conservative Macmillan looked towards France and its *Plan National* for inspiration, while Labour's Harold Wilson was impressed by Germany's corporatist system, which was perceived to have created the conditions for a well-functioning social market economy. Both leaders did not seem to think there was anything inherently wrong with Attlee's postwar settlement and worked within the broad outlines of the established consensus. They hoped to achieve faster growth by applying some of the lessons from their neighboring countries' economic ideas and policies; that is, they implemented incremental reform but did not rethink Britain's established postwar economic framework.

This mere tinkering with the consensus did not expel Britain's declinist fears, as the country continued to lag behind its industrial competitors into the 1960s. A more genuine challenge to the postwar consensus came from Edward Heath in 1970. For Heath's Conservatives, Britain's decline could be reversed by doing two things: first, through a general unleashing of market forces, which were thought to be held back by an overextended state; second, by membership of the European Economic Community (EEC). At the time, Brussels – where the EEC had its headquarters – was considered a bastion of market liberalization. With these new economic ideas, Heath and his Conservatives hoped to create a new institutional framework for Britain. Heath's shadow cabinet, preparing for a general election, consequently designed radical policy proposals that would provide the basis for the Tories' manifesto in 1970. Building on many of Enoch Powell's earlier ideas, the Conservatives promised to turn around Britain's decline with an active embrace of the free market.

Once in power, the Conservatives started to implement many of their plans, but in the face of the first real crisis in 1972 they quickly backed down. The miners' strike, combined with unemployment approaching the one million mark, resulted in a U-turn in Heath's government's economic policy. Rather than standing firm on their electoral commitment to embrace the free market, the Conservatives instead reached back to the old ideas institutionalized under Attlee. Heath accordingly set out to revive the economy through classic Keynesian demand stimuli, which led to an economic boom in 1973. Initial success gave way to runaway inflation after the OPEC oil shock of November 1973 and led to growing industrial unrest, power cuts, and another three day workweek. This series of events forced Heath to call early elections in February 1974 for a fresh mandate to reach a settlement with the National Union of Mineworkers. In that election, however, the Conservatives would lose their overall majority, having failed to convince the electorate that their ideas were the appropriate ones to address the ongoing economic crisis. Abandoned too was Heath's challenge of an alternative to the postwar consensus.

In this chapter I explain in detail the conditions under which Heath was able to formulate his challenge to the postwar consensus, and how he ended by failing in the face of economic difficulties. This chapter thus explores a case of missed opportunity for genuine policy realignment, and an "unsustainable equilibrium" situation, in which a leader comes to power opposed to the ideas of his predecessor, but is unable to break with the prevailing institutions. While the environment was vulnerable, Heath did not succeed in bringing about a real transformation of the existing economic arrangements. He could not convince the electorate that the economic downturn of 1973–1974 constituted a "real crisis" in need of his decisive intervention. Given the absence of such an intervention, underlying problems would continue to spiral out of control until a real break from the past was successful under Margaret Thatcher, who masterfully constructed the "winter of discontent" of the late 1970s as a crisis of the state that only her ideas could fix.

## Boom and bust: Britain's economy from 1946 to 1979

It is important to understand the economic context in which relative decline came to dominate British elite thinking.

Sterling played a critical role in postwar Britain's political economy. As discussed in the introductory chapter, obsession with maintaining a strong pound meant that most postwar governments were severely constrained in what they could do and de facto could not use monetary policy to manage domestic economic demand.[20] As a consequence, Keynesianism deviated substantially in Britain from how it was more routinely practiced in other countries. In Britain during this time, deflationary policies to defend the value of the pound usually trumped expansionary policies to sustain economic growth.[21] This was the opposite of what generally occurred elsewhere and was a result of Britain's unusual international position due to the significant sterling balances held by the commonwealth countries. Britain needed to run successive current account surpluses to be able to meet the frequent demands from those former empire countries to exchange sterling for US dollars or other European currencies.[22] This meant that even a small deficit on the current account could cause anxiety in the City about Britain's falling international reserves and trigger a run on the pound. This problem was further exacerbated by the Bank of England's decision in 1962 to allow foreign securities denominated in foreign currency to be issued in London. The effect of that decision was to make London the world's leading Eurodollar market: new Eurobond issues rose from $134 million in 1963 to more than $3.3 billion in 1968.[23] Hence, the slightest rumor could lead to enormous speculation against the pound, as many financiers sought to protect their sterling investments.

In practice, postwar British Keynesianism followed an habitual pattern: when unemployment figures rose even slightly, the government would introduce fiscal expansionary measures, which would feed into an economic boom. This usually led to imports growing much faster than exports, causing a current account deficit, which would swiftly be countered by deflationary fiscal policies. In other words: every "go" policy was followed a few years later by a "stop" measure, leading to a recurring economic cycle of peaks and troughs. This persistent "boom-bust" cycle is well illustrated in Figure 4.1, which plots economic growth and current account balance as a percentage of GDP. Every "boom" year (1951, 1955, 1960, 1964, 1968, and 1973) went hand in hand with a negative (or rapidly falling) current account balance, while every "bust" year usually saw a radical improvement in the current account (1952, 1958, 1962, 1966, 1971, and 1975) as a result of deflationary policies and falling imports. Furthermore, this pattern suspiciously seemed to follow the electoral cycle, causing concerns for the long-term impact of these policies on the real economy.[24]

Peter Hall has warned that one should not overemphasize the role and influence of the City of London in the postwar governments' stop-go policies.

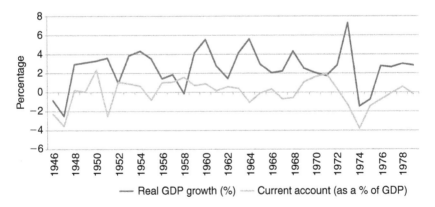

*Figure 4.1* British economy: economic growth and current account (1946–1979) (source: Liesner, *One Hundred Years of Economic Statistics, 1900–1987,* Tables UK.2 (p. 23), UK.16 (p. 53); and own calculations).

Instead, Hall points to the structural features of Britain's international position.[25] Although not denying the City's influence, Hall explains that successive governments understood that the balance of payments also depended on the City's invisible earnings of between £200 and £400 million annually, which might be threatened by devaluation. Also, devaluation would signify default for many Commonwealth nations that held sterling reserves – an effect that would be politically unthinkable.[26] By contrast, Alec Cairncross has argued that, whether the exchange rate was fixed or floating, the balance of payments would remain sensitive to both domestic and external pressures, downplaying the role that devaluation could have played at all. He cites for example two major devaluations, in 1949 and 1967, both of which had only temporary success in removing external pressure. It would not be until the discovery of North Sea oil starting in the late 1970s that the current account would start showing consistent and healthy surpluses.[27]

Regardless of which view one subscribes to, many analysts in the late 1950s started to question the British approach towards economic policy and the all but veto power of the City over the Treasury's decisions. The voices in defense of increased government support for industry became louder and a more long-term approach, like that of Germany and France, began to seem desirable. Once it became clear that Britain was lagging behind its major industrial competitors on the Continent (discussed in the next section), stop-go was singled out as one of the main reasons for the country's relative decline: the City's short-term preoccupation with the value of sterling prevented any type of longer term strategy for investment in the ailing manufacturing sector. The stop-go cycle was blamed for the relatively low level of investment in Britain, and calls for more planning in the economy soon began to carry the day. In 1959, after a triumphant election victory, it seemed time for Macmillan to put some of the ideas he earlier developed in *The Middle Way* into practice.[28]

## Relative decline

> Decline adds to the sense of precariousness which, in turn, freezes the nerve to do anything about it for fear of prestige loss and further, uncontrollable slippage. Substantial and sustained overseas defence commitments plus the cost of investing at home in the social and welfare programmes at the heart of the British New Deal had much to do with the UK's relative underperformance economically and help explain why Britain's 'Thirty Golden Years' were not so gilded as those of its western European neighbours, Germany, France, Italy and Benelux in particular.[29]

Macmillan rode to power at the same time as the British obsession with relative decline took root. There is a wealth of academic literature on the latter subject, which has been at the center of party political debate during much of the postwar period. This debate has focused not only on the state of the economy and its relation to other economies, but also on Britain's place and role in world politics.[30]

What is of relevance to our analysis is the effect of British decline on the evolv-ing relationship between the British economy and the state. This "political eco-nomic" sense is complicated by the fact that Britain viewed its decline in relative rather than absolute terms, comparing its performance to that of its major indus-trial competitors.[31] The belief that Britain has failed, or declined in some sense over the last 100 years has gained wide acceptance, even though failure and decline have seldom been adequately defined.

For the purposes of this book we take a political approach to relative decline. In a study of economic decisions and institutional change we are concerned with the juncture of the state and the economy, which depends more on perceptions than facts. Since most decisions in this field are more often than not politically motivated, the political approach to a consideration of relative decline is a more useful starting point.

Most economists would not understand this "political" approach to relative decline. Their main challenge is summed up by the "catch up and convergence" hypothesis. Joe Sanderson, among others, has pointed out that a country may be experiencing relatively poor economic performance not because it has weak-nesses, but because the countries that are performing more successfully are recovering from war, closing a technological gap, or transferring a factor of pro-duction from an important low-productivity sector to a high-productivity one. For example, France and Germany performed much better during the 1950s and 1960s because of the large transfer of a pool of underemployed agricultural labor to the manufacturing sector.[32] Barry Supple, one of the leading economists who has studied this subject, also emphasizes that assessments of apparent economic decline need to take some account of performance relative to what an economy "should" be capable of achieving. Since Britain's manufacturing sector was already well developed before the war started, it was impossible to achieve the kind of productivity gains that the countries on the continent experienced.[33] All these analyses implicitly follow the lead given by Alexander Gerschenkron in his seminal book, *Economic Backwardness in Historical Perspective*.[34]

This measured analytic approach to the consideration of Britain's decline is empirically valuable. However, in the period from 1959 to 1979, the British political elite was obsessed with Britain's weaknesses – cultural, political, eco-nomic and institutional – and an understanding of the thinking in these realms strengthens our analysis of why politicians made the decisions they did and enacted the policies they thought would "reverse" Britain's relative decline. It is therefore important to stress the fact that people's expectations and the way they think about the economy often directly influence actual economic outcomes.

In the previous chapter, I highlighted Britain's fine economic performance in the postwar years marked by record low unemployment, healthy growth rates, and relatively low inflation. As I shall discuss in the next subsection, however, the statistics show that the British economy by no means performed brilliantly when compared to the economies of Germany, France, Italy, Japan, and the United States. Consequently, there was a growing sense in Britain – rightly or wrongly – that the economy was not realizing its imagined full potential and was somehow falling behind or "failing." This political approach to a definition of decline necessarily assumes that this apparent failure occurred because the British economy had weaknesses that could be corrected be they economic, cultural, political, or institutional. Moreover, it assumes that if the political establishment could identify and correct these weaknesses, Britain could reverse its decline and match, and possibly even overtake, the economic performance of its competitors.[35]

## *The facts behind Britain's relative decline*

Let us look at the data behind Britain's relative decline that so preoccupied the policymaking elite. Table 4.1 compares economic growth in real terms between the United Kingdom, the United States, France, Germany, Italy, and Japan. For every single five year interval in the 1950s and 1960s, Britain was outperformed by France, Italy, Germany, and Japan, and in all but one by the United States. The 1970s show a more mixed picture: during the first three years, British growth performance was only outstripped by France and Japan, while the 1974–1975 recession was deeper in the United States, and Germany's was almost as deep as Britain's. During the last four years of the 1970s, however, Britain was again surpassed by all its major competitors, even after the 1976 devaluation of the pound during the Callaghan government and the subsequent recovery. In sum, the postwar growth performance and associated increase in living standards in Britain were impressive – at least when judged against its own historical standards. However growth rates of the other economies were much more impressive, and in the case of Japan truly spectacular – reminiscent of China's and India's growth performance during the 1990s and 2000s.

The next indicator of relative economic decline – growth in productivity – is shown in Table 4.2, which gives average growth rates for four periods: the 1930s, 1950s, 1960s, and 1970s. Here the data is even more astonishing than Table 4.1. Total productivity measures output per person employed in the whole economy (except for the United States, where output per man hour is used). Again, for all four periods, Britain clearly lags behind its direct competitors, except during the

*Table 4.1* Growth in real GDP (1950–1979)

|  | *Britain* (%) | *US* (%) | *France* (%) | *Germany* (%) | *Italy* (%) | *Japan* (%) |
|---|---|---|---|---|---|---|
| 1950–1955 | 3.2 | 5.2 | 4.7 | 10.6 | 6.1 | 9.4 |
| 1956–1960 | 2.5 | 2.2 | 5.0 | 6.5 | 5.5 | 8.6 |
| 1961–1965 | 3.2 | 4.6 | 5.8 | 4.9 | 5.2 | 9.9 |
| 1966–1970 | 2.5 | 3.0 | 5.4 | 4.2 | 6.2 | 11.6 |
| 1971–1973 | 4.4 | 4.3 | 4.9 | 3.9 | 4.0 | 6.9 |
| 1974–1975 | –0.8 | –0.9 | 1.4 | –0.7 | 0.3 | 0.7 |
| 1976–1979 | 2.7 | 4.3 | 3.5 | 3.8 | 3.8 | 5.1 |

Source: T. Liesner, *One Hundred Years of Economic Statistics, 1900–1987*, New York: Facts on File, 1989, Tables UK.2, US.2, F.2, G.2, It.2, J.2; and own calculations.

*Table 4.2* Growth in total productivity (1929–1980)

|           | Britain (%) | US (%) | France (%) | Germany (%) | Italy (%) | Japan (%) |
|-----------|-------------|--------|------------|-------------|-----------|-----------|
| 1929–1938 | 0.8         | 1.3    | 2.8        | 2.3         | 3.0       | 3.4       |
| 1950–1960 | 2.1         | 2.7    | 4.8        | 5.3         | 4.3       | 6.5       |
| 1960–1970 | 2.4         | 2.7    | 4.6        | 4.3         | 6.0       | 8.6       |
| 1970–1980 | 1.3         | 1.2    | 3.1        | 2.8         | 2.5       | 3.7       |

Source: Liesner, *One Hundred Years of Economic Statistics*, Table IV.2, p. 304.

1970s when it marginally beats the United States. In the 1930s France, Germany, Italy, and Japan saw their productivity increase more than three times as fast as the UK, while productivity in those countries grew more than twice as fast in the 1950s, 1960s, and 1970s. One of the principal consequences of Britain's slower productivity growth was a loss in international competitiveness – a major explanation for Britain's waning share in world trade – caused by the gradual decline in its manufacturing sector during the postwar period.

Given the fact that Britain's unemployment figures were about the OECD average, its slower overall GDP growth explains part of its poor productivity performance, but by no means all of the difference. What was the cause?

### Causes of relative decline

The causes of Britain's relative decline – especially its low productivity growth – have been widely studied by economists, political scientists, sociologists, and historians. The essence of economic decline is usually directly derived from relative economic efficiency and international competitiveness. However, the economic measure of performance cannot be approached solely in terms of growth rates and changes in productivity; it is often also a matter of subjective perception, as Supple has pointed out.[36]

Why did decline occur in the first place? The causes of relative decline are vehemently disputed even today. Trying to make sense out of the different arguments from the vast body of academic literature is complicated, especially since causes and effects of relative decline are often confused in these arguments and lead us to a somewhat hopeless chicken-and-egg scramble. Below I will briefly discuss four major areas of academic debate as to the causes of relative decline: economics, politics, culture, and institutions.

#### Economics

The characteristic most often noted about the British economy is the relatively low level of investment compared to its continental competitors. Neoclassical economists view the rate of investment as the crucial determinant of a country's level of growth, but interestingly enough most economists see this low level of investment more as an effect of decline rather than a direct cause of it.[37] Directly related to this low level of investment is the lack of interest on the part of Britain's financial sector to invest in British industry in the long term due to the historically large overseas orientation of the City of London.[38] The successful lobbying of British finance against devaluation is sometimes seen as the reason for British industry's lack of competitiveness in world markets, which further reinforces low preference to invest in domestic industry.[39] Add to that the government's adverse demand management and the damaging effects of the stop-go policies, and Britain has succeeded in creating a negative climate for long-term investment in industry, which in most other countries was the main source of economic renaissance and productivity growth in the 1950s.[40]

Other explanations for the decline point to the slow growth of British markets in the Commonwealth in the 1950s and 1960s compared with the rapidly expanding markets of continental Europe. The failure to join the European Economic Community when it was founded by the original six, with the signing of the Treaty of Rome in 1957, is seen as a clear missed opportunity. The logic of this argument is that faster integration with the continent would have forced Britain to become more competitive, and a much wider market for its exports would have allowed the country to reap the benefits of economies of scale.[41] Also often mentioned is the expansion of the British state at this time, especially after the reforms of the Attlee governments, which supposedly harmed the dynamism of the British economy. Since all major industrial economies saw vast increases in the size of their respective state sectors, often exceeding those in Britain, this argument, however, can hardly be taken seriously in accounting for Britain's relative decline.[42]

*Politics*

Besides economics, there are many political explanations for Britain's relative decline. First, there is the adversarial political party system. Postwar Britain saw leapfrogging Labour and Tory governments attempting to undo what the other had achieved in power; the persistent de- and renationalization of the steel industry is a prime example of this.[43] However, this explanation suffers from a lack of credibility given the broad postwar Keynesian consensus that emerged after 1945.[44] As I have argued in the two previous chapters, both parties agreed on the main goals of economic policy and only occasionally tried to make adjustments to the country's institutional setup. These adjustments were usually made after mostly symbolic ideological battles during general election campaigns.

A second political reason was failure to create a long-term institutional framework; one which could have accommodated greater economic harmony between capital and labor, and consumers and producers.[45] Examples of such a framework at the time included planning, a policy which seemed so successful in France; or the implementation of a coherent industrial policy which would align the interests of industry and finance, as in Germany.

The geopolitical realm is another example cited in relative decline literature, as was the determination to maintain a significant overseas military presence, even after the dismantling of the British Empire.[46] As Paul Kennedy argued in

*The Rise and Fall of the Great Powers*, diverting too large a proportion of resources away from wealth creation towards military purposes is likely to weaken the economy substantially, thereby further decreasing a country's national power in the long run.[47] The advent of the Cold War in the late 1940s meant that Britain was forced to sustain a military presence whose scale and sophistication exceeded a level that was justified given its reduced global role.[48] Britain's pretensions as a great power in the postwar world were to be increasingly unsustainable, and the high level of defense spending was to prove a crippling burden.[49] Hence, for pure political reasons of global status and international prestige, and in an effort to maintain the country's "special relationship" with the United States, all postwar governments faced the traditional "guns and butter" dilemma and found it very difficult to reallocate large funds from military spending towards, for example, a more serious industrial policy.

## Culture

Substantial scholarship has been devoted to the role of culture in Britain's relative economic decline. The underlying theme of most contributions to this line of thought is the assertion that there is something peculiar about British culture that makes it hostile to industrial development or innovation in general. Some observers stress the decline of the "industrial spirit" among the middle classes since the Victorian period, while others see the laziness or obstructionism of the British workforce as a major cause of decline.[50] Additionally, some authors stress the continuing cultural hegemony of the British aristocracy that somehow drew resources and talent away from industrial activity and towards arguably less productive pursuits in banking or finance.[51] This was also reflected in the country's education system where the Oxbridge elite were more likely to be attracted by the study of "soft" subjects such as literature, history, philosophy, and the arts, than to pursue degrees in "hard" subjects more applicable to the country's economic development such as business, science, or engineering.[52]

The cultural explanation suffers from what Dennis Kavanagh calls the "individualistic fallacy," i.e. the tendency to ascribe to the wider community the characteristics of certain individuals.[53] Nevertheless, despite all kinds of conceptual and methodological problems, the cultural explanation has been one of the most powerful and bipartisan explanations for decline in postwar Britain. It has been put forward equally by Labour and Conservative governments, opposition leaders, business leaders, and leading trade unionists.[54]

The main problem with the cultural thesis, unfortunately, is that it fails to explain why attitudes that were conducive to fast economic growth and rapid industrialization, which presumably made Britain into the "workshop of the world" by the mid-nineteenth century, somehow gave way to much less productive states of mind in the twentieth century.[55] And since the discussion here aims to explain the difference between Britain's economic performance and its more successful competitors, monocausal cultural explanations have only limited utility. However, many analysts still maintain that they should probably not be entirely dismissed.[56]

*Institutions*

Peter Hall has rejected all the above phenomena as effects rather than explanations, whose causes need to be explained in their own right. Hall sees nothing wrong with the role of the state, industrial investment, or the attitudes of British workers because they seem to show perfectly rational behavior within the institutional framework that they faced. Therefore, Hall points out, it is necessary to look at the "particular institutional setting of the markets facing British firms" in order to understand relative economic decline.[57] Britain's experience as the world's first industrial nation left British firms in specific institutional positions in relation to banks, the state, and the educational system. Hall breaks down Britain's historical legacy into four separate components: the industry–finance nexus, product markets and industrial structure, firm organization and performance, and the structure of the labor market and shop floor power.[58] Hall concludes that within this particular institutional context, individuals were responding in a predictable manner to the incentives they faced, and that the behavior of British capital and labor was therefore perfectly rational. Unfortunately, as Hall states, the British economy suffered in the long run from the actions of individuals who were maximizing their respective behaviors.[59] The conclusion from this analysis seems clear: in order to reverse decline, Britain needed a dramatic overhaul of its institutions.

All four types of existing explanations concerning the causes of relative decline provided the ideational background for the attempts to reverse it by Macmillan, Wilson, and Heath. Each of these prime ministers focused on one or two causes they thought to be the most important, and which they could reconcile with their broader party ideology. Macmillan and Wilson found the "economic" and "political" explanations the most compelling and focused on the low levels of investment and lack of planning. Wilson, consistent with Labour ideology, even tried to weaken some of the powers of the City by setting up another economic department that would offset the Treasury's narrow focus on finance. Heath also tried to change the institutions of postwar Britain by trying to shift the balance of power away from the state and back to the market, and through comprehensive industrial relations reform.

## Tweaking the consensus: economic policies addressing decline in the 1960s

As mentioned, the influence of relative decline on the psyche of the policymaking elite started to take a firm hold in the late 1950s, when Whitehall embraced different policy proposals in an effort to reverse the country's slower growth and diminishing international competitiveness. Some explanations for the decline were deemed more important than others, but there was an emerging consensus on the need for more long term national planning, a coherent industrial policy to revitalize British industry, and the establishment of less hostile relations between capital, labor, and the state. All ideas shared the goal of achieving faster economic growth. With an active "growth advocacy network" of journalists, academic economists, think tanks, and pressure groups providing the ideas, "growthmanship" was to become the battleground of British party politics in the next decade.[60]

During the 1960s, these ideas were put into practice. However, they always stayed within the broader framework of the ideas of the postwar consensus with the ultimate goal of full employment. It was not until Heath took power that a larger overhaul of the system was attempted. In the early 1960s, Macmillan began with small adjustments through an attempt at "growth through planning," with the establishment of the National Economic Development Council (NEDC), which would guide the economy towards a higher growth path. When Labour was voted back into office in 1964, Harold Wilson tried to take away part of the power of the Treasury over the economy by founding a new Department of Economic Affairs (DEA) that would put forward a "National Plan." We discuss both these episodes in greater detail below, before turning to Heath's challenge.

### Macmillan's attempt at national planning

The "64,000 dollar question," Macmillan wrote in his diary in 1963, "was how to Boom without Busting."[61] Against the backdrop of the frustrations of stop-go in the 1950s and the acute awareness of Britain's relative economic decline, the answer for Macmillan was through "a wholesale overhaul of economic objectives and policy instruments, more ambitious growth targets and a new institution that would coordinate national economic development: the National Economic Development Council."[62] The NEDC, proposed by Chancellor Selwyn Lloyd in the summer of 1961, was a tripartite consultative body consisting of ministers, peak level employers' organizations, and representatives of the Trades Union Congress (TUC). The Council began to hold regular meetings in March 1962. The NEDC was served by a staff of officials independent of the government who made up the National Economic Development Office (NEDO).[63]

The superior performance of the French economy and Jean Monnet's *Plan National* was thought to demonstrate that planning led to faster growth. Over the course of 15 years, France had succeeded in turning its economy from the sick man of Europe into a dynamic one that grew fast through high levels of investment. Admiring glances and business trips across the English Channel only increased the belief that the British had something to learn from the French.[64] The steady pursuit of long-term objectives, which planning entailed, was contrasted with the regular stops that occurred in the absence of planning. Macmillan also believed that the stops were usually the result of balance of payments problems, due to rising wage costs and to the problem of external liabilities, i.e. sterling balances. He thus expected that more constructive discussions with the unions in the context of more rapid growth might bring wages within the overall framework of planning and thereby help to eventually eliminate the stops.[65] The

NEDC was thus an attempt to put government–industry–labor relations on a much more constructive footing and create a national sense of direction towards growth. The Council went on to produce a five year economic plan for the British economy.[66]

The major problem with the NEDC, however, was that there was no mechanism for compulsory responsibilities on the part of business or labor.[67] In other words, firms or workers were never forced to accept the broad planning frameworks that were formulated by the NEDC.[68] Despite certain superficial similarities, the NEDC was fundamentally different from the French *Commissariat du Plan*, which had close links to the French state and a well-developed network of connections to the private sector. The NEDC basically continued a voluntaristic tradition according to which the state left matters of industrial reorganization largely to the private sector alone.[69] Since the NEDC was not very well integrated into the economic policymaking process, it had no power to press for the implementation of its detailed national plan. In the end, the Council acted as the principal forum for the negotiation of income policies, while the often insightful reports they published proved to have very little impact on actual economic policymaking.[70]

### Wilson's corporatist hopes

Wilson continued to attempt incremental, though different, changes to the existing framework, which met with equally limited success. Labour's election manifesto for the 1964 general election, *The New Britain*, had ambitious plans for the economy.[71] Maintaining full employment while achieving a faster rate of industrial expansion could only be secured by "a deliberate and massive effort to modernise the economy; to change its structure and to develop with all possible speed the advanced technology and the new science-based industries with which our future lies. In short, they will only be achieved by socialist planning."[72] In order to take away the overwhelming power of the Treasury over the economy, Labour promised to set up two new ministries: a Ministry of Economic Affairs with the duty of formulating, in unison with representatives of capital and labor, a national economic plan; and a Ministry of Technology to guide and stimulate a major national effort to bring advanced technology and new processes into industry.[73] The 1964 election was characterized by the customary ideological battle between Tories and Labour, but once Labour won its narrow election victory, their accession to power hardly signaled a fundamental shift towards *dirigisme*, let alone socialism. Harold Wilson, the new prime minister, who had promised to "reforge Britain in the white hot heat of the scientific revolution,"[74] set out to implement a program that was broadly similar to that attempted by Macmillan.[75]

Labour inherited a fast growing economy from the Tories in 1964, albeit a shaky one: the current account deficit was again widening. Apparently, outgoing Chancellor Reginald Maudling told his successor at the Treasury, James Callaghan, that he was "sorry to leave it in such a mess."[76] To his dismay, Callaghan would soon realize that Maudling was not referring to the state of the actual Treasury building, but to the British economy itself.[77] Since Wilson was well aware that Labour had been the party of devaluation and economic incompetence, he was determined to push through the national plan and avoid devaluation at all costs. George Brown was appointed to lead the Ministry of Economic Affairs, which published the National Plan in September 1965 after elaborate consultations with both sides of industry and the NEDC apparatus. Brown set the goal of sustained growth at 4 percent, which was not totally unrealistic at the time, since it had been surpassed in both 1963 and 1964.[78]

The talk of "creative tension" between the DEA, which represented the real economy, and the Treasury, representing the financial side of the economy, soon began to sound hollow. During the summers of 1965 and 1966, a deteriorating balance of payments induced a rapid depreciation of sterling. Instead of adhering to the National Plan's strategy of ignoring the balance of payments constraint on economic growth, Wilson was forced to abandon the National Plan in favor of deflation, cutting public spending and reining in consumer demand.[79] In retrospect, it seems that the grip of the Treasury, with its massive expertise and its hold over the entire Whitehall machine, was never really loosened. Given the chronic weakness of sterling, the Chancellor of the Exchequer – in this case, Callaghan – was bound to prevail. As the failure of the National Plan became evident, Wilson tried to take a more proactive approach to industrial planning by setting up the Industrial Reorganization Corporation in 1966, a new agency directed by an independent group of businessmen, and by the enactment of the Industrial Expansion Act in 1968, which was to provide new ways to finance industrial growth.[80] However, both of these new institutions lacked the necessary funds to make a substantial shift in Britain's economic structure possible.

Another fundamental weakness of Labour's National Plan was the innate assumption that wage restraint would function to combat inflation without enforcement mechanisms ensuring that the unions would implement this objective. When it became clear that this would not work in 1966, the government created the National Board for Prices and Incomes, which immediately imposed a statutory wage freeze lasting six months followed by a further two years of severe wage restraint, now backed by a new "statutory policy."[81] By the summer of 1967, after yet another sterling crisis, Wilson and Callaghan were finally forced to devalue the pound from $2.80 to $2.40, which further exacerbated the growing problem of rising prices. Labour tried to keep inflation and the increasingly restless trade unions in check, through a compulsory incomes policy and by means of legal restraints contained in Barbara Castle's white paper, *In Place of Strife*,[82] which ultimately failed to pass the House of Commons due to ardent lobbying by the unions.[83]

In the end, both Macmillan's and Wilson's attempts were seen as failures, since they were unable to break the firm grip of financial interests over the government's economic policy. However, both governments set out to create a far greater degree of state involvement in the economy than had been thought necessary in the 1950s. Both adopted a kind of "half way house" between

Keynesianism and Corporatism.[84] As observed by Hall and others, however, a strategy based on voluntary cooperation with state sponsored policies was bound to fail. Not only did it overlook the lack of control that union leaders had over their members on the shop floor, or the difficulty of achieving coordination in Britain's non hierarchical and highly competitive industry, it failed to trump the power of the City of London, which kept its de facto veto power over the country's economic decision making process.[85]

## Edward Heath's challenge to the postwar consensus

> Heath was par excellence a technocrat. He was not particularly interested in ideas, with the single exception of the idea of Europe, which was the thing that mattered most to him. [...] There was a technocratic solution to every problem; that is how he saw government.[86]

Edward Heath became leader of the Conservative Party in 1965, after Sir Alec Douglas-Home resigned and changed the party rules to allow for the first direct contest of Tory leadership.[87] To the surprise of many party members, Heath beat the favorite, Reginald Maudling. Heath was first elected to the House of Commons in 1950, where he made a name for himself as the Conservatives' chief whip under Anthony Eden, and Minister of Labour and Lord Privy Seal under Macmillan. In this last function, he was responsible for leading the first round of negotiations to secure Britain's accession to the Common Market. He was fervently pro-European, but was bound to fail in his first attempt at British EC membership given the standing veto of France's Charles de Gaulle.[88]

Heath was considered to be more on the liberal side of the party. He had bolstered his market credentials as President of the Board of Trade under Douglas-Home, where he oversaw the abolition of retail price maintenance in 1963. This was seen at the time as a free market move. In short, although Heath was clearly a confidant of Macmillan and a product of the postwar consensus, he was also willing to embrace some of the free market ideas that were continually espoused by the party's dark horse Enoch Powell, especially when he started to realize that existing planning attempts proved woefully futile in reversing the country's relative decline.[89]

Although the Conservatives lost substantially in the face of Labour's landslide election victory in 1966, Heath was allowed to stay on as party leader for the Tories, and used the time in opposition to develop a more detailed and radical program for a new Conservative government. By late 1967, after Labour's decision to devalue the pound, it was clear that both Macmillan's and Wilson's attempts at planning had failed to revitalize British industry, make an end to stop-go, and reverse decline. Heath and his shadow cabinet, which included Sir Keith Joseph and Margaret Thatcher, were to develop a new policy framework that – for the first time – was to challenge some of the founding principles of the postwar consensus and cause many right-wing Conservatives to speak with full enthusiasm of a "quiet revolution."[90]

### Back to the market: the ideas of Selsdon Park

In January 1970, Heath convened a brainstorming session with his Conservative shadow cabinet in the Selsdon Park hotel near Croydon, Surrey.[91] The purpose of the meeting was to knock into shape the party's manifesto for the anticipated general election later that year. Many Conservative Party members, not least Heath himself, had come to the conclusion that the state activism employed by both parties during the 1950s and 1960s had not only failed to reverse the country's relative economic decline, but actually made it worse. The task they set for themselves was to rebalance the state–market relationship in favor of the market.[92] For the first time since the 1930s, a major political party in Britain started to talk favorably about "the creative forces of the free market" in a concentrated effort to stimulate higher growth.[93] Certain policies found broad consensus within the party: tax cuts; the abandonment of Labour's incomes policy, which was seen as a huge failure in curbing inflation; the need for industrial relations reform in the spirit of Castle's white paper, *In Place of Strife*; and the need to resist – at all cost – any further nationalizations of ailing industries or so-called "lame ducks."[94]

Although the party's manifesto during the Selsdon Park meetings was still largely a work in progress, the meetings received massive media attention and were used as evidence by the British press as an unambiguous swing to the right by Heath's Conservatives. Indeed, Harold Wilson saw it as a clear vote loser for the Tories and coined it "Selsdon Man,"[95] describing Heath as a dangerous reactionary who wished to take the country back to a less civilized age of "unfettered jungle capitalism."[96] Wilson publicly announced that

> Selsdon Man is not just a lurch to the right; it is an atavistic desire to reverse the course of twenty-five years of social revolution. What [the Conservatives] are planning is a wanton, calculated and deliberate return to greater inequality.[97]

This was of course a huge exaggeration. Heath probably did not regard the meeting at Selsdon Park as embracing a new and radical economic philosophy.[98] As many observers have pointed out, he was a man who saw a technocratic solution to every problem, and the goals of economic policy – faster growth and full employment – were more important than any specific ideology on how to achieve them. On the other hand, he did little or nothing to contradict the free market impression that was given. It did clearly serve his purpose at the time, which was to be seen as an opposition leader who offered a new direction to the country with fresh policies that would reverse Britain's relative economic decline.[99]

Although there is still considerable disagreement over the ultimate role of the Selsdon Park meetings in the eventual Tory platform, there is no doubt that the Conservatives' 1970 manifesto, *A Better Tomorrow*, heralded a significant change in approach towards the economy from the Macmillan years.[100] Free market ideas figure prominently in the manifesto, emphasizing the benefits of economic freedom and highlighting their overall theme "to replace Labour's restrictions with Conservative incentive."[101] As the country was facing the highest rates of inflation in 20 years, the Conservatives emphasized that the need to curb inflation was more important than measures to maintain full employment. Heath blamed Labour for the rise in prices caused by the 1967 devaluation of sterling. The Tories unreservedly rejected the philosophy of compulsory wage control and hoped to achieve the same objective through trade union reform, an area where Labour had failed.[102] Heath was also well aware of his predecessor's broken promises: "Our policies are not, like Labour's, a collection of short lived devices. [...] Nor are they a set of promises made only to be broken. The last Conservative Government kept all its promises. So will the next."[103]

Heath's ideas for reversing the country's decline can be summarized in seven points, which were all featured prominently in the manifesto. First, he wanted to lower taxes and establish a simplified overall tax system. Second, he wanted more savings to create the "capital-owning democracy of the future." Third, the Conservatives stressed that there had been too much government under Labour and promised to cut government spending, starting with a reduction in government ministers. Fourth, they would tackle inflation not by the failed compulsory wage control, but by policies to stimulate growth and through better industrial relations. The government would also take the lead in curbing wages in the public sector. Fifth, they were to introduce a comprehensive Industrial Relations Bill, which would provide a proper legal framework for improved relations between management and unions so that strikes would become the means of last resort. Sixth, there would be government assistance in training for better jobs. And finally, emphasizing that "competitive free enterprise ensures choice for the consumer," they were to pursue a vigorous competition policy and would "progressively reduce the involvement of the state in the nationalized industries."[104]

### The 1970 election

At the start of 1970, Labour had been in government for almost six years. After having won a ringing endorsement from the electorate with a large majority in the 1966 general election, they began to trail consistently behind the Tories in the opinion polls.[105] However, towards the end of 1969, the polls were beginning to show Labour back in the lead and it was expected that Wilson would call an election sometime in 1970 to capitalize on this change of mood and on the economic recovery engineered by his Chancellor, Roy Jenkins, who had finally achieved a small balance of payments surplus by the end of 1969. By May 1970, Labour had convincingly won the local elections, and once Wilson announced a general election for late June, 67 percent of the population was convinced that Labour would win it.[106] At the time, British sociologists wrote reasoned dissertations suggesting that Wilson had created an enduring Socialist majority. Many people went along with the idea, apart from Edward Heath himself.[107]

In the end, many traditional Labour voters – angered by *In Place of Strife* and overall government cuts in social welfare – stayed at home, in the safe know-ledge that Wilson had won anyway. To everyone's consternation, Edward Heath's Conservatives won the 1970 general election with 46 percent of the vote and 330 seats, compared to 43 percent for Labour and 287 seats. Turnout was down from 76 percent in 1966 to 72 percent, which was seen at the time as particularly damaging for the Labour Party.[108] Heath had a comfortable majority of just over 30 seats and was called upon to form a new government. For the first time in over 30 years, a party that had openly campaigned on a free market plat-form had won a general election. Heath's coming to power was to mark the first major challenge to the reigning postwar consensus. Once in power, he would have the opportunity to translate the promises and ideas of the Conservatives' manifesto into actual government policy. Heath's surprise victory thus seemed to indicate the dawn of a new era in British economic policymaking.[109]

### Heath's experiment: 1970–1972

The first two years of the Heath government saw a flurry of legislative and policy initiatives that were to underline the Conservatives' broad *laissez-faire* orienta-tion.[110] The guiding assumption to his initiatives were that, left to its own devices, the market would regenerate industry and create the rapid economic growth necessary for an extensive welfare state to be maintained.[111] There were four elements to the new government's market-based economic policy: the with-drawal of the state from the private sector's day to day business; industrial rela-tions reform and free collective bargaining; control of public spending; and finally, Heath's personal decision to apply again for full membership of the European Economic Community.[112]

The first policy innovation was based on Heath's belief that the government could learn from the new "managerial" techniques and structures in the private sector, rather than the other way around. A number of government functions were passed on to autonomous agencies outside the Whitehall machine, and one of his loyal lieutenants, Peter Walker, was given almost carte blanche in his effort to streamline local government.[113] Furthermore, the degree of state inter-vention at the microeconomic level was dramatically reduced by abolishing the National Board for Prices and Incomes (NBPI), the Monopolies Commission and the Land Commission, as well as the elimination of many regional and sec-toral Economic Development Councils first set up by Macmillan.[114] In addition, state aid to ailing industries and regions was cut back to allow firms to make their investment and location decisions based on market signals, while credit controls were removed in order to give the financial sector more freedom to maneuver.[115]

The most controversial reform came in industrial relations. Since Heath had abolished the NBPI, the government had to provide private sector employers with some degree of protection as they tried to reach wage settlements with the trade unions.[116] Although Minister of Labour Robert Carr preferred a piecemeal approach, he was forced by Heath's cabinet to propose one big bill. This would later turn out to be a big strategic mistake.[117] The 1971 Industrial Relations Act was passed despite the vehement opposition of the TUC and – to many Tories' surprise – bitter denunciations by Barbara Castle, who had tried to push through very similar legislation two years earlier, but now in opposition had had an apparent change of heart.[118] The main effect of the act was to outlaw unofficial, wildcat strikes – a measure which Heath claimed would "grease the wheels of the labor market."[119] Also, a new Industrial Relations Court was established with wide-ranging powers to enforce ballots and so-called "cooling-off periods" on registered unions. There was, however, a legal loophole that the TUC shrewdly exploited: if unions refused to register, they would remain beyond the powers of the court.[120] By the time the Act was passed in parliament, the public standing of trade unions stood at its highest level for three years, and Heath was soon to realize that he had the worst of all possible worlds: a heavily disputed Act that passed at immense political cost without any apparent pay-off.[121] The TUC won the institutional battle to prevent its constituent unions from registering, and the successfully set up Industrial Court had virtually no work since most employers shied away from it.[122]

The third part of Heath's free market strategy was the general retreat of the state from the economy. This was emphasized by the appointment of John Davies, director-general of the Confederation of British Industries (CBI), to the newly created Department of Trade and Industry, in an effort to underline the government's free market image.[123] The government refused help to a number of enterprises in difficulties, such as the Docks and Harbours Board.[124] Heath replaced Labour's statutory incomes policy with free collective bargaining between management and employees in the private sector, while surreptitiously maintaining an incomes policy in the public sector, with the hope of setting an example for the rest of the economy.[125] Wilson's Industrial Expansion Act was repealed, and investment grants were replaced by tax allowances. Also, there was an overall cut in taxes that halved the selective employment tax and cut corporation tax.[126] However, Davies' strategy proved a hard act to follow. The government faced a moment of truth in early 1971 when Rolls Royce faced bankruptcy and took the painful decision to nationalize the company, which clearly delighted a cheering opposition.[127] And when the collapse of Upper Clyde Shipbuilders threatened Glasgow with heavy unemployment, Heath again would come to the rescue.[128]

Finally, Heath saw membership of the European Community (EC) as a way out of Britain's economic doldrums.[129] The EC had already agreed at the end of 1969 to reopen negotiations as to a British entry in June 1970.[130] The main stumbling blocks during the entry talks were pretty much the same as during the abortive 1967 bid by Labour. They included agriculture and fisheries, New Zealand, Commonwealth sugar, and the length of the transition period. The negotiations were completed in record time: the EC system of agricultural support would replace the British system of deficiency payments while prices would be gradually raised to EC levels, British tariffs would be brought into line with the EC's common external tariff by 1977, New Zealand would enjoy concessions for butter and cheese during the transition period, and there would be arrangements for Commonwealth sugar.[131] EC membership was finally achieved in January 1973, giving Britain complete free market access to the major economies of continental Western Europe. EC accession was not only a personal triumph for Heath, but also undoubtedly his most lasting achievement in government.

All these pro-market reforms were pushed through by the Conservatives against the backdrop of accelerating inflation, with wages rising over 10 percent and prices increasing at about 7 percent in 1970. This was followed by yearly increases in wages of no less than 13 percent in the next two years – an alarming rate to say the least. This sustained increase in prices was, of course, part of the global inflation that started to get under way in the late 1960s and was fuelled by US President Johnson's expansionary fiscal policies and the Vietnam War.[132] Furthermore, the world economy faced renewed international currency insecurity after the collapse of the Bretton Woods system in August 1971, when US President Nixon suspended the convertibility of the dollar, closed the gold window, and introduced an uncertain era of floating exchange rates. Nixon also imposed a surcharge of 10 percent on imports and a 90 day freeze of wages, prices, and dividends in the US.[133] The global economic climate was becoming increasingly volatile, and Heath's brave market policies were unable to turn the inflationary tide in Britain.

### Crisis and U-turn: 1972

Heath's market reputation was already bruised after the broken promises not to save "lame ducks," and rapidly accelerating inflation was proving to be the root of all trouble. With wages increasing faster than prices and no great gains in productivity to make up for the difference, the danger of a further inflationary spiral became evident.[134]

There were three other factors that were to worsen the situation. The first was the decision of the Bank of England in late 1971 to abandon ceilings on bank credit, in a move to allow for more competition between clearing banks and other financial agencies. This left the Bank of England with much less direct control over credit creation and the stock of money.[135] The immediate effect of this decision was to allow bank advances to increase sharply: in the 1960s, bank lending had increased by an average rate of 12 percent, in 1972 it increased by 37 percent, and in 1973 by 43 percent.[136] The second factor was the floating of the pound in June 1972, which led to its depreciation by about 8 percent vis-à-vis the deutschmark. This obviously meant that import prices from continental Europe, which surged after EC accession in January 1973, were to increase substantially. The last factor was that, due to Heath's policies of financial liberalization, there was increasing speculation in the property market. Rather than investment in industry or job creation, Heath's free market policies during his first two years in office had fuelled a real estate boom, which only made an already bad inflationary situation worse.[137]

The political costs of Heath's economic strategy began to seem enormous. Inflation in property prices and consumer goods, with its obvious implications for the general cost of living, led to increasing social unrest and demands for higher wages among workers. Increased worker militancy was further aggravated by the legal restrictions on strike action after the 1971 Industrial Relations Act.[138] In September 1971, a dispute over pay began between the National Coal Board (NCB) and the National Union of Mineworkers (NUM), which led to a seven week national strike in early 1972.[139] The NUM's new strategy of concentrated mass picketing made coal stocks inaccessible, and with overwhelming support and sympathy from the general population, the miners "felt much more powerful than the Conservative government."[140] Heath declared a state of emergency, which gave him the power to put industry on a three day week as part of a campaign to conserve energy. But as Peter Clarke later observed: "this was an improvisation which failed to halt the slide into darkness."[141] In the end, the government capitulated and the miners' earnings jumped by 16 percent in 1972, more than twice the rate of inflation at the time.

The Industrial Relations Act had achieved the opposite of its original goal: instead of making the labor market function more smoothly, it had radicalized organized labor, leading to a massive increase in strike activity with damning implications for output and productivity in an already weak industrial base.[142] Soon, the government's hope that each successive pay settlement in the public sector would be smaller than the one before proved groundless. The rise in wages was undiminished, and unemployment started to grow, nearly touching the emotive figure of one million in 1972. It was then that Heath – already badly battered by the miners – decided to dramatically change his priorities in economic policy. First, and most embarrassingly, he sought to mitigate inflation by persuading the TUC to lend its support to an incomes policy.[143] And if no agreement proved possible, a statutory incomes policy would be imposed; if the unions did not want to do business with him, the government would have to do its duty single-handed. To the great embarrassment of the Tories, the Industry Act of 1972, which implemented the new incomes policy, was welcomed by born-again socialist Tony Benn in the Commons as "a sign that the Tories too were at the brink of conversion to socialism."[144] Second, Heath aimed at a growth rate of 5 percent through a significant fiscal expansion in the budget of 1972, which would prove sufficient to bring down unemployment to below half a million.[145]

In retrospect, Heath's U-turn was quite spectacular. After less than two years of trying to unleash the creative forces of the market and building a more liberal economy, the first minor crisis – a dispute with the NUM – forced his government to dramatically change course. Heath apparently came to believe that the Conservative approach simply did not work in managing inflation and wanted to return to an interventionist, neocorporatist approach that sought active cooperation from the unions. Widely berated by many of his Conservative colleagues for his apparent weakness, Heath himself did not see it in this way. As already pointed out, he was first and foremost a technocrat who believed in a technocratic, administrative solution to most economic problems. When one solution failed, the government had to try an alternative one.[146]

*The Barber boom: 1972–1973*

In order to achieve an output goal of 5 percent, Chancellor Anthony Barber enacted significant tax cuts. Previous Labour Chancellor Roy Jenkins had bequeathed a big budget surplus in 1970 at over 5 percent of GDP; by 1973, the Heath government faced a deficit of over 3 percent.[147] The tax cuts caused government tax revenue to fall as a proportion to GDP by at least 7 percent.[148] This fiscal stimulus – every Keynesian's dream – was unprecedented by historical standards. The stimulus was not just fiscal, but also monetary. While the money supply (M3) had grown by around 25 percent during the whole three year period up to 1970, M3 now showed increases of that magnitude in each of the years 1972 and 1973.[149] This led to the *Barber Boom*, named after its Chancellor. The British economy expanded by 7.4 percent in 1973 as compared to an average of 2 percent in the period 1969–1972. The resulting fall in unemployment was welcomed by both business and unions. Again, that year's fast growth was part of a global boom in 1973, but seemed even more extravagant in Britain given its relatively weak growth performance over the last two decades.[150]

Emerging troubles lay ahead despite the boom. It was to stimulate inflation even further, and the unions – confident of their growing power, especially now that unemployment was down – became increasingly restless and tried to negotiate ever higher wage settlements.[151] To make matters worse, by late 1973 the oil exporting countries of the Middle East, enraged by the aftermath of the Yom Kippur War, formed an international oil cartel which resulted in a quadrupling of world oil prices. Another crisis, this time much greater than the miners' strike in 1972, was clearly in the making, and talk of early elections started to dominate the corridors of Whitehall and Westminster.

## A year of crisis: Britain's unsustainable equilibrium of 1974

The Barber boom was soon to come to a dramatic ending with the oil shock in November 1973. The first phase of Heath's statutory incomes policy consisted of a wage freeze, which allowed the government to maintain the boom. The second phase allowed the unions to negotiate better deals and, with unemployment again at half a million, they could do so under favorable circumstances.[152] Heath had hoped to strike a deal with the TUC, but the NUM – again – rejected the settlement and a second national strike soon became inevitable. The following year, 1974, was to be a year of protracted state failure and deep economic crisis with no clear solutions for bringing the country out of the recession.[153]

*The crisis: who governs?*

The Middle East oil embargo triggered a fresh economic crisis in Britain. First, there were increasing strains on the country's balance of payments including a deficit on the current account of a record £1 billion in 1973, which was soon to triple to a new high of £3 billion in 1974.[154] Second, the oil price hike had altered the relative price of energy. Overnight, coal was transformed into a relatively cheap form of energy, giving all the more power to the NUM, which had started an over-time ban in November 1973.[155] This time the Heath government thought that it was better prepared: it preemptively instituted a three day week for British industry to conserve energy. This tactic was met with initial success, and the government claimed that "Britain could take it."[156] Unfortunately, a deal with the miners became increasingly elusive, and when, on January 24, 80 percent of the miners voted in favor of another national strike to start on February 10, the situation became unten-able. Heath was forced to call a general election in February against his better judg-ment. He had come to the conclusion that there was no alternative.[157]

Many Conservative partisans had long dreamt of a confrontation in which "the unpopular unions would be subjected to the just wrath of the electorate,"[158] and they were to get their opportunity now to ask the electorate "who governs Britain?" The Conservative Party manifesto, *Firm action for a fair Britain,* talked about dealing with the "danger from outside" (the oil crisis) and "the danger from within" (mili-tant trade unions) and berated the "excessive wage increases at home."[159] Labour's manifesto *Let us work together – Labour's way out of the crisis* blamed Heath's stubbornness for the crisis, stating that the government called the election in a moment of panic. Wilson stated that the Conservatives are "unable to govern and are not telling the people the truth."[160] Wilson promised to end to the crisis with a fair settlement for the miners and to revive British industry when Labour was back in power.[161] Heath's fate seemed sealed: there was no way of getting around the impression of an incompetent government, hamstrung by another three day week and presiding over double digit inflation.[162]

The outcome of the election was inconclusive and resulted in a hung parlia-ment. The Conservatives received 37.9 percent of the vote and 297 seats, Labour got 37.1 percent of the vote and 301 seats. The great winner of the election was the Liberal Party with 19.3 percent but, due to Britain's "first past the post" electoral system, it received only 14 seats. The Conservatives lost 8 percent of the vote compared to 1970, while Labour lost 6 percent, with the Liberals gaining 12 percent.[163] Heath interpreted this result as having a narrow mandate, and tried to form a coalition government with Jeremy Thorpe, the leader of the Liberals.[164] This would soon prove to be impossible, and the Queen summoned Labour's Harold Wilson again to form a minority government with the silent approval of the Liberals and the other small regional parties from Scotland, Wales, and Northern Ireland. Wilson had a minority of 30 in the House of Commons, but since none of the other parties wanted Heath back, Wilson's posi-tion was actually stronger than it seemed at the time. Wilson hoped soon to repeat his electoral performance of 1966 when he achieved a large majority after initially having had a much smaller mandate in 1964.[165]

### Wilson back in power

Initially, Wilson seemed like a miracle worker. Within a few days of his first cabinet meeting in early March, the miners' strike was over, the three day week was abolished, and the economy was back on a full-time footing with the state of emergency ended. Of course, Labour inherited an economy in shambles: 1974 was the worst year since World War II. GDP fell by 1.5 percent in real terms, inflation was over 16 percent, and the current account deficit stood at an extraordinary 3.8 percent of GDP.[166] Denis Healey, the new chancellor, was forced to significantly raise taxes in his first budget presented in March. Also, Wilson got rid of the Pay Board and abolished Heath's controversial Industrial Relations Act. Instead, Labour set up the Advisory Conciliation and Arbitration Service (ACAS), which took a much more conciliatory tone towards the trade unions.[167] In September, after the annual conference of the TUC, Wilson and the unions agreed on moderate wage settlements for the coming year. Ever since their return to power in March 1974, and in eager anticipation of an early general election, Labour had been working ferociously on a *Social Contract*, as their way of showing the country that they would deal successfully with the unions.

And indeed, Wilson would call the next general election for October 1974. In Labour's manifesto, *Britain will win with Labour*, the "Social Contract" figured prominently.[168] The Social Contract described detailed commitments in the field of social policy, the "fairer sharing of the nation's wealth," and the determination to restore and sustain full employment. It recognized that the unions had a "newly restored" right of free collective bargaining, but acknowledged that their loyalties were not just to their members, but also to the community as a whole.[169] The Conservative manifesto, *Putting Britain First*, called for a national policy to fight inflation, which it called "a moral, political, social as well as economic evil."[170] For the Tories, everything else was secondary to the battle against inflation, and in order to achieve that goal, the country needed a "comprehensive price stabilisation programme."[171] They proposed to rigorously control public spending and the money supply, and claimed that Labour's "restraint and restriction" were "only palliatives."[172]

Although Wilson had hoped for a replay of the 1966 election, it turned out to be a rerun of the 1964 one with a splinter thin majority for Labour of just three seats. Labour had 39.2 percent of the vote and 319 seats, compared to the Conservative Party with 36.9 percent and 277 seats, while the Liberals lost 1 percent and one seat.[173] Although narrow, Wilson had a mandate from the country to restore confidence in the economy and put into effect the provisions of the Social Contract. Wilson's victory also heralded the restoration of the postwar consensus, which was briefly and unsuccessfully challenged during the first two years of the Heath government. The fight against unemployment came first again, and inflation would be solved through deliberate wage restraint by the country's major unions.

In the end, Heath was not able to convince the electorate that the Conservatives had the right answers to get the economy out of the enduring crisis. Wilson cunningly changed the focus of the debate away from the fundamental problems of the British economy to the political problem of dealing with the trade unions. In that respect, Labour's "Social Contract" was a stroke of genius: it proved that only Labour could be trusted to handle the unions, of which Wilson kept emphasizing that "they" were not the problem, as the Tories seemed to suggest. Britain in 1974 saw the worst economic crisis since World War II, but that did not signify a break with the prevailing institutional settlement. The Conservatives had the ideas in 1970, but reversed gears in the face of the first crisis and resorted to familiar Keynesian remedies to revive the economy. After 1972 when they had abandoned their free market ideas, the only thing the Conservatives could attempt was crisis containment. The year 1974 would, however, prove to be an "unsustainable equilibrium" for the country: Labour's Social Contract could mitigate the crisis in the short term, but was unable to cure the deep vulnerabilities of the British economy, which were partly caused by the postwar consensus.

## The gradual disintegration of the postwar consensus: 1975–1979

During the next five years, the postwar consensus gradually unraveled. Despite all of Labour's promises, it eventually was not able to manage the unions better in the late 1970s than the Conservatives had in the early 1970s.[174] Once the economy finally started to get out of its two year recession in 1976, the Labour government faced another sterling crisis and would be forced to call in the help of the International Monetary Fund in the autumn of 1976 to secure an emergency loan. Taxes had drastically fallen under the Heath government and spending was up due to the much higher unemployment, which now stubbornly refused to fall below 5 percent. Labour soon lost its overall majority after a series of by-elections, but secured a working coalition with the Liberals, the "Lib-Lab pact," which lasted from the spring of 1977 until late 1978. The economy eventually recovered and inflation and unemployment came down gradually. However, in the winter of 1978–1979, a series of major public sector strikes robbed Labour of its monopoly on social peace, and sowed the seeds of its eventual defeat in the May 1979 general election.[175]

In honoring its Social Contract, Labour soon abolished Heath's Pay Board. But the ongoing crises laid the foundations for an enormous wage explosion, with union leaders only making matters worse. Industrial earnings, which had increased by 15 percent in 1973, went up by 19 percent in 1974, and 23 percent in 1975. However, the number of days lost in strikes declined to only a fraction of its previous level, which gave substance to Labour's claim of being the party of social peace. After two thirds of Britons had endorsed membership of the EC in 1975, Tony Benn and others of the hard left were marginalized in the cabinet, dampening fears of a "siege economy" based on Benn's "alternative economic strategy."[176] In June 1975, Jack Jones and Hugh Scanlon – the powerful leaders of Britain's two biggest unions, the Transport and General Workers Union (TGWU) and the Amalgamated Engineering Union (AEU) – came up with a proposal for wage restraint.[177] Carefully avoiding the term "incomes policy," the Wilson government cut a deal with the TUC on moderate flat rate rises across the board, in an effort to break the inflationary spiral which had caused the cost of living to increase by 24 percent in 1975.[178]

To everyone's surprise, Wilson announced his resignation at the age of 60 in April 1976 and was succeeded by James Callaghan who beat Michael Foot, Denis Healey, Tony Crosland, and Tony Benn in Labour's leadership contest. He inherited an all but impossible economic situation from his predecessor: over 1.25 million unemployed, annual inflation at 16 percent, a record budget deficit of over 6 percent of GDP, a balance of payments deficit again approaching £1 billion, and the value of the pound down to $1.57. In a widely reported speech for the Labour Party Conference in Brighton, written by his son-in-law Peter Jay, Callaghan was to announce the end of the Keynesian postwar consensus. Rejecting the idea that Labour could still spend their way out of recession by "a stroke of the Chancellor's pen," Callaghan laid the foundations for what would come to be known as "monetarism." However, one has to be careful not to look at this "pragmatic" shift to monetarism as a full-fledged paradigm shift away from Keynesianism. As Robert Skidelsky has suggested,

> the reluctance to put the whole burden of the fight against inflation on monetary policy reflects both a vestigial political commitment to full employment and an analytic commitment to the cost-push theory of inflation. It was the collapse of the incomes policy in the "winter of discontent" in 1978–9, leading to the election of the much more ideologically intransigent Conservative Party under Mrs. Thatcher, which finally put policy Keynesianism to sleep.[179]

In April 1976, Denis Healey had imposed substantial spending cuts, but by the summer of the same year, confidence in the economy was badly shaken by another run on the pound, and the government needed to secure an emergency loan from the IMF to deal with the immediate crisis.[180] The IMF loan meant a further round of spending cuts in December of 1976, which obviously did nothing to improve Labour's popularity in the polls.[181] In his memoirs, Healey wrote the following:

> Economics is not a science. It is a branch of social psychology, which makes the absurd assumption that you can understand how people behave when they are making, buying, and selling things, without studying the society in which they live, and all the other ways in which they spend their time.[182]

Healey maintains up until today that, if he were given accurate forecasts in 1976, he would not have needed to go to the IMF at all.[183]

The economy finally started to recover after the IMF episode. Growth was 1.1 percent in 1977 and a much healthier 3.7 percent in 1978. Inflation fell from 16.6 percent in 1976 to 8.7 percent in 1978 and the employment situation showed some modest gains. Nevertheless, the trade unions continued to dominate the government's day-to-day dealings. Union membership for most of the postwar period had been around 10 million, but by the mid-1970s it was up to 13 million.[184] From 1977, the number of days lost in industrial disputes started to rise again, threatening the initial success of Labour's incomes policy. In 1977, rises in industrial earnings were held below inflation, lowering workers' living standards. To Callaghan the choice was obvious: either the government could manage the crisis-prone economy through a prices and incomes policy, or the free market could do the job through rising unemployment. This situation created an unholy alliance between the socialist left and the monetarist right in defense of market forces in wage negotiation.[185]

In 1978, the Callaghan government proposed a pay norm set at 5 percent, a most unrealistic target.[186] The increasingly restless public sector unions, the National Association of Local Government Officers (Nalgo), and the National Union of Public Employees (NUPE) started to be in the frontline of industrial action. They argued that, unlike in the private sector, wage policy had been tightly monitored for them and that they were always the first to suffer from cuts in public spending. In the face of a series of public sector union strikes in the autumn of 1978, the Labour government's incomes policy collapsed: not only was the five percent norm rejected by the TUC, it was also rejected by its own party conference in September.[187]

These were the forebodings to the "Winter of Discontent," the period of massive public sector strikes during the winter of 1978–1979. The Conservative Party, now under the leadership of Margaret Thatcher, in unison with the right-wing tabloid press, did not waste any opportunity to point out to the public the piles of garbage that were left uncollected and the images of unburied dead bodies in Liverpool. In so doing, they successfully constructed the crisis, of a state "held to ransom by the unions."[188] A general election was called for May 1979 and was won by the Conservatives. Callaghan, who campaigned fiercely during the spring and even made up a lot of the lost ground between Labour and Conservatives, was proven right when he told an aide that he felt that there had been "a sea-change in the public mood."[189] The coming to power of Margaret Thatcher and her attack on the postwar consensus will be discussed in the next chapter.

## Conclusion

This chapter, the second case study of the book, has concentrated on Edward Heath's attempt to challenge the institutional setup of the postwar consensus. The relative decline of the British economy and the failed attempts to reverse it by Macmillan and Wilson created the conditions for a more radical approach. The ideas to inform the Conservative policy in 1970 were developed in Selsdon Park and formed the core of the Conservative manifesto's economic strategy for the 1970 general elections. During his first two years in power, Heath proved successful in bringing back market incentives to the economy through new policies and institutions. Taxes were cut; a whole machinery of government institutions that regulated industry was abolished; a new legal framework for managing industrial relations was set up; and Britain quickly concluded successful negotiations to join the European Community by January 1973.

However, during the first minor crisis, the government was forced to retreat and revive the economy through the familiar Keynesian formula. In 1972, with unemployment approaching the symbolic threshold of one million, it was not the ideas of Selsdon Park that would lead the way out of the crisis, but the familiar old ideas of the postwar consensus. The fiscal and monetary stimulus that followed created the Barber boom, which contained the seeds of the next crisis, which was exacerbated by the OPEC oil shock and resulted in the "Great Inflation." Although the crisis was widely perceived by the political elite and the public at large, it did not lead to a decisive intervention that would challenge the institutional setup of the state. Labour's Social Contract would bring only temporary relief from a much more deep-rooted problem of runaway inflation, which proved impossible to be solved in the long run through prices and incomes policies.

After 1974, Britain saw the gradual unraveling of the postwar consensus, starting with James Callaghan's speech for the 1976 Labour Party Conference, where he announced the end of Keynesian economic policymaking and the abandonment of the overarching goal of full employment. In the end, Labour was unable to keep the unions in check due to the continuing spiral of price and wage increases. During the winter of 1978–1979, ongoing strikes by the public sector unions ended the party's monopoly on harmonious industrial relations, and created the opportunity for Margaret Thatcher to come to power in a largely constructed "crisis of the state."

To sum up Heath: he was a "never again expansionist" in the mould of his mentor Harold Macmillan. He had served in World War II and above all else was frightened of mass unemployment.[190] What 1972 proves is that either the free market ideas of the Tory Party were not fully developed or that Heath did not really believe in them in the first place. Heath had considered the new approach useful in order to get elected and offer something different than Wilson, who in his opinion had failed. Also, the general public did not seem ready for radical free market institutions, given their general support for the unions. Heath was less troubled by the Tory U-turn on economic policies than he was by the economic mess he saw ahead of him. For Heath, the complex realities of Britain's economy had been inadequately grasped by Selsdon Park; in 1972, he became convinced that the only way to reconcile high growth with low unemployment and low inflation was through the adoption of an incomes policy. Subsequent events, however, would prove him wrong.

# 5 Margaret Thatcher's triumph (1975–1990)

## Inflation, Hayek, and the overhaul of the British state

Those who wish to preserve freedom should recognize [...] that inflation is probably the most important single factor in that vicious circle wherein one kind of government action makes more and more government control necessary. For this reason, all those who wish to stop the drift toward increasing government control should concentrate their efforts on monetary policy. There is perhaps nothing more disheartening than the fact that there are still so many intelligent and informed people who in most other respects will defend freedom and yet are induced by the immediate benefits of an expansionist policy to support what, in the long run, must destroy the foundations of a free society.

Friedrich von Hayek (1960)[1]

To us, as to all postwar governments, sound money may have seemed out-of-date; we were dominated by the fear of unemployment. It was this which made us turn back against our own better judgment and try to spend our way out of unemployment, while relying on incomes policy to damp down the inflationary effects. It is perhaps easy to understand; our postwar boom began under the shadow of the 1930s. We were haunted by the fear of long-term mass unemployment, the grim, hopeless dole queues and towns which died. So we talked ourselves into believing that these gaunt, tight-lipped men in caps and mufflers were round the corner, and tailored our policy to match these imaginary conditions. For imaginary is what they were.

Keith Joseph (1974)[2]

What's irritated me about the whole direction of politics in the last thirty years is that it's always been towards the collectivist society. People have forgotten about the personal society. And they say: do I count, do I matter? To which the short answer is, yes. And therefore, it isn't that I set out on economic policies; it's that I set out really to change the approach, and changing the economics is the means of changing that approach. If you change the approach you really are after the heart and soul of the nation. Economics are the method; the object is to change the heart and soul.

Margaret Thatcher (1981)[3]

The conclusion on which the present Government's economic policy is based is that there is indeed a proper distinction between the objectives of macroeconomic and microeconomic policy, and a need to be concerned with both of them. But the proper role of each is precisely the opposite of that assigned to it by the conventional post-War wisdom. It is the conquest of inflation, and not the pursuit of growth and employment, which is or should be the objective of macroeconomic policy. And it is the creation of conditions conducive to growth and employment, and not the suppression of price rises, which is or should be the objective of microeconomic policy.

Nigel Lawson (1984)[4]

## Introduction

After an internally divided Conservative Party proved unable to win a majority in either of the two general elections of 1974, the position of Edward Heath as party leader became untenable.[5] The Conservatives had lost four of the last five general elections and Heath was deemed responsible for three of those defeats. Members on the right of the party openly despised his "gutless" record in office during the early 1970s, blaming the government's U-turn in economic policy on his lack of courage and perseverance.[6] Sir Keith Joseph, who had publicly criticized Heath's record during a series of high profile speeches after the February 1974 election, declared that he had "always considered himself a conservative, but had only recently realized that he never properly understood what being a conservative actually meant."[7] Members on the center-left of the party, mostly loyal to Heath, recognized that their leader had become discredited in the eyes of the public and that he needed to be replaced, preferably by someone non-doctrinaire; someone who, in Harold Macmillan's words, "could reunite the party at the top."[8]

However, no senior party member – including center-left favorite William Whitelaw – was prepared to launch a direct challenge against Heath, and leadership change mechanisms were not yet institutionalized in the party. In the past, leadership successions had been decided through covert consultations and mysterious meetings at the highest level of the party, or what Iain MacLeod called the secret dealings of "the magic circle."[9] The party had only held one open election in 1965 when Heath had won. Former Prime Minister Alec Douglas-Home was asked to revise the party's rules in order to allow for the possibility of annual leadership contests. As a result of the ensuing electoral mechanism, senior party members concluded that the best way to force Heath to step down was to run someone credible against him in the first round of party elections. This scenario assumed that Heath would be damaged enough after the first round and would decide to quit. Then they would bring in the party heavyweights – who were loyal to Heath and reluctant to run against him – into the second round.

This meant that a credible candidate from the right of the party was needed in the first round. Keith Joseph soon ruled himself out after causing considerable outrage when he seemed to suggest in a speech that the solution to abolishing poverty was to limit the number of children born to poor families.[10] With Joseph out, the way was open for Margaret Thatcher, who had served under Heath as Education Secretary. Thatcher was visibly associated with Joseph, having cofounded the Centre for Policy Studies (CPS) – a free market think tank – with him in 1974, in an effort to provide an alternative source of ideas for the party.[11] Senior party members never considered Thatcher as a potential party leader; not only was she a woman, she was also on the far right of the party, while the establishment and the majority of its members were mostly center-left and committed to the main tenets of the postwar consensus. Thatcher's role was to force Heath out in the first round and allow the party's center-left favorite, William Whitelaw, to run in the second round. Thatcher's campaign strategy, skillfully conducted by Airey Neave, consisted of downplaying her chances of an outright victory in the first round, thus marketing her as a safe bet for members hoping to usher in a Whitelaw era.

Her strategy would work to perfection. Many center-left Tory MPs who wanted to send a clear signal to Heath voted for her in the first round, clearly expecting other, and more palatable candidates, to stand in the second round. Thatcher received 130 votes, just shy of an overall majority, while Heath got just 119.[12] By winning that first round, Thatcher had made the all-important psychological break with Heath, who duly stepped down. From that moment onwards the momentum was on Thatcher's side. The *Daily Telegraph* ran an editorial the next day headlined "Consider her Courage," and soon after there was seemingly no stopping her.[13] In the second round a week later, Thatcher beat her four male opponents with apparent ease, winning an outright majority with 146 votes, against 79 for establishment favorite Whitelaw, 19 for Jim Prior, 19 for Geoffrey Howe and 11 for John Peyton.[14]

Many Conservatives, especially on the center-left of the party, were stunned. They did not quite comprehend the sweeping process they had helped set in motion. Not only had they elected a woman as their leader for the first time in history, her election also marked a significant break with the postwar, paternalistic Tory tradition of Butler, Macmillan, and Heath (post-economic policy U-turn).[15] The conventional narrative of the Thatcher victory suggests that the party made a shift to the right without actually intending to. In their haste to get rid of the unpopular Heath, who was widely considered to be an electoral liability, party members had elected someone representing the "New Right," a radical minority within the party led by Joseph. This minority wanted to revolutionize the way policy had been conducted in Britain since the end of World War II, by cutting the size of the state and changing the fundamental priorities of economic policy away from full employment.[16]

Mark Wickham-Jones has challenged this "orthodox" account of the 1975 Tory leadership contest. He argues that most party members were well aware of Thatcher's right wing ideological leanings – she was always the first to challenge Heath in both cabinet and shadow cabinet meetings – and also questions the received wisdom that the outcome of the second ballot was somehow "inevitable."[17] According to Wickham-Jones, the Conservatives realized that they needed to change and without a doubt wanted that shift to be to the right. According to this view, one which I support, a majority of the party agreed with Norman Tebbit, who declared at the time that "there was little point in changing the leader if we were going to be stuck with the same policies."[18]

The sudden and unexpected arrival of Margaret Thatcher at the top of the Conservative Party marked the birth of a genuinely new era of Conservatism in Britain. Not only was she to break with the policies of the Heath government after 1972, she was to question the underlying logic of 30 years of postwar consensus politics in Britain. Initially she would move cautiously and with a healthy dose of pragmatism, but it is fair to say that from 1975 onwards, Thatcher would introduce a radical new way of thinking in the Tory Party, blended with a new populist style of leadership. Although the opinion polls gauging her leadership potential were much lower than Callaghan's at the beginning, giving many Tories reason to think that she was nothing but a temporary blip, she would soon take command of the party machine and gradually bring her radical changes to its ideology and governing structure. What many party members and other observers did not realize at the time is that Thatcher would permanently change the basic terms of the political and economic debate at Westminster, with truly global repercussions.

In this chapter I analyze the conditions under which Thatcher was able to launch her successful assault on the institutions of the postwar consensus. I begin with a look at the breakthrough of the monetarist ideas in the 1970s, which laid the ideational foundation for Thatcher's rise. The chapter continues with Thatcher's construction of the Winter of Discontent in the public imagination, when she effectively recruited supporters of her vision of Britain as a monolithic state held to ransom by irrational and wicked trade union leaders. Finally, I discuss the transformation of the British economic landscape under Thatcher and her "new right" Conservatives. From the moment they controlled the Whitehall machine, the Conservatives were to radically change the way economic policy was conducted, using their free market ideas to fight inflation and cut government spending in the midst of one of the deepest recessions since the 1930s.

## Back to the future: the breakthrough of monetarist ideas in the 1970s

To understand Thatcher's success, one must first understand the ideational backdrop to her rise: the ideas that were lying around in wait of a champion. During the late 1960s and early 1970s, when Britain saw unemployment and inflation rise simultaneously, the fundamental logic of the Keynesian ideas that had buttressed the postwar consensus started to come under increasing scrutiny. In order to understand the ascendancy of monetarist ideas – in Britain as well as in many other advanced economies – it is important to understand how Keynesian thought gradually evolved after World War II. Popular myth has it that the Keynesian consensus broke down in the 1970s because Keynesian ideas simply failed to explain the phenomenon of stagflation. This gave way to monetarist ideas that managed to topple Keynes' "hegemonic" position in macroeconomics and replace his ideas more permanently.

In this section, I will show that this account is largely erroneous. Competing ideas, rising to prominence due to the divisions and disagreements within the Keynesian school of thought, took hold of the electoral psyche coaxed into place by Margaret Thatcher. The internal divisions of the Keynesian school had presented Friedrich von Hayek and Milton Friedman with a window of opportunity to put forward a simpler, more intuitive, and attractively coherent theory of what had caused the economic crisis of the mid-1970s and what the adequate solutions were. They could sum up their basic creed in two simple words: "money matters." Through the tireless proselytizing activity of the many free market think tanks aided by a powerful financial press, monetarist ideas rapidly spread to the London based British political elite. But it would be through Thatcher's rhetoric that the broader electorate also became aware of the intrinsic virtues of monetarism.

### Internal divisions: the "hollowing out" of Keynesian ideas

Keynes, had he not died in 1946, would probably not have been a "Keynesian" himself. Robert Skidelsky, Keynes' chief biographer, has argued that Keynes' *General Theory* could be interpreted both ways: that is, both against inflation as well as against unemployment.[19] John Hicks, for example, was one of the first influential economists to argue that there were a number of possible models of the economy to be found within the *General Theory*.[20] Furthermore, some people contend that the Keynesian revolution was ruined by policy mistakes: politicians, trying to promote their party's interests and legitimize their chosen policies, used Keynesian ideas selectively to justify their actions.[21] A classic example of this apparent misuse of Keynesian ideas by politicians is the phenomenon of the "political business cycle:" the use of policy tools to stimulate the economy just prior to an election.[22]

What ultimately accelerated the demise of Keynesian theory was the gradual movement away from Keynes' original ideas towards what came to be known in the 1960s as the "neoclassical synthesis." What Joan Robinson called "bastard Keynesianism" resulted from a peace treaty between Keynesians and (mainly American) anti-Keynesians, stemming from their intrinsic discomfort with Keynes' description of the macro economy as fundamentally unstable and at the constant mercy of investors' "animal spirits."[23] This neoclassical synthesis meant in practice that the anti-Keynesians accepted the possibility of a short-run equilibrium with high unemployment in return for the Keynesians' acceptance that this short-run equilibrium was caused exclusively by downwardly rigid money wages.[24] Hence, to quote Skidelsky, "the *General Theory* turned out to be a 'special case' of the classical theory after all, but with important implications for policy."[25]

Jacqueline Best has pointed out that the fundamental error of the neoclassical synthesis was that it abandoned Keynes' basic assumption of the "intersubjective

nature of economic activity."[26] For neoclassical economists such as Paul Samuelson, Robert Solow, and James Tobin, economic problems had to be treated in a
"technical" rather than an "ideological" manner. This technical approach thus
separated economic questions from the subjective complications of politics and
ideas. The problem with this technical approach, according to Best, was that it
rested on the assumption that the market itself was essentially rational. This constituted a radical departure from Keynes' own beliefs, which saw economic
crises as central to a capitalist economy, and identified the "inter-subjective
nature" of investing behavior as a direct cause of these cycles.[27] To know
whether a regime is stable or successful depends crucially on whether its participants perceive it as such.[28] For Keynes, it was clear that economic activity was
driven by the not-always-so-rational psychology of investors; investors who
tended to be overoptimistic during periods of economic boom, and overpessi-
mistic during recessionary episodes. Given the limited information available to
make informed decisions, argues Best, the idea of a "rational" market becomes
simply untenable.[29]

Where Keynes emphasized the volatility and irrationality of investment, the
Samuelson school of neoclassical economics blamed short-run imperfections –
such as imperfect information and price stickiness – for the occasional failure of
the market system to reach full employment equilibrium on its own.[30] Best
explains how this neoclassical assessment of the causes of inflation and unemployment signified a serious "hollowing out" of Keynes' original ideas, especially since they called for a series of mere technical fixes. For Samuelson and
his followers, "the right combination of fiscal and monetary policy could alter
demand sufficiently to eliminate inflationary or deflationary gaps between
current and full-employment equilibria."[31] Keynes himself would never have
believed that fiscal and monetary policy could smooth out the natural economic
swings produced by speculative expectations. Instead, Keynes saw salvation in
"socializing the conditions of investment and strictly controlling capital flows."[32]

Although Keynes did make the distinction between "voluntary" and "involun-
tary" unemployment in his *General Theory*, this was to be largely ignored by his
followers in the 1950s and 1960s. Defining full employment as the "maximum
that could be reached by expansionary measures,"[33] Keynes himself had theo-
rized that if one tried to further lower unemployment beyond that point, the
economy would experience inflationary pressures.[34] Skidelsky correctly observed
that the early Keynesians lacked a serious theory of inflation, promoting an
income-expenditure model where "quantities adjusted, not prices."[35] In other
words, there were no supply constraints in their models.[36] Instead of a real theory
of inflation, Skidelsky suggested, Keynesians had to rely on a mere empirical
observation proposed by A.W. Phillips, which stated that there existed a negative relationship between levels of unemployment and inflation in the United
Kingdom.[37] Popularized through the "Phillips Curve," this gave politicians an
apparent menu of choice: they could trade lower unemployment for a bit of extra
inflation. The government could maintain the level of unemployment as close to
zero as possible and make use of incomes policy to control wage costs. Hence, at

full employment it was wage-push, rather than demand-pull, that was identified as the cause of inflation. Skidelsky concludes that the refusal of Keynesians to take supply constraints seriously "left them with cost control as their only weapon against inflation."[38]

The above-mentioned lack of a serious theory of inflation created an ideational vacuum in Keynesian thought. This vacuum was soon to be filled by Milton Friedman in 1967, when he developed the concept of the "natural rate of unemployment," which was determined by structural and institutional factors and could not be lowered permanently by a government's active fiscal or monetary expansion.[39]

### The ideas of Milton Friedman

Milton Friedman's theories were founded on a restatement of the classic quantity theory of money first stated by John Stuart Mill (expanding on the ideas of David Hume) and further developed by Irving Fisher in 1911, which established a direct relationship between monetary growth and inflation.[40] Friedman's work was based on four main assumptions that were to form the core of neoliberal thinking.[41] Friedman proposed that because every economy had an institutionally determined "natural rate of unemployment" (first assumption), and consumers and investors had "adaptive" rather than shortsighted expectations (second assumption), there was no long-run trade-off between inflation and unemployment (third assumption). Finally, according to Friedman, unemployment was voluntary (fourth assumption). These four assumptions enabled Friedman to state with some confidence that increased government spending would only temporarily create a higher level of employment, but permanently increase the rate of inflation.[42] Governments had been trying to hold unemployment below its natural rate by expanding the money supply by too much, while employment creation depended on the concept of "money illusion," i.e. on employed workers not asking for money wage increases in line with higher prices. Given adaptive expectations, once inflation is expected, money illusion disappears, resulting in higher unemployment.[43]

As Mark Blyth has pointed out, Friedman's timing was perfect, given the growing global inflationary pressures caused by increased American expenditure on defense during the Vietnam War, Lyndon Johnson's "Great Society," the rapid growth of the money supply, and the quadrupling of oil prices by the OPEC cartel that was triggered by the Yom Kippur War in the Middle East in November 1973. The global phenomenon of "stagflation" entailed the abrupt breakdown of the Phillips Curve. Keynesians, increasingly fighting amongst themselves, were unable to explain why this had happened.[44] Friedman's work on the consumption function made him assume that the demand for money was much more stable than Keynes had argued, and hence that the quantity theory of money was a reliable predictor of inflation. Friedman's simple rule that the rational guidance of monetary policy was to ensure that there was just enough money in the economy to finance what it was capable of producing, while savings and growth in productivity would maintain a high level of activity.[45] Because of the existence of a political business cycle, one simply could not trust the government – or any politician in general – with one's money. Since governments wanted to enhance their chances of being reelected and remain in power as long as possible, all they were doing was cynically causing higher inflation.[46]

Friedman expressed strong views on social as well as economic questions. In his landmark books, *Capitalism and Freedom* (1962) and *Free to Choose* (1980), he placed monetarist ideas firmly in a free market context. Both books present the reader with standard "new right" ideas: the characteristic inefficiency of big government programs, the virtues of lower taxes, and the need to denationalize, deregulate, and ultimately abolish all programs that are seen as barriers to the efficient workings of the market. Similar to Adam Smith, Friedman saw the role of governments limited to three functions: guaranteeing a country's national defense, maintaining an efficient judicial system (especially property rights), and providing certain public goods that would be undersupplied by the market itself.[47] He also claimed that there was a causal connection between capitalism and personal freedom, since markets disperse power and decisions whereas the political process had a tendency to concentrate them. Freedom for the individual entailed making choices in the absence of coercion. Only the capitalist system, with its voluntary interaction between consumers and producers of goods and services, permitted this economic freedom that Friedman saw as essential for political freedom.[48]

### The renaissance of Friedrich von Hayek

Even before Attlee's Labour government was elected in July 1945, Friedrich von Hayek was already warning the world with zeal against the dangers of socialist planning. In his first influential book, *The Road to Serfdom*, published in 1944 and dedicated "to the socialists of all parties," Hayek objected to central planning as politically dangerous and economically inefficient. Planning generally led to pressures for more controls, given that the logic of intervention fed on itself.[49] For Hayek, centralized economic planning by government heavily reduced individual and group liberties, which weakened the legislative role of Parliament by fortifying the role of the executive and ultimately undermined the rule of law by granting too much discretion to central authority.[50] Hayek's ideas in the *Road to Serfdom* inspired one of Winston Churchill's most famous speeches during the 1945 election campaign.[51] Margaret Thatcher claimed to have read the book as a young chemistry student at Oxford around the same time.[52]

However, the popular tide in 1945 was clearly in favor of governments managing the economy, and the debate between Hayek and Keynes on how to conduct economic policy seemed to be won decisively by the latter, as we discussed in Chapter 3. In 1947, a frustrated Hayek convened more than 30 like-minded scholars to meet at Mont Pelerin in Switzerland. The goal of the conference was to combat "the state ascendancy and Keynesian and Marxist planning that was sweeping the globe."[53] The group quickly became known as the "Mont Pelerin Society," their objective being "to facilitate an exchange of ideas between like-minded scholars in the hope of strengthening the principles and practice of a free society and to study the workings, virtues, and defects of market-oriented economic systems."[54] During most of the 1950s and 1960s, however, the group's influence was marginal, and most of their ideas were not taken very seriously by the majority of the economic and political elite.[55]

The most comprehensive explanation of Hayek's societal and economic ideas appeared in *The Constitution of Liberty*, which was published in 1960. Although denying that he was a conservative himself, Hayek wrote like a classic conservative about the need for submission to undersigned rules and conventions. Since we cannot know about more than just a tiny part of society, we should be constantly distrustful of interventions or efforts to alter these complex relationships.[56] Part III of *The Constitution of Liberty* deals with "freedom in the welfare state" and encompasses most of his economic theories. In chapter 21, "the monetary framework," Hayek emphasized that inflation had become the chief threat to the stability of the macro economy and was encouraged by the principal features of the welfare state. Labor unions put pressure on wages, which forced an increase in the money supply above the growth of production, further adding to existing inflation.[57] The solution, for Hayek, was to tie the hands of the authorities by applying a long-term mechanical rule. The point of this rule – although Hayek admitted that such a rule would be hard to implement in reality – was to make monetary policy and its effects as predictable as possible.[58]

When Hayek moved back to Austria in 1970, he was deeply depressed. The success of mixed economies in the United States, Japan, and all over Western Europe made his free market theories seem more irrelevant than ever. But the specter of global stagflation – exacerbated by the oil shocks of 1973 – together with the ultimate academic recognition of Hayek in 1974, when he was awarded the Nobel Prize for Economics, instantly revived interest in many of his teachings. With the world in its deepest downturn since the Great Depression, and Keynesian economists quarrelling over the likely causes of the crisis, Hayek appeared to have been right all along and his theories seemed vindicated. His ideas were to prove instrumental in the ideological revival of the American Republican Party under Ronald Reagan and the economic platform of the British Conservative Party under Thatcher. One particular incident underlined the importance of Hayek's ideas in the economic policy proposals the Tories were to adopt under Margaret Thatcher. At a key Conservative Party meeting in the late 1970s, one party member had prepared a paper arguing for a "middle way" as a pragmatic path for the Tory Party to follow. Before he had even finished presenting his paper, Thatcher reached into her briefcase and took out a book, Hayek's *The Constitution of Liberty*. Interrupting the speaker, she held it up for all members present to see and said sternly: "*this* is what we believe," after which she banged the book down on the table.[59]

### The spreading of monetarist and New Right ideas in Britain

Dennis Kavanagh has suggested that free market ideas gained a more sympathetic hearing among Conservatives in the 1970s principally because of the failure of Heath's economic policies after the U-turns of 1972 and the widespread disillusion caused by his subsequent electoral defeats of 1974.[60] The energetic driving force behind this conservative soul-searching was Sir Keith Joseph. He argued that the Conservative Party had to rediscover its free market roots, which it had forgotten during the years of Macmillan and Heath in its search for a "state-led economic utopia."[61] Frustrated with the Conservative Research Department, which had for a long time reflected the economic consensus views of former Chancellor Rab Butler, Joseph – with the initial blessing of Heath – founded the Centre for Policy Studies (CPS) after the first 1974 election defeat.[62] The idea behind the new organization was to provide the party with an alternative forum for discussing a wide range of free market ideas while keeping a distance from the Tory machine. Joseph made Thatcher president and Alfred Sherman became the CPS' first director. The political importance of the CPS was underlined when Joseph made his famous Preston speech in September 1974, openly distancing himself from the Heath government's record, and advocating the important role of the money supply in attacking inflation.[63] This was widely seen as a bid for the party's leadership. Of course, it would be Thatcher, and not Joseph, who would eventually topple Heath in February 1975.[64]

Another think tank that played an important role in changing public opinion in the mid-1970s was the Institute of Economic Affairs (IEA). The institute was founded in 1955 by Antony Fisher, a businessman, who was persuaded by Hayek that a research body would be the most effective way of countering the country's tendencies towards socialism and planning. In those early days, the institute was regarded as eccentric by the political establishment and only Enoch Powell showed an interest in their early work, followed later by Joseph and Geoffrey Howe.[65] The IEA, run jointly by Ralph Harris and Arthur Seldon, had two main recurring themes: one stressing the need to limit the role of government in those areas where markets could supply services, and the other emphasizing the virtues of competitive pricing and market mechanisms. Kavanagh observed that "by 1979 the IEA was firmly established as the intellectual home of free markets, economic liberalism and monetarism in Britain, and came into its own as the ideas of Keynes, Beveridge, and the Fabians were in retreat."[66]

Although think tanks often tend to overestimate their influence on public opinion and actual policymaking, the mid-1970s was exceptional in the sense that politicians like Joseph, Thatcher, and Howe were openly rallying the CPS and IEA to come up with practical policy proposals for a future Conservative government. There was a real sense among Conservatives that the old ideas had failed. The ideas proposed by the CPS and IEA were spread all over the country through the many public speeches first by Joseph in 1974, and later by Thatcher during her time as leader of the opposition. Furthermore, the right wing press, not least *The Times*, proved instrumental in disseminating monetarist and new right ideas. In addition, several financial journalists proved very effective at convincing large parts of the Conservative elite of the need for a radical new policy direction that would once and for all break with the consensus. Through the authoritative columns of Peter Jay in *The Times*, Samuel Brittan in the *Financial Times*, and Nigel Lawson in *The Spectator*, monetarist ideas gradually gained a wider hearing in the 1970s, although they had been advocated starting as early as 1967.[67] It was only the apparent failure of the economic policy framework in the mid-1970s, however, that gave real credibility to monetarism as a viable alternative to Keynesian demand management and incomes policy.[68]

## Thatcher's preparation for government (1975–1978)

After her election as leader of the Conservative Party in February 1975, Thatcher inherited a demoralized and divided party still traumatized by the 1974 double defeat under Heath. Although the Tories had climbed back from heavy defeats before, there was a profound sense of gloom and, on the face of it, very little about which the party could be even vaguely optimistic.[69] The task ahead seemed all but impossible for Thatcher: she needed to devise a new strategy for government and renew the party's self-confidence, assuming she could first overcome the party's prejudice against having a woman as leader.

From the very beginning, mindful of the innate suspicions of much of the party's male dominated "wet" establishment, she moved with caution.[70] Her supporters were clearly in the minority in the shadow cabinet she formed in 1975. However, she always took great care to appoint loyalists to key economic positions – with Howe as shadow Chancellor and Joseph in charge of overall economic policy – while keeping many moderate Heathites, such as Whitelaw, Jim Prior, Peter Walker, and Ian Gilmour firmly on the front bench. Heath himself refused to serve under her leadership and became her first and most vehement critic, a role he would play with considerable fervor from the Tory backbenches until her resignation in 1990.[71]

The key document that outlined the Conservative Party's new economic policy, *The Right Approach to the Economy*, was published in 1977. The document, although surprising in its lack of commitment to specific policies, nevertheless set out the radical course Thatcher wanted for her party. A year earlier, a much vaguer document, *The Right Approach* (1976), had already emphasized the need to "right the balance" away from government towards the "more efficient" private sector.[72] Alongside hard monetary and fiscal policies aimed at steadily reducing targets for money supply and public borrowing, *The Right Approach to the Economy* stressed the need for "realistic and responsible" collective bargaining.[73]

Howe, quickly becoming almost as influential as Joseph on economic policy, stressed the switch from direct to indirect taxes in fiscal policy and the adherence to rigid monetary growth targets in monetary policy. This Tory stance on monetary policy hardly seemed to break with the postwar consensus given that the Labour government had de facto implemented a monetarist policy after the IMF loan in the autumn of 1976.[74] The Conservatives, however, rightly emphasized that Labour's conversion to monetarism was purely the product of circumstance rather than of conviction.[75] Howe and Lawson pointed out that Denis Healey's "unbelieving monetarism" would be reversed at the earliest opportunity, a plausible hypothesis.[76] Arguing that Labour's monetary policy conversion was "too little, too late," the Conservatives wanted the monetary cure to go much further "if sound money was to be restored and if new life was to be breathed into the ailing economy."[77] Despite the fact that large-scale unemployment had, for the first time since the 1930s, made a reappearance in Britain in the 1970s, it was inflation that was prioritized by the Conservatives. And as E.H.H. Green astutely observed, far from being electorally expedient, this "was a conscious political choice."[78]

To Thatcher, the appeal of monetarism went far and beyond a simple set of techniques for controlling the money supply. For her, the monetarist ascendancy created an opportunity to reassert the case for a genuinely free society. Stable money was one of the foundations of a free society, but limits on public spending and the removal of administrative barriers to free competition were also central. She saw the spreading network of corporatist institutions as the main obstacle to achieving a free economy. Her main targets were the Labour government's increasingly statutory incomes policy, the influence of the trade unions on government policy, which she saw as "undemocratic," and the latest nationalization measures that were taken in the 1970s.[79] Throughout her speeches addressing economic policy, Thatcher made it abundantly clear that she intended to break with that corporatist style of management – not only of Wilson and Callaghan, but also of Heath after his economic policy U-turn. For Andrew Gamble, this turn in party policy was new in the sense that it was not done purely out of electoral expediency, but "was now also bolstered by a set of doctrines about how the economy worked and how British decline could best be reversed."[80]

One policy area where there was surprisingly little commitment from the Conservatives was industrial relations. Given the overwhelming popular feeling that it was industrial strife that had brought down Heath's government in the February 1974 "who governs?" election, Thatcher initially decided not to unnecessarily alarm union members and the electorate at large with overtly zealous promises of anti-union legislation.[81] After all, it was truly believed that Labour had narrowly carried the day in the 1974 elections, because they were the party that could be trusted to handle the unions, while the Tories were seen as too antagonistic towards them. The Social Contract had proven relatively successful in the beginning, and had seemingly formed the cornerstone of Britain's steady economic recovery under Labour. Indeed, while in opposition, the Conservatives had meticulously tried to dispel the idea that any future Tory government would be embroiled once again in a showdown with the unions.[82] However, Thatcher's gut instincts were never well disposed towards the trade unions, and together with Howe and Joseph she realized that if the Tories wanted to reverse economic decline once and for all, reform in the field of industrial relations would be essential, but only "when the time was right."[83] Howe wrote in his memoirs that all three were "convinced that this gigantic millstone [trade union reform] could not be forever neglected."[84] The strategic objective of the Tories was to transform the unions from Labour's secret weapon into its major electoral liability. They needed to engineer a dramatic shift in public perceptions that the unions were central to Britain's economic decline and any reversal could only be brought about through a drastic and permanent reduction of their power.[85]

How was this shift to come about? Joseph brought in John Hoskyns, a successful entrepreneur and one-time regular soldier, and Norman Strauss, one of Unilever's corporate planners, to produce an economic policy document for the party that could tackle trade union reform.[86] By mid-November 1977, they presented their report during a private dinner at Thatcher's home. Hoskyns and Strauss had called their document "Stepping Stones," emphasizing the cumulative and systematic nature of any serious strategic plan able to take on the unions. Although it was never published, and ultimately did not make it into the 1979 election manifesto, it does deserve some examination since it was to profoundly influence Thatcher's thinking in this particular policy area once she was in office.[87]

The ongoing debate in the party over industrial relations reform was between Prior, the "wet" Shadow Employment Secretary, and Joseph. Prior favored a gradual non-confrontational approach that would attempt some kind of accommodation with the unions, while Joseph favored a more radical overhaul of the existing system, similar to Barbara Castle's *In Place of Strife* or Heath's Industrial Relations Act. Hoskyns and Strauss argued that by floating some extreme ideas, more modest ones would cease to look as dangerous to the public, which was still seen as "in constant thrall of the TUC [Trades Union Congress]."[88] Their strategy consisted of deflecting the standard Labour charge that the Tories were only interested in confrontation between unions and government. Hoskyns advised the Tories "to kick with the other boot" and demonstrate the extent to which the Labour Party – chained by the narrow interests of bloodthirsty unions – had produced a "sick, impoverished, stupid, unfair and frightened society."[89] The purpose of "Stepping Stones" was thus to push forward the frontiers of the thinkable and to engage every member of the shadow cabinet in injecting this new line into the country's bloodstream.[90]

Prior, although not adverse to dialogue, was not convinced by "Stepping Stones" and still preferred the party to keep a low profile on trade union reform. For the time being, his views were echoed by Thatcher herself, who publicly promised to keep the unions out of the political arena if the Tories returned to Whitehall, even though she privately favored Hoskyns' approach.[91] However, the increasingly militant behavior of the public sector unions that resulted in a series of strikes during the winter of 1978–1979 changed the party's attitude towards this cautious approach. As public opinion openly began to demand a curb on the power of the unions by legal means, Thatcher and Prior would change their public stance. Like manna from heaven, the Winter of Discontent would prove to be Thatcher's unexpected and critical "stepping stone," which she would relentlessly exploit in her march to Downing Street.

## The British state in crisis: the construction of the winter of discontent

It is hard to overestimate the significance of the public sector strikes that erupted in the winter of 1978–1979 to the future course of Britain's political economy.[92] In July 1978, Prime Minister Callaghan announced a continuation of the statutory incomes policy, setting the maximum pay rise at 5 percent.[93] To the TUC, this seemed to be unreasonable and excessive wage restraint. Inflation stood well over 8 percent and there was widespread evidence that the weekly take-home pay for a worker on average earnings had been falling in real terms since 1974.[94] Also, the TUC was distressed by the fact that it had not even been consulted. The pay policy was duly rejected by the annual TUC conference in Brighton in September and, to his own astonishment, by Callaghan's Labour Party conference in October.[95] The night before the TUC conference, the prime minister had invited the leaders of the major trade unions for dinner to hear out their opinions on the forthcoming pay round and their ideas on when to call the next election.[96] All but one of the union leaders had advised Callaghan to call an election in the next few weeks, but the prime minister had already made up his mind to wait until the next year and left the union leaders in the dark. Denis Healey, among others, still believes that if Callaghan had been more open to the trade unions leaders about his electoral intentions, they might have made a greater effort to keep their members in line and that "history would have been different."[97]

What happened next requires careful examination. According to popular myth, the prolonged public sector strikes that followed, which provided the backdrop to the Winter of Discontent, were caused by a shift in attitudes of the TUC leaders against the government. This is not correct. Most of the national unions, and their leaders, continued to support incomes policy in principle, but found it almost impossible to keep their own members and local organizations in line. The TUC found itself in a hostage situation. With Labour's Social Contract looking increasingly fragile, it became almost impossible for the TUC to convince its members that there was a quid pro quo for their continued wage restraint. Rank-and-file trade unionists resented the gradual erosion of their standards of living and felt betrayed by a supposedly "fraternal" Labour government.[98] As David Marsh has observed, the Winter of Discontent was symptomatic not of union strength, but rather of profound union weakness.[99] After the Transport and General Workers Union (TGWU) finally smashed the 5 percent norm with big pay settlements, the public sector unions tried to catch up and multiple strikes erupted all over the country, from NHS workers to gravediggers, from dockworkers to dustmen.[100]

Both the Conservative Party – with Thatcher herself resolutely in the vanguard – and the right wing British tabloid press proved instrumental to constructing the Winter of Discontent as symptomatic of a more fundamental crisis of the state. The right wing tabloid press fomented a crisis atmosphere with iterative and hyperbolic headlines describing the human misery caused by the strikes day after day. Upon this the Tories were able to successfully build a compelling narrative of Britain as a state that was under siege by the trade unions. In his brilliant analysis of the social unrest during that infamous 1978–1979 winter in *Sociology*, Colin Hay explains how the media's biased reporting from a multitude of complexly related or independent events helped Thatcher and her Conservatives convince the electorate that the country was experiencing a crisis "that required a decisive intervention."[101] For Hay, the media's selection and coverage of the various "newsworthy events" – for example, the rubbish bins that were not emptied, the food shortages (due largely to panic buying), the industrial stoppages, and the dead that were left unburied – constitute the "primary narration." These seemingly unrelated events were then explained by the Tories as "symptoms" of a much larger phenomenon, in a subsequent process of abstraction and "secondary narration." In other words, diverse social contradictions all over Britain, such as NHS strikes in London and gravediggers' picketing actions in Liverpool, were all painted as micro level symptoms of a much larger and more fundamental crisis, i.e. a crisis of a bloated state system which was being held hostage by vicious and unreasonable trade union leaders, who were portrayed as the "enemies of the state."[102]

Furthermore, an influential section of the British media played a crucial role in juxtaposing Prime Minister Callaghan's reluctant handling of the crisis with Thatcher's apparent decisiveness and willingness to attack trade union power. An unlucky course of events would prove devastating for Callaghan, who had flown back from an important international summit in the Caribbean and, to questions from journalists inquiring about the ongoing crisis, answered "I don't think other people in the world would share the view [that] there is mounting chaos."[103] The next day, the front page of *The Sun* twisted his words, producing the famous headline depicting Callaghan as saying "Crisis, What Crisis?" Those three words created the impression of a prime minister who was not only not in charge but also unaware of the gravity of the social unrest. Numerous other tabloid headlines blamed Callaghan personally for the strikes, with the *Daily Express* calling him "INACTION MAN," The *Daily Mirror* proclaiming "Jim Callaghan – THIS IS YOUR STRIKE," and *The Sun* asking "WHAT THE BLOODY HELL'S GOING ON JIM?"[104] These headlines were contrasted with the perceived dynamism and determination of Thatcher. The *Daily Mail* mentioned Thatcher's "calls for curbs on strikers' cash," The *Daily Express* headlined "Maggie's Crisis Challenge," while *The Sun* titled a major article "Maggie's Attack on Union Power." The popular message from the tabloid press was clear and would fatefully inform the electorate's perception of what really happened during that winter: while "Sunny Jim" was passively tanning himself in the Caribbean, unaware of the deep crisis in the country he was leading, Thatcher was resolutely calling for legal action against excessive trade union power.[105]

As I have already emphasized in Chapter 2, crises are by no means self-evident phenomena. In order to justify a decisive intervention, crises need to be explained and placed within a coherent and convincing narrative. Therefore, the objective facts need not be as important as the subjective perceptions of crisis.

Particularly illustrative of this point is a comparison between the actual economic performance indicators of Britain during the crises of 1973–1974 (Heath's crisis), and of 1978–1979, respectively. Only the latter resulted in a decisive break with the preexisting institutional arrangement.

As Table 5.1 shows, it is obvious that – with the notable exception of unemployment – the major economic indicators were much more positive during the Winter of Discontent than during the February 1974 election. During 1973–1974, directly following the first oil shock, there was a deep recession, with negative growth of 1.5 percent, annual inflation over 16 percent, and a record current account deficit of almost 4 percent of GDP. In 1978–1979, on the other hand, Britain was experiencing a healthy growth rate of 3.5 percent, annual inflation of 8.3 percent and a current account surplus of 0.6 percent. The only exception was unemployment, which was more than double in 1979. However, unemployment had been steadily rising ever since 1974 and was a more widespread phenomenon tormenting all major industrial countries at that time, notably France, Italy, and the United States.[106] Furthermore, the monetarist remedies Thatcher and the Conservatives proposed in order to cure Britain's economic woes would hardly improve – and were not expected to improve – the employment situation in the short run.

The conclusion that the Winter of Discontent rested on a false and hugely exaggerated account of a full-blown economic crisis is an important observation and one with which two of Britain's leading political economists agree. For Colin Hay, the Winter of Discontent was the only really hegemonic moment for Thatcherism, whereby success was "premised upon the ability of the New Right to construct the moment of the late 1970s as a moment of crisis, in which a particular type of decisive intervention was required. In so doing, it proved itself capable of changing, if not the hearts and minds of the electorate, then certainly the dominant perceptions of the political context, recruiting subjects to its vision of the "necessary" response to the crisis of a monolithic state besieged by the trade unions."[107] Andrew Gamble has noted that Thatcher and Joseph seized on the events of that winter as a "symbol of the bankruptcy of social democracy."[108] It seemed to confirm everything they had been preaching regarding the impossi-

*Table 5.1* Comparison between crises of 1973–1974 and 1978–1979

|  | *1973–1974* | *1978–1979* |
| --- | --- | --- |
| Economic growth | −1.5% | +3.5% |
| Unemployment | 2.3% or 600,000 | 4.9% or 1,320,000 |
| Inflation | 16.1% | 8.3% |
| Current account | −3.8% or −£3 billion | +0.6% or +£964 million |
| Misery index[1] | **18.4%** | **13.2%** |

Source: T. Liesner, *One Hundred Years of Economic Statistics, 1900–1987*, New York: Facts on File, 1989, Tables UK.2 (p. 23), UK.12 (p. 44), UK.8 (p. 37), UK.16 (p. 53); and own calculations.

Note
1 The misery index measures the rate of unemployment plus the rate of inflation.

bility of saving the postwar consensus. Gamble thus concludes that "the myth of the Winter of Discontent, with its images of closed hospitals, rubbish piling up in the streets and dead bodies rotting unburied in graveyards, was a masterpiece of selective news reporting in the Conservative interest."[109]

The impact of this selective news reporting on public opinion was devastating for Labour. Initially in November 1978, the Gallup Poll findings showed 43 percent of the electorate intending to vote Tory and 48 percent planning to vote Labour. Just three months later in February 1979, 53 percent of the electorate declared that they would vote Conservative with just 33 percent intent on voting Labour.[110] The same observation was true for the approval ratings of Callaghan and Thatcher: in November 1978, 54 percent approved of Callaghan's perform-ance as prime minister, compared with only 33 percent approving of Thatcher's performance as leader of the opposition. In February 1979, Gallup polled an approval rating of 23 percent for Callaghan, and 48 percent for Thatcher.[111] The Winter of Discontent thus created the "critical juncture" Thatcher wanted to engineer so desperately.

## Analysis of the 1979 election

It was not the Winter of Discontent that led to the immediate downfall of the Callaghan government, but a vote of no confidence in the Callaghan government after the devolution referendum in Scotland was set aside because less than 40 percent of the Scottish population had cast their ballot. The Scottish National Party (SNP) tabled a vote of censure that the Labour government lost by one vote. They narrowly lost because one Labour MP was dying and one angry SDLP[112] member voted against.[113] This was the first time a government had been defeated on a vote of no confidence since the downfall of Ramsay MacDonald's Labour government in 1924.[114] Callaghan's position was untenable and he called a general election for May 3, 1979. It would be the most divisive general elec-tion since 1945. After Heath's aborted attempt to challenge the consensus, this time the Conservatives were determined to avoid policy U-turns and faithfully implement their full manifesto.

The Tory manifesto – unadventurously called "Conservative Manifesto, 1979" – contained all the major ideas set out in "The Right Approach to the Economy" in 1977. Reminiscent of many of the ideas put forward in Heath's manifesto of 1970, the principal aim of the Conservatives was to "restore the balance in society," which they saw as having been tilted too much in favor of the state at the expense of private enterprise.[115] The emphasis was on the control of inflation and trade union reform. In order to master inflation, the manifesto stated that monetary discipline was essential, "with publicly stated targets for the rate of growth of the money supply."[116]

At the same time, a gradual reduction in the size of the government's borrow-ing requirement was considered vital. On trade union reform, Thatcher proposed three rather modest reforms: picketing would be limited to "those in dispute picketing at their own place of work," the closed shop would be weakened by legal means, and wider use of secret ballots for decision making would be given active encouragement throughout the trade union movement.[117] Furthermore, in their effort to create "a more prosperous economy," the Tories proposed an income tax cut, a "simpler and less oppressive system of capital taxation," a withdrawal of the state from industry, and some modest measures of denationalization, notably British Aerospace and the National Freight Corporation.[118] Given the future radicalism of the Thatcher governments in the course of the 1980s, the 1979 manifesto stands out for its moderation, especially on trade union reform and privatization.[119] But, and with the benefit of hindsight, the most important policy proposal of the manifesto was to give families the "legal right to buy their homes,"[120] a policy that would prove tremendously popular with a majority of the electorate.[121]

Labour's manifesto, "The Labour Way is the Better Way," was designed by Callaghan in an effort to strengthen national unity and "overcome the evils of inequality, poverty and racial bigotry."[122] Labour's manifesto promised to fight inflation by strengthening the Price Commission, radical reform of the EC's common agricultural policy, and active cooperation with the trade unions. The manifesto also emphasized Labour's priority of returning to full employment, adding that this should "go hand-in-hand with keeping down inflation."[123] Furthermore, Labour clearly stated that they did not believe that "economic success [was] an end in itself," stressing fairness and their fight against all forms of social injustice. In order to achieve that end, Labour pledged an "all-out attack on tax evasion" and the introduction of "an annual wealth tax on the small minority of rich people whose total net personal wealth exceeds £150,000."[124]

For the first time, the Conservatives used the advertising agency Saatchi & Saatchi to conduct their campaign. Blaming Callaghan for Labour's inept handling of the economy, they had a very effective poster targeting the prevailing high unemployment figures, showing a long dole queue with the title "Labour isn't working."[125] Callaghan's otherwise brave campaign suffered from a hostile press. All major tabloid papers supported the Conservatives, with the notable exception of The *Daily Mirror*.[126] One revealing example of the crucial role played by the British press during general elections is a comparison between the campaigns of 1970 (when Heath won a majority of 30) and 1979. In 1970, both *The Sun* and the *Daily Mirror* – with a combined circulation of 6.2 million – endorsed the Labour Party, while the *Daily Express*, the *Daily Mail* and *The Daily Telegraph* – with a combined circulation of 6.9 million – supported Heath's Conservatives. The crucial difference between 1970 and 1979 was the switch in allegiance of *The Sun* from Labour to the Conservatives. Also, an important trend between 1970 and 1979 was the circulation of the *Daily Mirror*, which fell from 4.7 million to 3.8 million, while the circulation of *The Sun* increased from 1.5 million to a staggering 3.9 million. Adding up the numbers for 1979, the four popular papers that supported Thatcher's Conservatives could guarantee a national circulation of 10.1 million, while Labour's support from the *Daily Mirror* was just at 3.8 million.[127]

Given this unfavorable environment for Labour, the actual election outcome was not as bad as could have been expected. On May 3, the Conservative Party polled 43.9 percent of the vote, giving them 339 seats in the House of Commons, against 37 percent of the vote for the Labour Party which gave them 269 seats. Thatcher had an overall majority of 43 in the House – a comfortable one and, so she claimed, a clear mandate for change. In their authoritative analysis of the 1979 general election, Butler and Kavanagh observed that Conservative policies concerning taxes and law and order exerted an important influence on those who voted for them.[128] Furthermore, the national swing from Labour to Tory was subject to substantial regional variation. Although a North–South divide had been apparent in general elections ever since the 1950s, this was far more pronounced in 1979: the swing from Labour to Tory in the South was 7.7 percent compared to 4.2 percent in the North.[129]

In the end, 1979 proved to be a watershed election. For the first time since 1945 there was a sense that something new was going to happen in Whitehall, and this time it was not going to be another "progressive" stride towards increased solidarity and a much fairer society.[130] On the contrary, it would prove to be an often divisive return to classic conservative principles of freedom, duty, and responsibility. When she arrived on the steps of Downing Street the day after the general election, Margaret Thatcher tried to strike an unexpectedly hopeful tone of conciliation and unity. Quoting Saint Francis of Assisi, Thatcher stated: "Where there is discord may we bring harmony. Where there is error may we bring truth. Where there is doubt may we bring faith. Where there is despair may we bring hope."[131]

## Paradigm shift: Thatcher's monetarist experiment (1979–1983)

Once in power, Thatcher did not waste time celebrating her electoral triumph. She immediately began putting together her first government, ensuring a careful balance between skeptical "wet" party heavyweights and loyal "dry" lieutenants. Her first cabinet was a close copy of her shadow cabinet, with many of the "wets" again in prominent positions. However, Thatcher again took great care to have real believers who shared her economic vision in key economic positions. With Howe and Lawson at the Treasury, and Joseph as Secretary of State for Industry, the economy would be in safe "monetarist" hands, as the thinking went among Thatcher and her loyalists. Thatcher at all costs wanted to avoid having "wets" in key economic posts, and in discussing appointments with Howe and Joseph, she typically used to ask: "Is he one of us?"[132] The only exception to this approach was the appointment of the conciliatory Jim Prior as Secretary of State for Employment, reflecting Thatcher's initial fear of renewed strikes and industrial unrest. However, after two years when she felt strong enough to have a thorough cabinet "reshuffle," Prior was replaced by Norman Tebbit, a committed Thatcherite.[133]

The first two years in government would prove incredibly difficult for Thatcher. Britain endured its longest recession since the 1930s, with two consecutive years of falling national income in 1980 and 1981. The recession was widely seen at the time to have been worsened by Howe's merciless 1981 budget. The approval ratings of the Conservative government and that of its stubborn prime minister fell from 38 percent and 45 percent respectively in August 1979, to a despondent 18 percent and 25 percent in December 1981.[134] While 43 percent voted Tory in the May 1979 general election, by early 1982 only 23 percent of the electorate intended to vote for them again.[135] Predictions of U-turns were frequent at the time, but during a tumultuous 1980 Conservative Party Conference, Thatcher made it clear that she was "not for turning."[136] Her government, as she explained, would not be afraid to make things worse in order to make them better. With this attitude, Thatcher laid the foundations for a new economic settlement in Britain during her first four years in government, based on the ideas that had replaced the prevailing Keynesian orthodoxy in the 1970s. Her initial assault on the postwar consensus had three broad pillars: a major change in the conduct of fiscal and monetary policy, the conscious redefinition of the role of the state in the economy with a renewed emphasis on the virtues of the free market, and a gradual rebalancing of relations between labor and capital in favor of the latter.

### Monetary and fiscal policy

The central document that informed economic policymaking under Thatcher was the Medium Term Financial Strategy (MTFS), which was adopted by Howe as Chancellor in 1980, but drafted by Nigel Lawson, then Financial Secretary to the Treasury. It sought to apply a monetarist approach to the country's economic management, with the hope of bringing down inflation and creating the conditions for the sustainable growth of output and employment.[137] In order to achieve that end, the MTFS would "progressively reduce the growth of the money stock" and "pursue the policies necessary to achieve this aim." It established a target range of 7 to 11 percent growth for M3 for 1980–1981, with the hope of achieving a range of 4 to 8 percent by 1983–1984.[138] Paragraph three of the MTFS outlined the central doctrine:

> Control of the money supply will over a period of years reduce the rate of inflation. The speed with which inflation falls will depend crucially on expectations both within the UK and overseas. It is to provide a firm basis for those expectations that the Government has announced its firm commitment to a progressive reduction in money supply growth. Public expenditure plans and tax policies and interest rates will be adjusted as necessary to achieve the objective. At the same time, the Government will continue to pursue policies to strengthen the supply side of the economy by tax and other incentives, and by improving the working of the market mechanism.[139]

The secret of success lay therefore in teaching the markets – not least the labor market – that this time around, the government was truly committed to financial discipline, no matter how bad the economic situation became. The logic was that inflation could only be contained if a fixed amount of money was available. Workers who wanted higher wages would price themselves out of the labor market, and firms who charged too much would stop selling their goods and go out of business.[140] The goal of permanently lower inflation could only be achieved through a learning or adjustment process, causing a temporary fall in output and increase in unemployment. After a couple of years of staying the monetarist course, inflation would properly start to fall.[141] As is usually the case, this theory proved difficult to apply in practice. In 1980, inflation came close to 20 percent, base interest rates went up as high as 17 percent, and the M3 targets were widely overshot. This was largely due to the Thatcher government's insistence on fostering supply side incentives and freeing the economy from government control.

Geoffrey Howe's first budget delivered on the fiscal promise of switching from direct to indirect taxes, with the basic income tax rate coming down from 33 to 30 percent, the top rate falling from 83 to 60 percent, and value added tax (VAT) increasing from 8 to 15 percent. As Howe himself liked to put it at the time: "pay as you earn" was replaced by "pay as you spend."[142] Not only was Howe's first budget a regressive redistribution of the tax burden in favor of the rich, the increase in VAT also worked as a direct stimulus to inflation.[143] A range of other measures on the fiscal side signaled the new direction of government policy. Howe pledged to reduce the public sector borrowing requirement (PSBR) to £8.25 billion, while public expenditure itself was to be cut directly by £1.5 billion and annual cash limits were imposed on the government departments' spending programs, with the aim of reducing expenditure by a further billion.[144] There was, however, one serious constraint on cutting expenditure, and that was the previous Labour government's promise to substantially increase public sector pay, a commitment which the Conservatives had pledged they would honor if elected to office. The implementation of the recommendations of the so-called "Clegg Commission," which was set up to bridge the increasing gap between public and private sector pay meant sizeable additions to the already high public sector budgets.[145]

In 1979–1980 the government's fiscal balance was 5 percent in deficit, and this worsened to 6 percent in 1980–1981, mainly because of increases in social security payments due to soaring unemployment, consistent with an economy in recession.[146] Unsatisfied with the towering interest rates, overvalued pound, and too-large government deficit, Howe and Lawson thought it crucial to lower the PSBR. In a determined effort to reduce the deficit by 2 percent of GDP, the 1981 budget was deflationary, with even deeper cuts on the spending side and additional increases on a whole range of taxes (excepting income tax).[147]

The rejection of Keynesianism was unmistakable. In the midst of a recession, with unemployment as high as 2.8 million (9.4 percent) and negative economic growth, Howe's budget allowed for further spending cuts and tax increases, placing the government's priority firmly with fiscal balance over countercyclical demand management.[148] A majority of the country's academic economists – 364 in total – were so outraged that they wrote a letter of protest to *The Times*.[149]

Thatcher and Howe emphasized that "there was no alternative" apart from engaging in ever more borrowing. Heath had done so in very similar circumstances in 1973, something Thatcher and Howe wanted to avoid at all costs.[150]

The monetary targets proved hard to meet and were continually revised upwards. The government could have realized at the time that liberalizing financial markets and a more general effort to deregulate the economy was to make control of M3 all but impossible. Monetarism as practiced by the early Thatcher government thus served as a useful mask for deflationary Keynesian policies. As an inflation strategy, however, Howe was eventually vindicated. Inflation gradually came down from 18 percent in 1980 to 4.5 percent in 1983. The question is whether that result was due to the Treasury's commitment to monetary targets or because of the deflationary effect of the recession itself. Unemployment had increased from 4.9 percent in 1979 to 11.7 percent in 1983, with an absolute decline in overall employment. As already mentioned in Chapter 2, about two million jobs were lost in the 1980–1981 recession, most of which were full-time unionized manufacturing jobs held by men in the industrial North.[151] Hence, it could be argued that the Phillips Curve was alive and well. The only real difference with the years of postwar consensus was the change in priority: low inflation and high unemployment were now chosen over low unemployment and higher inflation.

### Deregulation, liberalization, and limited privatization

The second pillar of Thatcher's first term economic policy was to set the economy free and unleash the creative forces of the market. The emphasis therefore had to change from demand management to supply side measures. Long before she came to power, Thatcher had identified overregulation, excessive state control, and unnecessary state ownership of many industries as the direct causes of Britain's relative decline. Government intervention drained the economy of productive capacity by increasing the burden of taxation and consequently crowding out private investment. "Rolling back the state" was regarded as essential to creating an enterprise economy.[152]

Thatcher's almost religious belief in the private sector proved to be just as dogmatic as Labour's faith in the public sector had been during the postwar years. Initially, there was great enthusiasm for deregulation, with an enormous number of "quangos" abolished,[153] among them the Price Commission. The regional support budget was cut by £233 million, one third of the total budget. The government also made plain that it was prepared for closures and redundancies in the public sector and eagerly backed tough management decisions for reform to restore profitability and make an end to subsidies.[154] Numerous companies were allowed to go bankrupt or significantly downsize, such as plants of the British Steel Corporation and British Leyland, resulting in absolute decreases in public sector employment during the first three years.

In pursuit of free markets, one of the more controversial early measures of financial liberalization was the abolition of exchange controls. A pet project of Lawson, exchange controls were first relaxed in July, and then completely withdrawn in October 1979. Lawson convinced a reluctant Howe that there was a case for encouraging more foreign investment at a time when disinvestment was occurring in the form of extraction of North Sea oil.[155] According to Lawson, this was a typical free market move, and would allow citizens to take out as much foreign currency as they wanted when traveling abroad and would permit financial institutions to diversify their investment portfolios. If British firms could invest abroad, it would ensure that investment in the UK would have to yield a worthwhile return. The economy had to compete.[156] Whatever capital outflow did occur at the time, it did not prevent a further rise in the effective exchange rate by over 10 percent in the 18 months following abolition of exchange controls.[157] Although it is unlikely that this was the intention at the time, one indirect consequence of the elimination of exchange controls was a further increase in unemployment due to the overvalued pound, which further harmed the competitiveness of British manufacturing.[158]

Although privatization did not figure prominently in the Conservatives' 1979 manifesto, the idea caught on during the first term. Not only did it fit the broader Thatcherite mindset of rolling back the state, it also brought in a significant amount of cash that helped reduce the budget deficit and made the idea of "popular capitalism" a reality since the population at large could buy shares. "Truly public ownership," it was argued, "meant putting shares in the hands of the public."[159] Privatization also opened the door to enterprise and brought a large tract of industry more immediately under the discipline of the market.[160] Part of the state holding in British Petroleum (BP) had already been sold off by Denis Healey to raise revenue after the 1976 IMF crisis. Thatcher's government accordingly sold more BP shares, as well as two other nationalized companies, Cable & Wireless and British Aerospace. These early privatizations were limited in scope. The first significant privatization would come after the 1981 cabinet reshuffle, when Lawson was piloted into the Department of Energy and success- fully completed the privatization of Britoil, which was sold for £1 billion.[161] However, the real enthusiasm for privatization was still to come in the latter years of the 1980s.

### *Industrial relations reform*

The third pillar of Thatcher's attack on the postwar consensus, industrial rela- tions reform, was the most politically sensitive of all. Despite her eagerness to "smash icons and break taboos," her radicalism only manifested itself initially when decisions could be implemented quickly and cost relatively little, such as closing down boards and eliminating public agencies.[162]

Taking on the unions was a political minefield. Heath's February 1974 defeat and the Winter of Discontent were still fresh in mind, and it was thought better to move slowly in this area. With the appointment of the "wet" Prior, Thatcher had already shown her prudence. She backed away from a conflict in the coal industry in 1981, instead preferring to buy off trouble for the moment and settle with the National Union of Mineworkers (NUM). However, the public sector strikes during the winter of 1978–1979 had served to harden public attitudes,[163] and there seemed to be some mandate for reform, although it had not changed Prior's determination to walk softly.[164] As Gamble observed, "there was no disposition at first to confront union power directly for fear of presenting the unions with the kind of issue around which they could rally effective protest, as had happened with the Heath government's Industrial Relations Act."[165]

The first trade union bill was passed in 1980 and found widespread approval for its minimal reform program. Jim Prior's Employment Act outlawed secondary picketing and required all new closed shops to be approved by four fifths of those affected. Also, public funds were made available to encourage unions to hold postal ballots.[166] These rather modest measures left many anti-union hardliners in the party dissatisfied, but they would get their way after the "wet" Prior was replaced at Employment by the "ultra dry" and uncompromising Norman Tebbit in 1981.[167] The Thatcher government's eagerness for more radical reform in industrial relations could not be better underlined than this change of leadership at the Department of Employment. In a notorious speech at the 1981 Conservative Party Conference, Tebbit clarified his government's stance on unemployment: "I grew up in the 1930s with an unemployed father. He did not riot. He got on his bike and looked for work, and he went on looking until he found it."[168]

Tebbit's 1982 Employment Act was a frontal attack on the closed shop. Trade unions now became liable for damages if they were the cause of unlawful industrial action. The Act also gave employers a legal right against industrial action "that was not mainly about employment matters" or that had mere "political motives."[169] In his memoirs, Tebbit describes the 1982 Employment Act as "his greatest achievement in government."[170] Incremental legislation during the next years went on to require membership ballots for elected officials as well as potential strikes. This piecemeal process would prove to be highly effective, and it avoided the fatal mistake Heath made in 1971, when he tried to do everything at once.[171]

### Economic recovery, war in the South Atlantic, and the revival of Thatcherism

After two years of negative economic growth, the economy started to show signs of recovery by early 1982. The recession had bottomed out in 1981, and growth resumed – first reluctantly by 1.5 percent in 1982, but approaching 4 percent in 1983. Of course, unemployment had risen to unprecedented levels, peaking at 3.2 million in January 1983, but falling just below the psychologically important number of 3 million by May of the same year. The Thatcher government, however, did deliver on its inflation promise: in just three years Howe's deflationary fiscal and monetary policies had managed to lower inflation from close to 20 percent to below 5 percent.[172] Also politically significant, mortgage rates fell by 4 percentage points in 1983. As a result, there was some comfort in 1983 for owner-occupiers who had kept their jobs, which was still a majority of the electorate.[173]

It was not just the revival of the economy's fortunes that would turn around Thatcher's electoral chances. All politicians who aspire to "make the weather" in a country's affairs have one thing in common: luck. Thatcher had her fair share of good fortune during her first term. First and foremost, the Labour opposition was in complete disarray. After Callaghan stepped down, the left wing Michael Foot narrowly beat Denis Healey and became the Labour Party leader in November 1980, while Tony Benn missed the deputy leadership by a whisker, which gave him renewed prominence as champion of an ascendant left wing coalition.[174] The years of Butskellism and consensus were visibly over, and viewed from the political center, the two main parties in British politics seemed to be in the hands of dangerous extremists. With an uncompromising Conservative leadership overflowing with "new right" rhetoric and the Labour Party controlled by the militant socialist left wing, there seemed to be an opening for a moderate middle road party.

The formation of the Social Democratic Party (SDP) in 1981 by the "Gang of Four" was therefore no great surprise.[175] The SDP was a serious attempt to "break the mould" of British politics, as Roy Jenkins himself put it. However, this was a mixed blessing for Thatcher, since the SDP proved to be a formidable electoral challenge to both Labour and Conservatives. Gallup polled the SDP (now in alliance with the Liberals) at an extraordinary 50 percent in December 1981, with Labour and Conservatives each at 23 percent. Luckily for Thatcher, this proved to be nothing more than short-term media hype, and the Alliance of Social Democrat Jenkins and Liberal David Steel soon dropped in the opinion polls to 29 percent in May 1982, and just 17 percent in May 1983.[176]

Secondly, there was the Falklands War. It is widely acknowledged that the "khaki effect" generated by the war with Argentina did much to improve Thatcher's electoral chances.[177] When General Leopoldo Galtieri's military junta invaded *Las Malvinas* in April 1982, Thatcher seized on the military crisis as the defining occasion to underscore her decisive leadership. Galtieri's invasion was her stroke of luck. The British military expedition was not without risk, and during the course of the war, Thatcher showed great courage and determination in the eyes of the public. The contrast with Heath was manifest. In many ways, Peter Clarke observed, "Thatcherite triumphalism was born in the Falklands war: a style of politics which, for good or ill, depended on taking the Iron Lady at her own valuation."[178] With victory secured by the end of June 1982, Thatcher, in a buoyant mood, made the following declaration: "We have ceased to be a nation in retreat. We have instead a newfound confidence – born in the economic battles at home and tested and found true 8,000 miles away."[179]

It was, of course, not the first time that a prime minister would move the electorate's attention away from ongoing domestic problems to a more pressing foreign policy matter during a period of economic trouble.[180] Thatcher cunningly linked victory in war abroad with a reversal of economic decline at home in the popular mind. She was able to do this because of the geographical and income distribution of Conservative votes. People at the bottom of the income distribution – who usually lived in Wales and the North of England, both traditional Labour strongholds – were not going to vote for her anyway. Patriotism trumped the pocketbook with the middle and upper class voters in the South of England and Greater London, most of whom had been able to hang on to their jobs, and who saw their situation beginning to improve by early 1982.

The swing in public opinion was stunning. While only 27 percent of the electorate intended to vote Conservative before the Falklands war in February 1982, by the time the war was over in late June 1982, 46 percent of the electorate declared to Gallup that they would vote Tory, compared to 27 percent for Labour and 24 percent for the SDP-Liberal Alliance.[181] A second Thatcher victory was starting to look more likely.

## Thatcherism vindicated: mass unemployment and the 1983 election

Although there were real signs of economic recovery by 1983, apart from a drop in inflation and a current account surplus, Thatcher and her government had very little to boast about. The current account surplus was mainly due to the lucrative exploitation of North Sea oil, and the reduction in inflation had come at a huge cost in unemployment, which was hovering somewhere between 12 and 13 percent in 1983, falling just below the 3 million mark in May 1983. Measured from peak to peak of the economic cycle, growth was only 0.6 percent in 1980–1983, barely a quarter of what had been the norm in Britain during the postwar era.[182] Interest rates were still over 10 percent, and the budget deficit was still more than 4 percent of GDP. Worst of all for a government that had pledged to "roll back the frontiers of the state" was the absolute increase in public expenditure from 44 percent of GDP in 1979–1980 to 47.5 percent in 1982–1983. This was mainly caused by higher social security payments for the unemployed, which easily overwhelmed some of Howe's cuts in public spending[183]. During Thatcher's first term, the size of the government had grown more than three times faster than the economy as a whole: public spending had increased by 6 percent in absolute terms.[184]

To sum up, this was not an economic record to be proud of, let alone confidently take to the electorate for approval. However, in just over a decade the perceptions of what was acceptable in Britain's political economy had radically changed. The unfortunate Heath was forced to make a policy U-turn away from his market solutions when he feared unemployment would top one million. Now, only ten years later, a new Conservative leader presided over an economy with more than three million unemployed. Most surprisingly of all, the odds of her winning an upcoming general election were quite good. The Tories had successfully persuaded 40 percent of the electorate that their solutions to tackle the inflationary crises of the 1970s were the right ones. Most of those 40 percent were not affected by the negative consequences of her policies. Thanks to the upsurge in patriotism after the successful recapture of the Falklands, Thatcher reveled in her newfound confidence. The opinion polls stayed heavily in her favor in early 1983, and there were signs of growth picking up and unemployment finally ceasing to rise. When the local elections on May 5 showed a comfortable Conservative position almost everywhere, Thatcher decided to call the next general election for June 9.[185]

In her foreword to the Conservative Party Manifesto, "The Challenge of Our Times," Thatcher defended the economic record of her government.[186] She immediately admitted that the universal and most intractable problem of the country was unemployment. She argued that the answer was "not bogus social contracts or government overspending" and stated that both simply destroyed jobs. "The only way to a lasting reduction in unemployment [was] to make the right products at the right prices, supported by good services." The role of government was to keep prices down through monetary policy and offer real incentives for enterprise.[187] The 1983 manifesto showed the "real Thatcherism" vowing to complete what the first government had set in motion in 1979. The first priority remained low inflation, which would be maintained with tight monetary policies and firm control of public spending and borrowing.[188] Second, Thatcher promised further trade union reforms to make unions more democratic and to further curb "the legal immunity of unions to call strikes without prior approval of those concerned through a fair and secret ballot."[189] Third, unemployment would be largely dealt with through labor market reform, encouraging "moves towards greater flexibility in working practices" and minimizing "legal restrictions which discourage the creation of jobs."[190] The main new proposal was the full-fledged privatization of British Telecom, British Airways, British Steel, and many other industries.[191]

Labour's manifesto, "The New Hope for Britain," was almost double the length of the Tories' and was famously called "the longest suicide note in history" by Gerald Kaufman,[192] a Labour shadow cabinet minister at the time.[193] Michael Foot, the opposition leader, attacked the Conservative government's record stating that "it is just not true that mass unemployment must be accepted."[194] Labour therefore promised a radical "emergency programme of action," including a massive government expansion program to foster a major rebuilding of British industry, increases in taxes for the rich to create a fairer Britain, a return to nationalization, and a repeal of all the Tories' industrial relations reform measures. By guaranteeing large increases in public expenditure and more central planning, the Labour Party committed itself to cutting unemployment to one million within five years. In addition to all of that, Labour wanted unilateral nuclear disarmament and complete withdrawal from the European Economic Community.[195]

The third party, the SDP-Liberal Alliance, struck a more conciliatory tone in its manifesto, "Working Together for Britain."[196] It also promised to cut unemployment – to two million in two years – by using government resources to further investment. Its threefold strategy included fiscal and financial policies for growth, direct action to provide jobs, and an "Incomes Strategy that will stick."[197]

Cecil Parkinson, once again with the support of Saatchi & Saatchi, took charge of the Conservative campaign and in one clever campaign ad which included the phrase "Like your manifesto, comrade!" compared the Labour manifesto with the Communist Party manifesto.[198] Both Labour and the SDP-Liberal Alliance seemed to suffer from internal strife. Foot, an unworldly, ageing, leftist idealist was the perfect out of touch opponent for a decisive and courageous prime minister. The Alliance had problems with its unappealing dual leadership – Steel for the Liberals and Jenkins for the SDP – which made the electorate question who was actually in charge of the political grouping. Thatcher's Conservatives again enjoyed favorable press coverage from four of the five main tabloids, which represented almost 10 million readers, while the circulation of the *Daily Mirror*, as ever faithfully supporting Labour, remained around 3.8 million.[199] By June, the only real question on people's minds was how large Thatcher's majority would be and which party would come in second, Labour or the Alliance, which had enjoyed a late surge in the opinion polls.[200] The choice was stark and, given that the misery index was still as high as 18 percent, many of the campaigners wondered whether the voters would apply narrow economic criteria to their electoral decision.[201]

The outcome of the election was hardly a surprise. Since Labour and the Alliance largely split the opposition vote, the "first-past-the-post" electoral system led to a landslide victory for the Tories. Turnout was down from 76 percent in 1979 to 73 percent. The Conservatives polled 42.4 percent, resulting in 397 seats. With 1.5 percent less in the popular vote compared to four years earlier, the party achieved 58 more seats in the House of Commons. Labour saw its worst result since 1918, polling 27.6 percent and only 209 seats. The Alliance got 25.4 percent of the vote and just 23 seats.[202] Thatcher thus had an increased absolute majority of 144 seats, giving her an apparent mandate to continue on her radical reform path. Not only had the Tories persuaded much of the public to connect success in the Falklands with its general political and economic strategy, they had managed to decisively win a general election based on the worst economic record since the Great Depression.[203]

It is simply impossible to overrate the importance of the 1983 general election outcome. Although Thatcher's was the first government to have served a full term and to be reelected since 1950,[204] one can hardly make the case that she won a resounding popular mandate for her radical economic policies considering that her party only received 42.4 percent of the vote. Had it not been for the Falklands, it is hard to imagine Thatcherism to have lasted much beyond 1983. What is obvious is that the electorate turned its back on Labour's strategy as a viable economic alternative and openly questioned Labour's fitness to govern. Furthermore, there is some truth in the fact that the Tories managed to shift the main economic debate away from unemployment towards inflation and privatization.[205] Thatcher herself, of course, would interpret the results as a ringing endorsement of her first four years in office. The remaining years of the 1980s would see the true face of Thatcherism in Britain. Determined to bring her free market crusade to a successful end, Thatcher's government would embark on a program of mass privatization, a more complete rebalancing of industrial relations in favor of capital, and further tax cuts, all part of an ongoing march towards a much fancied "classless, property-owning, share-owning democracy."[206]

## The transformation of Britain's economic landscape (1983–1990)

Thatcher's second government was unapologetically neoliberal in economic outlook. Lawson, a true believer of the first hour, was made Chancellor of the Exchequer, Tebbit was put back in the Employment Department, Parkinson was placed in Trade and Industry, and Joseph was put in Education and Science.[207] Most of the "wets" were gone, with the notable exceptions of Peter Walker (who agreed with Thatcher on trade union reform) and Michael Heseltine (who would resign over the Westland affair and later on trigger Thatcher's downfall in 1990). Thatcher's second term would complete her revolution in three important areas of "unfinished business:" industrial relations, privatization, and financial deregulation. As the world recovery started to gain momentum, the British economy was pushed onto a higher growth path, giving the impression that Thatcher's reforms had handsomely paid off. The years after 1983 saw a sustained economic recovery in which employment expanded for seven successive years. However, unemployment did not actually start to decrease until the end of 1986, when it would fall rapidly in just three years. Growth in Britain was fuelled by two main factors: an expansion of private sector investment and a large expansion in consumer spending boosted by a fall in personal savings and the wealth effects of a new housing boom.[208]

Under these much more favorable economic circumstances, Thatcher would find it much easier to win a third consecutive general election victory in 1987, which would allow her to complete her vision of Britain as a low tax, private enterprise economy "where the majority of people owned their homes and had shares on the stock market."[209] Lawson's 1988 budget would be the triumphant embodiment of Britain's newfound prosperity under Thatcher and would set in motion the familiar forces of accelerating inflation and boom and bust. Although Thatcher might not have the right to claim that she completely reversed Britain's relative decline, from 1983 onwards the economy grew noticeably faster than its major competitors. The big paradox is that the size of the state would actually increase during the first eight years of her long decade in power, a common observation to which I will return later in this chapter.

### Unfinished business I: industrial relations

In 1981, the Thatcher government had avoided a confrontation with the miners, who had figured prominently in Tory mythology since the early 1970s. The government had realized at the time that it could not win the battle, given that coal stocks were low and the miners were supportive of their moderate union leader, Joe Gormley.[210] After that regrettable "humiliation," the government began to build up coal stocks at vital power stations, convert power stations to dual oil-coal firing stations, and build up mobile police units.[211] These measures were based on a plan that was developed by Nicholas Ridley in opposition and consistent with the broader "Stepping Stones" approach to industrial relations.[212]

In September 1983, Thatcher appointed Ian MacGregor to head the coal industry. Meanwhile, the NUM leadership had changed from the moderate Gormley to the much more militant and populist Arthur Scargill, the former president of the Yorkshire miners. MacGregor clearly wanted to speed up closures of uneconomic pits, which would lead to major redundancies. In response, the NUM started an overtime ban in late October 1983. A controversial decision in April 1984 to close a major pit in Yorkshire – Scargill's old constituency – set off one of the longest major strikes since 1926. Thatcher, feeling strengthened by her fresh election victory in 1983, was in no mood to compromise. After Galtieri, she had found a brilliant new public opponent in Scargill who, with his unwavering class-war rhetoric, stood for everything she loathed about socialism and trade unions.[213] The government was prepared for a major confrontation, and at the beginning of that 1984 spring, the NUM embarked on a hopeless struggle that it could never realistically have won.[214] Opinion polls at the time showed that, unlike in 1974, the public did not completely take the miners' side.[215] The strike, which had at times been extremely bitter and violent, would finally come to an end in March 1985 "when the strikers marched to work with banners held high and bands playing, but without a settlement."[216] By the spring of 1985, the NUM had lost half its membership.[217]

Lawson described the miners' strike as "the central political event of the second Thatcher Administration."[218] Probably even more important than the humbling of the miners by the government was the subsequent defeat of the newspaper printers unions in 1986–1987 that had kept a tight hold over "Fleet Street" until that point. Rupert Murdoch, the Australian media magnate and personal friend of Thatcher, asserted his "right to manage" his own company and installed new computerized technology at a vast new plant in Wapping.[219] The battle with the print unions was the more significant in an economic sense, since it overcame union resistance to changes in working practices. Throughout most of this period the TUC was "frozen out of participation in central-government decision-making."[220] The government had made it clear that what it sought was "either union-free companies and industries or single-company unions with no-strike agreements."[221] During the second Thatcher government, a real paradigm shift thus took place in industrial relations that firmly switched the balance of power between capital and labor back in favor of the employers. What Heath failed to do with one all-encompassing Act, Thatcher accomplished over five years with three Acts, in 1980, 1982, and 1984. The "Stepping Stones" strategy had worked.

### Unfinished business II: privatization

Privatization, or "denationalization" as it was called at the time, was the most visible affirmation of the Thatcher revolution. Initially, during Thatcher's first term, privatization was seen as an easy means to raise additional revenue and reduce the public sector borrowing requirement. From 1979 to 1983, a modest £1.76 billion was raised in revenue.[222] But from 1983 onwards, with Lawson as Chancellor, the program gained its true coherence and momentum. Privatization soon became an obsession for the Thatcher government, with one success quickly leading to another. The Conservatives argued that they were "freeing the taxpayer from the burden of subsidizing the nationalized industries."[223] No less than ten major companies were privatized between 1984 and 1990, totaling over £25 billion in proceeds for the government (see Table 5.2).

The result was a cut in the share of the public corporations in the economy by more than half: it reduced employment in them from 8 to 3 million and cut their contribution to GDP from 10 to 5 percent.[224] The sales were justified on a number of grounds, but especially as "a means of making companies more efficient and competitive in an increasingly global marketplace."[225] It was also essentially a way of boosting "popular capitalism" by increasing the number of shareholders in the country.[226]

Alexander Cairncross, among others, has pointed out that "as had happened with nationalization [in 1945], the case [for privatization] rested heavily on ideology and rhetoric rather than on careful assessment of alternative industrial structures, industry by industry."[227] It was beyond dispute that some of the nationalized industries had made enormous losses that fell on the British taxpayer. However, this was largely because they had been forced to hold down prices for long periods as part of the government strategy in the 1970s for taming inflation, and they had been forced to maintain output levels in situations where such levels were highly unprofitable. As a consequence, the resulting losses did not necessarily reflect the inefficiency of their managements.[228] The real question was about future efficiency. Here it was far from obvious that large private

*Table 5.2* Privatization in Britain (1981–1990)

| Date | Company | Proceeds (£ million) | Equity sold (initially) (%) |
|------|---------|------------------------|------------------------------|
| October 1981 | Cable & Wireless | 224 | 50 |
| February 1982 | Amersham International | 71 | 100 |
| November 1982 | Britoil | 549 | 51 |
| February 1983 | Associated British Ports | 22 | 51.5 |
| June 1984 | Enterprise Oil | 392 | 100 |
| July 1984 | Jaguar | 294 | 99 |
| November 1984 | British Telecom | 3,916 | 50.2 |
| December 1986 | British Gas | 5,434 | 97 |
| February 1987 | British Airways | 900 | 100 |
| May 1987 | Rolls Royce | 1,363 | 100 |
| July 1987 | British Airports Authority | 1,281 | 100 |
| December 1988 | British Steel | 1,281 | 100 |
| December 1989 | Regional Water Companies | 5,110 | 100 |
| December 1990 | Electricity Companies | 5,092 | 100 |

Source: D. Childs, *Britain since 1945: A Political History*, 6th ed., London: Routledge, 2006, p. 204.

monopolies would outperform large public ones. As Lawson himself soon realized, in so far as privatization replaced public with private monopolies, it simply mirrored the Attlee nationalization process and stored up a very similar likelihood of "disappointing hopes for transformative change."[229] In the end, the Thatcher government cared more about fostering private ownership than the actual breaking up of monopolies.

The real goal, of course, was a "share-owning, property owning democracy."[230] The immensely popular policy of giving council tenants the right to buy their own homes at prices discounted according to their length of tenure, together with the sale of shares in the previously nationalized industries were the real tangible proof of Thatcher's vision of a popular capitalism. By 1987, over 1 million dwellings had been transferred from the public to the private sector, and the number of shareholders in Britain had almost tripled to a total of 9 million.[231]

### Unfinished business III: financial liberalization

The most important measure in the field of financial deregulation had already been implemented in 1979 by Howe: the abolition of exchange controls. This policy innovation – pushed through under the cloak of free market logic – allowed foreign capital to freely flow into the country, and Britons to invest abroad. In October 1986, most of the restrictive banking practices in the City of London were lifted in a series of changes that came to be known as the "Big Bang." In an effort to make London globally competitive, Big Bang triggered changes that released competition in the City, sweeping away centuries of tradition by admitting foreign brokers and jobbers and switching to a global standard of deregulation in place of the "gentlemanly conventions" of the past. This was pushed through by Lawson in alliance with Parkinson. The effect of the Big Bang meant that quite suddenly, the City of London became glamorous.[232] In the mid-1980s, as never before, it was in finance and finance-related activities, not in industry or the professions, where real money was to be made.[233] Transformed by the new technology, John Campbell noted, "the business of making money was no longer boring and respectable on the one hand, or shady and vulgar on the other, but fashionable and exciting."[234] London's later claim to be the world's leading financial center was underpinned by the growth of its business in cross border bank lending, foreign exchange, international bonds, and foreign equities trading – all largely made possible by those 1986 City of London reforms.[235]

### The 1987 general election victory, the 1988 budget, and the Lawson boom

Although it might not have seemed that way at the time, Thatcher's second term ran more smoothly than her first, and when she sought dissolution of parliament in the spring of 1987, the Conservatives entered the campaign as solid favorites.[236] The economy was growing, inflation had stayed within the 4 to 5 percent range, the pound was strong, and unemployment had finally started to fall.[237] Neil Kinnock replaced Michael Foot as Leader of the Labour Party in September 1983 and started the long and painful reform process that was to make Labour once again the "natural party of government." The outcome of the 1987 election showed very little change from the 1983 election. The Conservatives polled 42.3 percent (–0.1 percent), resulting in 376 seats (–17), Labour received 30.8 percent (+3.2 percent) and 229 seats (+21), while the SDP-Liberal Alliance had 22.5 percent (–2.8 percent) and 22 seats (–5).[238] The government's logical return to power was the electorate's reward for the growing prosperity and the result of the inability of Labour and the Alliance to offer a convincing alternative. Just like in 1983, this was an election victory achieved in the South of England, where Labour only retained three seats outside of Greater London.[239] A once again triumphant Thatcher thus became the first prime minister since Lord Liverpool in 1826 to win three successive general elections.[240]

In the afterglow of Thatcher's third victory, euphoria persisted for over a year, silencing the covertly simmering internal conflicts within the cabinet, especially between herself and Lawson over Europe and the question of the Exchange Rate Mechanism (ERM). There was one area, however, where both prime minister and her "brilliant" chancellor always found agreement: on the inherent virtue of tax cuts.[241] An exhilarated Lawson presented his 1988 budget to a stunned and roaring House of Commons: the top rate of income tax was cut from 60 to 40 percent, while the basic rate of income tax was lowered to 25 percent.[242] The Conservatives had thus fulfilled their pledge to cut income taxes, while the overall burden of taxation in Britain actually increased during the 1980s, as in most comparable countries. The 1988 budget had powerful redistributive effects, with the poor getting relatively poorer and the rich getting absolutely richer.[243] Lawson followed the supply side logic by the book: through creating such low tax incentives, the pace of growth would quicken and set in motion the mechanism for future wealth creation. In 1988, he could claim success on all possible fronts of the economy: low inflation and interest rates, fast growth, increasing employment, and to top it all off, a healthy budget surplus despite the tax cuts.[244]

Lawson's expansionary budget would overheat an economy that was already growing fast in 1986. From 4.4 percent in 1986, the British economy expanded by 4.8 percent in 1987 and by more than 5 percent in 1988. The "Lawson Boom" thus found its rightful place next to Maudling's "Dash for Growth" during the early 1960s and the "Barber Boom" in the early 1970s. Unfortunately for the Chancellor, Lawson's boom would also follow the "boom-bust" pattern of those earlier Conservative boom periods. The 1988 budget gave a boost to consumer demand, further stimulating inflation that was already accelerating in 1986. While inflation stood at 4 percent in early 1988, by the autumn of 1990 it was again over 10 percent. Furthermore, the economy saw a severe deterioration in the balance of payments as well as a genuine explosion in house prices. The seeds for the recession of 1990–1992 were sown in Lawson's hubristic budget. Two years later, Lawson, Howe, and Thatcher were all gone and a new economic crisis was at hand, with the structural flaws of Thatcherism laying out in the open. This episode will be examined in greater detail in the next chapter.

Many scholars have questioned the radicalism of Thatcher's governments, generally focusing on her reluctance to take on the main institutions of the welfare state, especially the National Health Service.[245] As proof of this contention, they usually point out the absolute growth in the public sector as a percentage of GDP, explaining this by powerful mechanisms of institutional path dependence. But that, I believe, is missing the point. The fact is that the distribution of income as a consequence of the regressive measures of cutting income tax and raising all kinds of indirect taxes became much more unequal. The Gini coefficient in Britain went from 0.25 in 1979 to 0.34 in 1990, the fastest increase in inequality of all OECD countries.[246] The industrial balance was firmly back in favor of capital compared to labor, full employment as the number one priority for economic policy was all but gone, 5 percent of GDP was transferred from the public to the private sector, and market mechanisms were introduced to all parts of economic life. From my own assessment, it should therefore be obvious that the Thatcher governments of the 1980s achieved nothing short of a revolution in economic policy: a real paradigm shift that ended the 30 years of postwar consensus in Britain.

## The virtues of Thatcherism

Since this chapter deals mainly with the so-called "virtues" of Thatcherism, it is useful to have another look at the country's economic performance in the 1980s in comparison to its major competitors in Europe and North America. Indeed, before the moment that all the shortcomings of Thatcher's free market experiment would become apparent in the long recession of 1990–1992, she could claim success on all three fronts: growth, unemployment, and inflation. Figure 5.1 plots the evolution of real GDP growth rates for Britain, the United States, Germany, France, and Italy. Although the recession during the early 1980s was by far the deepest in Britain, the country outperformed all the others in growth rates during 1983–1988 (with the exception of the United States and Germany in

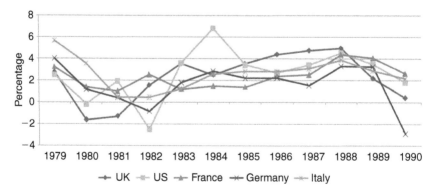

*Figure 5.1* Economic growth in the 1980s (source: OECD, *Historical Statistics,* Paris: OECD, 2001; and own calculations).

1984). This was something that was unheard of thus far in the postwar era, and of course Thatcher would cite the growth figures in 1983–1988 as evidence that Britain's decline had been reversed thanks to her free market reforms.[247]

Even in employment performance, Thatcher could claim that her policies had delivered in the end. Figure 5.2 shows Britain doing worse than the US, France, Germany, and Italy from 1981 to 1986. But after that, there was quite a dramatic fall in unemployment, from close to 12 percent in 1986, the highest rate of all five countries, to just over 5 percent in 1990, the lowest number of all. Although there has been valid criticism about the changes in measurement methods in the late 1980s in Britain, these cannot completely explain away the significantly improved performance of Britain's labor markets.

Finally, Figure 5.3 shows the inflation performance for all five countries in the 1980s. Here, all countries were successful in lowering inflation from double digits to approximately five percent in the late 1980s. However, it is in this area that Britain again got into trouble at the end of the decade when inflation crept up towards 10 percent.

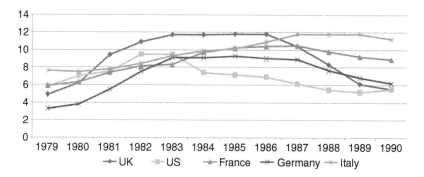

*Figure 5.2* Unemployment in the 1980s (source: OECD, *Historical Statistics,* 2001; and own calculations).

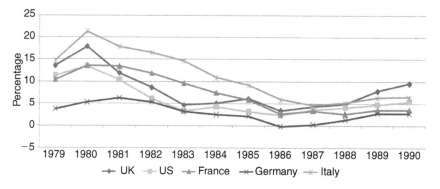

*Figure 5.3* Inflation in the 1980s (source: OECD, *Historical Statistics,* 2001; and own calculations).

One bone of contention remains: did Thatcher's reforms reverse Britain's relative economic decline or, for that matter, solve the country's underlying economic vulnerabilities? In Chapter 6, we will see how the Lawson boom sowed the seeds for the recession in the early 1990s. It will become clear that Thatcher and Lawson had not been able to break the familiar postwar "boom-bust" pattern that many Conservatives had so reviled in the 1960s and 1970s. Indeed, the recession of 1990–1992 exposed all the problems of Thatcherism – vulnerable short term consumer spending, unsustainable housing booms, underinvestment in industry and public services, increasing poverty, and widening income inequality. This would create the opening for new ideas and a rejuvenated Labour Party under a charismatic new leader, Tony Blair.

## Conclusion

In this chapter I have assessed Margaret Thatcher's attempt to change the reigning postwar economic consensus in Britain. After the failure of the Heath government to stick with his free market policies in the early 1970s, and the electoral debacles of 1974, the Conservative Party seemed ready for a change of course. Defying the odds, Thatcher was elected as their new leader and quickly started to introduce a radically different way of thinking in the party. Following the economic teachings of Hayek and Friedman, Thatcher eventually succeeded in bringing monetarism into mainstream economic thinking at Whitehall and Westminster.

The only way she proved successful in doing that, was because of the gradual "hollowing out" of Keynesianism. Hopelessly divided, Keynesian economists who subscribed to the new "neoclassical synthesis" seemed unable to explain the phenomenon of stagflation in the mid-1970s. The comforting logic of the Phillips Curve collapsed before their eyes, and the followers of Friedman could explain what had happened with apparent ease in two simple words: money matters. For them, inflation was always a monetary phenomenon in the long run and the only way to root out the problem was to directly control the growth of the money supply. Together with this new focus on inflation came a whole body of thought popularly associated with "new right" thinking, emphasizing free markets, the rolling back of the frontiers of the state, deregulation, liberalization, and privatization.

The indispensable economic crisis that could justify such a radical intervention based on monetarist ideas came, as we have discussed, in the winter of 1978–1979. Although by no means as deep or severe as the crisis in 1974, Thatcher and the Conservative Party, egged on by the rightwing tabloid press, convinced the electorate that the public sector strikes consisted of a crisis of the state that demanded a decisive intervention, nothing short of a complete overhaul of the existing institutional framework. The successful construction of the Winter of Discontent is a classic example of the fact that crises are by no means self-apparent phenomena, but events that need to be ably narrated or explained to the electorate. Through a process of selecting various "points of resonance" and linking several seemingly unrelated crisis events to a more coherent whole, anomalies in the political system suddenly become symptoms of a government that has lost all control over society. A decisive intervention, based on a different set of ideas, is needed to get out of that crisis. The election of 1979 was largely fought with the Winter of Discontent – a necessary though not determinant condition – looming in the background, and there was a significant swing in the electorate in favor of Thatcher.

Once in power, Thatcher implemented many of her economic ideas within the first six months. Fiscal and monetary policy were directed towards combating inflation, a whole set of market liberalizing measures were taken, industrial relations were decisively turned around in favor of employers, and a limited number of companies were privatized. Her first term was nothing short of an economic disaster, apart from the fact that inflation had been tamed. The 1983 election nevertheless saw another Thatcher victory, even with unemployment close to 3 million. The election seemed to have vindicated her ideas at least politically if not economically. In effect, she had managed to shift the dominant economic paradigm from full employment to low inflation. After her second victory, Thatcher tried to consolidate her victory over inflation while trying to complete her vision of a free enterprise economy. With a historic victory over the trade unions, financial liberalization, mass privatization, and a tax-cutting budget in 1988, the terms of the economic debate were changed forever. However, the failings of some of her policies had already become visible by late 1987 when the stock market crashed and inflation started rising. Although Thatcher had clearly changed the consensus, she had not yet cured Britain of many of its structural economic ills.

# 6 Thatcherism's flaws and Tony Blair's consolidation (1987–2005)

## From the Lawson boom to New Labour's "New Britain"

The idea that a Labour government in 1992 would have been good for Britain is hardly worth even taking the trouble to dismiss. Our victory ensured that our reforms over the previous thirteen years were made permanent. After some turmoil, it locked into place a new economic regime. With it came the benefits of recovery without inflation, a tremendous strength for Britain. It protected the country from the folly of Labour's grandiose spending plans, which would have meant either vast tax rises or the abandonment of all Labour had stood for on polling day. [...] Above all, our victory in 1992 killed socialism in Britain. It also, I must conclude, made the world safe for Tony Blair. Our win meant that between 1992 and 1997 Labour had to change. No longer is Britain trapped in the old two-party tango, with one government neatly undoing everything its predecessor has created. Unquestionably, this is good for the country.

John Major (1999)[1]

I used the term "third way," because you could say that there was a "first way" of traditional social democratic leftism, and there was a "second way," which was the Thatcherite reaction to that. People were looking for a third alternative, which reconciles effective competition in a global marketplace with limiting inequality and a decent element of social solidarity. [...] And this is not a "middle way" of any sort.

Anthony Giddens (2006)[2]

Our new economic approach is rooted in ideas which stress the importance of macro-economics, post neo-classical endogenous growth theory and the symbiotic relationships between growth and investment, and people and infrastructure.

Gordon Brown (1994)[3]

I have always believed that politics is first and foremost about ideas. Without a powerful commitment to goals and values, governments are rudderless and ineffective, however large their majority. Furthermore, ideas need labels if they are to become popular and widely understood. The 'Third Way' is to my mind the best label for the new politics which the progressive centre-left is forging in Britain and beyond.

Tony Blair (1998)[4]

## Introduction: a new Britain?

It is ironic that the final blow Margaret Thatcher would deal to Neil Kinnock and the Labour Party was her resignation. Celebrating her departure from Downing Street with champagne that night in his office, Kinnock told his staff and close allies: "It is right that we are celebrating here tonight: a great evil has left the land. [...] But so has our best asset!"[5] Ever since the 1983 electoral debacle, Kinnock had tried to get the Labour Party out of the doldrums: first with a difficult battle against Tony Benn and the militant left wing of the party and then through the Policy Review, which was supposed to bring the Labour movement back within the political mainstream. It was a long and painful process, but when Labour suffered a fourth consecutive defeat in the general election in 1992 – in the midst of a long economic recession that had laid bare all the troubles of Thatcher's often dogmatic market solutions – it was clear to many in the party that internal reform had not gone far enough.

The voters simply did not seem to trust Labour with the management of the economy, and they were willing to give Major the benefit of the doubt despite the Tories' own dismal economic record. In other words, crisis had not led to change in 1992 – let alone a decisive intervention – and it was clear that Kinnock's alternative had not convinced the British electorate. However, Major's victory would be short-lived. In September 1992, after another run on the pound, Britain was forced out of the European Exchange Rate Mechanism (ERM) and in one moment the Conservative Party lost its monopoly on economic competence. John Smith succeeded Kinnock as leader of the Labour Party, but when he died unexpectedly two years later in 1994, the torch was passed on to Tony Blair. An impatient Blair would take Kinnock's and Smith's reforms quickly to the next level: transforming the Labour Party and aiming to prepare it for office at the next general election.

In this chapter I analyze the conditions under which Tony Blair was able to come to power in 1997 supported by a substantially different economic platform than Labour had ever campaigned on in the past. The key moment for Labour to replace the Thatcherite ascendancy should have been the election of 1992, when the country was in the midst of a recession and another 1.8 million manufacturing jobs were lost. Kinnock's failure to construct a convincing crisis narrative and the rejection by the voters of his party's alternative approach to economic management, instigated a more radical process of reform that would see Labour move much more closely towards the reigning Thatcherite settlement. Over the next couple of years, they would de facto accept the Tories' underlying assumptions on how to run a modern economy. The creation of "New Labour" under Blair in 1994 was not just a repudiation of much of the party's past, but also an attempt to provide a credible alternative to the shortcomings of Thatcherism. That alternative would eventually be known as the "Third Way," but was only popularized as such after the 1997 election, in a typical effort to give a coherent framework to the party's economic policies post fact. Although some of the ideas that were floated in the mid-1990s – such as Will Hutton's "stakeholder-ism" and Anthony Giddens' "social investment state" that combined social justice with economic efficiency – provided genuine economic alternatives to Thatcherism, they would never quite make it into Labour's official manifesto out of fear of frightening "Middle England" and further advancing the party's pejo-rative "tax and spend" image. Once elected to power, Blair and Brown would stick to the Tories' monetary and fiscal policies for the first three years, even for-mally institutionalizing them. After 2000, some incremental changes to eco-nomic policy were implemented that achieved mixed results, but they always stayed within the broad framework that had been laid down by Thatcher.

## Neil Kinnock's Labour Party reforms (1983–1992)

When Neil Kinnock inherited the Labour Party from Michael Foot after the dis-astrous 1983 general election his task seemed almost impossible. First, with a pitiful 27.6 percent of the national vote, Labour had just delivered their worst electoral performance since 1918; as a consequence, the disarray in the party was substantial.[6] Second, Kinnock was immediately confronted with two formi-dable enemies, one internal and one external: a militant left wing faction in his own party that was resolutely determined to stick to their socialist principles, and a freshly vindicated Margaret Thatcher claiming a mandate for further radical reform. Although Kinnock himself was a man of the left – his father was a coal miner in Wales – he soon realized that he needed to move Labour back into the mainstream center of British politics if it was to survive at all given the new political economic atmosphere ushered in by Thatcher.[7]

Untarnished by government office during the Wilson–Callaghan period, Kinnock rose to prominence as shadow education secretary under Michael Foot.[8] When it became clear even before the 1983 election that Foot was to go, Kinnock emerged as the consensus candidate. With Benn temporarily out – he lost his seat in 1983 – there was no credible candidate from the hard left, and once the trade unions threw their support behind Kinnock's candidacy, the battle was over and Kinnock was left Labour's undisputed leader.[9]

The fact that he hailed from the left of the party made Kinnock vulnerable to criticism. The right of the party thought that he was not committed sufficiently to reform. Prominent members of the Labour left, like Eric Heffer and Tony Benn, scolded his "betrayal" of the Labour left and never forgave him for what they saw as his "lack of principle."[10] From 1983 to 1992, Kinnock had the thank-less task of taking the party along a long and painful journey out of the electoral wilderness to something resembling real "electability." In doing so, Kinnock would achieve something close to a revolution in the Labour Party, though the process would deeply scar him.[11] In the end, he himself forfeited the opportunity to lead a new Labour government. Although much of the socialist rhetoric remained in the party during the 1980s, the policies put forward in the Labour's 1992 manifesto were unrecognizable when compared to the "longest suicide note in history" that was the 1983 election manifesto.[12]

### *Kinnock's twin struggle with the Iron Lady and the "loony" left*

The first two years of Kinnock's tenure as Labour leader were completely domi-nated by Thatcher's intensifying assault on the power of the trade unions, which culminated in the long and bitter miners' strike in 1984–1985. Kinnock funda-mentally disagreed with Arthur Scargill's "undemocratic" hard line and openly urged the National Union of Mineworkers (NUM) to call a national ballot. Scargill – afraid of winning by only a very small margin – refused to do so, which fatally undermined the legitimacy of the miners' case in the eyes of the public.[13] Kinnock found himself torn between the left's traditional loyalty to the miners and the calls of a hostile press and the Tories to condemn the miners' violence. Of course, ardent NUM supporters regarded Kinnock's implicit criti-cism of the miners as disloyal.

The strike officially ended in March 1985. It was clear then that the tide had turned away from the miners, not only at the national level, but in the Labour party itself. Scargill, of course, never admitted defeat, and urged the Labour Party conference to promise that if elected they would reinstate all the miners who had lost their jobs and to reimburse the unions for fines incurred during the strike. Kinnock categorically resisted, arguing that binding a future Labour gov-ernment to such a course made no sense.[14] In so doing, Kinnock essentially con-ceded that the institutional foundations of the Labour Party, including their special ties with the trade unions, had to be abandoned. In the words of James Cronin, Kinnock realized that "Labour, if it were to win again, would not only have to be rebuilt, [...] it would have to be recreated on a new basis."[15]

To build a new, popular party of the center-left Kinnock had to marginalize the most radical elements of the so-called "hard left."[16] They were particularly strong in the local authorities, including London, Sheffield, and Liverpool. No one better realized this than Thatcher herself and, with the Rates Act of 1984, the Tories started a concerted effort to diminish the power of those local councils by "capping" local taxes on property. The triumph of a Tory-controlled parlia-ment over the Labour-controlled councils was unavoidable given the constitu-tional supremacy of parliament in Britain's unitary state.[17]

The struggle would be symbolized by the resistance of the Liverpool council against cuts in spending. The left in Liverpool was dominated by members of the "Militant Tendency," a Trotskyite organization determined to expose the evils of capitalism and the futility of efforts to reform it.[18] They advocated all-out con-frontation with the Thatcher government, claiming that it would "heighten capit-alism's contradictions" and advance the struggle for socialism.[19] Many hardliners on the Liverpool council argued that resistance against Whitehall would create a second front of popular protest, which together with the miners, would ulti-mately bring down Thatcher's government.

Continued resistance soon led to financial penalties, and by the autumn of 1985 the city of Liverpool ran out of money and was forced to lay off local authority workers. Throughout the conflict Kinnock had urged restraint, but had been on the defensive for the majority of the time. In his speech to the Labour

Party conference in Bournemouth in October 1985, Kinnock openly challenged the Militant Tendency. Amid howls of outrage from the left, a newly emboldened Kinnock stated: "You can't play politics with people's jobs and with people's homes... The people will not, and cannot, abide posturing. They cannot respect the gesture generals or the tendency tacticians."[20] The speech was widely praised by his supporters in the party and the media. It proved to be a decisive moment in Kinnock's tenure as Labour Party leader and placed him more firmly in the saddle.

Labour's internal reform was seriously delayed by constant battle against Thatcher's policy initiatives, the enduring strength of the hard left, and the difficult struggle to prevent the SDP-Liberal Alliance from replacing Labour as the main opposition party. It was only from the summer of 1985 onwards, after the miners' strike ended, that Kinnock was able to work more seriously on internal party reform.[21] Important appointments were Charles Clarke as his personal assistant, Patricia Hewitt as his press secretary, and John Reid as head of political research. All three soon produced blueprints for party reorganization and began to put their mark on the style, if not yet the policy substance, of the new leadership. [22]

The fact that presentation mattered had been clear to Kinnock from the very beginning, and he hired Peter Mandelson as director of communications. Mandelson drastically changed the way the party communicated with the press and the outside world, and put together a very effective campaign strategy for the 1987 elections. However, on economic policy the party moved very cautiously. In the summer of 1985, Kinnock hired Cambridge economist John Eatwell as his personal adviser on economic policy. Although he immediately acknowledged to Eatwell that he believed the party's whole stance on economic policy needed to change dramatically – including industrial policy, labor market policy, and policy towards Europe – he also gave Eatwell a small lecture on political reality. He told Eatwell that

> if [he] tried to do this now, the Party would fall apart. It was going to take a long time to explain to the many Labour Party members who are used to going out on wet Wednesday nights to argue about policies, that they had been wrong.[23]

### The 1987 election and the policy review

With 30.8 percent of the national vote in the 1987 general election, Labour did only marginally better than in 1983, but emerged as the main opposition party with 229 seats compared to the SDP-Liberal Alliance who achieved a mere 22.[24] The Conservatives maintained their comfortable majority of more than 100 seats in the House of Commons. In effect, Kinnock had ensured that Labour – and not the Alliance – would be the ones to provide a real alternative to the Tories, and if the latter were to lose support, it would be in Labour's favor. However, that prospect seemed far away in 1987: there were still too many skeletons in

Labour's closet and getting rid of them would require more than a clever marketing strategy.[25] Kinnock argued that Labour needed to continue its process of modernization by reshaping the party's program, policies and image much more thoroughly. The party needed nothing less than a "new identity."

After a period of reflection on the 1987 campaign, Mandelson came to the conclusion that the party's weakness lay in the product, not the presentation. In a speech in June 1987, Mandelson argued that Labour needed "an intellectually driven process of change" that would do for Labour what the Bad Godesberg Program had done for the German Social Democrats in 1959.[26]

Kinnock agreed with Mandelson's assessment and launched the Policy Review: a process that aimed to reverse the recent domination of policymaking by the hard left and "equip Labour with a conceptual framework, a rhetoric and a programme on which to base a renewed claim to the right to govern the nation."[27] He realized that Britain and the world had changed dramatically over the past 30 years, and that the party needed to come to terms with the material aspirations of the working classes and the fact that globalization had severely limited what one country could achieve by means of economic demand management.[28] Thatcher had clearly struck a sensitive chord with many blue collar workers in the country who wanted to buy their council homes and have more money in their pockets to spend on consumer goods. They were inherently suspicious of grand socialist designs and had always been skeptical of nationalization as a means towards greater prosperity. On economic policy, there would be a gradual shift on everything Labour had thus far stood for: nationalization, trade unions, Europe, and redistributive taxation. Kinnock was able to achieve this shift by stripping the party's union dominated National Executive Committee of its policy function.[29]

The final report of the Policy Review – "Meet the Challenge, Make the Change" – was overwhelmingly approved at the annual conference in 1989. The document recognized the market's role in driving innovation and consumer choice, called for a "fairer" tax system, and accepted that the government's role was to "create a framework for growth that would ensure adequate investment, proper training and infrastructure."[30] Kinnock himself started to embrace the concept of the "enabling state" and stressed the need to combine economic efficiency with social justice.[31] In order to achieve an enabling state, Kinnock proposed a "Medium Term Industrial Strategy," a program for growth, which would require more incentives for research and development, special loans for small businesses, a national training fund, and a national minimum wage.[32] Labour was not ready yet to give up its commitment to state ownership. It kept its long-standing critique of finance and the City of London and lamented the finance industry's short-term mentality of doing business. As Cronin pointed out, "what was different was their determination not to do anything very dramatic about it."[33]

The major shift in the Labour Party on the question of Europe came with the appointment of the French socialist Jacques Delors as president of the European Commission. By the mid-1980s, Kinnock had become convinced that "the path to economic recovery actually ran through Europe," and Delors' elaboration of a European Social Charter provided Labour with a new and more extensive set of worker rights than Britain enjoyed under Thatcher.[34] Delors was welcomed as a hero during the 1988 TUC conference and encouraged the unions to think of their future in European terms.[35]

This U-turn in Labour's policy towards Europe was revolutionary. The same Labour Party that had wanted to unilaterally withdraw from Europe five years earlier was now enthusiastically applauding a French Eurocrat. Delors' view that it was "necessary to improve workers' living and working conditions, and provide better protection for their health and safety at work"[36] directly appealed to the Labour Party faithful. The fact that Britain was in the midst of a Thatcherite assault on the state, and that Thatcher was fiercely against the European Economic Community exactly because she thought it would try to re-impose the state, gave Kinnock a window of opportunity to attack Thatcher in a way that would not alienate his electoral base.[37] This is probably why the Labour's NEC increasingly came around to embracing the idea of Europe.[38]

The sudden enthusiasm for the European project combined with a shift in monetary policy in favor of accession to the ERM committed the future Labour government to the battle against inflation while maintaining a rhetorical commitment to economic growth. On fiscal policy, Kinnock made it clear that a future Labour government would only spend "what the country can afford," while simultaneously vouching that people should not have to pay more than 50 percent of their incomes in taxes. However, overall Kinnock would accept the main contours of Lawson's direct and indirect tax structure.[39] Labour's updated policy program, "Looking to the Future," was made public in May 1990. It omitted any mention of the "Medium Term Industrial Strategy" and backed away from Keynesianism or any comprehensive macroeconomic goals for guaranteeing employment. Spending commitments were now made conditional, and the party stated that benefits would only grow "as rapidly as resources allow," while its commitment to the ERM and the fight against inflation became more unqualified.[40]

From 1990 onwards, with Thatcher's star waning, the careers of two young Labour MPs – Gordon Brown and Tony Blair – started to rise. Both were elected to the Commons in 1983 and from the start embraced Kinnock's leadership and his ideas to reform the party. Brown, two years Blair's senior, impressed the media and the party while on John Smith's shadow treasury team, often replacing him as shadow chancellor when he was ill. Blair caught Kinnock's attention as shadow employment spokesman and started the difficult process of diminishing the trade unions' sway over party policy.[41] At the 1990 party conference, Brown confidently declared that Labour saw a new role for government: "not government doing everything, not government doing nothing, not the government of the invisible hand of unrestrained market forces, not the government of the dead hand of centralized power; but the government of the helping hand."[42] During that same conference, Blair announced that a future Labour government would institute a "training revolution" with education and training at the core of its economic strategy.[43] All the talk of nationalization, redistribution, unilateral withdrawal from Europe, and higher taxation was gone by the early 1990s and Kinnock was in the driving seat to become Labour's next prime minister.

## The Lawson bust and the long recession

In the previous chapter, I discussed the "virtues of Thatcherism." Once recovery got under way in 1982, there was a gradual improvement in all major economic indicators. From 1986 onwards, Britain experienced a genuine economic boom, combining rapid growth with low inflation, high productivity, and falling unemployment. Already by late 1987, however, there were worrying signs that the Thatcherite engine had began to sputter. To understand why Labour moved closer to the Tories' economic platform rather than away from it even during the demise of Thatcherite growth, one must first understand the downside of Thatcherism itself.

### *The crumbling of Thatcher's brave new world*

The stock market crash of October 19, 1987 – Black Monday – that started in Wall Street but soon spread to the rest of the world, should have been a clear sign of the troubles that lay ahead. The Black Monday decline was the second largest one day percentage drop in stock market history. By the end of October, the London Stock Exchange had lost close to 27 percent of its total market value.[44] Although there is still substantial disagreement over the causes of that crash, it is beyond doubt that speculative behavior and irrational market psychology played a major role in the initial market hype that finally led to a major correction and squeezed out the "excess value." However, the markets quickly recovered, and after the announcement of Lawson's 1988 budget, the British economy seemed to be in thrall of an unstoppable boom, growing at 5 percent that same year.[45] Profits had risen steadily, and the average return on assets of industrial and commercial companies increased from 4.3 percent in 1981 to 10 percent in 1988.[46] This helped to finance fixed investment, which grew by almost one third between 1986 and 1989. Households borrowed heavily – by no means exclusively to buy a home – doubling the ratio of consumer debt to personal disposable income over the course of the 1980s. Household savings rates fell from 13.5 percent of disposable income in 1980 to 6.7 percent in 1989. The increase in debt was accompanied by a rise in asset values: house prices all but doubled between 1985 and 1989, while the value of average net personal wealth (real estate and financial assets) doubled in the same four years.[47]

But, as Table 6.1 illustrates, the boom started to slow down in 1989 with growth reduced to just 2.2 percent and inflation accelerating. By the second half of 1990, output actually started to fall, dropping further in 1991 and continuing into the second half of 1992, when the first signs of recovery finally appeared. Unemployment almost doubled in just two years from slightly above 5 percent in 1990 to just below 10 percent in 1992. As the Lawson boom came to an abrupt end, the expansionary measures that had fueled the boom went into reverse. Most borrowers, conscious of an increasing burden of debt, avoided new capital commitments.

Suddenly circumstances seemed to conspire to produce a severe monetary squeeze. Accelerating inflation, a growing current account deficit, and a slide in the exchange rate of the pound of more than 20 percent in 1989 were reason enough for a drastic hike in interest rates. The weakness of the pound was the main

*Table 6.1* Main economic indicators in Britain (1986–1992)

|  | 1986 | 1987 | 1988 | 1989 | 1990 | 1991 | 1992 |
|---|---|---|---|---|---|---|---|
| Economic growth[1] | 4.4 | 4.8 | 5.0 | 2.2 | 0.4 | −1.5 | 0.1 |
| Unemployment[2] | 11.8 | 10.4 | 8.3 | 6.1 | 5.5 | 7.9 | 9.7 |
| Inflation[3] | 3.4 | 4.2 | 4.9 | 7.8 | 9.5 | 5.9 | 3.7 |
| Current account[4] | −0.6 | −1.8 | −4.2 | −5.1 | −4.0 | −1.8 | −2.1 |

Source: OECD, *Economic Outlook*, No. 80, Annex Tables, Paris: OECD, 2006.

Notes
1 "Economic Growth" is measured as annual percentage change in real GDP.
2 "Unemployment" is the standardized unemployment rate.
3 "Inflation" is measured as the annual increase in consumer prices.
4 "Current Account" is measured as a percentage of GDP.

cause behind the gradual rise in short-term interest rates from 8 percent in June 1988 to 15 percent in October 1989.[48] Furthermore, Britain's ill-timed joining of the ERM – right after the fall of the Iron Curtain – added to the ongoing interest malaise. Helmut Kohl had made the largely political decision to finance the cost of German reunification through government borrowing, which led to skyrocketing German interest rates. Unfortunately this happened at a time of a looming world recession. With the deutschmark the anchor currency of the ERM, Britain was forced to follow the German lead and keep higher interest rates that were consistent with the fixed exchange rate set at 2.95 deutschmarks to the pound.

Higher interest rates not only deflated capital values and left borrowers with larger interest payments to make, they also severely affected investment, which fell by 15 percent between 1989 and 1992. Households now faced higher mortgage payments, which many home owners were then unable to meet. This led to a large number of house repossessions and a return of these homes to the housing market. For the first time in a generation, house prices started to fall. Under the influence of higher loan charges and the risk of loss, new housing starts in the private sector fell from 321,000 in 1988 to 120,000 in 1992.[49] The recession of 1990–1992 thus brought a grim end to the Lawson boom. It was obvious that the unhealthy boom-bust pattern of the British economy had not been cured by Thatcher's monetarist remedies, even though the Lawson bust did not quite follow the classic scenario of too much spending followed by a run on the pound.[50] Relative decline had not been reversed and Britain once again seemed to be the sick man of Europe. Thatcherite triumphalism dissolved in the midst of a severe economic crisis, and the many structural flaws of the British economy, which had been temporarily covered-up by the demand driven growth of the second half of the 1980s, were now revealed and more widely recognized.

### The effects of the 1990–1992 recession

Although the recession of the early 1990s affected the whole country through an increase in job losses and redundancies, it impacted the manufacturing sector the most. Manufacturing employment had already fallen dramatically during the 1980–1982 recession. A further 1.8 million jobs were lost in the 1990–1992 recession (or 30 percent of the whole manufacturing base of 1989).[51] Contrary to the early 1980s, when job losses were mainly concentrated in the North, Scotland, and Wales (traditionally Labour dominated constituencies), this time the job losses spread south as well. Not only were Northern and Midlands manufacturing jobs affected, but also service jobs in the previously prosperous, Tory-dominated, and "recession-immune" South East.[52] What is more, the restructuring of the British economy under Thatcher had added large-scale unemployment to the sources of renewed poverty in the 1980s and created new sectors of low-paid service employment that "trapped their occupants in paid labour and relative poverty at one and the same time," giving the country a growing class of "working poor."[53]

David Coates observed that by the mid-1980s, official reports were recording anywhere between 17 and 29 percent of the population living at or just above the supplementary benefit level, with as many as 12 million people close to poverty and at least 2.6 million living in acute poverty.[54] The cost of growing overall prosperity in Britain under Thatcher did not just come in the form of permanently higher unemployment and rising poverty, however, there was also a quickly rising level of income inequality. The gini coefficient, which measures income inequality between 0 and 1 (with 0 being "perfect equality" and 1 "perfect inequality"), rose from 0.25 in 1979 to 0.34 in 1990: this was the fastest increase recorded over the whole OECD, including the United States.[55] By 1991, as many as 4 million children in Britain were living in households whose total income was less than half the national average. The British economy thus stood alongside that of the United States and Canada in its propensity to generate poverty through low-wage employment.[56]

The manifest exposure of all these negative symptoms in the British economy made it clear that Thatcherism had created as many economic problems as it had solved. The recession of 1990–1992 might not have been the deepest since the Great Depression, but it lasted for almost two years. Upon her resignation in 1990 Thatcher left Major with an economy in tatters. Far from delivering a brave new economy, Thatcher's invisible hand had failed to break the damaging stop-go cycle of the British economy. In this period of renewed crisis, there was a space for new economic ideas. And Kinnock, at the helm of a rejuvenated and confident Labour Party, offered an attractive alternative to Thatcher's market fundamentalism: he offered an "enabling state" that would seek to combine the efficiency of the market with much higher levels of social justice.

## Economic crisis and the 1992 general election

The political situation in Britain drastically changed with the sudden departure of Margaret Thatcher from Downing Street in November 1990. Major's election as leader of the Conservative Party and prime minister was a breath of fresh air after 11 years of Thatcher domination. At least the electorate seemed to think so.

The Gallup poll in October 1990 showed that 34.3 percent intended to vote Conservative at the next general election against 46.4 percent for Labour. Just two months later, in December 1990, with Thatcher out of power, 44.6 percent of the electorate would have voted Tory compared to 39.1 percent for Labour.[57]

If Kinnock was correct in his analysis that the country was ready for change, John Major seemed to embody that change. He was so clearly not his predecessor. Where Thatcher thrived on conflict, Major sought consensus. However, with the British economy already sliding into a long recession, a new leader might not be enough for the Conservatives to win the next election. After seven years of often excruciating party reform and modernization, Labour was ready to fight and win the next election. It had accepted the role of the market in generating prosperity and the main goal of fighting inflation, but provided tangible solutions for the many structural failings of the country, especially in investment, education, health care, and poverty. Major called a general election for April 1992, and it was fought against the backdrop of recession and rising unemployment. Though most opinion polls showed Labour and the Conservatives neck and neck, Labour was widely expected to win.[58]

### Manifestos

The 1992 Conservative Party manifesto, "The Best Future for Britain," was a long and comprehensive document (almost three times longer than Labour's), commenting in detail on everything from Britain's role in the world, to health, housing, and education.[59] The first section of the manifesto, "taking responsibility for Britain," dealt with foreign policy and the changed world after the fall of communism. It stressed the need for British leadership in NATO and Europe, and Britain's role in providing foreign aid and humanitarian relief. On the economy, the manifesto was clear that it would consolidate the gains made under Thatcher in the 1980s and further "[set] the economy free" by extending privatization to British coal and major parts of the transportation industry including airports, ports, and rail services.[60] The manifesto further emphasized the virtues of low inflation, increased choice, property ownership, deregulation, and lower taxes, and promised to take steps towards a 20 percent base rate on income tax. Also, the "Citizen's Charter" was formally included in the manifesto, which was Major's personal program devised to improve quality in public services by extending people's rights and setting clear standards that addressed the needs of those who used them.[61] The manifesto did not deal with the direct and negative effects of the recession in Britain – the elephant in the closet – ostensibly assuming that the market would take care of it.

In sharp contrast, Labour's manifesto, "It's Time to Get Britain Working Again," directly addressed the recession and emphasized the need to get out of the enduring economic malaise.[62] Kinnock set the tone in his foreword: "This general election is a choice between a Conservative government paralysed by recession, and a Labour government determined to get on with building recovery."[63] The first section of the manifesto, "immediate action for national recovery," gave a list of ten points of action for jobs, skills, schools, the National Health Service, and children – providing incentive schemes for small businesses and investment in new machinery and plant in support of the manufacturing sector.[64] Labour's overall plan for the economy could be seen as the last attempt to modernize British industry. Underlining that they would be a "government which business can do business with," Labour promised to keep prices down and introduce a system of "fair taxes" that would keep the basic income tax rate unchanged at 25 percent and add a new top rate of 50 percent for individuals making more than £40,000 a year.[65] Furthermore, Labour pledged to strengthen Britain's regional economies, invest in modern transport, improve energy supplies, and "invest in people at work."[66]

In sum, voters had a clear choice between a center-right government that emphasized the virtues of the market, linking individual choice with responsibility, and a center-left government that promised an immediate action plan to bring the country out of recession, increase taxes on the rich, actively help industry to modernize, and heavily invest in skills and education. The election promised to be a referendum on Thatcherism: did the benefits outweigh the costs or were the costs too high?

Two fundamental issues were foremost in the public's mind in 1992. First, Thatcherism had not solved the boom-bust cycle and inflation had returned – even though it was already waning again in 1992. Second, it was unclear whether Thatcherism was creating the kind of society Britons wanted, given its low provision of public goods and widening income inequality. If the electorate fundamentally believed that the country was in a crisis that needed a decisive intervention based on new ideas, they would vote Labour. If not, they would vote for the Conservatives, who were determined to further build on Thatcher's legacy.

### *Campaign*

The campaign was launched with Norman Lamont's budget on March 10, which was countered by John Smith's shadow budget six days later. The latter admitted the need to increase direct taxation and thus handed the Tories a card that they knew all too well how to play.[67] Throughout the next month the Conservatives, aided by the tabloid press, harped on the theme that Labour would raise taxes.[68] Chris Patten, then chairman of the Tories, led a very effective campaign with one poster warning against "Labour's Tax Bombshell."[69] On the campaign trail, Major stood out as the antidote to Thatcher. He spoke from a soapbox during his public meetings all over Britain and assumed the role of the underdog.[70] This was clearly something the former prime minister would never have done, and it underlined the fact that Major was not Thatcher. However, he was prepared to defend her free market principles and he was widely perceived as a "compassionate" conservative who gave Thatcherism a much needed human face.

Although Labour was slightly ahead in the polls in March, it constantly had to fight the electorate's dormant fears about Labour's competence to govern.

These fears were shrewdly exploited by the Conservative Party machine. Kinnock proved himself to be a liability to his party, carrying tremendous baggage, even though he had devoted much of his career to exorcising it. The Tory jibe that he was nothing but a "Welsh windbag" seemed to stick and as Cronin observed, his "garrulous personality and long-winded style undermined his steady efforts to appear statesmanlike, and however controlled the performance, every once and a while the real Kinnock broke through unrestrained."[71] The most painful example of this was the infamous Sheffield rally on April 1 – partly modeled on François Mitterrand's campaign rallies in France – where Kinnock jumped onto the stage in an outburst of triumphalist enthusiasm.[72] While he probably gave one of his best speeches, the impression was created that "the Welsh boyo suddenly took over from the national statesman." Kinnock told that Sheffield rally the following:

> What's at issue in this election is not the soap boxes that people stand on, but the cardboard boxes that people live in. The decent British people are revolted by a government that has broken the consensus of 40 years – a government that has created poverty as a matter of policy, just as it has used unemployment as an instrument of economic management.[73]

As usual, the press was hostile to Labour, with four out of five major papers – *The Sun*, the *Daily Express*, the *Daily Mail*, and the *Daily Telegraph*: a circulation of almost 8 million – endorsing the Conservatives. *The Daily Mirror* – the only tabloid supporting Labour – had an all-time low circulation of 2.9 million.[74] None of the major tabloids was as violently anti-Labour or anti-Kinnock as *The Sun*. On the day before the election, they ran an eight page preelection special titled "Nightmare on Kinnock Street," while on polling day itself the front page featured Kinnock's head inside a light bulb asking: "If Kinnock Wins Today Will The Last Person in Britain Please Turn Out The Lights?"[75]

### Outcome

On April 9, 1992, Labour experienced its fourth consecutive defeat in a general election. The Conservatives polled 41.9 percent and won 336 seats, Labour just 34.4 percent and 271 seats; the Liberal Democrats received 17.8 percent of the votes and 20 seats.[76] Labour's narrow lead in the opinion polls had been trumped by a solid Conservative lead of 8 percent in the actual polls. Brushing aside *The Sun*'s sensationalism or Smith's candid shadow budget, Peter Clarke noted that this last minute upset for Kinnock was due to a "latent suspicion of a Labour Government."[77] He observed that "enough voters proved wary, in the event, not only of voting Labour but also of voting Liberal Democrat – for fear of letting Labour in by default."[78] Although Major scored the highest popular vote in British electoral history – more than 14 million – this would only translate into a 21 seat majority in Westminster given Britain's electoral seat counting system, denying Major the favorable terms that Thatcher had always benefited from.[79]

The consequences of the election were immense. It was a critical moment in the development of Britain's political economy. The basic principles of Thatcherism enjoyed the approval of 42 percent of the electorate, which in Britain's electoral system was usually enough to secure an overall majority in Parliament. The fact that the Conservatives – again – managed to win an election held in the midst of an economic recession meant that Thatcherism could be consolidated even more during the next five years as the principle of Britain's political economy. Major extended the Thatcher revolution with more privatizations and deregulation. By opting out of Europe's single currency and not signing Europe's Social Charter, he made it clear that he was, after all, Thatcher's rightful heir. However, under Major and his deputy Michael Heseltine, the Tories started to shave off the sharp edges of Thatcherism by showing more enthusiasm for interventions in the microeconomy. They invoked "the need to compete globally" as justification.[80]

Major would not get to enjoy his election victory for long. On September 16, 1992 Britain was forced to devalue the pound and leave the ERM after a speculative attack on sterling. With the humiliation of that Black Wednesday went the Tories' claim of having a monopoly on economic competence and their portrayal of Labour as the "party of devaluation." After the ERM debacle, however, devaluation seemed to solve many of the country's problems: the economy quickly started to recover and, fuelled by exports, Britain grew at an impressive rate for the next four years. With Kenneth Clarke at the Treasury from the beginning of 1993, the Major government had a popular and competent chancellor. However, the Conservatives would prove to be their own worst enemies in the 1990s. They tore themselves apart over the question of Europe. After a series of scandals, which popularized them as "the nasty party" mired in "sleaze," they would gradually lose all electoral appeal.[81]

## The end of socialism in Britain: from Kinnock to Blair

The result of 1992 meant that Labour would have to move even further towards the center ground of British politics and away from its socialist past to remain viable. More than ever, the Tories seemed to be the "natural party of government," and the conclusions many Labour modernizers drew from the loss in 1992 was that the internal reform process had not gone far enough.[82] To his credit, Kinnock immediately resigned as party leader and took full responsibility for Labour's loss; however, he made it clear that he preferred the party to continue with its process of transformation. As Cronin observed, "by coupling his resignation with an insistence on altering the institutional structure of the party, Kinnock gave his continued blessing to the 'modernising' project."[83] Kinnock was succeeded by Smith, the shadow chancellor, who won the leadership election by a large majority. By doing this, Labour avoided further infighting regarding the future direction of the party. Smith appointed Brown and Blair – key allies and fellow modernizers – to the frontbench positions of shadow chancellor and shadow home secretary respectively. Both quickly emerged as the stars of Labour's shadow team.[84]

### John Smith and OMOV

From the beginning it was obvious that Smith – though stemming from the right of the party – lacked the reformist zeal of Brown and Blair, who were both convinced that the entrenched role of the trade unions was a crucial anomaly. While Smith was happy enough to stand by, watch the Tories self-destruct, and enjoy the rising levels of support in the opinion polls, Blair and Brown wanted a more in-depth reform of the Labour Party's constitution. Smith's cautious approach contrasted sharply with the intensity of Kinnock, whose initiatives often became crusades if only because he was so embattled. Brown and Blair finally managed to convince a reluctant Smith to start working towards the abolition of the trade unions' "block vote" and to take up the campaign for "One Member, One Vote" (OMOV).[85]

Once Smith was on board he put his leadership at stake over the issue. The irony, of course, was that any proposal to diminish the power of the unions within the Labour Party would have to be approved by a party conference that was still dominated by those very same unions. Asking trade unions leaders to acquiesce to their own weakening would require a significant amount of horse trading and political skill.[86] After a careful compromise was crafted between Smith and John Prescott, a trade union man, the 1993 Labour conference grudgingly approved OMOV and gave Smith his victory.[87] This was a decisive step for the Labour Party, which was moving further away from its leftist past, and was widely recognized as a triumph for Smith.

Just eight months later the new Labour leader died of a heart attack, which opened up the leadership debate once again. Many members of the traditional left wing of the party were now convinced that Labour had reformed enough and that with the Tories en route to political oblivion, "one more haul" would suffice to get them back into power.[88] This view was not shared by the modernizers within the party, including Blair, Brown, and Mandelson. Those three still represented a minority view within the Labour Party, and were now convinced that the party needed to shed its socialist past once and for all.[89]

### Tony Blair, New Labour, and the rewriting of Clause IV

In an almost legendary deal at the Granita restaurant in Islington in May 1994, Brown agreed not to stand against Blair for the party's leadership. This was a concerted effort not to split the party's "modernizing" vote. In return, Brown would get a quasi monopoly on the party's foreign and domestic economic policy and would be an all-powerful Chancellor of the Exchequer if Labour was elected to power in 1997.[90]

Blair was the more energetic and charismatic of the two, and it had long been clear to Smith before he died that "it's got to be Tony."[91] Blair won the leadership election in July 1994 against Prescott and Margaret Beckett with 57 percent of the vote overall and a majority in all three sections of the party: among MPs and MEPs he achieved over 60 percent, among party members 58 percent, and among trade union votes 52 percent. Blair emerged from the leadership contest with his reputation enhanced, a solid mandate, and his most powerful rival – Gordon Brown – firmly on board as a key member of his team. Crucially, Blair had managed to become leader without having compromised on the key issues of the modernizers' agenda.[92] He surrounded himself with a shadow cabinet that had impressive credentials and enjoyed broad support from all sections of the party. Prescott enjoyed great popularity amongst the party faithful and the unions; he was elected deputy leader with a solid majority. The left-leaning Robin Cook took over foreign affairs, Jack Straw home affairs, George Robertson defense, and David Blunkett education, which was central to Blair's plans and rhetoric.

From the moment Blair was elected leader, it was clear that he would complete the modernization process Kinnock had started in 1983 instead of patiently waiting for the Tories to collapse in government. In September 1994, Blair told Philip Gould – a key ally – that "it [was] time we gave the party some electric shock treatment."[93] Blair would carry out the Labour Party's modernization to a point of no return; to achieve this, Labour's historic links with the trade unions could no longer be preferential. In an interview with the BBC, Blair stated that the unions "would have the same access [to a Labour government] as the other side of industry."[94]

The symbolic break with the past would come in the October 1994 party conference in Blackpool. Surrounded by signs and images that announced the birth of "New Labour, New Britain," Blair distanced himself from the old Labour Party of Wilson, Callaghan, Foot, Benn, and Kinnock.[95] With this symbolic break came a strategic decision: Blair decided to rewrite Clause IV of the party's constitution. This clause committed the party to

> secure for the workers by hand or by brain the full fruits of their industry and the most equitable distribution thereof that may be possible upon the basis of the common ownership of the means of production, distribution, and exchange, and the best obtainable system of popular administration and control of each industry or service.[96]

Before becoming leader of the Labour Party, Blair had written a pamphlet for the Fabian Society that criticized the wording of Clause IV for "confusing ends with means." Blair put forward a case for defining socialism in terms of a set of values. So the pamphlet read, the policies needed to achieve these values would have to change to account for a changing society.[97] After becoming leader, Blair announced at the conclusion of his 1994 conference speech that Labour needed a "new statement of aims and values," and that he would draw one up and present it to the party. The new version, which made very few tangible commitments, was finally adopted at a special Easter conference in 1995 and was the result of a long internal party debate.[98]

The question still remains as to why Blair pushed these radical reforms when the Conservative Party was imploding for all to see. Instead of alienating the

Labour Party faithful, Blair could have waited for the Tories to self-destruct and hand him the keys to Downing Street after the next general election. However, by insisting on treating the party with a dose of intellectual shock therapy, Blair and Brown showed that they had learned the lessons of Thatcherism. The power of her ideas was such that Labour, the main opposition party, was forced to adopt her economic framework, in effect making the next election about economic competence and fighting the credibility battles all over again, rather than generating any new economic ideas.

Tony Blair instinctively felt that Britain had changed irrevocably and beyond recognition after Thatcher. By one measure, the working class had declined from over 58 percent of the labor force in 1964, when Labour won, to 49 percent in 1979, when Thatcher came to power, to just over 34 percent in 1997.[99] Blair's hope was to make New Labour the "people's party." In order to achieve that, he believed that Labour needed to redefine its social base and appeal to the "broad mass in the middle of society."[100] A left wing manifesto would fail to appeal to enough voters to bring Labour back to power. Blair took away the veto power of the left in drafting the manifesto, and made sure to avoid the mistakes of his predecessors by not committing to specific policies that would prove to be impossible to realize once in power. But, in order to be ready to steer the economy, New Labour needed "a project" – an ideational framework or a governing philosophy – which would inform its future economic decisions. The ideas that provided the alternative to the outdated ideas of Old Labour, as well as to the shortcomings of Thatcherism, were all in existence in the mid-1990s, but would only later be known as the "Third Way."

## The Third Way

During the early and mid-1990s, there was a flurry of center-left writing on the role and ideas of social democratic parties and governments in a post-Reagan and post-Thatcher world. Out of a more general reckoning that the heyday of postwar Keynesian demand management was over, many academics and pundits started to think of a more general framework that could provide an alternative to the individualistic neoliberalism of Thatcher and the collectivist alternative of people like Benn. In Britain, two thinkers especially influenced the way Blair and Brown thought about the political economy: Anthony Giddens and Will Hutton. Both Giddens and Hutton tried to find a genuine social democratic alternative to Thatcherism.

However, Blair and Brown usually watered down those ideas in their speeches. Instead they emphasized their macroeconomic credentials and stayed within the ideational framework created by Thatcher and Lawson. The neoliberal ideas proved to be so hegemonic that anything that veered away from them too much never made it into the 1997 New Labour manifesto. The irony of the Third Way is that it only really caught on *after* Tony Blair's victory at the polls in 1997.

In this section, I will discuss the ideas of Giddens and Hutton and how both Blair and Brown would twist those ideas in their speeches, creating merely some kind of ideational framework for New Labour rather than adopting new economic ideas themselves. I conclude that for all the stimulating intellectual activity of the mid-1990s, the ideas that later became known as the Third Way – with minor exceptions – never translated into specific policies that New Labour could commit itself to once in power.

### *Anthony Giddens:* Beyond Left and Right

In *Beyond Left and Right*, Giddens set out to provide a framework for future radical politics.[101] Recognizing the shortcomings of socialism and neoliberalism, Giddens argued that the old divisions between left and right had become outdated. He based this on three sets of developments that had affected the industrialized world during the previous 20 or so years. First, there was intensifying globalization, meaning that day to day activities were increasingly influenced by events happening on the other side of the world. Second, Giddens saw the emergence of what he called a "post-traditional social order," where traditional family structures were replaced by all kinds of alternative social arrangements. Third, the expansion of "social reflexivity" introduced a dislocation between knowledge and control, which was a prime source of what Giddens called "manufactured uncertainty."[102] Based on those three assumptions, Giddens saw the need to fundamentally change the welfare state from negative to positive welfare. Negative welfare meant that the state was there to "protect the individual against misfortune," while positive welfare meant that the state would give each and every citizen the tools to be successful in a globalized, knowledge driven economy.[103]

Giddens himself did not like the term Third Way, but preferred to see his ideas as providing the framework for "the renewal of social democracy."[104] He emphasized that it was wrong to see his ideas as a middle road between Keynesian social democracy and Hayekian neoliberal economics. Instead, Giddens argued that his approach could be summed up by combining economic efficiency and market flexibility with high levels of social protection and an active state that limited poverty and income inequality.[105] The Third Way was thus a strategy based on the assumption that effective government had to work with, rather than against, the capitalist trends of the world economy. It did not resist the turn towards individualism in contemporary capitalism, but sought to empower individuals to actively participate within it.[106] Giddens thus developed the concept of the "social investment state:" by directing public investment into human capital and infrastructure, the government would equip Britain to compete in a "global, knowledge-based economy," while simultaneously "equipping individuals to prosper" within it and to profit from its steady expansion.[107]

If old style social democracy believed it could manage or even transform the economy in the interests of the working class, the Third Way would involve "rediscovering an activist role for government" within a framework that left the market mechanism the main driver for economic wellbeing.[108] The role of the state was therefore to better educate its citizens and train them to flourish in the information economy. In effect, an "active welfare state" would increase levels of labor market participation, while at the same time providing a safety net to protect them against the adverse shocks of globalization.[109]

This whole idea of an active welfare state is of course nothing new. It has underpinned the economic success of the Scandinavian countries for the past 60 years. Thus, Giddens' writings indirectly pointed Britain towards the "Scandinavian Model," where flexible labor markets would be offset by high levels of government spending, and the universal provision of public services such as health and education. In order for this view to work, the government required higher levels of general taxation: something to which both Blair and Brown were loath to commit.

### Will Hutton: The Stakeholder Society

In February 1996, Blair wrote a short pamphlet in the Fabian Review introducing "stakeholding" as a new concept in New Labour thinking.[110] Blair was strongly influenced by Hutton's *The State We're In*, a book that had emerged out of an ongoing debate in which New Labour thinkers were already deeply involved.[111] Hutton's main argument was that the source of Britain's economic weakness lay in its financial system, which was fundamentally biased towards short-term profits and disregarded the long-term needs of British industry. Hutton produced an insightful diagnosis of Britain's economic ills, building his claims upon two lines of existing research. The first line of research was the study of the powerful role of financial interests in British economic policymaking, which held the unholy triumvirate of City of London–Treasury–Bank of England responsible for favoring finance over industry.[112] The second line of research Hutton borrowed from was the study of "varieties of capitalism" which in the classic tradition of Andrew Shonfield explains economic success and failure based on the different institutional structures in which various economies are embedded.[113] The crucial assumption that Hutton borrowed from this latter line of research was that institutional structures with closer ties between business and state, and finance and industry, and more cooperative industrial relations, enhance overall economic performance.[114]

For Hutton, the solution was to radically transform the institutions of British capitalism: remake the financial system, change patterns of corporate governance and employment by empowering all of the "stakeholders" in the economy, and genuinely include workers, consumers, managers, owners, bankers, and the public at large.[115] A multiplicity of small reforms "ranging from the role of non-executive directors to the tax treatment of short-term capital gains, would help to push the system towards generating more committed, patient owners and bankers."[116] For Hutton, the tax system thus had to be used to promote long-term shareholding and somehow penalize speculative behavior. He also wanted legal and financial obstacles to hostile takeovers. Hutton admitted that he got his inspiration from the "best types of overseas forms of capitalism," which "struck the right balance between commitment and flexibility."[117] In other words, Hutton's solution pointed towards the corporatist arrangements of Germany and Austria, whose adoption would entail a radical transformation of Britain's political economy. Just like Giddens, Hutton stressed the fact that his approach was a genuine third way, and not a middle way as Macmillan had already tried to construct in his 1938 book.[118]

For Blair, Hutton's argument took on a less structural and more "individualist" character. Wary of taking on the powerful financial interests of the City, Blair promoted the concept of "stakeholding" as fitting within the so-called "training revolution."[119] Blair thus explained that

> the stakeholder economy is about giving you the chances that help you to get on and so help Britain to get on too: a job, a skill, a home, and opportunity – a stake in the success we all want for Britain.[120]

This watered down version of Hutton's ideas again brought nothing new, but an appeal to "investment, quality and trust."[121]

### The New Labour "project"

During the three years from 1994 to 1997, both Blair and Brown carefully avoided any detailed commitments on economic policy apart from Brown's flagship "welfare to work" program, which would be financed by a onetime windfall tax on the large profits the privatized utility companies had enjoyed. Their emphasis was instead on macroeconomic stability, which Brown made famous in the sound bite "prudence for a purpose."[122] However, the rhetoric was often different – inspired by "post-neoclassical endogenous growth theory," which Brown's most trusted economic advisor, Ed Balls, had explained to him. In a speech on economic policy for the Labour Party Conference, Brown summarized what a Treasury under New Labour would look like:

> The lesson of stop-go Conservative economics is that sound finances can be achieved and the problems of boom and bust can be solved only if the underlying weaknesses of the British economy are addressed. A Labour Treasury, therefore, must tackle the under-investment in people, industry and infrastructure which have brought both high unemployment and high inflation. So I want a Labour Treasury, working with other departments, to be an engine of new ideas in Government, a catalyst for long term change, and a modernising force making for a dynamic economy.[123]

How Brown would solve these "underlying weaknesses" was less clear, especially since he had committed a Labour government to adhere to Kenneth Clarke's austere spending plans for the first two years. Even Clarke himself later admitted that he would probably not have stuck with them, given the more favorable economic climate of the late 1990s.[124]

Although economic policy was the domain of Brown, Tony Blair set out his own vision for the British economy in a book he wrote in 1996 called *The New*

*Britain: My Vision of a Young Country*.[125] In chapter 11, "New Labour, New Economy," Blair stressed that the role of government in a modern economy was limited, but crucial. In his view, government should secure low inflation, promote long-term investment, ensure that business had well-educated people, provide for a first class infrastructure, work with business to promote regional development, and create a strong and cohesive society, "which removed the drag on the economy of social costs like unemployment and related welfare benefits."[126] Again, there were no specific commitments for a potential New Labour government, but an emphasis on low inflation, the efficient working of the market, and the limited role the state had to play. There were however, two significant boons for the left of the party: once in power New Labour would establish a legal minimum wage and sign on to the European Social Charter.[127]

The most revealing comparison is between the 1984 Mais Lecture by Lawson and the 1995 Mais Lecture by Blair.[128] Both Lawson and Blair fundamentally agreed on all aspects of macroeconomic policy. During that speech, Blair committed New Labour to the Thatcherite agenda of tough macroeconomic strategies to ensure the control of inflation. He also stressed the virtues of balanced budgets, restraint in public expenditure, and the disciplining effect of market competition.[129] Of course, there was still a lot of rhetoric about the flaws of the Tories' "neoliberal market fundamentalism" as well as the faults of the outdated "Keynesian collectivism" of Old Labour, but the commitment to Thatcherism was unmistakable. As Cronin has pointed out,

> situating the Third Way between such stark alternatives might be tactfully useful, but since the space that lay between these opposites was so vast, it said far too little about what the Third Way actually was; and it virtually invited cynical commentary about its vagueness and vacuity.[130]

To avoid this, Blair and Brown lost no opportunity to stress the importance of the macroeconomic fundamentals of the economy, the limited role of the state and the trade unions, and the virtues of the private sector in providing services. Those very same areas of economic policy had constituted the then radical core of Thatcherism in 1979.

The shift in ideas in the Labour Party under Blair is quite phenomenal, if one compares it with the Labour ideas of ten years earlier. The Labour Party had traditionally prided itself on the fact that it did not listen to popular opinion, but was on a mission to change society. The idea that the party would shrug off its socialist goals and principles in just a few years would have seemed impossible during the early 1980s. Both Blair and Brown, having first arrived in Westminster under the 1983 electoral program of Labour, suddenly were true believers of everything they had fought against in the mid-1980s. The two consecutive electoral losses in 1987 and 1992 convinced them that Thatcher had got many things right, and they felt compelled to embrace her ideas, even if there was no objective need for further change. What this shift shows, more than anything, is the supremacy and quasi-hegemony of Thatcherite ideas by the mid-1990s. Even

Smith had mentioned Labour's commitment to full employment when he was party leader. Once Blair was in power this was expediently dropped.[131]

Both Colin Hay and Richard Heffernan have explained this shift in ideas as the Labour Party becoming engaged for the first time in its history in "preference accommodation."[132] Labour had a long tradition of "preference shaping," going back to the founding of the party in 1919. The innovations of the Attlee government were its major achievement. Once it became obvious to the modernizers, from four successive electoral defeats and most opinion polls that a majority in Britain did not share their socialist ideals of equality and public ownership, and that for all their personal dislike of Thatcher, many voters did approve of many of her policies, Labour gave up its aspirations for social engineering and followed the Tory line on economic management. In this sense, New Labour's economic ideas proved to be directly path dependent with Thatcherism, while the few innovations it did propose could easily be reconciled with her basic economic governing philosophy.

Although New Labour's embrace of Thatcherism was in large part a response to the strategic logic of the political situation, there was more to it. According to John Gray, the pervasive influence of neoliberal ideas in the 1990s largely shaped the New Labour world view.[133] Blair, Brown, and Mandelson thus created New Labour in the neoliberal belief that only one economic system could deliver prosperity or, in other words, that there was no alternative. Gray points out that, just like Marxism, this neoliberal ideology "instills a dangerous conceit:" it encourages the illusion that history does not matter and that the past is simply a prelude to a radiant future. Gray points out that in this view "intractable conflicts are viewed as soluble problems, which with advancing rationality can be eradicated entirely. Politics therefore becomes a mere branch of technology."[134]

## Sea change: the 1997 general election

> Tony Blair is a man who won't let Britain down.
>            Margaret Thatcher, *Speech at the Reform Club* (January 1997)[135]

### Background

By any standard, it was remarkable that Major's government lasted as long as it did. From the ERM debacle in September 1992 onwards, Major's government stumbled from one political crisis to the next, losing one by-election after another, and eventually losing its overall majority in Parliament.[136] The forced devaluation of the pound in September 1992 was probably the single most important event of Major's five year term: on Black Wednesday, the Tories lost their cherished aura of economic competence. However, when Kenneth Clarke replaced Norman Lamont at the Treasury, the economy quickly recovered. Growth averaged 3.2 percent from 1993 to 1997, unemployment fell from 10.4 percent in 1993 to 7 percent in 1997, and inflation averaged just 2.3 percent.[137] In other words, Major and Clarke could boast an impressive economic record in 1997. Also, with Heseltine at the Board of Trade, Major's government started to

veer away from the "raw" Thatcherism of the 1980s, began addressing the issue
of underinvestment in health and education, and engaged in more active intervention in British industry, which Heseltine thought necessary to maintain global
competitiveness.[138] Of course, none of that seemed to actually matter since the
Tories had made themselves practically unelectable via multiple scandals, which
created a general impression of a party on its way out. Also, the internal rivalries
within the party over Britain's future in Europe were unmanageable by 1997.
Blair scoffed at Major during a debate in the House of Commons in early 1997:
"I lead my party, he follows his."[139]

With Blair, "New" Labour had a charismatic young leader – 27 years younger
than Margaret Thatcher – who promised to give Britain what it needed: a
welcome change in the country after 18 years of Conservative rule. From his
speeches and changes to the party's constitution, the days of socialism and class
struggle were seemingly over. New Labour now was the "people's party:" they
had equal ties to both sides of industry and were determined to banish their "tax
and spend" mantra to the dustbin of history.[140] Brown had promised to keep the
fight against inflation as the number one priority of Labour's new government
and committed to stick with the Tories' tax and spend plans for the first two
years if elected. Though both Brown and Blair often spoke of an economy "in
crisis" during the 1990s, it was more electoral rhetoric than anything else.[141]
Proof of that was their reluctance to commit to any kind of specific remedies
they deemed necessary to solve the so-called crisis. Both Blair and Brown went
out of their way to emphasize their macroeconomic credentials in order not to
frighten the financial markets and the readers of *The Sun* in Middle England.

### Manifestos

The Tories' 1997 election manifesto, "You Can Only Be Sure with the Conservatives," started by pointing out that Britain, once the sick man of Europe, was now
its most successful economy.[142] According to the manifesto, that was the achievement of 18 years of Tory rule, which was responsible for "the enterprising virtues
of the British people [having] been liberated from the dead hand of the state."[143]
On the economy, the Tories' manifesto committed itself to a "low tax economy,"
set a goal for the state to spend less than 40 percent of national income, and aimed
to achieve a basic rate of income tax of 20 percent while maintaining the top rate
at 40 percent. The goal of economic policy was to "double living standards" over
the next 25 years.[144] Furthermore, the Conservatives had an "education guarantee"
that set national targets for school performance and increased parents' choice of
schools, but they were vague as to how they would pay for it.[145] They also promised "world class Health and Public Services" and committed themselves to
increasing the real resources of the National Health Service, "so NHS spending
will continue to share in a growing economy."[146] Finally, they promised to hold a
referendum on potential membership in the EMU, but stressed that it was "in the
national interest to keep our options open." At the same time, the Tories underlined that "without sustainable convergence," Britain would not join.[147]

Labour's 1997 manifesto, "New Labour because Britain Deserves Better," began by stating that "in each area of policy a new and distinctive approach has been mapped out, one that differs from the old left and the Conservative right. This is why new Labour is new."[148] Arguing that they were a party of ideas and ideals and not of an outdated ideology, they made it clear that in government "what counts is what works." In his foreword, Tony Blair admitted that "some things the Conservatives got right." On the economy, Labour stressed especially what it would not do, for example "no increase in the basic or top rates of tax."[149] Education was the clear priority and the share of national income spent on education would increase under Labour. The one specific policy was to get 250,000 young unemployed off benefits and into work. Furthermore, Blair promised to "save the NHS" by raising spending in real terms every year. And of course, there was his trademark "tough on crime and tough on the causes of crime" sound bite for domestic affairs.[150] However, the fact that Brown had committed his Treasury to the same spending plans as Clarke for the first two years meant that there was no basic difference between the Tories and Labour on health and education. Finally on Europe, New Labour guaranteed that any decision about Britain joining the single currency "must be determined by a hard-headed assessment of Britain's economic interests."[151]

### Campaign

The Tories' internal troubles made it possible for Labour to make inroads among groups it had never before been able to reach. Blair and Brown made a special effort to court business and the overwhelmingly right wing tabloid press.[152] During the campaign, Blair visited the City of London and professed his belief that "economic activity is best left to the private sector" and stressed once again that "the postwar Keynesian dream is well and truly buried."[153] In April 1997, Labour published its business manifesto, "Equipping Britain for the Future," and recruited over 80 businessmen to endorse it.[154] Alastair Campbell, Blair's all-powerful press secretary, got Blair an invitation to address Rupert Murdoch's media empire in 1995. This paid off handsomely when *The Sun*, for the first time since 1970, came out in favor of Blair and New Labour in 1997. During the campaign, Blair was interviewed twice by *The Sun* and was invited to write seven articles for that paper.[155] In all, six of the ten major national newspapers backed Blair. Their combined readership was twice that of the papers backing Major and the Conservatives.[156] The Tories had been trailing Labour in the opinion polls ever since September 1992, and although Major fought a brave campaign, it was a lost battle from the start. Michael Heseltine made a courageous effort immediately before the election when he stated on national television that if all the "don't knows" came down on the right side, and if the polls were as mistaken as they had been in 1992, the Tories would have a majority of 60.[157] The media, scenting a Conservative massacre on election day, had already started to speculate about Major's future successor.[158]

*Outcome*

On May 1, 1997, New Labour won a landslide victory, winning 43.2 percent of the national vote compared to 30.7 percent for the Conservatives, with voting turnout at 72 percent. This translated into 418 seats in the House of Commons for Labour compared to just 165 seats for the Tories, 44 fewer seats than Labour in 1983. The Liberals recovered from 1992 and more than doubled their seats to 46 with 16.8 percent of the total vote.[159] Since some opinion polls had predicted as much as 50 percent for Labour, Blair's victory was less impressive than hoped for by some of the party faithful at the time, but the distribution of seats hugely exaggerated Labour's triumph.[160] It was the biggest electoral swing from Conservative to Labour since 1945. Labour's majority was the largest in its history, while the Tories' defeat was the worst since 1832.[161] With an overall majority of 177 seats in Parliament, Tony Blair and New Labour had a resounding mandate to govern and implement their policy agenda, even though nobody really knew what that policy agenda was.

The 1997 election has often been described as a "sea change" election. Geoffrey Wheatcroft observed that there have been three landslide victories in twentieth century British politics "when the whole mood of the country seemed to change, and the air people breathed felt different." He was thinking of the Liberal victory over the Tories in 1906, the Labour victory over the Tories in 1945, and New Labour's victory again over the Tories in 1997.[162] There is no doubt that the expectations of Blair were high. However, it should have been apparent from New Labour's manifesto and their statements over the previous three years that not much would change at Whitehall apart from the personnel: at least, not in the first two years. Blair and Brown had deliberately been campaigning to lower the electorate's expectations as to what they could achieve once in government. Prudence in economic policy would be "for a purpose," i.e. to reduce poverty and income inequality and create a dynamic knowledge-driven economy with first class healthcare, education, and other public services. In order to achieve that, they would need at least two terms.

## New Labour's economic policies (1997–2000)

During the first three years of New Labour government, Blair and Brown would continue the neoliberal economic policies of the Tories, especially in monetary, fiscal, and industrial policy. This also applied to their policy towards Europe apart from a largely symbolic commitment to the European Social Charter. In labor market policy, there was the "welfare to work" program for young unemployed people, which on the face of it was a "social democratic" policy, but was in fact radically different from the Scandinavian example.[163]

*Monetary policy*

Just five days after the general election, Brown announced in a press conference at the Treasury that the Labour government had decided to grant the Bank of England formal independence.[164] The move was widely acclaimed as a political masterstroke and gave the new government the immediate respect of the financial markets and foreign investors. The model that Brown preferred for the newly independent Bank of England was something of a hybrid between the Federal Reserve, the Bundesbank, and New Zealand's central bank. As shadow chancellor, Brown declared in 1995: "I am attracted to the openness of debate and decision-making which occurs in the US, the internal democracy of decision-making in the Bundesbank and the way in which the New Zealand government sets targets for the bank to pursue."[165] Brown set the British economy's inflation target at 2.5 percent with a provision that if the actual rate varied by more than one percentage point, the Monetary Policy Committee (MPC) would be required to explain its policy in a public letter to the Treasury. Of crucial importance was that the inflation target was "symmetrical," i.e. crafted to avoid both inflation and deflation.[166] The letter Bank of England governor Eddie George received from Brown made it clear that the MPC's overriding responsibility was to hit the inflation target, but that it should also "take account" of economic growth.[167] The Bank's independence won the Labour government the precious credibility Brown had been longing for in opposition: inflationary expectations and long-term interest rates fell. For example, the ten-year bond differential with Germany fell from 1.7 percentage points to average just 0.5 percentage points in 2001.[168]

Ed Balls has claimed that the May 1997 decision to hand over monetary policymaking to the Bank of England was the single most important decision taken by the Labour government, adding that the post-1997 arrangements made by Labour are far superior to the way the Tories conducted monetary policy under Major and Clarke.[169] That is an exaggeration. It is perhaps more useful to look at monetary policymaking as an evolving process over time, which changed in 1976 when the Callaghan government committed itself to fighting inflation through monetary targets. In many ways, Brown's decision built on the previous five years and was the logical next step.[170] From 1992 to 1997, the Tories did the hard work by reducing inflation to low single digits. Though both Major and Clarke had opposed formal independence for the Bank of England, previous Conservative chancellors Lawson and Lamont had been strong advocates of it, but always found their proposals rejected by 10 Downing Street.[171] Also, given the international tendency towards monetary policy independence, with an independent European Central Bank and Federal Reserve Board, the decision was probably inevitable. Brown nevertheless does deserve credit for having had the courage to make the decision. What most commentators did not realize at the time is that Brown's "genial" decision institutionalized the core of Thatcherist ideas, the supremacy of inflation control over full employment, and thus meant the formal death of Keynesian demand management through the manipulation of interest rates.

### *Fiscal policy*

After Brown had outsourced monetary policy to the Bank of England, he set about creating his "platform of stability" for fiscal policy.[172] During the campaign, New Labour had promised to abide by the Tories' spending plans in 1998 and 1999. Brown, a firm believer in rules, established a new "Code for Fiscal Stability" in 1998, which introduced his famous "Golden Rule." This meant that, over the economic cycle, the government would only borrow to invest and not to fund current expenditure. Additionally, there was a commitment to keep public debt as a percentage of national income at a "stable and prudent level."[173] Brown decided to tighten fiscal policy to correct what was seen as an "excessive level of borrowing," even though the underlying trend was favorable already. In his first budget speech in July 1997, Brown announced a plan to reduce the deficit with a combination of higher "stealth" taxes and a squeeze on overall public spending. With public spending coming in below planned levels and tax receipts higher than expected due to a booming economy, there was a significant improvement in the country's public finances during the first three years.[174]

Under pressure from Blair, Brown had promised no new taxes during the campaign, again underscoring the hegemony of the Tories' ideas on low income taxes. The only exception was the windfall tax on the privatized utilities to pay for the so called "New Deal" welfare-to-work program.[175] For Brown, employment was the vital bridge between economic efficiency and social justice. The idea of the Working Families Tax Credit was borrowed from the Clinton administration. Paid through the wage packet, the credit provided an automatic top up for those on low incomes. Its introduction was accompanied by a new minimum wage, a reduction in National Insurance Contributions at the bottom end of the income scale, and a new 10 percent starting rate of income tax. It was a basic carrot and stick approach – the carrot being the top up and the minimum wage, with the stick coming from a severe tightening of the benefit regime via the "gradual rolling out of the New Deal alternatives of work or training across all age groups."[176] Brown's fascination with the American approach to the supply side of the economy was in sharp contrast with his often quite open contempt for the European social model, even though much of the conditional benefit programs he admired had already been pioneered in the Netherlands and Scandinavia.

The penny pinching of those first three years should not be surprising given New Labour's lack of concrete commitments in their election manifesto. But Blair's first term restraint was extraordinary: New Labour presided over a slower rate of growth in public spending during its first term than had occurred during John Major's premiership. At 1.7 percent a year, the rate of growth was below the growth rate of the economy as a whole, which was around 2.5 percent during Blair's first four years.[177] Many have argued that New Labour's ambitions, at least for its first term in power, were limited to achieving economic competence and earning the respect of the financial markets.[178]

However, from a political point of view, for a Labour government that wanted to tackle the many structural weaknesses in the British economy and the chronic underinvestment in health and education, spending restraint was probably the wrong decision. Waiting three long years before starting to get serious about investing in doctors, nurses, and teachers – whose training takes many years – is almost inviting disappointment because of the slow progress and lack of initial results in the performance of the country's public services. Instead of building hospitals and schools, Brown was using the boom of the late 1990s to pay off government debt.[179] Obviously, this judgment comes with the benefit of hindsight. Brown and Blair were not aware in 1997 that they were to inherit such a buoyant economy with large surpluses in its public finances. Paying off debt eventually brought down long term interest rates, which benefited the economy overall.[180] However, one could argue that long term interest rates were already falling worldwide thanks to Clinton's fiscal austerity in the United States and the European fiscal tightening in the framework of the Maastricht Treaty. Brown's fiscal prudence probably had only a minor effect overall.

### Industrial policy

The Blair government's policy towards industry proved to be completely in line with its Conservative predecessors. It was not just a matter of grudgingly accepting that privatization and all the other Thatcher reforms were irreversible; Blair and Brown were wholeheartedly committed to competition as the principal driver of economic growth and productivity.[181] The contrast with Old Labour's activism and instinct to rescue "lame duck industries" could hardly be more striking. Of course, this did not mean that New Labour had a complete "hands off" approach towards industry. Again, Ed Balls' influence and ideas based on endogenous growth theory provided the rhetorical backbone to policy, though only very modestly. Brown repeatedly drew attention to the "productivity gap"[182] between Britain and other industrialized countries (especially Germany and France) and used his tax and spending powers to correct what he saw as the supply side weaknesses in the British economy: especially the lack of public investment in infrastructure and R&D.[183] However, during New Labour's first term in power, public sector capital investment, the need for which Gordon Brown had consistently advocated during all his years as shadow chancellor, was lower than in any previous comparable four-year period since the 1970s.[184]

### Economic relations with the European Union

Blair arrived in office in 1997 supported by a Labour manifesto that promised to give Britain leadership in Europe. Later, he would often talk about Europe as Britain's "destiny."[185] The single most important decision for Blair was whether he would make the case for British membership in Europe's Economic and Monetary Union (EMU). Although Blair seemed eager initially to once and for all end Britain's ambiguity towards Europe, Brown was more skeptical. By giving Brown veto power over the decision to join EMU, Blair lost de facto control over a process that was as much about politics as it was about economics.[186]

In October 1997, after a period of confusion, Brown announced the "five tests" that would have to be met before the government would recommend EMU entry in a referendum. The five tests included questions on business cycle convergence, potential improvement of the competitive environment for British firms, growth and stability, the impact on Britain's financial services industry, and the existence of sufficient flexibility in the advent of adverse economic shocks.[187] It was clear from the beginning that the five tests were vague enough to postpone EMU entry forever. When the euro was successfully launched in January 1999, Britain remained – again – outside the most important EU development in a generation, and Brown was excluded from the increasingly important meetings of eurozone finance ministers.[188] The continuity with Thatcher – maybe not in rhetoric, but definitively in actual policy – was striking.

## Incremental change (2000–2005)

The first three years of the New Labour government saw a consolidation of the neoliberal settlement in Britain. After seven years of Major and three years of Blair, it was clear that Thatcherism would long outlive Thatcher herself. But after their first three years in power – spent wooing the financial markets and foreign investors with a low inflation, low tax, low interest economy with flexible labor and capital markets – New Labour started to get more serious about their "public services agenda," especially in health and education.

### Prudence with a purpose

The second spending review Brown completed in the summer of 2000 showed a stark difference in spending from his first three years in office. Brown had always emphasized that the initial fiscal austerity was meant to provide long term economic stability with the goal of creating a stable macroeconomic framework within which later spending decisions could be taken. According to Philip Stephens, the 2000 spending review marked a "determined effort to demonstrate that a government committed to economic orthodoxy could nonetheless change the nature of society."[189] Setting the targets for 2001 to 2004, the Chancellor announced sustained increases of more than 6 percent a year in real terms for health and education, with an even sharper increase for transport infrastructure.[190] Overall, the review projected real increases of 3.25 percent a year in the government's overall budget, against a projected overall growth rate of the British economy of 2.5 percent.

The message of the Blair government was the following: the state could still make a difference by rebuilding the country's decaying infrastructure and by providing decent universal health, education and welfare provision.[191] The change in policy was within Brown's self-restraining "Golden Rule" and took time to translate into actual results in performance. The 2001 general election followed one year later and the result, in percentages as well as in seats, was almost identical as that in 1997.[192] With the Conservatives in continued disarray and a stellar economic record during the first four years, which included falling unemployment, the electorate was more than happy to see Labour in power for another four years. The most eye-catching statistic from that election was the complete collapse in voter turnout from 72 percent in 1997 to 59 percent in 2001. This is telling for a government that promised to bring politics closer to the people and emphasized the importance of building an inclusive community.[193]

The 2002 spending review announced an increase of 8.6 percent per annum in health and 5.2 percent in education, to be paid for by a significant increase in national insurance contributions. This was probably the most significant correction to the Thatcherite consensus. New Labour's focus groups had shown that the electorate was willing to pay higher taxes and contribute more, if it could see where the extra money was going. While Blair and Brown had been reluctant to raise taxes during their first term for fear of alienating their middle class electorate, that fear seemed to be gone in their second term.[194] The result was a ballooning government deficit, which joined an already widening deficit on the current account – broadly in balance in 1997 – including a record trade deficit of £57 billion.[195] There is no doubt that basic economic stability was achieved during the Blair-Brown years, but many have pointed out that Brown's budgets were characterized by endless tinkering and that the overly complicated British tax system became so complex that it actually harmed the country's overall competitiveness in world markets.[196] Surprisingly for such a pro-business Labour government, the IMD World Competitiveness rankings show the UK dropping from ninth place in 1997 to twenty-second in 2004.[197]

It needs to be mentioned, however, that Labour completely stayed away from talking about income redistribution. Given the huge rise in income inequality since 1979, there was clearly room for a more active state role, especially after the growth of the earlier years had again proportionately benefited the rich. The fact that Brown, and especially Blair, did not dare to raise the issue again underlines – among others things – the power of Thatcherite ideas.[198] They seemed to accept what Lawson thought about income inequality, namely that "it is a fact of life."[199]

### Mixed record on public service reform

The main test for Brown is whether his increased public spending actually led to significant progress in public service performance. Here, the record is mixed.[200] First, while health was generally considered to be a success, whether the reforms of the NHS and the vastly increased resources allocated to it produced a better and more responsive health system remains in contention. Second, in education there was a vast difference between progress in primary and secondary schools. Literacy and numeracy rates in primary schools improved quite significantly, but the progress in GCSE results and in the number of students remaining in education beyond the age of 16 was much more modest.[201] Third, on transportation the Blair years have been an overall disappointment. While a steady increase in capital expenditure saw some transport improvements, a lot remains to be done and it is interesting that the only real success in this area came from left wing London Mayor Ken Livingstone, who introduced the congestion charge in London, which significantly reduced traffic in the city.[202]

Where there was real continuity between Thatcher and Blair in their approach towards public services, was in their eagerness to introduce market mechanisms and competition. According to John Gray, the Blair government, while overseeing a marked expansion of the public sector, "renewed the Thatcherite project of reshaping autonomous social institutions as bureaucratic replicas of business enterprises."[203] Blair and Brown extended privatization well beyond anything Thatcher dreamed of – or thought desirable – in the 1980s, including the introduction of market forces in the justice system and parts of the prison service. In this, as in a number of other policies such as the deregulation of postal services and his push to inject market mechanisms into the NHS, Blair went further than Thatcher had wished to go while she was in office.[204] With Blair, Britain also saw the rise of the "audit state" with targets being introduced throughout the whole public sector. Schools and hospitals, universities and the police were all judged by performance, with only measurable results considered reliable. Gray points out that "as providers have altered their behaviour to meet targets, the needs met by public services have slipped from view. Predictably, the result has not been increased satisfaction by the users of services, but a pervasive mistrust."[205]

## The British economy under New Labour

The performance of the British economy under New Labour has often been the envy of the rest of continental Europe. From 1997 onwards, Britain saw healthy growth rates combined with low inflation and gradually falling unemployment. However, there has been a strong sense that Blair and Brown were claiming a little too much for their economic management. "The longest run of economic growth since 1701," cited by Brown in his 2005 budget, or 51 successive quarters by the time of the May 2005 election was indeed impressive, but more than one third of those were obviously achieved under the Conservatives.[206] Labour's claim that they inherited an economy in crisis and put it right is simply not true. Willem Buiter observed that "the foundations for greater macroeconomic stability were laid when the UK left the ERM and the Bank took up inflation targeting." Furthermore, Buiter argued, "that was Mervyn's work [Mervyn King, now governor of the Bank of England], long before Balls was even a twinkle in Gordon's eye."[207] Apart from the obvious strengths in the British economy, which brought about a general increase in the average standard of living, there were numerous weaknesses, most notably the lagging productivity figures and the loss of the country's industrial base. In the words of Mark Blyth, the British economy after Blair basically "consists of one third government, one third finance, and one third housing swaps."[208]

### Strengths

Figure 6.1 illustrates New Labour's impressive growth record compared to their immediate competitors during their first eight years in office. Averaging 3.3

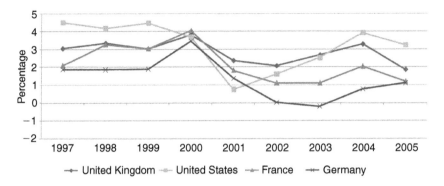

*Figure 6.1* Economic growth (1997–2005) (source: OECD, *Economic Outlook*, No. 80, Annex Tables, Paris: OECD, 2006).

percent during the first four years, the global slowdown in growth performance did not affect Britain in the manner that it did other industrialized countries, especially France and Germany.

The biggest achievement of New Labour is that it oversaw an economy that created over two million new jobs during its first eight years in office while the unemployment rate fell from 7 percent in 1997 to 4.8 percent in 2005 (Figure 6.2). This notable employment record was achieved without overheating the economy, and keeping inflation very low: between 1 and 2.5 percent (Figure 6.3).

No doubt, Blair and Brown's record on the economy was the basis for their successful bids for reelection in 2001 and 2005. A steady economic expansion pushed Britain's GDP per head above that of France and Germany by 2005. Jobless figures were the second lowest in the European Union and there was only very modest inflation. And sterling, the "Achilles heel of governments from Clement Attlee's to John Major's," vanished as a dominant issue in economic policymaking.[209]

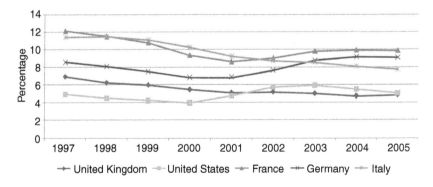

*Figure 6.2* Unemployment (1997–2005) (source: OECD, *Economic Outlook*, No. 80, Annex Tables).

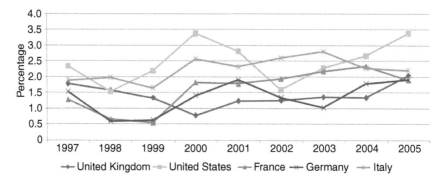

*Figure 6.3* Inflation (1997–2005) (source: OECD, *Economic Outlook*, No. 80, Annex Tables).

## Weaknesses

There were some serious flaws in New Labour's economic miracle, however, the most striking being the continuing underperformance in labor productivity (Figure 6.4), usually seen as the biggest single component defining a country's long run competitiveness.[210]

The Economic and Social Research Council, in an autumn 2004 assessment, concluded that the productivity gap in relation to competitor countries was as large as when Labour came to power.[211] The Council put forward a variety of explanations, including the following: a relative failure to invest, failure to innovate, poor labor relations, trade distortions given the legacy of the British

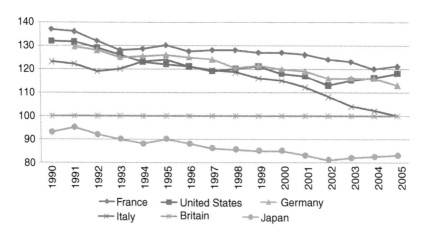

*Figure 6.4* Labor productivity[1] (1990–2005) (source: *The Economist*, "Britannia Redux: A Special Report on Britain," February 3, 2007).

Note
1  Productivity is measured in Output per Hour Worked (Britain = 100).

Empire, antagonism towards manufacturing, "short-termism" among business leaders and financial institutions, technological backwardness, lack of entrepreneurship, over-regulation of business, an overly instrumental attitude to work among employees, and the rigidities of the class structure. Furthermore, the report added that "the list [was] not exhaustive."[212]

In other words, the long-term structural weaknesses of the British economy, which Blair and Brown talked about so often while in opposition, were not addressed by New Labour. William Keegan, among others, has argued that excessive prudence by Brown during the first term contributed to an overvalued pound, which undermined the efforts of industrial exporters, who are traditionally fast growers when it comes to productivity.[213] Indeed, by the spring of 2005, one million more jobs had been lost in manufacturing compared to the sector's total labor force in May 1997.[214]

Also, what is worrying from a sustainability point of view is that growth in Britain during the Blair years was largely driven by aggregate demand. Figure 6.5 shows that during the first term, growth in private consumption was much faster than overall GDP growth, while during the second term growth was fuelled by a large expansion in public sector spending. Household savings rates fell from 10.2 percent in 1995 to just 3.7 percent in 2004, while household debt as a percentage of disposable income increased from 104 percent in 1996 to a staggering 159 percent in 2005, compared to 135 percent in the United States, 107 percent in France, and 89 percent in Germany.[215] This expansion in private consumption was fueled in large part by the continuing housing boom in Britain. This again raises the question as to how long the economy can sustain these above average growth rates.

Though Brown's budgets have been notable for their redistributive efforts, progress in the areas of poverty and income inequality, though real, have been rather modest during the Blair governments. New Labour's biggest ambition, what Polly Toynbee in *The Guardian* once called "the unshakable moral

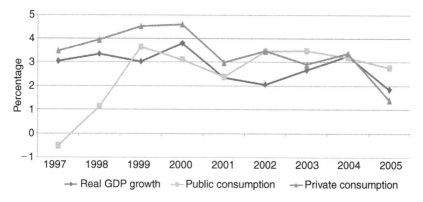

*Figure 6.5* Britain: growth of public and private consumption (1997–2005) (source: OECD, *Economic Outlook*, No. 80, Annex Tables; and own calculations).

underpinning of this government," was to cut and ultimately abolish child poverty.[216] New Labour has indeed lifted 700,000 children out of poverty but, as Peter Wilby has pointed out, 3.4 million remain there, which is a proportion of the child population higher than in all but seven of the 26 other EU members.[217] According to research conducted by the Joseph Rowntree Foundation, which Wilby mentions, current policies will keep child poverty at those levels until 2010.[218] Blair's target to cut child poverty by a quarter, which was originally set for 2004, will not be reached until 2020. Wilby also cites a study conducted by the Institute for Fiscal Studies (IFS) that considers "relative household spending" – sometimes seen as a better yardstick than income because it also includes savings, borrowings, and other assets – and concludes that by this measure, child poverty has actually grown since 1997.[219]

Furthermore, on income inequality, the progress under New Labour was very disappointing to say the least. According to the IFS, income inequality actually widened during Blair's first term in Britain, but was back to the 1997 level by 2005. Far from reversing the levels of income inequality, Britain under New Labour is a much less equal society than it was under Thatcher.[220] Of course, by comparison, income distribution was far more regressive during the Thatcher years. Interestingly enough, the government of Major was more directly redistributive from rich to poor than either of the Blair governments. Obviously, New Labour – like all neoliberal economists – will argue that it is better to have a "growing pie" for everyone than the same pie divided in a different fashion. But poverty and welfare are just as much relative concepts as they are absolute. Needs change over time, and what seemed like a luxury 20 years ago might be considered a necessity today.[221]

Finally, in a study on child well-being conducted by UNICEF in 2007, Britain is at the very bottom of the league of 21 advanced countries in the world, trailing the United States and Hungary.[222] According to the report, children growing up in the United Kingdom suffer greater deprivation, worse relationships with their parents, and are exposed to more risks from alcohol, drugs, and unsafe sex than those in any other wealthy country in the world. This is a devastating blow for a New Labour government that made child poverty and education its top priorities.[223]

## Conclusion

> One thousand days to prepare for a thousand years. Not just turning a page in history, but writing a new book. Building on the greatness of our nation through the greatness of its people. No more squandering the nation's assets. No more sleaze. No more cash for questions. No more lies. No more broken promises. I say to the Tories: enough is enough. Enough. Be done. The glory days of Britain are not over. But the Tory days are. Let us call our nation to its destiny. Let us lead it to our new Age of Achievement and build for us, our children, and their children, a Britain, united to win in the new millennium.
>
> Tony Blair (1996)[224]

In this chapter I have argued that due to the lack of an effective formulation of a crisis narrative by the Labour Party, transformational change was impossible for Blair to achieve. Although the weaknesses of the British economy – underinvestment in education, health, transportation, and public services; vulnerable short-term housing and consumer booms with massive and increasingly unsustainable levels of household debt; and growing poverty and income inequality – were clearly visible, Blair and Brown were unable or unwilling to sell this situation as a "real crisis" to the electorate. Thus there was also no need for a decisive intervention that would change the economic status quo. The economic ideas behind Thatcherism proved to be so dominant and persistent that the Labour Party under Blair felt the obligation to build its alternative within the broad contours of her neoliberal settlement. The fact that the anomalies in the economy were building up, but that nothing was done to correct them, thus makes Blair's government a "failure" according to Hay's crisis framework.

During the late 1980s, it became obvious that the Lawson boom was just as unsustainable as Maudling's "dash for growth" in the 1960s and the Barber boom in the 1970s. Thatcherism had not broken the postwar boom-bust cycle, and the long recession of 1990–1992 revealed the economy's chronic structural weaknesses. Kinnock had a chance in the 1992 election to break with the Thatcherite consensus since that election took place against the backdrop of economic crisis. The fact that Labour lost that election because they failed to construct a persuasive crisis narrative meant that the Labour Party adapted their ideology even further towards the Conservatives' guiding economic ideas. The policy elite that steered New Labour towards victory in 1997 had committed themselves to avoiding the mistakes of 1992. According to them, Kinnock lost because he lacked economic credibility. They were thus determined to do anything to achieve a status where the electorate would trust that the economy would be safe in New Labour's hands. By being so focused on achieving economic credibility, and thus adopting an austere fiscal and monetary framework, New Labour totally missed the changed political circumstances.

What were these changed political circumstances? By the mid-1990s, Major's Conservatives were virtually unelectable due to an overall feeling of fatigue and the atmosphere of scandal and infighting that surrounded the party. New Labour had memorized the lessons of Thatcherism so well that they made the 1997 election all about the economy but forgot the political reasons for the Tories' looming failure. In order to appeal to the middle classes of Middle England – who already had made up their minds not to vote Conservative at the next election – New Labour tied their own hands by committing themselves to Clarke's tax and spending programs. In effect, New Labour was fighting the battles of 1992 all over again in 1997, ignoring the new political context. By being unable to think differently from the Conservatives on the economy, the path dependence in Thatcherite economic policymaking continued.

What later became known as the Third Way was never able to challenge the core of Thatcherism, i.e. the primacy of inflation over employment, the virtues of the private sector, the limited role of the trade unions in the economy, and the absence of an actively redistributing role for the state. After 18 years of often divisive Tory rule, Britain was ready for change. The fact that Blair won a landslide victory in 1997 that was bigger than Attlee's thrashing of Churchill in 1945, together with his rhetoric of "building a new settlement for Britain," had created the illusory expectation of a real paradigm shift. But without a convincing narrative of an economy in crisis, there would be no impetus for radical change. New Labour thus consolidated many of Thatcher's innovations in economic policy, even making some of them all but irreversible. As a consequence, policy changes under New Labour were only possible as long as they "fitted" within the broader framework of the established economic wisdom under Thatcher.

New Labour can boast about presiding over a strong economy with an enviable record on growth, employment, and inflation. However, by 2005, there were major flaws in the British economy, and the structural weaknesses both Blair and Brown had attacked during their time in opposition were still rampant and showed no signs of going away. Furthermore, progress on many social indicators has been truly disappointing, especially for a Labour government, which explains the general feeling of lost opportunities and missed chances that surrounds New Labour after ten years of Blair.

# 7    Conclusion

## Made in Britain

### A constructivist approach towards Britain's political economy

In this book I have offered a comprehensive framework that brings theory and history together to explain continuity and change in Britain's postwar economic policy. To do so I necessarily went beyond a purely "structural" understanding of British economic decision making. Such a structural approach would have started from the assumption that the ideas of political leaders only matter insofar as they go together with existing institutional structures and traditions. If one pushes this assumption to the extreme, however, nothing ever changes, as we discussed in Chapter 2. But, of course, radical change does happen and those rare moments of rapid institutional change are interesting phenomena for social scientists to study; why and how they occur provides valuable insights for policymakers and pundits alike.

To go beyond existing or "standard" political science explanations for institutional continuity and change, I began the study of political economy of postwar Britain by approaching it from a constructivist point of view. By paying particular attention to the power of economic ideas and pointing out their transformative role during particular moments in time, I corrected for the intrinsic limitations of, and points of contention among, existing explanations. Far from denying that governments and their leaders often face severe constraints from their environments, including external factors such as the dynamics of an increasingly globalizing economy and the pressures of intensifying trade and capital flows, I tried to show how, during periods of protracted state crisis and economic collapse, ideas play a central role in defining what future institutional path the state will follow.

In my analysis I applied Stephen Skowronek's insightful typology[1] of political regimes to the case of Britain. A limited model by definition, this typology nonetheless simplifies a complex series of events, personalities, and circumstances into a digestible format with which to analyze postwar Britain. According to Skowronek, political leaders come to power within distinctive complexes of existing institutions and ideas that can either prove vulnerable or resistant to change. Every new head of government will therefore face a set of institutional conditions, shaped by his or her predecessors, which they seek to change or affirm. In other words, different periods in time have different dynamics, and we need to explain the decisions made by governments within the context of each distinct period. However, each of these periods can be classified, and thus do not need to be considered disparate "special cases." Consequently, we arrive at four distinct political contexts: reconstruction, disjunction, preemption, and articulation.

Borrowing from the existing literature on crisis, ideas and path dependence, I argued that if we want to understand sweeping change and broad institutional continuities, we need to complement the study of institutions with an analysis of the role of old and new economic ideas in constructing economic crises. It is just as important to understand the process that leads to the "hollowing out" or "delegitimation" of the old ideas, as well as the mechanisms that lead to a body of new ideas becoming influential. Obviously, not every period of economic turmoil will lead to radical change. In order to understand when ideas will be genuinely path altering, I argued that one needs to take a closer look at the narrative that is constructed to explain a crisis. This book adds to existing literature on ideas and crisis by explaining both continuity and change as well as analyzing crisis and crisis narration within the same intellectual framework.

During economic downturns there is a real chance for political leaders to achieve a breakthrough if they manage to link their ideas with a solution that can lead the economy out of the impasse. Usually, those leaders who achieve paradigmatic change will be remembered as the great innovators and are therefore often treated much more favorably by historians than the consolidators who did not achieve any deep-seated transformations. In the United States, Franklin Delano Roosevelt and Ronald Reagan immediately come to mind as path shaping presidents; while in France we can think of Charles de Gaulle, who was instrumental in laying the foundations of the Fifth Republic.

The theoretical framework I developed in this book I have called a "punctuated evolution" model. This model assumes that there are certain points in time that are more important than others, which are periods of much more rapid change than is usually the norm. This punctuated evolution model focuses on "critical junctures." I define a critical juncture as a particular moment in time when the contradictions in the existing system are widely perceived and a decisive intervention is called for. I argue that an economic downturn can cause a critical juncture if a political leader can construct a persuasive crisis narrative. Such a narrative puts in plain words why things fell apart, recruits adherents to a political vision and to a body of economic ideas, and creates a mandate for more radical reform. Also, I pointed out that political leaders pick and choose economic ideas from the available economic theories that they find attractive and try to reconcile them with their parties' guiding ideologies. Alternatively, political leaders might try to change their parties' ideologies since they think it electorally expedient by arguing that their ideas need to be adapted to the changed political and economic context.

During moments of crisis, new ideas will vie for dominance with old ideas, which – on the face of it – can no longer explain the continuing accumulation of anomalies in the system. New ideas, however, will be able to clarify what went wrong in the system, and formulate answers on how the crisis can be solved. The new ideas will then function as a blueprint for what the future institutional setup of the state will look like. However, when an economic downturn does not lead to a critical juncture, either because the contradictions in the system are left unacknowledged or because there is an absence of a crisis narrative sufficiently convincing to persuade voters that a radical alternative is called for, the significance of new ideas will only be marginal. In such a case, new ideas will only play a role insofar as they fit within the current institutional setup and can be reconciled with the reigning paradigm. Under these circumstances, there will at most be incremental changes to the system; the overarching goals and priorities of the economic system will not be called into question.

Most of the time, however, there is broad institutional stability and continuity, which is also explained by the punctuated evolution model I developed. Traditionally, stability was explained by institutional stickiness, positive feedback mechanisms, and the path dependent nature of existing institutions. I illustrated that institutional stability over time is not only possible because of the existing institutions themselves, but also – and often more importantly – because of the strong path dependent tendencies caused by the ideas that underpin them. When a body of old ideas is marginalized by a more appealing body of new ideas, they will be hard to change once they are established in the minds of the political elite. Thatcher, for example, partly succeeded in giving her neoliberal ideas exactly such a dominant status by repeating over and over again at every opportunity she had that there was no alternative. The fact that her ideas were picked up by Blair and Brown after 1992 illustrates that both thought it was impossible to win an election without abiding by her basic economic assumptions.

To maintain a dominant status, ideas need to be continually dispersed and reiterated. There is a central role played here by "ideational carriers," such as think tanks, politicians, and the media. For example, Hayek often complained to many of his like-minded colleagues that their socialist opponents were so much better organized in spreading and promoting socialist ideas that it was almost impossible to compete with them for popular attention. Additionally, Hayek added that socialists more strongly *believed* in the virtue of their cause.[2] By founding think tanks of their own, and by spreading their ideas through influential journalists in the quality and popular press, the New Right tried to fight socialism with its own means. It eventually prevailed and pushed most socialist ideas to the margins of the political economic debate.

In this book I applied this theoretical punctuated evolution model to the political economy of Britain during the period from 1945 to 2005. By examining four different governments, all coming to power from opposition with a potential chance to bring about a paradigm shift, I gained new insights into the reasons why some governments were successful in achieving radical change in the British institutional architecture, and while others were not, despite facing similar opportunities. Consequently, the theoretical framework explained why

Attlee and Thatcher practiced what Skowronek calls the "politics of reconstruction;" why Heath's term in office was characterized by the "politics of preemption" during the first two years and the "politics of disjunction" during his last two years; and finally why the Blair governments are a good illustration of the "politics of articulation," especially since he de facto affiliated himself with the core ideas of his Conservative predecessors.[3] I will summarize my main findings of the four cases in the next section by revisiting the six propositions formulated in Chapter 2.

### The six propositions revisited

#### Propositions one and two

The first two propositions argue that a period of economic downturn is a necessary though not sufficient condition to bring about a paradigm shift. Downturns and recessions are by no means self-evident phenomena. In order to eventually lead to paradigmatic change, they need to be constructed by a persuasive and intuitive crisis narrative to the voting population. If the political elite and the electorate at large are convinced by the narrative, and recognize that there is a real crisis – a moment in need of a decisive intervention – then the conditions are created for large scale paradigm shifts.

In the case of Clement Attlee, there was a clear crisis narrative that called for an intervention. Attlee convinced the electorate that the economic collapse of the Great Depression and the high levels of unemployment of the 1930s together with the experience of total war from 1940 to 1945 delegitimated the old regime. The critical juncture came during the general election in the summer of 1945, when Attlee and Labour argued that the Conservative settlement post World War I was bankrupt and that the levels of unemployment during the 1930s were unacceptable. Churchill saw the future path of Britain's political economy evolving into an improvement of its existing structures, which he believed to be fundamentally legitimate and sound. He missed the tide of public sentiment, skillfully guided by Labour's campaign, which portrayed the status quo ante as unacceptable. Labour's campaign then explained how only a Labour government able to establish new institutions and shift the balance of power from capital to labor, would succeed in building a completely new society based on fair shares, or a "New Jerusalem."

When he came to power in 1970, Edward Heath was not facing a sharp downturn in economic conditions that could justify a radical departure from the postwar consensus. However, when the first economic problems arose in 1972, caused by a miners' strike and rising levels of unemployment, Heath – the quintessential technocrat – showed that he was not wedded to free market orthodoxy. When it proved to be politically expedient, he abandoned the market and reached back for the ideas of the old consensus. Two years later, when there was a much deeper economic downturn – now with record balance of payments deficits, runaway inflation, power cuts, a three-day week, and another miners' strike –

Heath called a snap election, but failed to persuasively narrate the recession as a state crisis that needed his decisive intervention. Labour, on the other hand, made the case that 1974 was a "political" crisis – the Tories were unable to handle the unions – and needed a political answer, i.e. the Social Contract. When the Tories lost their majority in the general election of February 1974 and Labour formed a minority cabinet that patched up the ailing system, 1974 became an example of an unsustainable equilibrium where the contradictions in the system were widely perceived, yet no decisive intervention was made.

When Thatcher was campaigning during the May 1979 election, overall economic conditions in Britain had been improving quite significantly during the previous two years. However, she had seized on the events of the Winter of Discontent of 1978–1979 a couple of months earlier – and the images of garbage piling up in the streets, dead bodies that were left unburied, and hospitals that were not treating patients – as a crisis of the state that needed her intervention. Although, by any objective means, the economic indicators in 1979 were much better than in 1974, she managed to come to power on a platform promising fundamental change to economic policy. Together with Joseph and Howe, she narrated that infamous winter (rife with public sector strikes and union militancy) as the symbol of the bankruptcy of social democracy and the consensus policies of the postwar years in Britain. Through selective media coverage and by linking seemingly unrelated events, Thatcher and the Tories pointed to a much deeper crisis that was not objectively measurable when looking at actual economic performance. With just over 43 percent of the vote, they claimed a mandate for change.

When Blair came to power in 1997, the long recession of 1990–1992, which saw unemployment going up from 5 to 10 percent in the course of only two years, was over. Labour leader Neil Kinnock had failed to frame that recession as a real crisis in need of different solutions, and despite the increasing amount of unemployed and working poor, he had lost the general election of 1992. Five years later, after the economy was freed from its ERM chains and had started to grow again, it would be hard for Blair and Brown to convince the electorate that their growing prosperity was a sign of deep economic crisis. Instead, they framed 1997 as a crisis of governance and trust in the government and thus did not ask for a mandate to radically change the country's economic institutional setup. Given that the underlying structural weaknesses of the economy were all still there, New Labour could have made the case for more radical change, but since they were fighting the 1997 election on a Tory economic platform, the shortcomings of the economy were left unacknowledged and no intervention was taken. According to Hay's crisis terminology, this situation is considered to be a "failure."[4]

*Propositions three and four*

Propositions three and four are about the transforming role of economic ideas. First, I proposed that during periods of economic crisis (as defined by Hay), economic ideas play a decisive role. They explain what went wrong, how to fix it, and provide a blueprint for new institutions (as argued by Blyth). Furthermore, I proposed that political parties only make selective use of the available bodies of economic theory and usually pick those ideas that they see as reinforcing their parties' guiding ideological traditions.

In 1945, Labour used the ideas of John Maynard Keynes, William Beveridge, and the Fabians as their "weapons" during the general election. Keynes' *General Theory* provided some of the ideas on how Labour was to conduct its economic policies, Beveridge's 1942 Report gave the party a popular blueprint for constructing a universal welfare state, and the Fabians' ideas on nationalization and economic planning, together with the successful wartime planning experience, gave Labour the rationale for shifting the center of gravity in the economy decisively from the market to the state. However, both Keynes and Beveridge, being staunch Liberals, were not in favor of such a far-reaching socialist system and never advocated the nationalizations Labour eventually implemented. By using Keynes' arguments about the instability of the capitalist system, Labour justified a greatly enhanced role for the state and shifted the balance away from capital and towards labor. Once elected, Attlee's Labour government proved very successful in using these ideas to establish a new framework for economic policy and found new political and economic institutions.

When Heath came to power in 1970 he was determined to turn around Britain's relative economic decline with a reversal of many of the postwar consensus policies moving from state intervention to market mechanisms, with the choice for EEC membership firmly within this line of thought. The key document describing the Conservatives' new approach in 1970 was the Selsdon Park document, which accepted the idea that there was relative decline because of the rigidity in British institutions that gave a lack of incentive to entrepreneurship and economic activity. Despite the absence of an economic recession when he was elected, Heath proved to be relatively successful in implementing many of these ideas during his first two years of government. However, in the face of the first economic downturn in 1972, he reached back for the old ideas of Keynesian demand management and reflated the economy with a combination of monetary and fiscal stimuli. The resulting Barber boom eventually led to accelerating inflation, which was further fueled by the OPEC oil shock. The Heath government's policies during its first two years in power was an effort to bring the party back to the liberal economic traditions of the 1920s and 1930s. This had long been preached by Enoch Powell in the 1950s and 1960s. In that sense, the return to the market fitted with the party's ideological roots.

Thatcher, from the moment she was elected leader of the Conservative Party, enthusiastically recruited the views of many neoliberal thinkers, especially those of Milton Friedman and Friedrich Hayek. Thatcher instinctively agreed with Friedman, since he was seen as the key opponent of Keynes – who was associated with the postwar consensus – and his views on sound money as a way to tame inflation struck a chord with her. She also liked the views of Hayek, especially since he was so opposed to planning and socialism. The writings and theories of both thinkers provided her with the intellectual framework to plan for her time in government while she was still in opposition. With the U-turn and eventual failure of Heath still fresh in her mind, she was determined to avoid his mistakes and proved successful in using ideas to explain what had gone wrong with the British economy in the 1970s. Once in power, she established a monetarist framework for conducting economic policy, broke the power of the unions, and embarked on a program of significant economic liberalization and privatization, in fact undoing much of the Attlee settlement. Most of her policies were directly inspired by neoliberal writings and thought.

While Blair and Brown initially tried to frame their ideas as an alternative to Thatcherism, their Third Way ideas were very close to it, and were much more of an attempt to ban the ghosts of Labour's left wing past, especially the traumatic experience of the party's fourth consecutive election loss in 1992. Many in the Labour Party interpreted Kinnock's loss as a punishment for their perceived lack of economic competence and credibility. New Labour's policy elite – including Mandelson, Blair, Brown, and Balls – memorized the economic lessons of Thatcherism so well that they had become totally blind to the changed political and economic context. First, since the Tories made themselves practically unelectable by 1995 because of a series of moral scandals and internal battles over Britain's role in Europe, Labour did not have to court the Middle England voters who had already given up on the Tories. Second, because of their obsession with economic prudence, Blair and Brown tied themselves to a rigorous fiscal rule that denied their core constituents much needed improvements in public services – at least for their first three years in government. While one could argue that the Conservatives themselves, especially with Michael Heseltine at the Board of Trade, were already veering away from the sharp edges of Thatcherism, once Labour came to power, Blair and Brown reinforced the Thatcherite settlement of the 1980s. The ideas of economic prudence were only very reluctantly accepted by a party that was desperate, after four consecutive election losses, to get back into power. However, Brown justified them as prudence for a purpose, with the goal of building a more economically fair and socially just society. However, the disappointing results in poverty reduction and high income inequality did not vindicate the rationale behind Brown's initial prudence.

*Propositions five and six*

The last two propositions are concerned with institutional stability over time. First, I propose that in the absence of an economic downturn or perceived crisis, ideas only matter insofar as they fit within the existing paradigm and will at most bring about incremental change. Second, I argue that ideas, just as much as institutions, show strong path dependent tendencies and give continuing legitimacy to the existing paradigm. Systemic stability is maintained until the moment that a new crisis calls into question the legitimacy of the existing institutional arrangement.

There were two broad institutional settlements in Britain after World War II that each lasted for more than two decades and covered both Conservative and Labour governments. The initial settlement was established by Attlee's governments from 1945 to 1951. This led subsequently to the long and prosperous period of the postwar consensus. The main elements of that consensus included a commitment to full employment as the overarching goal of economic policy, the management of aggregate demand through Keynesian policies, the important role of the state in controlling the commanding heights of the economy, active state intervention in the free market, and the relative power of the trade unions vis-à-vis employer's organizations. These principles were accepted subsequently by Winston Churchill, Harold Macmillan, and Harold Wilson. While there were numerous attempts to tinker with the consensus in order to increase growth and improve competitiveness, the overall idea of maintaining full employment proved to be the binding commitment between all those postwar governments. It was only when Heath came to power that many of the theoretical underpinnings of the consensus came under attack. However, once the commitment to full employment became endangered in 1972, Heath himself proved to be a "never again" expansionist. This underlined once more the ideational path dependence of the reigning Keynesian ideas.

The second institutional transformation, started by Thatcher in 1979, overthrew the postwar settlement by calling into question the main principles that had justified its foundation in 1945. After Thatcher came to power, the overarching goal of economic policy was to maintain stable prices. The political commitment to full employment was dropped. The main ingredients of Thatcherism were a monetarist macroeconomic policy aimed at keeping prices down, a much smaller role for the state in the economy, tax cuts, a limited role for trade unions, liberalization of product and factor markets, and a program of mass privatization. These principles eventually came to be broadly established as the Thatcherite consensus and were consolidated under Major and Blair. Although many ideas of the Third Way intellectual movement in the 1990s challenged the Thatcherite assumptions on how to manage a modern economy, they were only adopted by Labour insofar as they fitted within the broader neoliberal goals. The path dependent power of neoliberal ideas led to a New Labour government with a large majority in Westminster that did almost nothing for three years to reduce poverty and inequality or improve the provision of public services. Once their neoliberal economic credentials were established, Blair and Brown increased taxes by stealth and engineered a sizeable increase in public spending: perhaps the only significant incremental change to the Thatcherite settlement, which even the Conservatives under David Cameron accepted in 2007. But this steady increase in public spending hardly called into question the main underlying principles of the Thatcherite settlement.

## Suggestions for further research

The concept of crisis and the role of ideas have been studied in many academic fields. In this section, I suggest four areas of the social sciences where the theoretical framework and punctuated evolution model that was developed in Chapter 2 could be of relevance and maybe even provide the analytical foundations for various case study applications. The four areas are foreign policy and security studies, domestic politics and the rise of populist and extreme right parties, economic development and institutional change, and health and environment policy studies.

In international relations and foreign policy the study of crises is a central research area. My framework suggests that crises will only lead to an intervention if they have a convincing narrative about what went wrong and how it can be fixed. The US-led invasion of Iraq in 2003 makes for an interesting case study. No objective crisis was widely perceived. But through the constant repetition of a crisis narrative about the "potential dangers" Iraq could pose under its leader Saddam Hussein, especially if equipped with weapons of mass destruction, the US and its "coalition of the willing" were able to justify a military intervention. The idea that played a central role in the Iraq war was that the absence of democracy led to a potentially unstable country that was hostile to the West, and only through a comprehensive process of democratic institution-building would the country become a stable and integral part of the global economy.[5] There are numerous other case studies in the field of international relations where powerful states fabricate a crisis or seize upon one in order to justify a foreign intervention.[6]

The second area is in domestic politics, especially related to populism and extreme right parties in Europe and elsewhere. The electoral appeal of extreme right parties is based on exaggerations of existing situations, e.g. the inherent threat to national cultures and traditions from mass immigration. They thus construct a crisis of identity of the state that requires nothing less than drastic solutions. Most of the time, these solutions include radical curbs on immigration, tough action against crime and other perceived anti-social behavior, and a return to nationalist traditions and values such as self-help and sovereignty. The ideas of most populist parties are often rather simplified accounts on what went wrong with modern society and give easy solutions on how things can be set straight.[7]

The third area of interest is international development. In many developing countries, quick fixes to the current system will not provide lasting poverty reduction. Usually, what is needed is a more comprehensive overhaul of the existing institutions. In order to bring about such radical change, civil servants from international organizations often find it useful to help create a crisis in client countries that justifies their intervention. Richard Stern, a senior investment policy officer at the World Bank and former economist at the IMF, explained in an interview how the Bank assisted the government of Yemen in fabricating a fiscal crisis that demonstrated the need to implement a working modern fiscal system.[8] Since the country had no functioning tax system to provide a steady source of income for the government, the crisis provided the justification to establish a whole new system. Yemen is just one example of many in the developing world where the book's model is useful in analyzing institutional continuity and change. Another more poignant example is the discursive demolition of the Asian development model. Rodney Bruce Hall illustrated how key actors, such as the IMF, the US Treasury, and the Kim Dae-Jung administration in South Korea were able to delegitimate the Asian model by constantly associating it with "cronyism" and corruption. Hall points out that the manner in which those narratives constructed the causes of the Asian crisis accelerated the eventual demise of the whole Asian model.[9]

The fourth area where my theoretical framework could stimulate further research is in health and environment policy studies. It has often been noted that government action in both areas is usually reactionary rather than preventive. Tough decisions, usually involving increases in taxes, are often only taken by governments after a serious crisis has illustrated the need for decisive action. In other areas where we know the potentiality of a disaster but cannot provide unambiguous proof, the narrative of the looming crisis might be instrumental in causing real change. Global warming is the obvious example of a future disaster that demands radical measures today. The only way people will change their behavior is when governments and advocates overplay the potential impact.[10]

Since this book is first and foremost a study of postwar British political economy, there is much more research that needs to be done on the Blair governments. The first three cases of this book – Attlee, Heath, and Thatcher – have been widely analyzed and there is a multiplicity of secondary literature and academic work. One area for future research is the apparent disappearance of the threat of balance of payments crises in Britain. It is very interesting that an issue that held all postwar governments hostage ostensibly disappeared. What happened in the structure of the British economy that can explain the fact that the high value of the pound and the chronic current account deficits ceased to be perceived as potential crises? Brown would probably claim the credit for himself, pointing to the stable macroeconomic framework he has built over the last ten years. But there must be more to it than that. Perhaps it is the changing structure of the British economy from manufacturing to services and the significant capital market liberalization that has taken place over the last 25 years. But does that make Britain less vulnerable to speculative attacks and balance of payments crises? Future research could provide answers.

In summary, this book explained that while economies often go through recessions and economic downturns, they go through actual crises much more rarely. I have argued that paradigmatic change in a country's institutional setup is only possible if economic downturns are perceived by the political elite and the public at large as an actual crisis that calls for a decisive intervention. Additionally, since crises are by no means self-evident events, they need to be constructed in a convincing crisis narrative that explains where things went wrong and what can be done about it. In those rare moments, the choices governments have are delineated by the available stock of economic ideas. Ideas will inform the future shape of the state's new institutions and, together with those new institutions, will guarantee relative economic stability over time.

# Postscript

## Gordon Brown, the "Great Recession," and the future of neoliberalism

### The dangers of linear thinking

On May 11, 2005, I attended a conference about "Europe's Global Role" at The Brookings Institution in Washington, DC. As a graduate student in international political economy preparing to write my doctoral dissertation on how economic ideas translated into economic policy in postwar Britain, I was especially interested in the first panel, "Britain between America and the European Union." The panel was chaired by Phil Gordon and consisted of three distinguished speakers: Anatol Lieven from the New America Foundation, Gerard Baker from the London *Times*, and Charles Grant from the London-based Centre of European Reform. Less than a week earlier, Tony Blair had triumphantly returned to 10 Downing Street for the third consecutive time after yet another general election victory for his Labour Party. Tory leader Michael Howard duly resigned, setting in motion the fourth leadership contest in the Conservative Party in just eight years.[1] In addition, the British economy in 2005 – combining healthy growth rates, low inflation, and unemployment well under 5 percent – was the envy of Continental Europe. Chancellor Gordon Brown, Blair's inevitable successor as prime minister, openly boasted about presiding over the longest economic expansion in the country since records began. These reasons combined made it difficult, if not impossible, to see an end to New Labour's hegemony over Westminster and Whitehall. To borrow Macmillan's phrase, the country in 2005 "had never had it so good."

This triumphant mood Britain found itself in at the time was reflected in the remarks of the Brookings panelists, with the notable exception of historian Lieven. To my surprise, Baker and Grant stressed the unqualified virtues of the British economy, suggesting that there was no end to Labour's economic success story, with Brown likely to win the next general election after having taken over from Blair in due course. After the presentations I asked the panel what would happen to future Prime Minister Brown's credibility when the inevitable recession hit Britain and how rising unemployment would affect his electoral prospects. Baker was quick to respond that Britain had been growing much faster than the rest of Europe because of deregulation and sound monetary policy, which made it more capable than the rest of Europe to respond to long run changes in the global economy. He ended his response to my question by saying:

I don't share your pessimism. Sure there are threats out there. There could be a downturn in the British economy, but I don't think it's inevitable that Britain is headed for some sort of spectacular 1931-style crash at any point in the next ten years.[2]

Grant also pointed out the fundamental strengths of the British economy, but went even further when he ended with the following comment: "I don't think there will be a recession. You talked about the inevitable recession. Actually, I think Gordon Brown has abolished recessions."[3]

About three years later, in early September 2008, an opinion piece by Martin Wolf in the *Financial Times* on the future prospects of the British economy caught my attention. I cite Wolf:

The [OECD] suggested this week that the UK, alone among the group of seven leading high-income countries, was likely to experience negative growth in the third and final quarters of this year. If so, this would end a run of 64 consecutive quarters of positive growth. For Gordon Brown, the return of boom and bust has to be an embarrassment. Yet did anybody else believe the business cycle could be eliminated? Market economies are never as stable as that.[4]

It is interesting that Wolf would publish such an opinion. Only a few years earlier, many policy wonks and pundits – the best and the brightest – all over London and Washington had believed exactly that: namely that business cycles in Anglo-Saxon economies had been banished to the dustbin of history. I wrote Wolf an email mentioning the exchange I had had at Brookings three years earlier. He had the good grace to write me back, saying: "Yes, it was a strange time of euphoria. But stuff always happens, as Rumsfeld said."[5]

The above anecdote illustrates the inherent danger in the self-fulfilling power of economic ideas. Many analysts truly believed for quite some time that countries only had to follow a laundry list of rules from the neoliberal bible (or what would come to be known as the "Washington Consensus" in the 1990s) to have a successful economy.[6] New York Times columnist Thomas Friedman popularized this idea when he coined the term "golden straightjacket" in *The Lexus and the Olive Tree* in 2000.[7] According to Friedman, any country could be a winner in globalization as long as its government wrapped itself in that gilded jacket of neoliberal ideas. This entailed making private sectors the primary engine of economic growth, maintaining a low rate of inflation through independent central banks, shrinking the state bureaucracy, deregulating capital markets, opening their banking systems to private ownership and competition, and removing all restrictions on foreign investment.[8]

So the popular belief at the time was that if countries followed Friedman's advice, all would be well – perhaps not immediately in the short run, but certainly in the long run. For Friedman it was clear: "When it comes to the question of which system today is the most effective at generating rising standards of living, the historical debate is over. The answer is free-market capitalism."[9] Hence, in our brave new globalized and neoliberal world, it would be unthinkable for any economy that followed his prescriptions to collapse. Such a government would "have done all the right things." And arguably, no other country in the world had been a better acolyte of the neoliberal creed since 1979 than Britain. By any standard, the British economy had been performing very well.[10]

One lesson is apparent: there is an innate danger in times of economic boom that people begin to believe that the boom will never end. The longer a boom period lasts, the fewer people there are who actively remember a recession. Soon enough, the belief grows that the economy is meant to follow a linear path based on the trajectory of the previous ten years. This is an inherent weakness in the quantitative methods economists use to make their predictions about the future trajectory of the aggregate economy. The primacy of the market reigns high and soon becomes vulnerable to self-fulfilling prophesies and built-in optimism. But when economics trumps politics, history is quickly forgotten, leading to the idea that "we live in different times," in a new era where different rules and policies apply. Before we know it, economic discourse is dominated by a kind of Manichean view of the world economy. In this world divided between the past and the future, if you follow the new rules, your future must necessarily be better.[11] The old rules are no longer valid. If you continue to follow the old rules you will miss the train of progress and will be irrevocably left behind. Interestingly enough, free market capitalism does not believe in a free market of economic ideas.

Success also breeds hubris, and contempt for the countries that do not follow this new set of ideas. The hubris of one man in particular, Gordon Brown, knew no limits, both at home and abroad. He was at his best during debates in the House of Commons when he could remind the Tories how all their past economic policies had resulted in the same pattern of "Tory boom and bust,"[12] mocking the earlier Maudling, Barber, and Lawson booms as unsustainable, short-lived, and all ending in ruin. During the Ecofin Council meetings, which bring together the economics and finance ministers of the 27 European Union member countries, Brown never let an opportunity pass to lecture his continental colleagues on the many virtues of a "modern market economy" like Britain. It is understandable that most of his European colleagues found him "arrogant," since he often refused to listen to their opening remarks and ostentatiously kept off his simultaneous translation headphones. While he kept them on to listen to his French and German counterparts, he never seemed to take them too seriously, as he would just repeat verbatim his earlier statement to the council when it was his turn to respond. Unsurprisingly, and soon enough, the idea of Cool Britannia as a "model" economy for the rest of Europe gained in ascendancy. This was especially true after the elections of Angela Merkel in Germany in 2005, and Nicolas Sarkozy in 2007 in France. Both Merkel and Sarkozy went out of their way during their campaigns to praise the dynamism of the British economy.[13]

Pride comes before the proverbial fall, and in 2008, the "unthinkable" happened. The hubris of neoliberalism acolytes was sanctified when Nassim Taleb's "black swan" made her entry into the world economy,[14] putting a larger than life question mark over everything economic policymakers had come to take for granted for well over 20 years, and giving a completely new meaning to the idea of "Knightian" uncertainty.[15] Enter the "great crash" of 2008.

## The crash of 2008 and the crisis of neoliberalism

What started as a problem in the US housing market in 2007 soon spread to the world economy as a whole. Once it was clear how a "global inverted pyramid of household and bank debt" was built on a narrow range of feeble American sub-prime mortgages, the "debt balloon started to deflate, at first slowly, [but] ultimately with devastating speed."[16] Banks soon stopped lending, both to each other and to their private customers, which caused a credit crunch in early 2008 and put an astonishing amount of pressure on the financial sector. Bear Stearns all but collapsed in March 2008, and was rescued by JP Morgan Chase, which only bought Bear Stearns after US government support. By the summer of 2008 commodity prices started to fall and giant American mortgage lenders Fannie Mae and Freddie Mac were taken into public ownership.[17] These events were part of the run up to the mindboggling events of September 2008, when the world economy was at the edge of the abyss and flirted with total collapse: Lehman Brothers fell down, Merrill Lynch narrowly avoided bankruptcy by dissolving into Bank of America, and big banks all over the world had to be rescued by their governments, all in the midst of a US presidential campaign. Stock markets plunged, and the financial crisis soon translated into a massive slide of the real economy, leading to falling output levels, rapidly increasing unemployment, and increasing savings resulting in a Keynesian liquidity trap.

Talk of a new Great Depression was rife in the world's major capitals. Only one thing was certain in the midst of the chaos: governments had to step in to rescue their banking systems and guarantee most of the deposits in those banks if they were to avoid an accelerated slide into a certain Great Depression. Central banks slashed interest rates to close to zero, and governments – in haste – put together fiscal stimulus packages of a magnitude unprecedented in peacetime. However, the world would be unable to avoid its first global contraction in output since World War II. The world economy shrank 1.1 percent in 2009, according to the International Monetary Fund: the advanced economies contracted by 3.4 percent on an annual basis, while emerging and developing economies grew at a scant 1.7 percent in 2009.[18] While it narrowly steered clear of another Great Depression, the world was definitely grappling with a "Great Recession," and a fierce debate over what had caused the dramatic series of events leading up to it quickly entered into full swing.

What was seen as the main cause of the financial crisis that led to our "Great Recession?"[19] First, most analysts focused on the US housing market and the role played therein by subprime mortgage lending. Exotic interest-only and adjustable-rate mortgages, for instance, helped extend credit to prospective buyers with dubious credit histories. As more actors entered the market a positive feedback loop of rising home prices, falling lending standards, and speculation was created. It was therefore no coincidence that the regions with the fastest rate of home price appreciation also had the highest rates of subprime lending.[20]

Second, the debate moved to what was perceived to be "irresponsible" monetary policy by the Federal Reserve. In the wake of the 2001 recession, Fed Chairman Alan Greenspan slashed the target US federal funds rate to 1 percent and, despite early evidence of an emerging housing bubble, he kept that target rate to fight deflation and maintain investment growth. According to this "monetary policy caused the crisis" explanation, cheap credit fueled the housing bubble. Failure to raise interest rates thus exposed Greenspan's ideological bias: the Fed only targeted core consumer prices, ignoring asset price inflation.

The third explanation pointed at distorted incentives in the banking system, both for financial institutions and for individuals. "Quasi governmental" agencies such as Fannie Mae and Freddie Mac took advantage of their implicit (and later explicit) government solvency guarantee to borrow cheaply in the capital markets. Investment banks gamed the rating agencies' methodology and created triple-A rated securities out of bonds of dubious credit quality, while the financial sector relied on risk models that grossly underestimated the probability of disjointed price movements in asset prices: so-called "black swan" events. Meanwhile, homeowners tapped into their home equity, often taking out second or third mortgages, and established home equity lines of credit which fueled a consumption binge. Liberalization and deregulation of the financial industry had spurred the creation of new financial products, such as "credit default swaps" (CDSs) and "derivatives." Very few people fully understood such products; as early as 2003, financier Warren Buffett described derivatives as "financial weapons of mass destruction."[21] Many of those products were perceived to be at the heart of the crisis that caused Lehman's collapse and many other banks' solvency problems.

Fourth, analysts moved towards the persistent US current account deficit and global macroeconomic imbalances as the main explanation of the crisis. This explanation had two sides to the same coin. One side was the idea of a global savings glut, which was mopped up by the American consumer and government, allowing the US economy to live beyond its means, which in turn functioned as the main engine for world economic growth. The other side was the deficient US savings view combining the "twin deficit" idea – large US federal government deficits had to be financed by savings from abroad – and the historically low savings of US households.[22]

With different explanations for the causes of the crisis being floated at different times, the blame game for who bore ultimate responsibility began.[23] Depending on the flavor of the day, different economic actors were seen as the main culprits. First and foremost, the bankers were blamed for their "reckless" behavior; they were perceived to be gambling away people's hard earned savings in a casino capitalist system. When they needed to be bailed out by the taxpayer after their institutions had come close to the brink of collapse, bankers were on the receiving end of the public's scourge and outrage at a system characterized by the "privatization of profits and the socialization of risk." Next to be blamed were the credit-rating agencies, like Moody's and Standard & Poor's, who gave unjustly high ratings to tranches of subprime mortgage backed "collateralized debt obligations" (CDOs), hence misleading those who were buying these financial products into thinking they were safe. The perverse incentives of a system where the ratings agencies were paid by the banks that they were supposed to rate were exposed by the crisis. Then the blame shifted to the hedge fund managers whose short-selling behavior was seen to do nothing but damage to the real economy... then to the regulators who were thought to be asleep while all this had been going on... then the central bankers who kept interest rates too low for too long... and then of course to the governments, which had allowed it all to happen...[24]

While there is truth behind all of the arguments above, I ultimately agree with Robert Skidelsky that the financial crisis that triggered the "Great Recession" was first and foremost a crisis of ideas.[25] Most of what happened in the economy in 2008 and 2009 was thought, quite simply, to be an impossible situation to have occurred in the new neoliberal world we lived in – a world that we largely constructed. The Queen of England herself asked the obvious question to a gathering of economic theorists and policymakers: "Why did nobody see this coming?" The answer is that most economists believe in efficient markets that always clear, in a system that correctly prices risk, and in people's rational expectations: beliefs that encourage them to ignore the writing even when exposed so plainly on the wall.[26] Quite simply, their firm faith in their ideas made any alternative eventuality an impossibility. The triumph of the 1990s, the minor recession of 2001, and the success of the consecutive years created a self-fulfilling prophecy. For most policymakers, the world began in 1989 with the fall of communism and the heyday of the ideas of the Washington Consensus. Britain was no exception. As pointed out in Chapter 6, New Labour's enthusiasm for Thatcher's market reforms, her neoliberal ideas, and the wealth-creating powers of the City of London encouraged Blair and Brown to institutionalize her neoliberal settlement. In a cruel twist of fate, the financial crisis would hit the British economy particularly harshly.

Starting in April 2008 and ending in September 2009, the UK economy saw six consecutive quarters of negative growth, with the last quarter of 2009 seeing barely any growth at all.[27] In 2009, the UK economy shrank by 4.8 percent, leading to an increase in the rate of unemployment from 5.6 percent in 2008 to an estimated 8.4 percent in 2010.[28] The 6 percent decline in Britain's GDP between its pre-crisis peak and the last quarter of 2009 is the third highest in the group of seven leading high income countries, after Italy and Japan.[29]

Since Britain is so dependent upon financial services, the country was hit harder than most of its European counterparts. With a full quarter of all British tax receipts paid by the financial sector, the crisis unavoidably led to a fall in total government revenues by 18.1 percent between 2008 and 2009.[30] This resulted in a skyrocketing in British net government borrowing, not only because of the fall in tax revenues from the financial sector, but also after the effect of the automatic stabilizers. Britain's general government balance went from a deficit of 4.9 percent of GDP in 2008, to one of 12.2 percent in 2009, and is predicted to be as large as 14 percent in 2010.[31] The "Green Budget" of the independent Institute for Fiscal Studies notes that

> the UK's level of borrowing in 2010 and the increase in its borrowing between 2007 and 2010 are both forecast to be the highest as a share of national income in the G20. [...] While the UK had the tenth-highest debt out of 19 countries in the G20 in 2007, by 2014 it is forecast to have the fourth highest (behind Japan, Italy and the US).[32]

This has dire consequences for the country's future and its future government, and will undoubtedly entail a prolonged period of austerity – the only viable option.

Looking at Britain's economic situation in the *Financial Times*, Martin Wolf concluded that "the UK has not only had a financial crisis, with the usual severe impact on output and the public finances, but that the UK has also been a 'monocrop' economy, with finance itself acting as the 'crop.'"[33] As Wolf noted further, "countries that depend heavily on output and exports for commodities whose markets are volatile are all too familiar with the cycles these crops can create."[34] In other words, just as a country like Nicaragua is overly dependent on coffee and banana production making it vulnerable to fluctuating world coffee and banana prices, so has Britain made the mistake of being excessively exposed to financial shocks given its heavy dependence on the financial sector. Hence, during an economic downturn, the once fashionable idea that "what is good for the City is good for the country" starts to ring increasingly hollow.

However, as this book has shown, any crisis that is a crisis of ideas is an opportunity for policy realignment, as long as a convincing crisis narrative can explain what went wrong and how things can be fixed. Thus, in many ways, the financial crisis has created the conditions for Prime Minister Brown to establish a new settlement for the British economy. How did Brown respond to the financial crisis and does it signify a lasting and permanent break with Thatcher's neoliberal settlement – a settlement of ideas so obviously unprepared to deal with the crisis?

## Brown's economic policies

Ever since New Labour came to power in 1997 there has been a division of responsibility between Blair and Brown, with the former focusing on foreign affairs and domestic issues such as justice and security, and the latter left to deal with the economy. This division of labor only intensified after the terrorist attacks of September 11, 2001, when Blair spent most of his time globetrotting and soon became intimately involved with the US-led invasion of Iraq in the spring of 2003. As already discussed in Chapter 6, from the beginning of New

Labour's reign it was clear that Brown's approach to the economy would be very cautious. He hardly touched any policies that were left in place by his Conservative predecessors John Major and Kenneth Clarke. Brown kept Clarke's fiscal plans in place for the next three years, institutionalized price stability as the main goal of government economic policy by making the Bank of England independent in May 1997, and created the Financial Services Authority (FSA), which was put in charge of banking supervision. The FSA would later be criticized for its excessively laissez-faire attitude towards the banks and was singled out by many analysts who preferred to blame the regulators for the crisis.

The response of Brown and his Chancellor, Alistair Darling, to the financial crisis was to announce a massive rescue package on October 8, 2008 with a notional value of £400 billion (equal to 28 percent of Britain's GDP). This package paved the way for the partial nationalization of a number of the country's largest banks and was expected to restore some stability to the country's financial sector. The Bank of England cut its base rates in November 2008 to 3 percent, with further cuts in the ensuing months that resulted in a base rate of 0.5 percent in February 2009 – the lowest rate since 1694 when the Bank was founded. Furthermore, the Bank of England announced its "quantitative easing" program, a nice-sounding term for what is basically printing money.

On January 19, 2009, Brown announced a second rescue package, which included a fresh £50 billion in guarantees for asset-backed securities including corporate debt and mortgages held by private banks, an insurance scheme to underwrite banks' toxic assets, and an extension of the £250 billion credit guarantee scheme. Brown's government also revealed a £2.3 billion support package for the failing automotive industry, receiving simultaneous criticism from the left that it was doing too little, and from the right that it was doing too much. In April 2009, Darling announced a tax increase from 40 to 50 percent for the top earners, i.e. those who make more than £150,000 a year, a move that would have been unthinkable only two years earlier. Later in the year, in what is generally seen as a "populist" move, Darling also announced a "supertax" on bankers' bonuses above £25,000.[35]

The future of the country's tripartite financial regulatory system – the Bank of England (BoE), the Financial Services Authority (FSA), and the Treasury – remains unclear up until today. Tensions between the FSA and the BoE have mounted to the point of policy paralysis, with each blaming the other, or analysts blaming the Labour Party for creating the FSA in the first place.[36] In a remarkable speech during the annual City Banquet in September 2009, Adair Turner, the FSA chairman, criticized the City of London's activities as "socially useless."[37] Turner suggested that London had grown too large, claiming that the job of the FSA was to regulate the City, and not to protect its competitiveness, and that the preponderance of finance had destabilized the British economy.[38] Turner's remarks raised objections from members of Brown's government, not least Brown himself, who rejected Turner's calls for a Tobin tax.[39]

Differences of opinion continue between the FSA and the BoE over how to best prevent future financial crises. Mervyn King, governor of the Bank of

England, supports a British version of the US Glass–Steagall Act that would divide commercial and investment banks, with the former receiving implicit support in times of need from the BoE and the latter being free to fail. The FSA, on the other hand, supports imposing tighter regulations, such as higher capital and liquidity requirements on all financial institutions. The difference in opinion basically comes down to the FSA's belief in risk versus the BoE's emphasis on uncertainty in finance. If you think the economy is relatively stable and that it behaves in predictable ways, you are likely to subscribe to the FSA view. Of course, since the FSA is itself a regulator, it basically has to believe in risk. How else could it do its job and be on top of it all? However, to be fair, Turner himself goes quite far along the uncertainty road in his critique of risk management. If you believe in the persistence of "black swans" and the dangers of banks that are too big to fail, you will probably subscribe to the BoE view.[40] From this book, and the central importance of "Knightian" uncertainty during economic crises, it should come as no surprise that I come down in favor of the latter. Of course, one can have segmentation and countercyclical capital charges. Both views are not mutually exclusive. You can limit building society growth to cool house prices regardless of anything going on in investment banks.

In early November of 2009, Brown had an apparent change of heart and seemed to indicate his endorsement of a Tobin-style tax. Such a Tobin tax, which would entail a levy on global financial transactions, is promising both as a means to raise revenue and as a way to discourage reckless speculation, even though its implementation on a global scale might be difficult. During a speech at St Andrews, Brown called for "a better economic and social contract between financial institutions and the public based on trust and a just distribution of risks and rewards."[41] As Mark Blyth puts it,

> originally intended to 'put sand in the wheels of finance' and perhaps fund development in the Global South, Brown's version [of the Tobin tax] is an implicit admission that the bust will happen again. Asking bankers to tax themselves to provide for a fund to insure against future blow ups admits the inevitability of the blow-up. It's not if, but when. As such, regulation to avoid a boom-bust gives way to insurance for the next time the cycle occurs. It is to admit 'too big to bail' and ask for help by the very agents causing the problem.[42]

Brown's speech immediately won plaudits from fellow EU leaders, with France's Sarkozy enthusiastically backing such a move. However, such a tax would be impossible to implement without the backing of the United States, and all indications from the Obama Administration and US Treasury Secretary Timothy Geithner suggest that the US government will not back a Tobin-style tax. In addition, the managing director of the IMF, Dominique Strauss-Kahn, said he thought such a move was unlikely to be adopted in the near future.[43]

Looking at the economic policies of the past two years – nationalization of banks, re-regulation of the financial sector, tax increases for the rich, proposals to break up banks that are too big to fail, as well as a tax on financial transactions – we see a substantial break from the policies of the previous 30 years. Does this fact mean that Brown is using the current crisis to bring about a real paradigm shift in Britain's economic policy?

## Crisis and paradigm shift: the dog that does not bark?

My answer is no. In this book, I problematized the notion of economic crises as self-apparent and material phenomena. I proposed that we need to look at crises as political constructions that require decisive interventions. During the social construction of a crisis, the movement of the data by itself is not always as important as the "narration" of the movement in the data. What exactly defines whether a moment in time constitutes a crisis in need of a decisive intervention is delimited by the stock of available economic ideas. And here, it would be wrong to see economic ideas as mere technical knowledge or a simple correspondence theory of the world. Rather, they are seen as what one could call "simplifying devices" politicians use in moments of uncertainty to define "what exactly has gone wrong" and "what to do in order to fix it."

All the elements of crisis are there with the advent of the "Great Recession," but the dog has yet to bark. What Brown lacks – indeed what all the current global leaders lack – is not only a convincing narrative of the current crisis, but also a coherent body of economic ideas which he could tap into. Given the absence of a dominant narrative and the deficiency of innovative ideas, all we can expect in the current situation is small incremental fixes. The current neoliberal settlement thus is being "tweaked" rather than overhauled. All Brown's policies – nationalization of banks, higher taxes for the rich, and taxes on bonuses – are temporary measures, in the hope that things will go back to business as usual in the near future. There is no way we can call this a new permanent settlement. The behavior of today's bankers, who were happily cashing in their bonuses in 2009 while the rest of the economy was in a standstill, is a case in point: nothing fundamental seems to have changed.

The tragedy of Gordon Brown lies in the fact that the crisis of 2008 came 16 years too late. If the current crisis were to have occurred during the 1992 general election, after 13 years of Thatcherism, Brown's old ideas would have carried the day, creating the space for a paradigm shift. Unfortunately, Brown and Blair, like so many others, were carried away during the 1990s by the intrinsic attraction of neoliberal ideas, losing their earlier skepticism about the self-healing powers of markets, and actually started to believe in the main tenets of Thatcherism. Brown especially, whose instincts were always more social democratic than Blair's, should have trusted his earlier beliefs that what is good for the City eventually does harm to the real economy.

Of course, on entering the Treasury building in May 1997, Brown would soon realize how dependent the British government is on revenues from the financial sector. It is therefore perfectly understandable that he would not directly set out to implement policies that would do harm to banks.

The problem, however, lies deeper. Brown's instincts and beliefs are fundamentally neoliberal, and after 11 years of neoliberal policies, Brown himself is an integral part of the settlement Thatcher created and he himself institutionalized. Many analysts doubt whether he has the credibility to transform the current system because of his past behavior. That seems wrong-headed for the obvious reason that the fiercely anti-communist Richard Nixon was the only man who could have credibly opened up relations with communist China, and Keith Joseph and Margaret Thatcher – who had been part of Heath's government – could take on Attlee's postwar settlement. If Brown really believed a complete overhaul of the system were called for, he would be the man to do it, given his neoliberal credentials, and it would make him a stronger politician. Yet, so far, he has resisted. He still believes that he has done all the right things and – just like John McCain during the US presidential campaign in September 2008 – that the fundamentals of the economy are strong.

Neoliberalism might be dead, but it is still too early to tell what a new settlement for Britain will look like. As opposed to the 1970s, when the 2008 crisis hit there was no comprehensive body of ideas lying around that was readily available to be put to use. Why is that?

During a conference on the financial crisis in Washington, DC in the spring of 2009, a Japanese analyst told me that it was striking how China and India had shrugged off their earlier ideologies and were marching full speed ahead, with pragmatic solutions and responses to the crisis, while the United States and Britain still seemed flabbergasted by events and were struggling to come up with answers from outside the neoliberal framework. How could it be that India and China, who had been so ideological under Nehru and Mao during the 1950s and 1960s, managed to be pragmatic, while the once so pragmatic United States and United Kingdom were still obsessed with their failed neoliberal ideology today?[44] Since old ideas need entrepreneurs to dust them off, repackage, and update them for new realities – like Friedman and Hayek did so skillfully in the 1970s – a lack of such entrepreneurs leaves the West in an economic ideational vacuum. It could well be the case that the new ideas will not come from the United States or Britain this time around, but from emerging Asia.

However, there has been a serious shift in perception on what a new settlement will need – even in the West. Keynes is back in vogue, the state as regulator of the financial system and overseer of the real economy has entered mainstream thinking again, and the contours of a new neo-Keynesian settlement are beginning to take shape. All over the world people have started to draw lessons from the crisis. You know something has really changed when even the IMF itself, that sacred temple of neoliberal economics, has started to rethink macroeconomic policy, in person of chief economist Olivier Blanchard. In an IMF staff position note, Blanchard indicated that the focus on low inflation has been excessive in the past, that counter-cyclical fiscal policy is an important tool, and that financial regulation as we know it contributed to the amplification that transformed the decrease in US housing prices into a major world economic crisis.[45]

For Britain in particular, it is perhaps time to start rethinking the economic framework by going back to old principles that were "tried and tested," as Churchill would have said in 1945,[46] and putting them back at the heart of economic policymaking. The idea of a country having a comparative advantage in finance and hence needing to specialize in financial products has serious flaws, as Wolf's monocrop metaphor has indicated. Creating a prosperous economy will only be achieved if there are incentives for long term investment in the real economy and if the dogmatic beliefs in the magic powers of self-regulating markets are shelved once and for all. To have a better chance of weathering an economic storm, an economy needs to diversify its production and consumption portfolios, balance public and private sectors, actively limit income inequality, and invest in its long-term growth potential. An economy that does so has a much better chance than one that is heavily exposed to one particular industry and to financial speculation.

In closing, as we start our quest for a new and better paradigm, we should keep in mind what Raymond Aron once observed about politics. According to Aron, politics "is never a conflict between good and evil, but always a choice between the preferable and the detestable."[47] Historian Tony Judt picked up on this theme when delivering the Second Annual Raymond Aron Lecture at Brookings in Washington, DC. To quote Judt:

> The detestable can take many forms in the public realm, past and future. But it is always characterized by its attraction to one big theory, one big model, one big view of how things are, how they work, and how they should work. It is always very sure of itself. It is almost invariably dangerously smug in its incontrovertible theoretical superiority and moral rectitude.[48]

So, what is the preferable according to Judt? "The preferable is always a compromise [...] caught somewhere between the lessons of memory and the distractions of prosperity, between prophylactic social provisions and the attraction of maximizing profit. Like all such compromises, it is deeply contradictory and flawed."[49]

In our quest for a new economic settlement that is preferable rather than detestable, it is always a good idea to start by taking history seriously. We ignore its lessons at our own peril.

# Appendix

## List of interviewees

(in alphabetical order)
BENN, Tony (Secretary of State for Industry and Energy, 1974–1979)
BRITTAN, Samuel (*Financial Times*)
BURNS, Terence (Former Permanent Secretary to the Treasury)
CLARKE, Kenneth (Chancellor of the Exchequer, 1993–1997)
EATWELL, John (Cambridge and former economic adviser to the Labour Party)
GAMBLE, Andrew (then at University of Sheffield)
GEORGE, Edward (Governor of the Bank of England, 1993–2003)
GIDDENS, Anthony (London School of Economics)
HARRIS, Ralph (Head of the Institute of Economic Affairs, 1957–1987)
HAY, Colin (then at University of Birmingham)
HEALEY, Denis (Chancellor of the Exchequer, 1974–1979)
HEFFERNAN, Richard (Open University)
HENNESSY, Peter (College of Queen Mary)
HESELTINE, Michael (Deputy Prime Minister, 1995–1997)
HEYWOOD, Jeremy (Civil Service adviser to Tony Blair, 1997–2001)
HOBSBAWM, Eric (Birkbeck College)
HOWE, Geoffrey (Chancellor of the Exchequer, 1979–1983)
HUTTON, Will (The Work Foundation)
KINNOCK, Neil (Leader of the Labour Party, 1983–1992)
LAMONT, Norman (Chancellor of the Exchequer, 1990–1993)
LAWSON, Nigel (Chancellor of the Exchequer, 1983–1989)
LEIGH-PEMBERTON, Robin (Governor of the Bank of England, 1983–1993)
LIEVEN, ANATOL (King's College London and New America Foundation)
LYTTELTON, Adrian (son of Oliver Lyttelton, Professor of History, Pisa)
PARKINSON, Cecil (Chairman of the Conservative Party, 1981–1983)
PEMBERTON, Hugh (University of Bristol)
RICHARDSON, Gordon (Governor of the Bank of England, 1973–1983)
RIDDELL, Peter (*The Times*)
ROSS, Fiona (University of Bristol)
SELDON, Anthony (Wellington College)
SKIDELSKY, Robert (University of Warwick and House of Lords)
SKINNER, Dennis (Labour MP)

SMITH, Andrew (Secretary of State for Work and Pensions, 2002–2004)
STERN, Richard (FIAS, World Bank Group, Washington, DC)
TEBBIT, Norman (Secretary of State for Employment, 1981–1983)
THOMPSON, Helen (University of Cambridge)
WHEATCROFT, Geoffrey (author and columnist)
WICKHAM-JONES, Mark (University of Bristol)

# Notes

## 1 Continuity and change in British economic policymaking

1 C. Attlee, *Campaign Speech to the Labour Party Conference*, Scarborough, October 1951.
2 E. Heath, *Speech to the Conservative Party Conference*, Blackpool, October 1970.
3 M. Thatcher, *Speech to the Conservative Party Conference*, Brighton, October 1980.
4 Tony Blair interview before the 2005 general election as quoted in P. Riddell, "Impressions of the Election," *Political Quarterly* 76 (3), July 2005, p. 320.
5 In 2001, New Labour had a slightly reduced overall majority of 167 seats, while in 2005 its majority fell to 66 seats. What was remarkable for a government that promised to "bring democracy closer to the people" was the low turnout of the 2001 and 2005 general elections: 59 percent and 61 percent respectively. These turnout figures stand in stark contrast compared to the general elections of 1992 and 1997, when turnout was as high as 78 percent and 71 percent respectively.
6 T. Blair, *New Britain: My Vision of a Young Country*, London: Harper Collins, 1996.
7 The intellectual foundations of "The Third Way" were best expressed in *Beyond Left and Right* by Anthony Giddens (1994), a prominent British sociologist; and to a lesser extent the writings of Will Hutton in *The State We're In*, first published in 1995. (A. Giddens, *Beyond Left and Right: The Future of Radical Politics*, Cambridge: Polity Press, 1994; and W. Hutton, *The State We're In*, London: Jonathan Cape Ltd, 1995.)
8 Blair, *New Britain*, pp. ix–xiii.
9 R. Heffernan, *New Labour and Thatcherism: Political Change in Britain*, New York: Palgrave, 2001.
10 A. Seldon, "The Second Blair Government: The Verdict," in A. Seldon and D. Kavanagh (eds.) *The Blair Effect, 2001–2005*, Cambridge: Cambridge University Press, 2005, p. 411.
11 Ibid.
12 A. Marr, *A History of Modern Britain*, London: Macmillan, 2007, pp. 507–509 and W. Hutton, "The Stakeholder Society," in D. Marquand and A. Seldon (eds.) *The Ideas that Shaped Postwar Britain*, London: Fontana Press, 1996, pp. 290–308.
13 P. Riddell, *The Unfulfilled Prime Minister*, London: Politico's, 2005, pp. 3–7.
14 P. Clarke, *Hope and Glory: Britain 1900–2000*, second edition, London: Penguin Books, 2004, pp. 44–45.
15 Of course, Keynesian demand management was only formally introduced after the devaluation of 1949 in Britain. Before that, there was an attempt at planning under Hugh Dalton at the Treasury, but given the severe financial constraints, this effort was soon aborted.
16 D. Yergin and J. Stanislaw, *The Commanding Heights: The Battle for the World Economy*, New York: Touchstone, 2002, pp. 1–28.
17 Riddell, *The Unfulfilled Prime Minister*, p. 6.

18 D. Childs, *Britain Since 1945: A Political History*, sixth edition, London: Routledge, 2006, p. 163.

19 Interviews with Nigel Lawson (London: Marble Arch, September 12, 2006), Geoffrey Howe (London: House of Lords, October 10, 2006), Norman Tebbit (London: House of Lords, October 10, 2006), Ralph Harris (London: House of Lords, October 11, 2006), and Cecil Parkinson (London: House of Lords, October 11, 2006).

20 The concept "crisis" is defined as a moment of decisive intervention in the process of institutional change. Conceptualized as such, crisis is revealed as a strategic moment in the transformation of the state and as a moment in which a tendential unity is reimposed upon the state. This will be further elaborated in Chapter 2. The definition is borrowed from Colin Hay. Full reference: C. Hay, "Crisis and the structural transformation of the state: interrogating the process of change," *British Journal of Politics and International Relations* 1 (3), October 1999, pp. 317–344.

21 See M. Blyth, *Great Transformations: Economic Ideas and Institutional Change in the Twentieth Century*, Cambridge: Cambridge University Press, 2002, pp. 35–45.

22 For Dennis Kavanagh and Peter Hall it is the former, i.e. a "self-evident state of affairs," for Colin Hay, Mark Blyth and myself, it is the latter.

23 The term "institutions" will be used as defined by Peter Hall, who refers to the "formal rules, compliance procedures, and standard operating practices that structure the relationship between individuals in various units of the polity and economy." (See P. Hall, *Governing the Economy: The Politics of State Intervention in Britain and France*, Oxford: Oxford University Press, 1986, p. 19.)

24 See P. Pierson, *Politics in Time: History, Institutions and Social Anaylsis*, Princeton: Princeton University Press, 2004, pp. 1–16.

25 D. Coates, "The New Political Economy of Postwar Britain," in C. Hay (ed.) *British Politics Today*, Cambridge: Polity Press, 2002, p. 157.

26 C. Hay, "Continuity and Discontinuity in British Political Development," in D. Marsh et al. *Postwar British Politics in Perspective*, Cambridge: Polity Press, 1999, pp. 23–27.

27 Although one could question the extent of Clement Attlee's charisma, he was widely admired and respected in the British electorate for his competence (he ran domestic affairs during the War with great success) and statesmanship. Heath, Thatcher and Blair all brought a fresh face to the top of British politics.

28 Coates, "The New Political Economy of Postwar Britain," pp. 157–184.

29 M. Blyth, "The Transformation of the Swedish Model: Economic Ideas, Distributional Conflict, and Institutional Change," *World Politics* 54 (1), October 2001, p. 3.

30 See M. Blyth, "When Liberalisms Change: Comparing the Politics of Deflations and Inflations," in R. Roy, A. Denzau and T. Willett (eds.) *Neoliberalism: National and Regional Experiments with Global Ideas*, New York: Routledge, 2007.

31 J. Campbell, *Institutional Change and Globalization*, Princeton: Princeton University Press, 2004, p. 21.

32 David Ricardo, Thomas Malthus, Richard Cobden, Karl Marx, John Stuart Mill, Alfred Marshall, John Hicks, John Maynard Keynes, and Friedrich von Hayek are just a handful that immediately come to mind.

33 P. Hall and D. Soskice, *Varieties of Capitalism: the Institutional Foundations of Comparative Advantage*, Oxford: Oxford University Press, 2001.

34 Pierson, *Politics in Time*, p. 47.

35 Heath's successful accession to the EEC in 1973 and Blair's stable macroeconomic record come to mind.

36 For a discussion of "innovators" and "consolidators" in modern British political history, see S. Beer, *Britain Against Itself: The Political Contradictions of Collectivism*, New York: W.W. Norton, 1982; and S. Beer, *British Politics in the Collectivist Age*, New York: Knopf, 1965.

37 G. King, R. Keohane and S. Verba, *Designing Social Inquiry: Scientific Inference in Qualitative Research*, Princeton: Princeton University Press, 1994, p. 208.

38 S. Van Evera, *Guide to Methods for Students of Political Science*, Ithaca: Cornell University Press, 1997, pp. 50–53.
39 Op. cit., p. 54.
40 S. Berman, "Review: Ideas, Norms, and Culture in Political Analysis," *Comparative Politics* 33 (2), January 2001, p. 244.
41 A. George and A. Bennett, *Case Studies and Theory Development in the Social Sciences*, Cambridge: MIT Press, 2005, p. 67.
42 See M. Blyth, "Great Punctuations: Prediction, Randomness, and the Evolution of Comparative Political Science," *American Political Science Review* 100 (4), November 2006, pp. 493–498.
43 J.S. Mill, "Of the Four Methods of Experimental Inquiry," chapter eight in J.M. Robson (ed.) *A System of Logic*, Toronto: Toronto University Press, 1973, pp. 388–406.
44 Van Evera, *Guide to Methods for Students of Political Science*, p. 57.
45 Bennett and George, *Case Studies and Theory Development in the Social Sciences*, p. 99.
46 Ibid.
47 A complete list of interviewees is provided in the Appendix.
48 W. Quandt, "The Middle East on the Brink: Prospects for Change in the 21st Century," *The Middle East Journal* 50 (4), Winter 1996, p. 10.

## 2 Crisis, ideas, and path dependence: theoretical framework and postwar Britain's changing political economy

1 M. Friedman, *Capitalism and Freedom*, Chicago: University of Chicago Press, 40th Anniversary Edition, 2002, pp. xiii–xiv.
2 C. Hay, "Crisis and the Structural Transformation of the State: Interrogating the Process of Change," *British Journal of Politics and International Relations* 1 (3), October 1999, pp. 317–318.
3 M. Blyth, *Great Transformations: Economic Ideas and Institutional Change in the Twentieth Century*, Cambridge: Cambridge University Press, 2002, p. 11.
4 P. Pierson, *Politics in Time: History, Institutions, and Social Analysis*, Princeton: Princeton University Press, 2004, pp. 10–11.
5 See for example D. Marsh et al., *Postwar British Politics in Perspective*, Cambridge: Polity Press, 1999.
6 P. Addison, *The Road to 1945: British Politics and the Second World War*, London: Cape, 1975, pp. 14–15.
7 P. Hennessy, "The Attlee Governments 1945–1951," in P. Hennessy and A. Seldon (eds.) *Ruling Performance: British Governments from Attlee to Thatcher*, Oxford: Blackwell, 1987, p. 33.
8 C. Hay, "British Politics Today: Towards a New Political Science of British Politics?" in C. Hay (ed.) *British Politics Today*, Cambridge: Polity Press, 2002, pp. 1–13.
9 D. Kavanagh, *The Reordering of British Politics: Politics after Thatcher*, Oxford: Oxford University Press, 1997, p. 29.
10 B. Pimlott, "The Myth of Consensus," in L.M. Smith (ed.), *The Making of Britain: Echoes of Greatness*, London: Macmillan, 1988, pp. 129–141.
11 P. Kerr, *Postwar British Politics: From Conflict to Consensus*, London: Routledge, 2001.
12 R. Lowe, "The Second World War Consensus and the Foundation of the Welfare State," *Twentieth Century British History*, 1 (2), 1990, p. 156.
13 S. Ball and A. Seldon (eds.), *The Heath Government 1970–74: A Reappraisal*, London: Longman, 1996.
14 Op. cit., p. 2.

15 Kavanagh, *The Reordering of British Politics*, pp. 85–109.

16 P. Clarke, *Hope and Glory: Britain 1900–2000*, second edition, London: Penguin Books, pp. 367–379.

17 P. Pierson, *Dismantling the Welfare State? Reagan, Thatcher, and the Politics of Retrenchment*, Cambridge: Cambridge University Press, 1994.

18 D. Marsh and R. Rhodes (eds.), *Implementing Thatcherite Policies: Audit of an Era*, Buckingham: Open University Press, 1992, p. 187.

19 P. Hall, "Policy Paradigms, Social Learning and the State: The Case of Economic Policymaking in Britain," *Comparative Politics* 25 (3), April 1993, pp. 275–296.

20 Interview with Nigel Lawson, London: Marble Arch, September 12, 2006.

21 N. Lawson, *The View From No. 11: Memoirs of a Tory Radical*, London: Corgi Books, 1993, p. 28.

22 C. Hay, "The 'Crisis' of Keynesianism and the Rise of Neo-Liberalism in Britain: An Ideational Institutionalist Approach," in J. Campbell and O. Pedersen (eds.), *The Rise of Neoliberalism and Institutional Analysis*, Princeton: Princeton University Press, 2001, pp. 193–218.

23 R. Skidelsky, "Mrs. Thatcher's Revolution," in D. Calleo and C. Morgenstern (eds.) *Recasting Europe's Economies*, Lanham, MD: University Press of America, 1990, pp. 105–108.

24 C. Hay, *The Political Economy of New Labour: Labouring Under False Pretences?* Manchester: Manchester University Press, 1999, pp. 66–71.

25 See Kavanagh (1997), Hay (*The Political Economy of New Labour*, 1999) and Heffernan (*New Labour and Thatcherism: Political Change in Britain*, 2001) in particular.

26 A. Gamble, "Commentary: The Meaning of the Third Way," in A. Seldon and D. Kavanagh (eds.), *The Blair Effect 2001–2005*, Cambridge: Cambridge University Press, 2005, pp. 430–438.

27 Founded by Lord Hollick in 1986, the Institute for Public Policy Research (IPPR) has become the leading progressive think tank in Britain and has profound links and influence with the Labour Party.

28 Interview with Anthony Giddens, London: the London School of Economics, October 31, 2006.

29 H. Macmillan, *The Middle Way*, London: Macmillan, 1938.

30 A. Giddens, *The Third Way*, Cambridge: Polity Press, 1998. Of course, the puzzle of how to combine flexibility and globalization with economic growth and equity has been the essence of Scandinavian social democracy since the 1940s. In many ways, Giddens' ideas therefore pointed Blair and Britain in the direction of the Scandinavian model. In this sense, his ideas are not very new; however, applied to the case of Britain they were.

31 Interview with Will Hutton, London: The Work Foundation, October 19, 2006.

32 W. Hutton, "The Stakeholder Society," in D. Marquand and A. Seldon (eds.), *The Ideas that Shaped Postwar Britain*, London: Fontana Press, 1996, p. 299.

33 Giddens himself, however, rejects this judgment. See A. Giddens, "It's time to give the Third Way a second chance," *The Independent*, June 28, 2007.

34 M. Freeden, "The Stranger at the Feast: Ideology and Public Policy in Twentieth Century Britain," *Twentieth Century British History* 1 (1), 1990, pp. 9–34.

35 Op. cit., p. 11.

36 Ibid.

37 D. Marsh et al., *Postwar British Politics in Perspective*, Cambridge: Polity Press, 1999.

38 Ibid.

39 R. Keohane and H. Milner (eds.) *Internationalization and Domestic Politics*, Cambridge: Cambridge University Press, 1996, pp. 243–258.

40 J. Frieden and R. Rogowski, "The Impact of the International Economy on National Policies: An Analytical Overview," in Keohane and Milner (eds.) *Internationalization and Domestic Politics*, p. 25.

41 S. Berman, *The Social Democratic Moment*, Cambridge: Harvard University Press, 1998, p. 202.

42 P. Gourevitch, *Politics in Hard Times: Comparative Responses to International Economic Crisis*, Ithaca: Cornell University Press, 1986 and R. Rogowski, *Commerce and Coalitions: How Trade Affects Domestic Political Alignments*, Princeton: Princeton University Press, 1989.

43 J. Legro, *Rethinking the World: Great Power Strategies and International Order*, Ithaca: Cornell University Press, 2005, p. 45.

44 J. Frieden, "Invested Interests: the politics of national economic policies in a world of global finance," *International Organization* 45 (4), Autumn 1991, pp. 425–451.

45 K. McNamara, *The Currency of Ideas: Monetary Policy in the European Union*, Ithaca: Cornell University Press, 1999, pp. 32–34.

46 K. Sikkink, *Ideas and Institutions: Developmentalism in Brazil and Argentina*, Ithaca: Cornell University Press, 1991, p. 7.

47 Berman, *The Social Democratic Moment*, p. 203.

48 P. Hall, *Governing the Economy: The Politics of State Intervention in Britain and France*, Oxford: Oxford University Press, 1986, p. 19.

49 Ibid.

50 M. Weir and T. Skocpol, "State Structures and the Possibilities for 'Keynesian' Responses to the Great Depression in Sweden, Britain and the United States," in P. Evans, D. Rueschemeyer and T. Skocpol (eds.) *Bringing the State Back In*, Cambridge: Cambridge University Press, 1985, p. 125.

51 "Second generation" path dependence scholars include Tim Büthe, Abraham Newman, Elliot Posner, and Orfeo Fioretos.

52 "Ideational Institutionalist" is Colin Hay's term. Mark Blyth would prefer "Constructivist Political Economy".

53 J. Campbell, *Institutional Change and Globalization*, Princeton: Princeton University Press, 2004, p. 65.

54 Pierson, *Politics in Time*, pp. 1–16.

55 Op. cit., p. 27.

56 D. North, *Institutions, Institutional Change and Economic Performance*, Cambridge: Cambridge University Press, 1990.

57 Pierson, *Politics in Time*, pp. 10–13.

58 P. Pierson, "The Study of Policy Development," *The Journal of Policy History* 17 (1), January 2005, pp. 34–51.

59 Campbell, *Institutional Change and Globalization*, p. 87.

60 Op. cit., p. 76.

61 K. Thelen, "Historical Institutionalism and Comparative Politics," *Annual Review of Political Science* (2), 1999, p. 385.

62 Ibid.

63 Pierson, *Politics in Time*, p. 52.

64 North, *Institutions, Institutional Change and Economic Performance*, pp. 98–99.

65 Ibid.

66 G. Peters, J. Pierre, and D. King, "The Politics of Path Dependency: Political Conflict in Historical Institutionalism," *The Journal of Politics* 67 (4), November 2005, p. 1277.

67 Ibid.

68 Sikkink, *Ideas and Institutions*.

69 See for example Mark Blyth ("'Any More Bright Ideas?' The Ideational Turn of Comparative Political Economy," *Comparative Politics* 29 (2), January 1997), Kathleen McNamara (1998), and Sheri Berman (1999).

70  P. Hall (ed.), *The Political Power of Economic Ideas: Keynesianism across Nations*, Princeton: Princeton University Press, 1989, pp. 3–26.

71  P. Hall, "Introduction," in Hall, *The Political Power of Economic Ideas*, p. 8.

72  Weir and Skocpol, "State Structures" in Evans, Rueschemeyer and Skocpol (eds.), *Bringing the State Back In*, pp. 107–163.

73  Hall, "Introduction," pp. 10–11.

74  Op. cit., pp. 11–12.

75  See for example Gourevitch, *Politics in Hard Times*.

76  Hall, "Introduction," pp. 12–13.

77  Ibid.

78  Blyth, "'Any More Bright Ideas?' The Ideational Turn of Comparative Political Economy," pp. 229–231.

79  Op. cit., p. 235.

80  Op. cit., p. 237.

81  Op. cit., p. 246.

82  Blyth, *Great Transformations*, p. 38.

83  Blyth, "Any More Bright Ideas?", p. 246.

84  See for example, Jeffry Frieden (1991) and Keohane and Milner (1996).

85  Berman, *The Social Democratic Moment*, p. 20.

86  Op. cit., pp. 20–21.

87  Op. cit., pp. 32–33.

88  Campbell, *Institutional Change and Globalization*, p. 91.

89  Blyth, *Great Transformations*, pp. 27–34. This is, of course, a point made much earlier by Karl Marx.

90  A. Wendt, *The Social Theory of International Politics*, Cambridge: Cambridge University Press, 1999.

91  See Hall, *Governing the Economy,* pp. 17–20.

92  Blyth, *Great Transformations*, p. 41.

93  Blyth, "The Transformation of the Swedish Model: Economic Ideas, Distributional Conflict, and Institutional Change," *World Politics* 54 (1), October 2001 p. 4.

94  The neoliberal ideational consensus can be summed up as the belief in price stability as the main goal of a government's economic policy. That goal would be achieved by an independent central bank that would either control the money supply directly or use some kind of target (interest rate or inflation rate) to keep prices stable over time. The broader neoliberal consensus also encompasses a limited but strong state, recognizing the private sector as the main actor in generating economic growth.

95  McNamara, *The Currency of Ideas*, pp. 122–158.

96  S. Berman, "Review: Ideas, Norms, and Culture in Political Analysis," *Comparative Politics* 33 (2), January 2001, p. 232.

97  Legro, *Rethinking the World*, pp. 24–48.

98  Mill once noted that "ideas, unless outward circumstances conspire with them, have in general no very rapid or immediate efficacy in human affairs" (quoted in Berman, *The Social Democratic Moment*, p. 25).

99  Legro, *Rethinking the World*, p. 40.

100 Blyth, *Great Transformations*, p. 35.

101 Op. cit., pp. 40–42.

102 D. Wincott, "Review of Mark Blyth's *Great Transformations*," *West European Politics* 26 (4), October 2003.

103 Berman, "Review: Ideas, Norms, and Culture in Political Analysis," pp. 237–239.

104 Campbell, *Institutional Change and Globalization*, p. 107.

105 Blyth, *Great Transformations*, p. 229.

106 Op. cit., pp. 229–230.

107 Op. cit., p. 35.

108 James Callaghan, on the other hand, saw that during his final days in office, the world in which he had spent most of his political life was about to change quite radically. He famously remarked to one of his aides: "There are times, perhaps every 30 years, when there is a sea change in politics. I suspect that there is now such a sea change, and it is for Mrs. Thatcher.".

109 Legro, *Rethinking the World*, p. 28.

110 Frank H. Knight presided over the Department of Economics at the University of Chicago from the 1920s to the late 1940s (jointly with Jacob Viner). In his famous dissertation, *Risk, Uncertainty and Profit* (published in 1921), Knight made a distinction between "risk" (randomness with knowable probabilities) and "uncertainty" (randomness with unknowable probabilities).

111 Blyth, *Great Transformations*, pp. 9–10.

112 Hay, "Crisis and the Structural Transformation of the State," pp. 317–319.

113 Op. cit., p. 327.

114 W. Outhwaite (ed.), *The Blackwell Dictionary of Modern Social Thought*, Malden, MA: Blackwell Publishing, 2003, p. 132.

115 Ibid.

116 Ibid.

117 Op. cit., p. 133.

118 Berman, *The Social Democratic Moment*, p. 20.

119 Blyth, *Great Transformations*, p. 39.

120 Op. cit., p. 40.

121 I want to thank Erik Jones at the Johns Hopkins SAIS Bologna Center for pointing this out to me.

122 Berman, "Review: Ideas, Norms and Culture in Political Analysis," p. 236.

123 Hay, "Crisis and the Structural Transformation of the State," p. 333.

124 Op. cit., p. 335.

125 C. Hay, "Narrating Crisis: The Discursive Construction of the 'Winter of Discontent,'" *Sociology* 30 (2), Spring 1996, p. 253.

126 Op. cit., p. 254.

127 Blyth, *Great Transformations*, pp. 40–41.

128 Blyth, *Great Transformations*.

129 Friedman, *Capitalism and Freedom*, 2002, pp. xiii–xiv.

130 S. Skowronek, *The Politics Presidents Make: Leadership from John Adams to George Bush*, Cambridge: Harvard University Press, 1993.

131 Op. cit., p. 35.

132 Op. cit., p. 36.

133 See Chapter 1 for a reference to Samuel Beer's distinction between innovators and consolidators. The US examples that most closely correspond to Clement Attlee and Margaret Thatcher are Franklin Delano Roosevelt and Ronald Reagan.

134 The US equivalents are Herbert Hoover and Jimmy Carter.

135 In the US, good examples are Woodrow Wilson and Richard Nixon.

136 In the US, the examples that come to mind are Lyndon Johnson, George H.W. Bush and Bill Clinton. For a full discussion of the four cases in US presidential politics, see Skowronek, *The Politics Presidents Make*, pp. 34–39.

137 Hay, "Crisis and the Structural Transformation of the State," p. 318.

138 Clarke, *Hope and Glory*, pp. 44–45.

139 D. Yergin and J. Stanislaw, *The Commanding Heights: The Battle for the World Economy*, New York: Touchstone, 2002.

140 J. Sanderson, "Britain in Decline?" in A. Cox, S. Lee and J. Sanderson, *The Political Economy of Modern Britain*, Cheltenham: Edward Elgar, 1997, p. 45.

141 D. Coates, "The New Political Economy of Postwar Britain," in C. Hay (ed.) *British Politics Today*, Cambridge: Polity Press, 2002, p. 160.

142 OECD Historical Statistics, Paris: OECD, 2000 and Wales, *Economic Statistics Monthly*, March 2010, online, available at www.wales.gov.uk/docs/statistics (accessed May 3, 2010).

143 J. Wells, "Uneven Development and De-industrialization in the UK since 1979," in F. Green (ed.) *The Restructuring of the UK Economy*, Hemel Hempstead: Harvester Wheatsheaf, 1989, p. 25.

144 World Trade Organization, *International Trade Statistics*, Geneva: WTO, 2006.

145 S.N. Broadberry, "Employment and Unemployment," in R. Floud and D. McCloskey (eds.) *The Economic History of Britain since 1700, Volume 3, 1939–1992*, second edition, Cambridge: Cambridge University Press, 1994, p. 199.

146 This makes Britain the "leading" services economy in the world.

147 Coates, "The New Political Economy of Postwar Britain," p. 162.

148 Op. cit., pp. 163–164.

149 This should be seen in light of a growing regionalization of the world economy, quite different from the current received wisdom that we live in a "globalized" world that is flat. See, for example, T. Friedman, *The World is Flat*, New York: Farrar, Strauss and Giroux, 2005. For an excellent critique of Friedman, see J. Gray, "The World is Round," *The New York Review of Books* 52 (13), August 11, 2005.

150 J. Buller, "Britain's Relations with the European Union in Historical Perspective," in D. Marsh et al., *Postwar British Politics in Perspective*, pp. 115–124.

151 For an analysis of Britain's economic and political options in the 1960s, see D. Calleo, *Britain's Future*, New York: Horizon Press, 1968.

152 Interview with Samuel Brittan, London: *Financial Times*, September 26, 2006.

153 Hall, *Governing the Economy*, pp. 25–47.

154 P. McCarthy, "Britain: The Melancholy Pleasure of Decline," in P. McCarthy and E. Jones (eds.) *Disintegration or Transformation? The Crisis of the State in Advanced Industrial Societies*, New York: St. Martin's Press, 1995, pp. 179–197.

155 A. Gamble, *Britain in Decline: Economic Policy, Political Strategy and the British State*, fourth edition, Basingstoke: Macmillan 1994, p. 14.

156 Clarke, *Hope and Glory*, p. 270.

157 Sanderson, "Britain in Decline?" p. 46.

158 It is interesting that, compared to France, Germany, and Japan, the United States was performing rather poorly too. On two indicators, productivity and unemployment, even the UK does far better than the US.

159 Gamble, *Britain in Decline*, p. 17.

160 Sanderson, "Britain in Decline?" p. 55; this point is discussed at greater length in Chapter 4.

161 Hall, *Governing the Economy*, pp. 25–47.

162 A. Gerschenkron, *Economic Backwardness in Historical Perspective*, Cambridge: Harvard University Press, 1962.

163 One could argue that it is still a major problem, even though it has disappeared from the daily discourse in the British financial press.

164 For further discussion, see S. Brittan, *Steering the Economy*, Harmondsworth: Penguin, 1970.

165 Hall, *Governing the Economy*, p. 58.

166 Interview with Samuel Brittan.

167 S. Blank, "Britain: The Politics of Foreign Economic Policy, the Domestic Economy, and the Problem of Pluralistic Stagnation," *International Organization* 31 (4), Autumn 1977, pp. 673–721.

168 For example, the proposal of the Bank of England to float the pound in 1952 ("Operation Robot") was essentially voted down by Churchill's cabinet for political reasons: any weakening of the pound was seen as an abdication of Britain's duty to the overseas holders of sterling (Hall, *Governing the Economy*, p. 58).

169 Interview with Robin Leigh-Pemberton (governor of the Bank of England from 1983–1993), London: House of Lords, October 11, 2006.

170 Hay, "Crisis and the Structural Transformation of the State," p. 328.

171 Hay, "Narrating Crisis," pp. 253–254.

## 3 Clement Attlee's postwar "settlement" (1945–1970): depression, war, Keynes, Beveridge, and a new consensus

1 J.M. Keynes, *Essays in Persuasion*, New York: W.W. Norton, 1963, p. 312 (the essay, "The End of Laissez-faire," was first published by Keynes in 1926).

2 W.H. Beveridge, *Social Insurance and Allied Services*, HMSO, November 1942, Cmd. 6404.

3 Labour Party, "Let Us Face the Future: A Declaration of Labour Policy for the Consideration of the Nation," *1945 General Election Manifesto,* London: Labour Party, 1945.

4 P. Hennessy, *Having It So Good: Britain in the Fifties*, London: Allen Lane, 2006, p. 22.

5 Note that the term "invincible armada" was not a Spanish one; it was a sarcastic phrase employed by later English commentators.

6 P. Clarke, *Hope and Glory: Britain 1900–2000*, second edition, London: Penguin Books, 2004, p. 197.

7 See P. Hennessy, *Never Again: Britain 1945–1951*, revised second edition, London: Penguin Books, 2006; and D. Thomson, *England in the Twentieth Century 1914–1963*, Harmondsworth: Penguin Books, 1965, p. 218.

8 Even though Neville Chamberlain's reforms as Chancellor of the Exchequer from 1931 onwards were relatively successful compared to other countries (e.g. France), Britain saw high unemployment throughout the 1930s with especially high numbers of unemployed in the industrial north of England, Wales, and Scotland.

9 A.J.P. Taylor, *English History 1914–1945*, The Oxford History of England Part XV, New York: Oxford University Press, 1965, pp. 599–600.

10 A. Marr, *A History of Modern Britain*, London: Macmillan, 2007, p. 3.

11 Clarke, *Hope and Glory*, p. 215.

12 D. Childs, *Britain since 1945: A Political History*, sixth edition, London: Routledge, 2006, pp. 2–5.

13 Interviews with Tony Benn, London: Holland Park, October 13, 2006, and Denis Healey, London: House of Lords, October 12, 2006.

14 See M. Foot, F. Owen and P. Howard writing as "Cato", *Guilty Men*, first published in Britain in 1940 and cited in Clarke as the title of his sixth chapter of *Hope and Glory*, pp. 182–215.

15 Thomson, *England in the Twentieth Century*, pp. 217–223. For an alternative interpretation of that period in Britain, see W.K. Myers, "A Rationale for Appeasement: A Study of British Efforts to Conciliate Germany in the 1930s," *PhD Dissertation*, Baltimore: Johns Hopkins University, 1972.

16 J.M. Keynes, *The General Theory of Employment, Interest and Money*, Amherst, NY: Prometheus Books, 1997.

17 Beveridge, *Social Insurance and Allied Services*.

18 Hennessy, *Having It So Good*, pp. 22–23.

19 Clarke, *Hope and Glory*, pp. 224–225. However, there would never be a clear majority in favor of it.

20 Taylor, *English History 1914–1945*, p. xxiv, figure 4.

21 E. Hobsbawm, *Industry and Empire: From 1750 to the Present Day*, New York: The New Press, 1999, p. 185.

22  See, for example, T. Rooth, *British Protectionism and the International Economy: Overseas Commercial Policy in the 1930s*, Cambridge: Cambridge University Press, 1992.

23  D. Landes, *The Unbound Prometheus*, Cambridge: Cambridge University Press, 1969, pp. 368–369.

24  M. Thomas, "The Macro-economics of the Inter-war Years," in R. Floud and D. McCloskey (eds.) *The Economic History of Britain since 1700, Volume 2: 1860–1939*, second edition, Cambridge: Cambridge University Press, 1994, pp. 321–322.

25  S.N. Broadberry, *The British Economy Between the Wars: A Macroeconomic Survey*, Oxford: Basil Blackwell, 1986, pp. 67–70.

26  S. Pollard, *The Development of the British Economy, 1914–1980*, third edition, London: Edward Arnold, 1983, pp. 108–119.

27  See Broadberry, *The British Economy Between the Wars*, p. 30 and J. Kuczynski, *A Short History of Labour Conditions in Great Britain, 1750 to the Present Day*, London: Frederick Muller Ltd, 1946, p. 120.

28  Pollard, *The Development of the British Economy*, pp. 66–82.

29  Clarke, *Hope and Glory*, p. 176.

30  Among the worst affected towns was Jarrow where unemployment led to the famous Jarrow Hunger March in which unemployed workers marched 300 miles to London to protest against unemployment.

31  In *The Road to Wigan Pier*, George Orwell described life for the unemployed in northern England during the depression:

> Several hundred men risk their lives and several hundred women scrabble in the mud for hours … searching eagerly for tiny chips of coal in slagheaps so they could heat their homes. For them, this arduously-gained "free" coal was more important almost than food.

Although Orwell's book is not quite the documentary record it purports to be, it is still a fitting literary monument to the darker side of 1930s Conservative Prime Minister Stanley Baldwin's "beloved England".

32  C. Webster, "Health, Welfare and Unemployment during the Depression," *Past and Present* 109, November 1985, pp. 204–230.

33  Of course, the people of Britain themselves would not care much about that, for the simple reason that they did not compare themselves to other countries.

34  B. Eichengreen, "Tariffs and Flexible Exchange Rates: The Case of the British General Tariff of 1932," *PhD Dissertation*, New Haven: Yale University, 1979.

35  For more detailed analysis, see S.N. Broadberry, *The British Economy Between the Wars*, pp. 66–74.

36  Clarke, *Hope and Glory*, p. 132.

37  L. Seabrooke, "The Everyday Social Sources of Economic Crises: From 'Great Frustrations' to 'Great Revelations' in Interwar Britain," *International Studies Quarterly* 51 (4), 2007, pp. 795–810.

38  Ibid. Seabrooke points out that Keynes publicly countered this argument by stating that the construction of a crisis around the value between sterling and gold, like the gold itself, "was wearing thinner" (as quoted in *The Times*, May 26, 1925).

39  S.N. Broadberry, "The Emergence of Mass Unemployment: Explaining Macroeconomic Trends in Britain during the Trans-World War I Period," *Economic History Review* 43, 1990, pp. 279.

40  For a critique of Churchill's decision, read J.M. Keynes, *The Economic Consequences of Mr. Churchill* (1925), reprinted in Keynes, *Collected Writings Volume 9*, second edition, London: Palgrave, 2000.

41  Keynes, *The General Theory*, chapters 1, 2, 10–12, and 16.

42  Pollard, *The Development of the British Economy*, pp. 141–145.

43 Clarke, *Hope and Glory*, pp. 180–181.
44 Thomson, *England in the Twentieth Century*, pp. 185–189.
45 Interview with Tony Benn.
46 R. Middleton, *Government versus the Market: The Growth of the Public Sector, Economic Management and British Economic Performance, c. 1890–1979*, Cheltenham: Edward Elgar, 1996, pp. 418–420.
47 Capital Expenditure is the sum of expenditure on consumption, war and non-war capital formation. Government expenditure is the sum of government expenditure on non-war current services (part of consumption) and government war expenditure (part of war).
48 P. Howlett, "The Wartime Economy, 1939–1945," in R. Floud and D. McCloskey (eds.) *The Economic History of Britain since 1700, Volume 3, 1939–1992*, second edition, Cambridge: Cambridge University Press, 1994, pp. 1–4.
49 Bread only went on ration after the war, in July 1946. In order to avoid an imminent famine in Germany, the British found themselves in the ironic situation of having to feed the Germans they had just defeated.
50 Pollard, *The Development of the British Economy*, p. 227.
51 Ibid.
52 Clarke, *Hope and Glory*, p. 209.
53 T. Judt, "The Future of Decadent Europe," *The Brookings Institution*, US–Europe Analysis Series, February 2006. Judt points out that Britain in World War II lost 1 person for every 125 people in their population; compared to 1 in 5 in Poland, 1 in 8 in Yugoslavia or 1 in 11 in Greece.
54 Taylor, *English History 1914–1945*, p. 599.
55 Childs, *Britain since 1945*, pp. 7–8.
56 P. Clarke, "The Keynesian Consensus and its Enemies," in D. Marquand and A. Seldon (eds.) *The Ideas that Shaped Postwar Britain*, London: Fontana Press, 1996, p. 68 and author's personal conversations with Robert Skidelsky in March 2007 in Washington, DC.
57 Clarke, "The Keynesian Consensus and its Enemies," p. 69.
58 For a full account of Keynes' life and work, see the brilliant three volume biography by Robert Skidelsky on *John Maynard Keynes* (*Volume 1: Hopes Betrayed (1883–1920)*; *Volume 2: The Economist as Saviour (1920–1937)*; *Volume 3: Fighting for Britain (1937–1945)*; London: Penguin, 2002.
59 Keynes, *The General Theory*, chapter 24, p. 372.
60 P. Clarke, *A Question of Leadership: From Gladstone to Blair*, second edition, London: Penguin Books, 1999, p. 166.
61 See Keynes citation at the very beginning of this chapter.
62 Clarke, *A Question of Leadership*, p. 167.
63 Eddie George pointed out in an interview with the author that the "national income machine" at the economics library in Cambridge does not have any supply constraints (interview with Eddie George, City of London, October 11, 2006).
64 R. Skidelsky, "Keynes' Legacy," *Lecture at Princeton University*, November 2006.
65 Beveridge, *Social Insurance and Allied Services*, paragraphs 303–309.
66 Clarke, *Hope and Glory*, p. 213.
67 Hennessy, *Never Again*, p. 128.
68 Pollard, *The Development of the British Economy*, p. 229.
69 Beveridge, *Social Insurance and Allied Services*, Cmd. 6404, paragraph 441.
70 Op. cit., paragraph 301 and part VI.
71 Op. cit., paragraph 440.
72 Clarke, "The Keynesian Consensus and Its Enemies," pp. 70–71.
73 J. Tomlinson, *Democratic Socialism and Economic Policy: The Attlee Years 1945–1951*, Cambridge: Cambridge University Press, 1997, pp. 4–5.

74 For an overview of the debate between different factions on the left at that time, see S. Berman, *The Primacy of Politics: Social Democracy and the Making of Europe's Twentieth Century*, New York: Cambridge University Press, 2006.

75 D. Hart, "Editor's Introduction," in G.B. Shaw and H.G. Wilshire, *Fabian Essays in Socialism*, New York: Humboldt, 2003.

76 Fabian Society, "A History of the Fabian Society," online, available at: www.fabian-society.org.uk/About/Fabian_History.pdf (accessed January 22, 2009).

77 Taken from Hennessy, *Never Again*, p. 79.

78 M.E. Murphy, "The Role of the Fabian Society in British Affairs," *Southern Economic Journal* 14 (1), July 1947, pp. 14–23. For a discussion on how exactly these ideas were adopted in Labour's manifesto, see Hennessy, *Never Again*, pp. 80–81.

79 Interview with Tony Benn.

80 F.A. von Hayek, *The Road to Serfdom*, London: Routledge, 1944.

81 Tomlinson, *Democratic Socialism and Economic Policy*, p. 134.

82 Clarke, "The Keynesian Consensus and its Enemies," p. 77.

83 Tomlinson, *Democratic Socialism and Economic Policy*, pp. 134–135.

84 A.C. Pigou, "Review of *The Road to Serfdom*," *Economic Journal* 54, 1944, pp. 217–219.

85 P. Kerr, *Postwar British Politics: From Conflict to Consensus*, London: Routledge, 2001, p. 41.

86 HM Government's *White Paper on Employment Policy*, May 1944, Cmd. 6527, paragraph 80.

87 Conservative Party, "Mr. Churchill's Declaration of Policy to the Electors," *1945 General Election Manifesto*, London: Conservative Party, 1945.

88 Ibid.

89 Labour Party, "Let Us Face the Future."

90 Ibid.

91 Ibid.

92 Ibid.

93 Interview with Denis Healey.

94 A. Mitchell, *Election '45: Reflections on the Revolution in Britain*, London: Fabian Society, 1995, p. 8 and p. 23.

95 D. Butler and G. Butler, *British Political Facts, 1900–1994*, seventh edition, New York: St Martin's Press, 1994, pp. 498–499.

96 Marr, *A History of Modern Britain*, p. 5.

97 Hennessy, *Never Again*, p. 82.

98 Marr, *A History of Modern Britain*, p. 6.

99 Interview with Ralph Harris at the House of Lords, London, October 11, 2006.

100 Butler and Butler, *British Political Facts, 1900–1994*, p. 247.

101 Mitchell, *Election '45: Reflections on the Revolution in Britain*, p. 14.

102 Marr, *A History of Modern Britain*, p. 8.

103 K. Jefferys, *Finest and Darkest Hours: The Decisive Events in British Politics from Churchill to Blair*, London: Atlantic Books, 2002, p. 67.

104 Tomlinson, *Democratic Socialism and Economic Policy*, pp. 23–67.

105 For a much more complete and comprehensive analysis of the Attlee governments' economic policies from 1945 to 1951, see Tomlinson, *Democratic Socialism and Economic Policy*.

106 Pollard, *The Development of the British Economy*, pp. 266–267.

107 Childs, *Britain Since 1945*, pp. 15–16.

108 Jefferys, *Finest and Darkest Hours*, p. 65.

109 Hennessy, *Never Again*, pp. 132–144.

110 Childs, *Britain Since 1945*, p. 16.

111 Clarke, *Hope and Glory*, pp. 224–225.

112 Pollard, *The Development of the British Economy*, pp. 268–269.

113  Hennessy, *Never Again*, pp. 163–174.
114  A. Cairncross, "Economic Policy and Performance, 1945–1964," in Floud and McCloskey (eds.) *The Economic History of Britain Since 1700, Volume 3, 1939–1992*, second edition, Cambridge: Cambridge University Press, 1994, p. 52.
115  A. Marwick, *Britain in the Century of Total War*, London: Penguin, 1968, p. 357.
116  Clarke, *Hope and Glory*, p. 141.
117  Childs, *Britain Since 1945*, p. 19.
118  I. Richter, *Political Purpose in Trade Unions*, London: George Allen, 1973, p. 246.
119  Childs, *Britain Since 1945*, p. 13.
120  Barbara Castle described the rationale of nationalization in an interview during a documentary on PBS: "You know, it seemed to people who'd been to the war, it seemed to them natural justice. Why not pool your resources? And so we broke into the concept of the sacredness of private property.", online, available at: www.pbs.org/wgbh/commandingheights/shared/ minitextlo/tr_show01.html#7 (accessed October 3, 2006).
121  Pollard, *The Development of the British Economy*, p. 258.
122  Clement Attlee during the Labour Party Conference in Bournemouth on June 10, 1946. Quoted in Hennessy, *Never Again*, p. 198.
123  Clarke, *Hope and Glory*, p. 225.
124  Cairncross, "Economic Policy and Performance, 1945–1964," pp. 51–52.
125  Pollard, *The Development of the British Economy*, p. 258.
126  Clarke, *Hope and Glory*, p. 226.
127  Op. cit., p. 225.
128  Interview with Samuel Brittan at the *Financial Times* in London, September 26, 2006.
129  Pollard, *The Development of the British Economy*, p. 259.
130  François Mitterrand rode to power in France in 1981 promising mass nationalizations. At the time, this was nothing short of radical. Even though he had to reverse most of it in 1983, it would be wrong to gloss over it as a mere hiatus in France's "normal" institutional path.
131  Clarke, *Hope and Glory*, p. 224.
132  Interviews with Neil Kinnock (London: Fielden House, October 12, 2006), Denis Healey and Tony Benn.
133  Cairncross, "Economic Policy and Performance, 1945–1964," pp. 46–47.
134  As quoted in Cairncross, "Economic Policy and Performance, 1945–1964," p. 49.
135  Keynes, *The General Theory*, chapter 24, p. 376.
136  Clarke, *Hope and Glory*, pp. 226–227.
137  Tomlinson, *Democratic Socialism and Economic Policy*, pp. 304–305.
138  Pollard, *The Development of the British Economy*, p. 237.
139  Thomson, *England in the Twentieth Century*, p. 223. It was, of course, not just devaluation that corrected Britain's dollar deficit. By then, significant funds were available from Marshall Aid, combined with military assistance through NATO.
140  See Addison (P. Addison, *The Road to 1945: British Politics and the Second World War*, London: Cape, 1975), Marwick (1968), and Kerr (2001).
141  A. Calder, *The People's War: Britain 1939–1945*, London: Pimlico, 1969, p. 531.
142  Opinion polls are cited by Childs in *Britain Since 1945*, p. 17.
143  For a good study on the swing in public opinion towards Labour and a more elaborate discussion of some of the arguments made here, see W. Harrington and P. Young, *The 1945 Revolution*, London: Davis Poynter, 1978.
144  J.D. Hoffman, *The Conservative Party in Opposition, 1945–1951*, London: Macgibbon and Kee, 1964, p. 235.
145  The result of the 1951 general election was closer than many had anticipated. On a high turnout, there was a small swing of 1.1 percent across the country, which was sufficient to give Churchill's Conservatives a small parliamentary majority of 17 seats. Labour actually had 200,000 more votes than the Conservatives, a result of huge Labour majorities in urban strongholds. See Clarke, *Hope and Glory*, p. 80.

146  For a very good overview of this period in Britain, see V. Bogdanor and R. Skidelsky (eds.) *The Age of Affluence, 1951–1964*, London: Macmillan, 1970.
147  John K. Galbraith, *The Affluent Society*, 40th anniversary edition, New York: Mariner Books, 1998.
148  Interviews with Eddie George, and Robin Leigh-Pemberton (London: House of Lords, October 11, 2006).
149  Interview with Robin Leigh-Pemberton.
150  P. Hall, *Governing the Economy*, Oxford: Oxford University Press, 1986, p. 67.
151  The Conservatives dropped their opposition to the Labour nationalizations after 1951 and sought to maintain peaceful, non-confrontational relations with the labor unions for most of the 1950s and 1960s.
152  See, for example, D. Kavanagh, *The Reordering of British Politics: Politics after Thatcher*, Oxford: Oxford University Press, 1997.
153  Hennessy, *Having It So Good*, p. 22.
154  Op. cit., p. 23.
155  Of course, this was not true in comparison with the rest of Western Europe and Japan. The issue of relative decline will be discussed at greater length in Chapter 4.
156  As quoted in D. Brinkley, "Dean Acheson and the 'Special Relationship': The West Point Speech of December 1962," *Historical Journal* 33 (3), September 1990, pp. 599–608.

## 4  Relative decline and the unraveling of consensus (1959–1979): from "having it so good" to the "winter of discontent"

1  H. Macmillan, *Speech at Bedford football ground*, July 20, 1957.
2  H. Wilson, *Speech at the Labour Party Conference*, Scarborough, October 1, 1963.
3  E. Heath, "A Better Tomorrow", *1970 General Election Manifesto*, London: Conservative Party, 1970.
4  J. Callaghan, *Speech at the Labour Party Conference*, Brighton, September 28, 1976. (This speech was written by his son-in-law and future BBC economics correspondent, Peter Jay).
5  See E.H.H. Green, *Ideologies of Conservatism*, Oxford: Oxford University Press, 2004, chapter 6, pp. 157–191 for an overview of Macmillan's view of Britain's political economy.
6  For a very good assessment of the Conservative period from 1951–1964, see V. Bogdanor and R. Skidelsky (eds.) *The Age of Affluence, 1951–1964*, London: Macmillan, 1970.
7  P. Hennessy, *Having It So Good: Britain in the Fifties*, London: Allen Lane, 2006, pp. 557–559.
8  Interview with Robin-Leigh Pemberton, London: House of Lords, October 10, 2006.
9  P. Clarke, *Hope and Glory: Britain 1900–2000*, second edition, London: Penguin Books, 2004, pp. 268–269.
10  D. Thomson, *England in the Twentieth Century*, Harmondsworth: Penguin Books, 1965, p. 261.
11  A. Cairncross, "Economic Policy and Performance, 1945–1964," in R. Floud and D. McCloskey (eds.), *The Economic History of Britain Since 1700, Volume 3, 1939–1992*, second edition, Cambridge: Cambridge University Press, 1994, p. 58.
12  Hennessy, *Having It So Good*, p. 569.
13  He had delivered that famous line already two years earlier, in a speech at Bedford football ground.
14  Clarke, *Hope and Glory*, p. 270.
15  "Supermac" was the subject of a cartoon – "Introducing Super-Mac" – by "Vicky" (Victor Weisz, 1913–1966) in the *Evening Standard* on November 6, 1958. With its rather dismissive caption, "How to Try to Continue to be Top without Actually

Having Been There," it depicted Harold Macmillan in the guise of the comic-book hero Superman.

16  Interview with Samuel Brittan, London: *Financial Times*, September 26, 2006.

17  R. Middleton, *Government versus the Market: The Growth of the Public Sector, Economic Management and British Economic Performance, c. 1890–1979*, Cheltenham: Edward Elgar, 1996, pp. 443–451.

18  A. Booth, *The British Economy in the Twentieth Century*, Basingstoke: Palgrave, 2001, pp. 6–7.

19  Interview with Peter Hennessy, London: Mile End Road, November 1, 2006.

20  Interview with Samuel Brittan.

21  Middleton, *Government versus the Market*, pp. 575–578.

22  P. Hall, *Governing the Economy*, Oxford: Oxford University Press, 1986, p. 77.

23  S. Strange, *Sterling and British Policy*, London: Oxford University Press, 1971, p. 205.

24  R. Middleton, *The British Economy Since 1945: Engaging with the Debate*, Basingstoke: Macmillan, 2000, pp. 70–71.

25  Hall, *Governing the Economy*, p. 78.

26  Ibid.

27  A. Cairncross, *The British Economy since 1945*, second edition, Oxford: Blackwell Publishers, 1995, p. 12.

28  A. Cox and J. Sanderson, "The Political Economy of Britain since 1939," in A. Cox, S. Lee and J. Sanderson, *The Political Economy of Modern Britain*, Cheltenham: Edward Elgar, 1997, p. 20.

29  Hennessy, *Having It So Good*, p. 41.

30  See, for example, Hobsbawm (*Industry and Empire: From 1750 to the Present Day*, New York: The New Press, 1999), Alt (*The Politics of Economic Decline: Economic Management and Political Behaviour in Britain since 1964*, Cambridge: Cambridge University Press, 1979), Beer (*Britain Against Itself: The Political Contradictions of Collectivism*, New York: W.W. Norton, 1982), Pollard (*The Development of the British Economy 1914–1980*, third edition, London: Edward Arnold, 1983), Gamble (*Britain in Decline: Economic Policy, Political Strategy and the British State*, fourth edition, Basingstoke: Macmillan, 1994), and Hennessy (2006).

31  Gamble, *Britain in Decline*, p. 14.

32  J. Sanderson, "Britain in Decline?" in Cox, Lee and Sanderson, *The Political Economy of Modern Britain*, Cheltenham: Edward Elgar, 1997, pp. 55–58.

33  B. Supple, "British Economic Decline since 1945," in R. Floud and D. McCloskey, *The Economic History of Britain since 1700, Volume 3: 1939–1992*, second edition, Cambridge: Cambridge University Press, 1994, pp. 318–320.

34  A. Gerschenkron, *Economic Backwardness in Historical Perspective*, Cambridge: Harvard University Press, 1962.

35  Interview with Andrew Gamble, University of Sheffield, October 17, 2006.

36  Supple, "British Economic Decline since 1945," p. 326.

37  Cairncross, *The British Economy since 1945*, p. 19.

38  For a more elaborate discussion of the role of the City, see S. Lee, "The City and British Decline," in Cox, Lee and Sanderson, *The Political Economy of Modern Britain*, pp. 206–256.

39  S. Pollard, *The Development of the British Economy*, pp. 274–292.

40  Hall, *Governing the Economy*, pp. 30–32.

41  Cairncross, *The British Economy since 1945*, pp. 19–20.

42  Hall, *Governing the Economy*, pp. 28–30.

43  Interview with Andrew Gamble.

44  See Chapters 2 and 3.

45  For further discussion of industrial policy, see S. Lee, "Industrial Policy and British Decline," in Cox, Lee and Sanderson, *The Political Economy of Modern Britain*, pp. 108–160.

46  For an in-depth analysis of this problem of "overstretch," see S. Blank, "Britain: The Politics of Foreign Economic Policy, the Domestic Economy, and the Problem of Pluralistic Stagnation," *International Organization* 31 (4), Autumn 1977, pp. 673–721.

47  P. Kennedy, *The Rise and Fall of the Great Powers*, New York: Random House, 1989.

48  Discussions with Robert Skidelsky, Washington, DC, March 2007.

49  Clarke, *Hope and Glory*, p. 442.

50  Hall, *Governing the Economy*, pp. 33–34.

51  S. Lee, "British Culture and Economic Decline," in Cox, Lee and Sanderson, *The Political Economy of Modern Britain*, pp. 65–67.

52  Interview with Robin Leigh-Pemberton.

53  D. Kavanagh, "Political Culture," in V. Bogdanor (ed.), *Blackwell Encyclopedia of Political Institutions*, Oxford: Basil Blackwell, 1987, p. 447.

54  Lee, "British Culture and Economic Decline," p. 65.

55  Hall, *Governing the Economy*, p. 34.

56  Lee, "British Culture and Economic Decline," p. 102.

57  Hall, *Governing the Economy*, p. 37.

58  For further discussion, see Hall, *Governing the Economy*, pp. 38–47.

59  Ibid.

60  H. Pemberton, *Policy Learning and British Governance in the 1960s*, London: Palgrave Macmillan, 2004.

61  K. Theakston, "Review of Hugh Pemberton's *Policy Learning*," *Public Administration* 84 (1), 2006, p. 243.

62  Op. cit., pp. 242–244.

63  Cairncross, "Economic Policy and Performance, 1945–1964," pp. 59–60.

64  A. Ringe and N. Rollings, "Responding to Relative Decline: The Creation of the National Economic Development Council," *Economic History Review* 53 (2), 2000, pp. 331–353.

65  Cairncross, *The British Economy since 1945*, p. 140.

66  Thomson, *England in the Twentieth Century*, p. 263.

67  Interview with Samuel Brittan.

68  Cox and Sanderson, "The Political Economy of Britain since 1939," p. 21.

69  Hall, *Governing the Economy*, p. 87.

70  Ibid.

71  Labour Party, "The New Britain," *1964 General Election Manifesto*, London: Labour Party, 1964.

72  Op. cit., p. 5.

73  Interview with Tony Benn, London: Holland Park, October 13, 2006.

74  As quoted by Hall in *Governing the Economy*, pp. 87–88.

75  Cox and Sanderson, "The Political Economy of Britain since 1939," p. 21.

76  Interview with Samuel Brittan.

77  Ibid.

78  Clarke, *Hope and Glory*, p. 300.

79  Cox and Sanderson, "The Political Economy of Britain since 1939," p. 22.

80  Cairncross, *The British Economy since 1945*, p. 172.

81  Clarke, *Hope and Glory*, pp. 309–310.

82  Barbara Castle named her White Paper "In Place of Strife" in homage to Aneurin Bevan's political testament, *In Place of Fear* (1952). Many critics pointed out that it was mainly "in place of incomes policy." (Interview with Ralph Harris, London: House of Lords, October 11, 2006).

83  C. Crouch, *The Politics of Industrial Relations*, London: Fontana Press, 1979, pp. 66–72.

84  Cox and Sanderson, "The Political Economy of Britain since 1939," p. 23.

85  Ibid. and Hall, *Governing the Economy*, p. 88.

86 Interview with Nigel Lawson, London: Marble Arch, September 12, 2006.
87 For a comprehensive study of the Heath government, see S. Ball and A. Seldon (eds.) *The Heath Government 1970–74: A Reappraisal*, London: Longman, 1996.
88 Discussions with Robert Skidelsky, March 2007.
89 Interviews with Cecil Parkinson and Norman Tebbit, London: House of Lords, October 10, 2006.
90 Clarke, *Hope and Glory*, p. 330 and interviews with Geoffrey Howe (London, House of Lords, October 10, 2006), Kenneth Clarke (London, Portcullis House, October 12, 2006), and Norman Tebbit.
91 A. Seldon, "The Heath Government in History," in Ball and Seldon (eds.) *The Heath Government*, p. 6.
92 Green, *Ideologies of Conservatism*, p. 231.
93 Interview with Geoffrey Howe.
94 Cox and Sanderson, "The Political Economy of Britain since 1939," p. 24.
95 J. Ramsden, "The Prime Minister and the making of policy," in Ball and Seldon (eds.) *The Heath Government*, p. 29.
96 Clarke, *Hope and Glory*, p. 331.
97 A. Havighurst, *Britain in Transition: The Twentieth Century*, Chicago: University of Chicago Press, 1985, p. 541. See also Edward Heath, *The Course of My Life: The Autobiography of Edward Heath*, London: Coronet, 1999.
98 Seldon, "The Heath Government in History," pp. 13–15.
99 Interviews with Michael Heseltine (London, September 27, 2006), Geoffrey Howe, Norman Tebbit, Nigel Lawson and Kenneth Clarke.
100 Seldon, "The Heath Government in History," p. 7.
101 Conservative Party, "A Better Tomorrow," *1970 General Election Manifesto*, London: Conservative Party, 1970.
102 Op. cit., pp. 4–5.
103 Ibid.
104 Op. cit., pp. 5–9.
105 D. Butler and G. Butler, *British Political Facts 1900–1994*, seventh edition, New York: St. Martin's Press, 1994, pp. 252–253.
106 *Time Magazine*, "Unexpected Triumph," June 29, 1970.
107 Ibid.
108 Clarke, *Hope and Glory*, p. 448.
109 After only one month in office, the government suffered a serious blow due to the death of Chancellor Ian McLeod, a brilliant mind and political heavyweight in the Conservative Party. He was replaced by a political lightweight, Anthony Barber, "a most ridiculous appointment" according to Kenneth Clarke. This meant that Heath would personally dominate all economic policymaking during his term in office (interview with Kenneth Clarke).
110 J. Ramsden, "The Prime Minister and the making of policy," p. 31.
111 Cox and Sanderson, "The Political Economy of Britain since 1939," p. 25.
112 Interview with Geoffrey Howe.
113 Clarke, *Hope and Glory*, p. 334.
114 Cairncross, "The Heath Government and the British Economy," in Ball and Seldon (eds.) *The Heath Government*, p. 110.
115 Interview with Michael Heseltine.
116 See R. Taylor, "The Heath Government and Industrial Relations: Myth and Reality," in Ball and Seldon (eds.) *The Heath Government*, pp. 161–190.
117 Clarke, *Hope and Glory*, p. 331.
118 Interview with Geoffrey Howe.
119 Cox and Sanderson, "The Political Economy of Britain since 1939," p. 25.
120 Interviews with Geoffrey Howe and Norman Tebbit.
121 Interview with Dennis Skinner, London: House of Commons, October 12, 2006.

122  Clarke, *Hope and Glory*, p. 331.
123  R. Taylor, "The Heath Government, Industrial Policy and the 'New Capitalism'," in Ball and Seldon (eds.) *The Heath Government*, pp. 148–155.
124  The company's debenture holders then were to find out that they did not have the government guarantee of their holding which they had assumed.
125  Cox and Sanderson, "The Political Economy of Britain since 1939," p. 25.
126  Cairncross, *The British Economy since 1945*, p. 189.
127  Taylor, "The Heath Government, Industrial Policy and the 'New Capitalism'," p. 150.
128  Clarke, *Hope and Glory*, p. 332 – Upper Clyde Shipbuilders was at first denied assistance, but after a sit-in strike, the company was reorganized on a basis that allowed work to continue at all four yards involved.
129  J. Young, "The Heath Government and British Entry into the European Community," in Ball and Seldon (eds.) *The Heath Government*, pp. 259–263.
130  H. Young, *This Blessed Plot: Britain and Europe from Churchill to Blair*, London: Macmillan, 1998, pp. 224–230.
131  Cairncross, *The British Economy since 1945*, p. 200.
132  The United States Congress approved a huge tax cut in 1964 and, after the Civil Rights Legislation, government spending was substantially increased to finance Lyndon Johnson's "Great Society." For a more in-depth analysis of the inflationary effects of these policies, see David P. Calleo, *The Bankrupting of America*, New York: Morrow, 1992.
133  Cairncross, *The British Economy since 1945*, p. 190. In the end, price controls were to last much longer, until January 1973.
134  S. Blank, "Britain: The Politics of Foreign Economic Policy, the Domestic Economy, and the Problem of Pluralistic Stagnation," pp. 710–711.
135  Hall, *Governing the Economy*, pp. 90–93.
136  Cairncross, *The British Economy since 1945*, p. 191.
137  Cox and Sanderson, "The Political Economy of Britain since 1939," p. 25.
138  Op. cit., p. 26.
139  Cairncross, *The British Economy since 1945*, p. 191.
140  Interview with Dennis Skinner.
141  Clarke, *Hope and Glory*, p. 334.
142  Cox and Sanderson, "The Political Economy of Britain since 1939," p. 26.
143  Cairncross, "The Heath Government and the British Economy," p. 135.
144  Interview with Tony Benn.
145  Cairncross, *The British Economy since 1945*, p. 191.
146  Interviews with Nigel Lawson, Kenneth Clarke, Norman Tebbit and Geoffrey Howe.
147  Cairncross, "The Heath Government and the British Economy," pp. 117–122.
148  Hall, *Governing the Economy*, pp. 89–90.
149  Cairncross, *The British Economy since 1945*, p. 191.
150  Cox and Sanderson, "The Political Economy of Britain since 1939," p. 27.
151  Interview with Dennis Skinner.
152  R. Taylor, "The Heath Government and Industrial Relations: Myth and Reality," pp. 183–189.
153  Professor Mark Wickham-Jones told the author in an interview at the University of Bristol on September 28, 2006 that the events of 1974 made him decide that he wanted to become a political scientist.
154  Clarke, *Hope and Glory*, p. 338.
155  Interview with Dennis Skinner.
156  Interview with Norman Tebbit.
157  K. Jefferys, *Finest and Darkest Hours: The Decisive Events in British Politics from Churchill to Blair*, London: Atlantic Books, 2002, pp. 180–181.
158  Clarke, *Hope and Glory*, p. 339.

159 Conservative Party, "Firm Action for a Fair Britain," *February 1974 General Election Manifesto*, London: Conservative Party, 1974.

160 Labour Party, "Let Us Work Together – Labour's Way Out of the Crisis," *February 1974 General Election Manifesto*, London: Labour Party, 1974.

161 Ibid.

162 Interview with Tony Benn.

163 Butler and Butler, *British Political Facts*, p. 218.

164 Jefferys, *Finest and Darkest Hours*, p. 181.

165 D. Childs, *Britain since 1945: A Political History*, sixth edition, London: Routledge, 2006, pp. 179–180.

166 T. Liesner, *One Hundred Years of Economic Statistics, 1900–1987*, New York: Facts on File, 1989, Tables UK.2 (p. 23), UK.11 (p. 42), and UK.16 (p. 53).

167 Childs, *Britain since 1945*, p. 180.

168 Labour Party, "Britain will Win with Labour," *October 1974 General Election Manifesto*, London: Labour Party, 1974.

169 Op. cit., p. 4.

170 Conservative Party, "Putting Britain First," *October 1974 General Election Manifesto*, London: Conservative Party, 1974.

171 Op. cit., p. 2.

172 Ibid.

173 Butler and Butler, *British Political Facts*, p. 218.

174 Blank, "Britain: The Politics of Foreign Economic Policy, the Domestic Economy, and the Problem of Pluralistic Stagnation," p. 711.

175 For a comprehensive reassessment of the policies of the Labour governments from 1974–1979, see A. Seldon and K. Hickson (eds.) *New Labour, Old Labour: The Wilson and Callaghan Governments, 1974–79*, London: Routledge, 2004.

176 Interview with Tony Benn.

177 Clarke, *Hope and Glory*, p. 349.

178 Cairncross, *The British Economy since 1945*, pp. 201–206.

179 R. Skidelsky, "The Fall of Keynesianism," in D. Marquand and A. Seldon (eds.), *The Ideas that Shaped Post-War Britain*, London: Fontana Press, 1996, p. 62.

180 C. Hay, "The 'Crisis' of Keynesianism and the Rise of Neo-Liberalism in Britain: An Ideational Institutionalist Approach," in J. Campbell and O. Pedersen (eds.) *The Rise of Neoliberalism and Institutional Analysis*, Princeton: Princeton University Press, 2001, pp. 193–218.

181 Interview with Denis Healey, London: House of Lords, October 12, 2006.

182 D. Healey, *The Time of My Life*, London: Politico's, 2006, p. 377.

183 Healey was to sum up his misgivings about economic forecasts in his November 1976 Treasury statement:

> Like long-term weather forecasts they are better than nothing ... But their origin lies in the extrapolation from a partially known past, through an unknown present, to an unknowable future according to theories about the causal relationships between certain economic variables which are hotly disputed by academic economists, and may in fact change from country to country or from decade to decade.
>
> (Healey, *The Time of My Life*, p. 381)

184 Interview with Dennis Skinner.

185 Interview with Denis Healey.

186 Hay, "The 'Crisis' of Keynesianism and the Rise of Neo-Liberalism in Britain," pp. 211–212.

187 Interviews with Nigel Lawson and Geoffrey Howe.

188 C. Hay, "Narrating Crisis: the discursive construction of the 'Winter of Discontent'," *Sociology* 30 (2), Spring 1996, p. 253.

189 Interview with Neil Kinnock, London: Fielden House, October 10, 2006.
190 P. Hennessy, *The Prime Minister: The Office and its Holders since 1945*, London: Penguin Books, 2000, pp. 331–356.

**5 Margaret Thatcher's triumph (1975–1990): inflation, Hayek, and the overhaul of the British state**

1 F.A. von Hayek, *The Constitution of Liberty*, London: University of Chicago Press, 1978 reprint, pp. 338–339.
2 K. Joseph, "Inflation is Caused by Governments," Speech at Preston, September 5, 1974, online, available at: www.margaretthatcher.org/archive/ displaydocument. asp?docid=110607 (accessed March 7, 2010).
3 M. Thatcher, "Interview," *Sunday Times*, May 3, 1981.
4 N. Lawson, "The British Experiment," *Mais Lecture*, London: City University Business School, June 18, 1984, online, available at: www.margaretthatcher.org/commentary/displaydocument.asp?docid=109504 (accessed June 3, 2009).
5 Hugo Young wrote that the year 1974 "encompassed the long-drawn-out death throes of Edward Heath's Conservative Party." See H. Young, *One of Us*, London: Pan Books, 1991, p. 81.
6 Interview with Norman Tebbit, London: House of Lords, October 10, 2006.
7 Interview with Ralph Harris, London: House of Lords, October 11, 2006.
8 Lord Stockton, *The Times*, October 9, 1975, as quoted in A. Gamble, *The Free Economy and the Strong State: The Politics of Thatcherism*, second edition, London: Macmillan, 1994, p. 93.
9 G. Wheatcroft, *The Strange Death of Tory England*, London: Allen Lane, 2005, pp. 1–20.
10 In Edgbaston, Joseph made a speech mentioning "the high and rising proportion of children... being born to mothers least fitted to bring children into the world." His remarks were instantly denounced at the time, much as Enoch Powell's "rivers of blood" speech had been. See G. Howe, *Conflict of Loyalty*, London: Pan Books, 1995, p. 89.
11 P. Clarke, *Hope and Glory: Britain 1900–2000*, second edition, London: Penguin Books, 2004, p. 360.
12 Hugh Fraser, the third candidate, received 16 votes. Therefore, Thatcher received 49 percent of the vote, Heath 45 percent, and Fraser 6 percent.
13 Gamble, *The Free Economy and the Strong State*, p. 91.
14 Howe, *Conflict of Loyalty*, p. 93.
15 E.H.H. Green, *Ideologies of Conservatism*, Oxford: Oxford University Press, 2004, pp. 236–237.
16 Julian Critchley, a veteran Tory MP, called the election a "peasants' revolt," stating that "the party did not vote for Margaret, they voted against Ted Heath." See J. Critchley, *Westminster Blues*, London: Future Press, 1986, pp. 121–130.
17 M. Wickham-Jones, "Right Turn: A Revisionist Account of the 1975 Conservative Party Leadership Election," *Twentieth Century British History* 8 (1), 1997, pp. 74–89.
18 N. Tebbit, *Upwardly Mobile*, London: Weidenfield and Nicolson, 1988, p. 142.
19 R. Skidelsky, "The Fall of Keynesianism," in D. Marquand and A. Seldon (eds.) *The Ideas that Shaped Post-war Britain*, London: Fontana Press, 1996, pp. 44–45.
20 J.R. Hicks, "Mr. Keynes and the 'Classics': A Suggested Interpretation," *Econometrica* 5, April 1937, pp. 147–159.
21 See T.W. Hutchinson, *Economics and Economic Policy in Britain 1946–1966*, London: George Allen & Unwin, 1968, pp. 121–122.
22 However, empirical evidence for the existence of the "political business cycle" is nonexistent. Furthermore, if one takes into account the assumption of rational expectations, it becomes incredibly complex to even imagine it.

23 Skidelsky, "The Fall of Keynesianism," p. 54.
24 Interview with Robert Skidelsky, London: House of Lords, October 25, 2006.
25 Ibid.
26 J. Best, "Hollowing out Keynesian Norms: How the Search for a Technical Fix Undermined the Bretton Woods Regime," *Review of International Studies* 30 (3), 2004, pp. 383–404.
27 J. Best, *The Limits of Transparency*, Ithaca: Cornell University Press, 2005, p. 19.
28 See also R.L. Heilbroner, *The Worldly Philosophers: The Lives, Times and Ideas of the Great Economic Thinkers*, revised seventh edition, New York: Simon and Schuster, 1999, pp. 275–277.
29 Best, "Hollowing out Keynesian norms," pp. 387–388.
30 Op. cit., p. 389.
31 Op. cit., p. 390.
32 Op. cit., pp. 390–391.
33 J.M. Keynes, *The General Theory of Employment, Interest and Money*, Amherst, NY: Prometheus Books, 1997, chapter 21, "The Theory of Prices," p. 295.
34 Keynes, *The General Theory*, chapters 2 and 19.
35 Skidelsky, "The Fall of Keynesianism," pp. 54–55.
36 Eddie George, former governor of the Bank of England, in an interview with the author in the City of London (October 11, 2006) pointed out that the "national income machine" – on display at the economics library in Cambridge University – suffered from one serious flaw: it had no supply constraints.
37 See A.W. Phillips, "The Relations between Unemployment and the Rate of Change of Money Wage Rates in the United Kingdom, 1861–1957," *Economica* 25, 1958, pp. 283–299. The Phillips relationship that was found for the UK case, was later confirmed by US data.
38 Skidelsky, "The Fall of Keynesianism," p. 55.
39 Op. cit., p. 56.
40 M. Friedman, "The Role of Monetary Policy," *American Economic Review* 58 (1), March 1968.
41 M. Friedman, *Capitalism and Freedom*, Chicago: University of Chicago Press, 1982, p. vii. See also M. Blyth, "One Ring to Bind Them All: American Power and Neoliberal Capitalism," in S. Steinmo and J. Kopstein (eds.) *Growing Apart: America and Europe in the 21st Century*, Cambridge: Cambridge University Press 2007, pp. 109–135.
42 M. Friedman, "Inflation and Unemployment: the New Dimensions of Politics," in M. Friedman, *Monetarist Economics*, London: Institute of Economic Affairs, 1991.
43 H. Johnson, "The Keynesian Revolution and the Monetarist Counter-Revolution," in E. Johnson and H. Johnson (eds.) *The Shadow of Keynes*, Chicago: University of Chicago Press, 1978, pp. 194–195.
44 Blyth, "One Ring to Bind Them All," pp. 118–120.
45 Skidelsky, "The Fall of Keynesianism," p. 55.
46 Blyth, "One Ring to Bind Them All," p. 121.
47 A. Smith, *An Inquiry into the Causes and the Nature of the Wealth of Nations*, Amherst, NY: Prometheus Books, 1991, book V, chapter 1, parts I, II, and III, pp. 468–475.
48 D. Kavanagh, *The Reordering of British Politics: Politics After Thatcher*, Oxford: Oxford University Press, 1997, p. 95.
49 F.A. von Hayek, *The Road to Serfdom*, Fiftieth Anniversary Edition, Chicago: University of Chicago Press, 1994, pp. 63–75.
50 Kavanagh, *The Reordering of British Politics*, p. 92.
51 This was the speech where he used the term "Gestapo".
52 Young, *One of Us*, p. 22.

53  Interview with Ralph Harris, London: House of Lords, October 11, 2006.
54  For a history of the Mont Pelerin Society, see R.M. Hartwell, *A History of the Mont Pelerin Society*, Indianapolis: Liberty Fund, 1995.
55  Interview with Ralph Harris.
56  Kavanagh, *The Reordering of British Politics*, p. 93.
57  Hayek, *The Constitution of Liberty*, pp. 324–340.
58  Op. cit., p. 337.
59  J. Ranelagh, *Thatcher's People: An Insider's Account of the Politics, the Power, and the Personalities*, London: HarperCollins, 1991, p. ix.
60  Kavanagh, *The Reordering of British Politics*, p. 90.
61  Interview with Ralph Harris.
62  Howe, *Conflict of Loyalty*, p. 86.
63  Joseph, "Inflation is Caused by Governments".
64  Kavanagh, *The Reordering of British Politics*, pp. 102–103.
65  Interview with Ralph Harris.
66  Kavanagh, *The Reordering of British Politics*, p. 97.
67  N. Lawson, *The View from No. 11: Memoirs of a Tory Radical*, London: Corgi Books, 1993, p. 8.
68  For an analysis of why Heath's policies failed, see Chapter 4.
69  Gamble, *The Free Economy and the Strong State*, pp. 92–93.
70  The term "wet" was English public school slang for someone judged to be weak, feeble or "soppy." It was used both as a noun and an adjective: "wets" espoused "wet" policies, i.e. increased public spending and incomes policy. The term's adoption was followed by creation of the "dries" – those who opposed the "wets," and supported "dry" policies, such as reducing public spending, cutting taxes, keeping down inflation, lowering interest rates, tightly controlling the money supply, and reducing the regulatory power of the state.
71  Young, *One of Us*, pp. 100–106. Edward Heath's role as a backbencher in the House of Commons from 1974 onwards was described as "the long sulk".
72  D. Butler and D. Kavanagh, *The British General Election of 1979*, London: Macmillan Press, 1980, pp. 78–79.
73  Howe, *Conflict of Loyalty*, p. 101.
74  For an excellent analysis of the 1976 IMF episode in Britain, see S. Ludlam, "The Gnomes of Washington," *Political Studies* 40 (4), December 1992, pp. 713–727.
75  Interview with Geoffrey Howe, London: House of Lords, October 10, 2006.
76  Interview with Nigel Lawson, London: Marble Arch, September 12, 2006.
77  Gamble, *The Free Economy and the Strong State*, p. 99.
78  E.H.H. Green, *Thatcher*, London: Hodder Arnold, 2006, p. 65.
79  Op. cit., pp. 100–101.
80  Interview with Andrew Gamble, University of Sheffield, October 17, 2006.
81  Young, *One of Us*, pp. 114–117.
82  Gamble, *The Free Economy and the Strong State*, p. 102.
83  Interview with Geoffrey Howe.
84  Howe, *Conflict of Loyalty*, p. 104.
85  Young, *One of Us*, p. 116.
86  Howe, *Conflict of Loyalty*, p. 104.
87  Young, *One of Us*, p. 115.
88  Gamble, *The Free Economy and the Strong State*, p. 102.
89  Young, *One of Us*, p. 116.
90  Green, *Thatcher*, pp. 115–117.
91  Interview with Geoffrey Howe.
92  Larry Lamb, then editor of *The Sun*, immortalized that winter in Britain as the "Winter of Discontent".
93  Clarke, *Hope and Glory*, p. 356.

94  R. Taylor, "The Trade Union 'Problem' in British Politics," in B. Pimlott and C. Cook (eds.) *Trade Unions in British Politics*, London: Longman, 1982, p. 207.
95  D. Childs, *Britain since 1945: A Political History*, sixth edition, London: Routledge, 2006, p. 204.
96  Interview with Dennis Skinner, London: House of Commons, October 12, 2006.
97  Interview with Denis Healey, London: House of Lords, October 12, 2006.
98  What many union members engaged in at the time was called "wildcatting," i.e. strikes without the approval of the officials of their union.
99  D. Marsh, *The New Politics of British Trade Unionism: Union Power and the Thatcher Legacy*, London: Macmillan, 1992, p. 62.
100 Clarke, *Hope and Glory*, p. 356.
101 C. Hay, "Narrating Crisis: The Discursive Construction of the 'Winter of Discontent'," *Sociology* 30 (2), Spring 1996, pp. 253–277.
102 Op. cit., p. 269.
103 As quoted in BBC News, *Crisis? What Crisis?* London: BBC, September 12, 2000 online, available at: news.bbc.co.uk/2/hi/ uk_news/politics/921524.stm (accessed June 4, 2007).
104 Hay, "Narrating Crisis," p. 271.
105 Ibid.
106 In 1979, unemployment in Britain was 4.9 percent, compared to 5.8 percent in the United States, 5.9 percent in France and 7.6 percent in Italy (source: OECD).
107 Hay, "Narrating Crisis," p. 255.
108 Gamble, *The Free Economy and the Strong State*, p. 103.
109 Ibid.
110 D. Butler and G. Butler, *British Political Facts, 1900–1994*, seventh edition, New York: St. Martin's Press, 1994, p. 255.
111 Ibid.
112 Social Democratic and Labour Party (Northern Ireland).
113 Childs, *Britain since 1945*, p. 208.
114 P. Joyce, *Politico's Guide to UK General Elections 1832–2001*, London: Politico's, 2004, p. 341.
115 Conservative Party, "Conservative Manifesto, 1979," *1979 General Election Manifesto*, London: Conservative Party, 1979.
116 Op. cit., pp. 3–4.
117 Op. cit., pp. 5–6.
118 Op. cit., pp. 7–9.
119 Gamble, *The Free Economy and the Strong State*, p. 102.
120 Conservative Party, "Conservative Manifesto, 1979," p. 13.
121 Discussions with Robert Skidelsky, March 2007.
122 Labour Party, "The Labour Way is the Better Way," *1979 General Election Manifesto*, London: Labour Party, 1979.
123 Op. cit., p. 4.
124 Op. cit., p. 7.
125 This poster was to haunt the Tories later on in 1983, when unemployment was three times as high.
126 Childs, *Britain since 1945*, p. 209.
127 Butler and Butler, *British Political Facts, 1900–1994*, p. 498.
128 Butler and Kavanagh, *The British General Election of 1979*, p. 340.
129 Joyce, *Politico's Guide to UK General Elections 1832–2001*, p. 348.
130 Interview with Geoffrey Wheatcroft, Bath, October 22, 2006.
131 J. Campbell, *Margaret Thatcher, Volume Two: The Iron Lady*, London: Jonathan Cape, 2003, p. 1.
132 Young, *One of Us*, pp. ix–xii.
133 Clarke, *Hope and Glory*, p. 369.

134 Butler and Butler, *British Political Facts, 1900–1994*, pp. 255–256.
135 Ibid.
136 Clarke, *Hope and Glory*, p. 372.
137 Interview with Nigel Lawson.
138 Howe, *Conflict of Loyalty*, pp. 161–164.
139 As quoted in Nigel Lawson, *The View from No. 11*, p. 68.
140 Interview with Geoffrey Howe.
141 Clarke, *Hope and Glory*, p. 370.
142 Interview with Geoffrey Howe.
143 A. Cairncross, *The British Economy since 1945*, second edition, Oxford: Blackwell Publishers, 1995, pp. 236–244.
144 Gamble, *The Free Economy and the Strong State*, pp. 108–115.
145 Howe, *Conflict of Loyalty*, pp. 153–154.
146 Clarke, *Hope and Glory*, p. 371.
147 Cairncross, *The British Economy since 1945*, p. 244.
148 Interview with John Eatwell, Cambridge: Queen's College, October 18, 2006.
149 Interview with Geoffrey Howe.
150 Cairncross, *The British Economy since 1945*, p. 245.
151 Clarke, *Hope and Glory*, p. 372.
152 Kavanagh, *The Reordering of British Politics*, p. 126.
153 Quango is an acronym (variously spelt out as quasi non-governmental organization, quasi-autonomous non-governmental organization, and quasi-autonomous national government organization) used notably in Britain, Ireland, and Australia to label colloquially an organization to which government has devolved power. In Britain the official term is "non-departmental public body" or NDPB.
154 Gamble, *The Free Economy and the Strong State*, p. 109.
155 Interview with Nigel Lawson.
156 Lawson, *The View From No. 11*, p. 41.
157 Cairncross, *The British Economy since 1945*, p. 238.
158 There clearly was a knock on effect throughout the whole economy of a de facto non-accommodating stance coming from an open capital account.
159 Clarke, *Hope and Glory*, p. 381.
160 Cairncross, *The British Economy since 1945*, p. 269.
161 Clarke, *Hope and Glory*, p. 382.
162 Gamble, *The Free Economy and the Strong State*, p. 112.
163 E.H.H. Green has noted that in 1978, opinion polls showed that 78 percent of the British electorate felt that trade unions had too much power and that trade union leaders were the most powerful figures in the country. This would fall to 17 percent in 1990, when Thatcher left office (Green, *Thatcher*, p. 123).
164 Clarke, *Hope and Glory*, p. 369.
165 Gamble, *The Free Economy and the Strong State*, p. 112.
166 Childs, *Britain since 1945*, p. 219.
167 Interview with Michael Heseltine, London, September 27, 2006.
168 Interview with Cecil Parkinson, London: House of Lords, October 11, 2006.
169 Childs, *Britain since 1945*, p. 219.
170 N. Tebbit, *Upwardly Mobile*, London: Futura, 1991, p. 233.
171 Clarke, *Hope and Glory*, p. 369.
172 OECD, *Historical Statistics*, Paris: OECD, 2001.
173 Clarke, *Hope and Glory*, p. 376.
174 Childs, *Britain since 1945*, pp. 220–221.
175 First, there was the "Gang of Three" – i.e. David Owen, Shirley Williams, and William Rodgers – who rallied the social democratic wing of the Labour Party, leading to an actual split. After his stint with the European Commission, Roy Jenkins joined them to make the "Gang of Four." Jenkins was later elected leader of the Social Democratic Party.

176  Butler and Butler, *British Political Facts, 1900–1994*, p. 256.

177  However, many Conservatives have pointed out economic recovery got underway in early 1982, and that the Conservatives would have won the 1983 election without it. It probably did have an effect on the relatively poor performance of the SDP, compared to Labour. If it wasn't for the Falklands, the SDP might have been the main opposition party after 1983. (Discussions with Robert Skidelsky, Washington, DC, March 2007.)

178  Clarke, *Hope and Glory*, p. 375.

179  M. Thatcher, "Speech to Conservative Rally at Cheltenham," *Margaret Thatcher Foundation*, July 3, 1982, online, available at: www. margaretthatcher.org/speeches/ displaydocument.asp?docid=104989 (accessed June 4, 2007).

180  US President George W. Bush did this remarkably well in 2003 when he focused the US national debate away from the economy towards the potential threat of Saddam Hussein's Iraq.

181  Butler and Butler, *British Political Facts, 1900–1994*, p. 256.

182  Clarke, *Hope and Glory*, p. 372.

183  Cairncross, *The British Economy since 1945*, p. 246.

184  Measured as total government spending divided by GDP.

185  D. Butler and D. Kavanagh, *The British General Election of 1983*, New York: St. Martin's Press, 1984, p. 43.

186  Conservative Party, "The Challenge of Our Times," *1983 General Election Manifesto*, London: Conservative Party, 1983.

187  Op. cit., p. 1.

188  Op. cit., pp. 3–4.

189  Op. cit., pp. 4–5.

190  Op. cit., pp. 5–6.

191  D. Butler, *British General Elections since 1945*, second edition, Oxford: Blackwell, 1995, p. 38.

192  As cited in D. Healey, *The Time of My Life*, London: Politico's, 2006, p. 500.

193  Labour Party, "The New Hope for Britain," *1983 General Election Manifesto*, London: Labour Party, 1983.

194  Op. cit., p. 4.

195  Op. cit., pp. 6–8.

196  SDP–Liberal Alliance, "Working Together for Britain," *1983 General Election Manifesto*, London: SDP-Liberal Alliance, 1983.

197  Op. cit., pp. 4–5.

198  Butler and Kavanagh, *The British General Election of 1983*, p. 104.

199  Butler and Butler, *British Political Facts, 1900–1994*, p. 498.

200  Childs, *Britain since 1945*, p. 231.

201  Butler and Kavanagh, *The British General Election of 1983*, p. 13.

202  Clarke, *Hope and Glory*, p. 449.

203  Butler and Kavanagh, *The British General Election of 1983*, p. 294.

204  It was the first full government with the same prime minister. The Tories had won two elections in 1955 and 1959 after having served a full term, but during both occasions a different Prime Minister started the new term.

205  Interview with Cecil Parkinson.

206  Ibid.

207  Cecil Parkinson was forced to resign in October 1983 to avoid a sex scandal, and was replaced by Tebbit. In the same reshuffle, Tom King replaced Tebbit at Employment, and Nicholas Ridley replaced King at Transport.

208  Cairncross, *The British Economy since 1945*, pp. 258–259.

209  Interview with Ralph Harris.

210  Childs, *Britain since 1945*, p. 236.

211  Lawson, *The View from No. 11*, p. 148.

212 P. Routledge, *Scargill: The Unauthorized Biography*, London: Harper Collins, 1994, p. 129.
213 Clarke, *Hope and Glory*, p. 378.
214 Interview with Dennis Skinner.
215 Childs, *Britain since 1945*, p. 238.
216 Ibid.
217 Clarke, *Hope and Glory*, p. 378. Of course, the NUM lost half of its membership after most of the industry closed down.
218 Lawson, *The View from No. 11*, p. 161.
219 Clarke, *Hope and Glory*, p. 379.
220 Gamble, *The Free Economy and the Strong State*, p. 126.
221 Ibid.
222 Childs, *Britain since 1945*, p. 244.
223 Ibid.
224 Clarke, *Hope and Glory*, p. 382.
225 Interview with Cecil Parkinson.
226 Gamble, *The Free Economy and the Strong State*, p. 125.
227 Cairncross, *The British Economy since 1945*, p. 270.
228 Ibid.
229 Interview with Nigel Lawson and Clarke, *Hope and Glory*, p. 382.
230 Interview with Cecil Parkinson.
231 Clarke, *Hope and Glory*, pp. 382–83.
232 Campbell, *Margaret Thatcher, Volume Two: The Iron Lady*, pp. 241–244.
233 Op. cit., p. 244.
234 Ibid.
235 S. Hogg, "How the Big Bang made a City Boom," *The Independent*, October 20, 2006.
236 There were some major battles that could have brought the government down, including the resignation of Michael Heseltine during the Westland affair, the miners' strike, and the abolition of the Greater London Council.
237 Butler, *British General Elections since 1945*, p. 39.
238 Clarke, *Hope and Glory*, p. 449.
239 Op. cit., p. 393.
240 Butler, *British General Elections since 1945*, p. 41.
241 Interview with Michael Heseltine.
242 Ibid.
243 By 1990–1991 individual taxpayers paid £27 billion less than at 1978–1979 rates; more than half of this remission went to the 4 million taxpayers currently earning over £20,000 a year, with the remainder divided among the other 22 million taxpayers. More generally, by 1989 the managing director of any medium-sized firm could expect to earn over £50,000 a year, a rise of well over a third in ten years, after allowing for inflation; and taxpayers in this range benefited from reduced income taxes to the tune of £9,000 a year (source: Clarke, *Hope and Glory*, p. 395).
244 Interview with Nigel Lawson.
245 See, for example, P. Pierson, *Dismantling the Welfare State?*, Cambridge: Cambridge University Press, 1994.
246 M. Brewer, A. Goodman, J. Shaw and L. Sibieta, "Poverty and Inequality in Britain: 2006," *Institute for Fiscal Studies*, Commentary no. 101, 2006.
247 Interviews with Nigel Lawson, Geoffrey Howe, and Cecil Parkinson.

## 6 Thatcherism's flaws and Tony Blair's consolidation (1987–2005): from the Lawson boom to New Labour's "New Britain"

1 J. Major, *The Autobiography*, London: Harper Collins, 1999, p. 401.
2 Interview with Anthony Giddens, London: London School of Economics, October 31, 2006.

3 Brown made that comment during a speech at an economic seminar on September 27, 1994 in London (source: M. White, "The Gift of Tired Tongues," *The Guardian*, September 30, 1994).

4 T. Blair, "The Third Way," *Fabian Society Pamphlet*, London: Fabian Society, 1998.

5 Interview with Neil Kinnock, London: Fielden House, October 11, 2006.

6 P. Clarke, *Hope and Glory: Britain 1900–2000*, London: Penguin Books, 2004, pp. 445–449.

7 Interview with John Eatwell, Cambridge: Queen's College, October 18, 2006.

8 Interview with Neil Kinnock.

9 Interview with Tony Benn, London: Holland Park, October 13, 2006.

10 Interview with Denis Healey, London: House of Lords, October 12, 2006.

11 J. Cronin, *New Labour's Pasts: The Labour Party and its Discontents*, Harlow: Pearson Education, 2004, p. 246.

12 B. Jones and D. Kavanagh, *British Politics Today*, seventh edition, Manchester: Manchester University Press, 2003, p. 43.

13 Interview with Dennis Skinner, London: House of Commons, October 12, 2006.

14 Interview with Neil Kinnock.

15 Cronin, *New Labour's Pasts*, p. 263.

16 Interview with Neil Kinnock.

17 Cronin, *New Labour's Pasts*, pp. 255–258.

18 P. Jenkins, *Mrs. Thatcher's Revolution: The Ending of the Socialist Era*, Cambridge: Harvard University Press, 1988, pp. 246–250.

19 Cronin, *New Labour's Pasts*, p. 258.

20 Op. cit., p. 261.

21 Interview with Neil Kinnock.

22 Cronin, *New Labour's Pasts*, p. 275.

23 Interview with John Eatwell.

24 Clarke, *Hope and Glory*, p. 449.

25 Cronin, *New Labour's Pasts*, p. 286.

26 D. Macintyre, *Mandelson and the Making of New Labour*, London: Harper Collins, 1999, p. 174.

27 Cronin, *New Labour's Pasts*, p. 291.

28 François Mitterrand's 1983 U-turn de facto ended the idea of Keynesian demand management in one country. Of course, one of the main reasons why Mitterrand's reflation did not work was that both the United Kingdom and the United States had abolished controls and were deflating.

29 Cronin, *New Labour's Pasts*, pp. 293–294.

30 Op. cit., p. 295.

31 Interviews with Neil Kinnock and John Eatwell.

32 Cronin, *New Labour's Pasts*, p. 295.

33 Ibid.

34 Interview with Neil Kinnock.

35 Cronin, *New Labour's Pasts*, p. 350.

36 Jacques Delors, "Speech for the Trades Union Congress," September 1988, as quoted in *Europe and the TUC*, online, formerly available at: www.ukwatch.net/article/europe_and_the_tuc (accessed February 14, 2007). As at May 2010, the gist can be found at http://hansard.millbanksystems.com/lords/1993/jul/22/european-communities-amendment-act-1993.

37 This episode also neatly coincides with Labour's review of NATO policy: not quite embracing nuclear weapons, but dropping the proposed budget and unilateral withdrawal clauses.

38 For a thorough account of this episode in Labour Party history, see R. Holden, *The Making of New Labour's European Policy*, New York: Palgrave, 2002.

39  Cronin, *New Labour's Pasts*, p. 295.
40  Op. cit., p. 312.
41  Interview with Tony Benn.
42  Cronin, *New Labour's Pasts*, p. 314.
43  Labour Party, *Report of the Labour Party Annual Conference*, London: Labour Party, 1990, p. 75.
44  N. Lawson, *The View from No. 11: Memoirs of a Tory Radical*, London: Corgi Books, 1993, p. 746.
45  See table 6.1.
46  A. Cairncross, *The British Economy since 1945*, Oxford: Blackwell Publishers, 1995, p. 277.
47  Op. cit., pp. 277–278.
48  Op. cit., p. 278.
49  Ibid.
50  The Lawson boom was qualitatively different from the classic boom-bust pattern in the British economy. Due to the drastic changes in the country's political economy under Thatcher – the growing importance of services (especially finance), the fall in manufacturing, the increasing amounts of household debt, and the flattening out of the lower-end wages – the recession hit people much more directly than the earlier "stops."
51  In the 1980–1982 recession, manufacturing employment fell from 7.4 million to 5.4 million jobs, a reduction of 2 million or 27 percent of the 1979 manufacturing labor force. (J. Wells, "Uneven Development and De-industrialisation in the UK since 1979," in F. Green (ed.), *The Restructuring of the UK Economy*, Hemel Hempstead: Harvester Wheatsheaf, 1989, p. 25.)
52  D. Coates, "The New Political Economy of Postwar Britain," in C. Hay (ed.), *British Politics Today*, Cambridge: Polity Press, 2002, p. 161.
53  Op. cit., p. 168.
54  Ibid.
55  M. Brewer, A. Goodman, J. Shaw and L. Sibieta, "Poverty and Inequality in Britain: 2006," *The Institute for Fiscal Studies*, Commentary no. 101, 2006, p. 24.
56  Coates, "The New Political Economy of Postwar Britain," p. 168.
57  D. Butler and G. Butler, *British Political Facts, 1900–1994*, seventh edition, New York: St Martin's Press, 1994, p. 258.
58  D. Butler and D. Kavanagh, *The British General Election of 1992*, London: Macmillan, 1992.
59  Conservative Party, "The Best Future for Britain," *1992 General Election Manifesto*, London: Conservative Party, 1992.
60  Op. cit., pp. 14–15.
61  Op. cit., p. 18.
62  Labour Party, "It's Time to Get Britain Working Again," *1992 General Election Manifesto*, London: Labour Party, 1992.
63  Op. cit., p. 1.
64  Op. cit., pp. 4–5.
65  Op. cit., p. 5.
66  Op. cit., p. 7.
67  Clarke, *Hope and Glory*, p. 406.
68  D. Butler, *British General Elections since 1945*, second edition, Oxford: Blackwell, 1995, p. 43.
69  Butler and Kavanagh, *The British General Election of 1992*, p. 148.
70  Cronin, *New Labour's Pasts*, p. 324.
71  Ibid.
72  Clarke, *Hope and Glory*, p. 406.
73  Butler and Kavanagh, *The British General Election of 1992*, p. 126.

74  Butler and Butler, *British Political Facts, 1900–1994*, p. 498.

75  Cronin, *New Labour's Pasts*, p. 325.

76  Clarke, *Hope and Glory*, p. 450.

77  Op. cit., p. 406.

78  Ibid.

79  One factor was that Labour constituencies, often located in declining parts of the country, were shrinking and thus, pending the drawing of new boundaries, over-represented in Parliament. Conversely, with a larger share of the national vote than in 1987, the Tories found their majority cut from 100 to 21.

80  Interview with Michael Heseltine, London, September 27, 2006.

81  Interview with Kenneth Clarke, London: Portcullis House, October 12, 2006.

82  Interview with Neil Kinnock.

83  Cronin, *New Labour's Pasts*, p. 334.

84  Clarke, *Hope and Glory*, p. 410.

85  Cronin, *New Labour's Pasts*, pp. 343–348.

86  Interview with Andrew Smith, London: Portcullis House, October 11, 2006.

87  Interview with Dennis Skinner.

88  Interview with Tony Benn.

89  Interview with Neil Kinnock.

90  W. Keegan, *The Prudence of Mr. Gordon Brown*, Chichester: Wiley Publishers, 2004, p. 124.

91  J. Rentoul, *Tony Blair: Prime Minister*, London: Little, Brown, 2001, p. 218.

92  Cronin, *New Labour's Pasts*, p. 380.

93  P. Gould, *The Unfinished Revolution: How the Modernisers Saved the Labour Party*, London: Little, Brown, 1998, pp. 216–218.

94  Rentoul, *Tony Blair: Prime Minister*, p. 248.

95  Cronin, *New Labour's Pasts*, p. 382.

96  The original version of Clause IV was drafted by Sidney Webb in November 1917, and adopted by the Party in 1918 (source: interview with Peter Hennessy, London: Mile End Road, November 1, 2006).

97  T. Blair, "Socialism," *Fabian Society Pamphlet*, 1994, available in P. Richards (ed.), *Tony Blair: In His Own Words*, London: Politico's, 2004, pp. 81–88.

98  For a discussion of this debate, see Cronin, *New Labour's Pasts*, pp. 383–388.

99  In many ways, this is a contradiction (see next endnote).

100  Cronin, *New Labour's Pasts*, p. 401. However, given the fast rise in income inequality, the "median person" in British society was becoming relatively poorer over time.

101  A. Giddens, *Beyond Left and Right: The Future of Radical Politics*, Cambridge: Polity Press, 1994.

102  Op. cit., pp. 4–7. Giddens explains that "manufactured risk" is a result of human intervention into the conditions of social life and into nature. The uncertainties (and opportunities) it creates are largely new. They cannot be dealt with by age-old remedies; but neither do they respond to the Enlightenment prescription of more knowledge, more control. Put more accurately, the sorts of reactions they might evoke today are often as much about *damage control* and *repair* as about an endless process of increasing mastery.

103  Interview with Anthony Giddens.

104  Ibid.

105  Ibid.

106  Cronin, *New Labour's Pasts*, p. 427.

107  A. Giddens, *The Third Way*, Cambridge: Polity Press, 1998, p. 62; All this was also part of the modernization of the Democratic Party in the United States, and the idea of "reinventing government" by people like Robert Reich and Ira Magaziner.

108 A. Giddens, "Introduction," in A. Giddens (ed.), *The Global Third Way Debate*, Cambridge: Polity Press, 2001, p. 6.

109 Cronin, *New Labour's Pasts*, p. 427.

110 T. Blair, "The Stakeholder Society," *Fabian Review*, London: Fabian Society, February 1996.

111 W. Hutton, *The State We're In*, London: Jonathan Cape, 1995.

112 Cronin, *New Labour's Pasts*, pp. 395–396.

113 A. Shonfield, *Modern Capitalism: The Changing Balance of Public and Private Power*, Oxford: Oxford University Press, 1965.

114 Interview with Will Hutton, London: The Work Foundation, October 19, 2006.

115 Cronin, *New Labour's Pasts*, p. 396.

116 W. Hutton, "The Stakeholder Society," in A. Seldon and D. Marquand (eds.), *The Ideas that Shaped Post-War Britain*, London: Fontana Press, 1996, p. 299.

117 Op. cit., p. 300.

118 See Chapters 3 and 4.

119 Cronin, *New Labour's Pasts*, p. 396.

120 Ibid.

121 Blair, "The Stakeholder Society".

122 Keegan, *The Prudence of Mr. Gordon Brown*, preface, pp. ix–x.

123 G. Brown, "New Policies for the Global Economy," *Speech to the Labour Party Conference about the Treasury under Labour*, Brighton, June 25, 1995.

124 Interview with Kenneth Clarke.

125 T. Blair, *New Britain: My Vision of a Young Country*, London: Harper Collins, 1996.

126 Op. cit., pp. 107–117.

127 Interview with Andrew Smith.

128 Discussions with Robert Skidelsky, Washington, DC, March 2007.

129 M. Kenny and M.J. Smith, "(Mis)understanding Blair," *The Political Quarterly* 68 (3), 1997, p. 221.

130 Cronin, *New Labour's Pasts*, p. 430.

131 Op. cit., p. 353.

132 See R. Heffernan, *New Labour and Thatcherism: Political Change in Britain*, New York: Palgrave, 2001 and C. Hay, *The Political Economy of New Labour: Labouring under False Pretences?* Manchester: Manchester University Press, 1999.

133 J. Gray, "Blair's Project in Retrospect," *International Affairs* 80 (1), 2004, p. 42.

134 Ibid. One famous author who actively promotes this "technological determinism" is Thomas Friedman. See especially his book, T. Friedman, *The World Is Flat: A Brief History of the Twenty-First Century*, New York: Farrar, Strauss and Giroux, 2005.

135 Rentoul, *Tony Blair: Prime Minister*, pp. 276–277.

136 Butler and Kavanagh referred to those five Major years as "The Longest Parliament" in their authoritative assessment of the British General Election of 1997.

137 OECD, *Economic Outlook* No. 80, Paris: OECD, 2006, Annex Tables, online, available at: www.oecd.org/document/61/0,2340,en_2649_201185_2483901_1_1_1_1,00. html (accessed March 12, 2007).

138 Interview with Michael Heseltine.

139 BBC News, "In Quotes: Blair's Leadership." London: BBC, May 11, 2007, online, available at: news.bbc.co.uk/2/hi/uk_news/politics/3750847.stm (accessed March 13, 2007).

140 Interview with Geoffrey Wheatcroft, Bath, October 22, 2006.

141 Brown would continue to do so once in power. For example, even during his Labour Party conference speech in Manchester in 2006, he stated that Labour "inherited a Britain of economic instability, unemployment and chronic underinvestment in public services" in 1997, implying that the Tories left them with an economy in crisis. Gordon Brown, "Speech to the Labour Party Conference," Labour Party,

Manchester, 2006, as quoted by BBC News, online, available at: http://news.bbc.co.uk/1/hi/uk_politics/5378312.stm (accessed May 13, 2010).

142 Conservative Party, "You Can Only Be Sure with the Conservatives," *1997 General Election Manifesto*, London: Conservative Party, 1997.

143 Op. cit., p. 1.

144 Op. cit., p. 5.

145 Op. cit., p. 17.

146 Op. cit, p. 21.

147 Op. cit, pp. 39–40.

148 Labour Party, "New Labour because Britain Deserves Better," *1997 General Election Manifesto*, London: Labour Party, 1997.

149 Op. cit., p. 5.

150 Op. cit., p. 19.

151 Op. cit., p. 34.

152 Cronin, *New Labour's Pasts*, pp. 404–405.

153 Op. cit, p. 404.

154 D. Butler and D. Kavanagh, *The British General Election of 1997*, London: Macmillan, 1997, p. 109.

155 Macintyre, *Mandelson and the Making of New Labour*, pp. 372–376.

156 Butler and Kavanagh, *The British General Election of 1997*, p. 156.

157 Op. cit., p. 111.

158 Interview with Kenneth Clarke.

159 Clarke, *Hope and Glory*, p. 450.

160 Interview with Andrew Smith.

161 Cronin, *New Labour's Pasts*, p. 408.

162 G. Wheatcroft, "The Tragedy of Tony Blair," *The Atlantic Monthly* 294, June 2004, p. 59.

163 For a good analysis on how the Swedes organize it, see G. Esping-Andersen, *Politics against Markets: the Social Democratic Road to Power*, Princeton: Princeton University Press, 1985. Brown's "welfare to work" is based on "recommodifying labor" to make a non-market agent (i.e. disabled, unemployed, disaffected youth) into a market agent. The Swedish system was based upon improving the skills and mobility of already engaged labor market actors.

164 For a detailed analysis of Brown's decision, and the central influence of his economic adviser Ed Balls, see Keegan, *The Prudence of Mr. Gordon Brown*, pp. 151–197.

165 P. Stephens, "Chapter 9: The Treasury under Labour," in A. Seldon (ed.), *The Blair Effect: The Blair Government 1997–2001*, London: Little, Brown, 2001, p. 190.

166 Interview with Eddie George, City of London, October 11, 2006.

167 Stephens, "The Treasury under Labour," p. 190.

168 Op. cit., p. 191.

169 P. Riddell, *The Unfulfilled Prime Minister*, London: Politico's, 2005, p. 75.

170 Ibid.

171 Interview with Norman Lamont, London: Green Park, November 1, 2005.

172 Keegan, *The Prudence of Mr. Gordon Brown*, p. 237.

173 Stephens, "The Treasury under Labour," p. 191.

174 Riddell, *The Unfulfilled Prime Minister*, p. 77.

175 Again, one could argue that the "welfare to work" program was hardly an innovation. The ideas go back to Ronald Reagan's early years in making benefits conditional on accepting a job. What New Labour did – as well as the Clinton Democrats – was to give actual teeth to these programs.

176 Stephens, "The Treasury under Labour," pp. 197–198.

177 Keegan, *The Prudence of Mr. Gordon Brown*, p. 250.

178  D. Smith, "The Treasury and Economic Policy," in A. Seldon and D. Kavanagh (eds.), *The Blair Effect: 2001–2005*, Cambridge: Cambridge University Press, 2005, pp. 179–180.

179  Also, it is doubtful that in a world of open capital flows, paying back some debt will cause interest rates to fall. This was part of a more global phenomenon due to the fall in US rates. Many countries that increased debt still had falling rates.

180  Interview with Neil Kinnock.

181  G. Owen, "Chapter 10: Industry," in A. Seldon (ed.), *The Blair Effect: 1997–2001*, p. 209.

182  Despite Britain's apparent economic success during the last ten years, the economy still lags in one crucial measure: labor productivity. Part of the explanation is the rather radical deindustrialization that has gone on in Britain over the last three decades: manufacturing employment has drastically fallen, and most of the jobs in that sector were highly "productive," in that they produced a lot of output per man hour.

183  Owen, "Chapter 10: Industry," p. 209.

184  Keegan, *The Prudence of Mr. Gordon Brown*, p. 250.

185  P. Riddell, "Europe," in A. Seldon and D. Kavanagh (eds.), *The Blair Effect: 2001–2005*, p. 362.

186  For a brilliant analysis of Britain's relations with Europe since World War II, see H. Young, *This Blessed Plot*, London: Macmillan, 1998.

187  J. Glover, "The Five Tests," *The Guardian*, September 29, 2000, online, available at: www.guardian.co.uk/EMU/Story/0,2763,375315,00.html (accessed July 20, 2005).

188  Riddell, "Europe," p. 366.

189  Stephens, "The Treasury under Labour," p. 194.

190  HM Treasury, *Spending Review 2000*, Cmd. 8047, London, 2000.

191  Stephens, "The Treasury under Labour," p. 195.

192  For an analysis of the 2001 general election, see D. Butler and D. Kavanagh, *British General Election of 2001*, London: Palgrave Macmillan, 2001.

193  Clarke, *Hope and Glory*, p. 450.

194  A. Seldon, "The Second Blair Government: The Verdict," in Seldon and Kavanagh (eds.), *The Blair Effect: 2001–2005*, p. 418.

195  Smith, "The Treasury and Economic Policy," p. 178.

196  Interview with Norman Lamont.

197  Smith, "The Treasury and Economic Policy," p. 179.

198  Other factors are the political clout of the City of London, and the influence of the conservative press barons.

199  Interview with Nigel Lawson, London: Marble Arch, September 12, 2006.

200  Riddell, *The Unfulfilled Prime Minister*, pp. 106–108.

201  Seldon, "The Second Blair Government: The Verdict," p. 419.

202  Op. cit., p. 421.

203  Gray, "Blair's Project in Retrospect," p. 39.

204  Op. cit., p. 43.

205  Ibid.

206  Smith, "The Treasury and Economic Policy," p. 177.

207  D. Smith, "Brown to Break Record," *Sunday Times*, June 6, 2004.

208  Discussions with Mark Blyth, Baltimore, March 2007.

209  *The Economist*, "Britannia Redux: A Special Report on Britain," London, February 3, 2007.

210  Paul Krugman puts it as follows: "productivity isn't everything, but in the long run it's almost everything." (quoted in Smith, "The Treasury and Economic Policy," p. 175).

211  Smith, "The Treasury and Economic Policy," p. 177.

212  See R. Vaitilingham, *The UK's productivity gap: What research tells us and what we need to find out*, London: Economic and Social Research Council, September 2004.

213 Keegan, *The Prudence of Mr. Gordon Brown*, p. 333.
214 Smith, "The Treasury and Economic Policy," p. 181. Of course, these job losses in the manufacturing sector were replaced by service sector jobs, which were not always better paid or more "productive" from an economic point of view.
215 OECD, *Economic Outlook*, No. 80, Paris: OECD, 2006, Annex Tables.
216 P. Toynbee, "We Will Never Abolish Child Poverty in a Society Shaped Like This One," *The Guardian*, July 7, 2006, online, available at: www.guardian.co.uk/commentisfree/2006/jul/07/comment.labour (accessed July 14, 2010).
217 P. Wilby, "Thatcherism's Final Triumph," *Prospect*, October 2006, p. 29.
218 Ibid.
219 Ibid.
220 Brewer et al., "Poverty and Inequality in Britain: 2006," p. 24.
221 Op. cit., pp. 19–20.
222 BBC News, "UK is Accused of Failing Children," London: BBC, February 14, 2007, online, available at: news.bbc.co.uk/2/hi/uk_news/6359363.stm (accessed February 14, 2007).
223 S. Boseley, "British Children: Poor, at Greater Risk, and More Insecure," *The Guardian*, February 14, 2007, online, available at: www.guardian.co.uk/society/2007/feb/14/childrensservices.politics (accessed July 14, 2010).
224 T. Blair, "Labour Party Conference Speech," Blackpool, 1996.

**7 Conclusion: made in Britain**

1 S. Skowronek, *The Politics that Presidents Make: Leadership from John Adams to George Bush*, Cambridge: Harvard University Press, 1993.
2 Interview with Ralph Harris, London: House of Lords, October 11, 2006.
3 Skowronek, *The Politics that Presidents Make*.
4 C. Hay, "Crisis and the Structural Transformation of the State: Interrogating the Process of Change," *British Journal of Politics and International Relations* 1 (3), October 1999, pp. 317–344.
5 See, for example, A. Flibbert, "The Road to Baghdad: Ideas and Intellectuals in Explanations of the Iraq War," *Security Studies* 15 (2), April–June 2006, pp. 310–552.
6 See also Z. Brzezinski, "Terrorized by 'War on Terror': How a Three-Word Mantra Has Undermined America," *The Washington Post*, March 25, 2007, p. B01.
7 See, for example, M. Blyth and R. Katz, "From Catch-all Politics to Cartelisation: The Political Economy of the Cartel Party," *West European Politics* 28 (1), January 2005, pp. 33–60.
8 Interview with Richard Stern, Washington, DC: FIAS, World Bank Group, April 5, 2007.
9 See R.B. Hall, "The Discursive Demolition of the Asian Development Model," *International Studies Quarterly* 47, 2003, pp. 71–99; and also R. Wade, "From 'Miracle' to 'Cronyism': Explaining the Great Asian Slump," *Cambridge Journal of Economics* 22, 1998, pp. 693–706.
10 For an example on water, see K. Conca, *Governing Water: Contentious Transnational Politics and Global Institution Building*, Cambridge: MIT Press, 2005.

**Postscript: Gordon Brown, the "Great Recession," and the future of neoliberalism**

1 John Major was succeeded as Conservative Party leader in 1997 by William Hague. In 2001, Hague resigned and was replaced by Iain Duncan Smith, who was in turn ousted in 2003 in favor of Michael Howard. In 2005, Howard resigned and David Cameron took over at the helm of the party.

2  G. Baker, "Europe's Global Role," *Second Annual CUSE Conference at the Brookings Institution*, Washington, DC, May 11, 2005, online, available at: www.brookings.edu/fp/cuse/events/2annualconf20050511.pdf, pp. 54–55 (accessed February 1, 2010).

3  C. Grant, "Europe's Global Role," *Second Annual CUSE Conference at the Brookings Institution*, Washington, DC, May 11, 2005, online, available at: www.brookings.edu/fp/cuse/events/2annualconf20050511.pdf, p. 55 (accessed February 1, 2010).

4  M. Wolf, "Why the Sky may not be Falling," *Financial Times*, London, September 4, 2008.

5  M. Wolf, "Re: Your two op-eds in the *FT* this week," email, September 5, 2008.

6  J. Williamson, "What Washington Means by Policy Reform," in J. Williamson (ed.) *Latin American Adjustment: How Much Has Happened?*, Washington, DC: Peterson Institute for International Economics, 1990, chapter 2, online, available at: www.iie.com/publications/papers/print.cfm?doc=pub&ResearchID =486 (accessed June 4, 2009).

7  T. Friedman, *The Lexus and the Olive Tree*, New York: Anchor Books, 2000, pp. 101–111.

8  Ibid.

9  Op. cit., p. 103.

10  The OECD called the British economy the "new Goldilocks economy" in September 2006, suggesting that it should replace the United States as the example to follow for the rest of the OECD members. Source: A. Seager, "UK Hailed as the New Goldilocks Economy," *The Guardian*, September 6, 2006, online, available at: www.guardian.co.uk/business/2006/sep/06/politics.economicpolicy (accessed March 12, 2010).

11  T. Judt, "The Future of Decadent Europe," *The Brookings Institution*, US-Europe Analysis Series, February 2006, online, available at: www.brookings.edu/fp/cuse/analysis/judt20060210.pdf (accessed June 3, 2007).

12  M. Wolf, "The British Election that Both Sides Deserve to Lose," *Financial Times*, March 12, 2010.

13  When Angela Merkel was elected Chancellor, there were a lot of comparisons between her and Margaret Thatcher, soon (wrongly, it would turn out) earning her the nickname "iron chancellor" or "Germany's iron lady." Nicolas Sarkozy went out of his way to praise Blair and Brown's economic policies, mentioning that the UK economy was the envy of many French. (See, for example, J. Keaten, "Blair, Sarkozy Show Unity over Europe," *Washington Post*, May 11, 2007, online, available at: www.washingtonpost.com/wp-dyn/content/article/2007/05/11/AR2007051101584.html (accessed March 13, 2010)).

14  N.N. Taleb, *The Black Swan: The Impact of the Highly Improbable*, New York: Random House, 2007.

15  Remember from Chapter 2 that Knight made a distinction between "risk" (randomness with knowable probabilities) and "uncertainty" (randomness with unknowable probabilities).

16  R. Skidelsky, *Keynes: The Return of the Master*, London: Allen Lane, 2009, p. 4.

17  Op. cit., pp. 4–5.

18  IMF, *World Economic Outlook – Sustaining the Recovery*, Washington, DC: IMF, October 2009, p. 169.

19  An overview of the causes of the financial crises was given by the author during a presentation at the SAIS Bologna Center. See M. Matthijs, "Macroeconomic Imbalances, Neoliberal Ideas, and the Global Financial Crisis: Lessons and Policy Implications," *Johns Hopkins SAIS Bologna Center Lecture Series*, October 15, 2009.

20  For example, in the US, the subprime share of mortgage originations (as a percentage of total originations) went from below 8 percent in 2003, to 18.5 percent in 2004, and 20 percent in both 2005 and 2006 (source: Mortgage Bankers' Association; see M. Matthijs, "Macroeconomic Imbalances.").

21  BBC News, "Buffett Warns on Investment 'Time Bomb'," London: BBC, March 4, 2003, online, available at: news.bbc.co.uk/2/hi/2817995.stm (accessed March 14, 2010).

22 For an overview, see B. Eichengreen, "The Blind Men and the Elephant," *Issues in Economic Policy*, The Brookings Institution, January 2006, online, available at: www.brookings.edu/views/papers/200601_iiep_eichengreen.pdf (accessed June 3, 2009).

23 Skidelsky, *Keynes: The Return of the Master*, pp. 22–27.

24 Ibid.

25 Op. cit., p. 28.

26 To be fair, there were a lot of economists that did see it coming. For an overview, see James K. Galbraith, "Who Are These Economists, Anyway?" *The NEA Higher Education Journal*, Fall 2009, pp. 85–97.

27 Yet the UK's recession has not been more severe than that of other high-income countries. As noted by Alistair Darling in his speech on the pre-Budget report, the cumulative contraction in the recession, up to the third quarter of 2009, has been 3.2 percent in the US, 5.6 percent in Germany, 5.9 percent in Italy, and 7.7 percent in Japan (source: M. Wolf, "How to Share the Losses: The Dismal Choice Facing Britain," *Financial Times*, December 16, 2009).

28 Economist Intelligence Unit, *UK Country Report: February 2010*, London: EIU, February 2010.

29 Wolf, "The British Election that both sides deserve to lose.".

30 IMF, *State of Public Finances: Cross Country Fiscal Monitor*, Washington, DC: IMF, November 2009, p. 18.

31 Economist Intelligence Unit, *UK Country Report, February 2010*, p. 18.

32 Institute for Fiscal Studies, "The IFS Green Budget," London: IFS, February 2010, online, available at: www.ifs.org.uk/publications/4732 (accessed March 12, 2010).

33 Wolf, "How to Share the Losses: The Dismal Choice Facing Britain" .

34 Ibid.

35 A. Darling, "Chancellor of the Exchequer's Budget Statement," HM Treasury, April 22, 2009, online, available at: www.hm-treasury.gov.uk/bud_bud09_ speech.htm (accessed March 5, 2010).

36 Economist Intelligence Unit, *UK Country Report: July 2009*, London: EIU, July 2009.

37 A. Turner, *Mansion House Speech*, London: Financial Services Authority, September 22, 2009, online, available at: www.fsa.gov.uk/pages/Library/Communication/Speeches/2009/0922_at.shtml (accessed March 5, 2010).

38 Ibid.

39 The Tobin Tax is a proposal for an international tax on currency transactions floated by the economist James Tobin in the 1970s, but was never implemented.

40 Keynes also made the distinction between risk and uncertainty. See Skidelsky, *Keynes: The Return of the Master*, pp. 83–88 and p. 193.

41 A. Sparrow and L. Elliott, "Alistair Darling Backs Brown's Tobin Tax Despite Cold Shoulder from the US," *The Guardian*, November 8, 2009, online, available at: www.guardian.co.uk/business/2009/nov/08/darling-brown-tobin-tax-obama (accessed March 5, 2010).

42 Blyth, M., "Re: tobin tax," email, March 8, 2010.

43 Ibid.

44 This is particularly striking, since most people in both US and UK would patently deny that they are "ideological" in any sense.

45 O. Blanchard, G. Dell'Ariccia and P. Mauro, "Rethinking Macroeconomic Policy," IMF Staff Position Note, SPN/10/03, Washington, DC: IMF, February 12, 2010, online, available at: www.imf.org/external/pubs/ft/spn/2010/spn1003.pdf (accessed March 5, 2010).

46 See Chapter 3.

47 J. Jennings, "Introduction: Raymond Aron and the Fate of French Liberalism," *European Journal of Political Theory* 2 (4), 2003, p. 369.

48 Judt, "The Future of Decadent Europe".

49 Ibid.

# Bibliography

Addison, P., *The Road to 1945: British Politics and the Second World War*, London: Cape, 1975.

Alt, J., *The Politics of Economic Decline: Economic Management and Political Behaviour in Britain since 1964*, Cambridge: Cambridge University Press, 1979.

Attlee, C., *Campaign Speech to the Labour Party Conference*, Scarborough, October 1951. Labour Party archives are available at the British Library on microfilm, via: www.bl.uk/services/document/microrescoll/rescola.html.

Baker, G., "Europe's Global Role," *Second Annual CUSE Conference at the Brookings Institution*, Washington, DC, May 11, 2005, online, available at: www.brookings.edu/fp/cuse/events/2annualconf20050511.pdf, pp. 54–55 (accessed February 1, 2010).

Ball, S. and A. Seldon (eds.), *The Heath Government 1970–74: A Reappraisal*, London: Longman, 1996.

BBC News, "Crisis? What Crisis?" London: British Broadcasting Corporation, September 12, 2000 online, available at: news.bbc.co.uk/2/hi/uk_news/ politics/921524.stm (accessed June 4, 2007).

BBC News, "Buffett Warns on Investment 'Time Bomb'," London: British Broadcasting Corporation, March 4, 2003, online, available at: news.bbc.co.uk/2/hi/ 2817995.stm (accessed March 14, 2010).

BBC News, "UK is Accused of Failing Children," London: British Broadcasting Corporation, February 14, 2007, online, available at: http://news.bbc.co.uk/1/hi/ uk/6359363.stm (accessed February 14, 2010).

BBC News, "In Quotes: Blair's Leadership." London: British Broadcasting Corporation, May 11, 2007, online, available at: news.bbc.co.uk/2/hi/uk_news/ politics/3750847.stm (accessed March 13, 2007).

Beer, S., *British Politics in the Collectivist Age*, New York: Knopf, 1965.

Beer, S., *Britain Against Itself: The Political Contradictions of Collectivism*, New York: W.W. Norton, 1982.

Berman, S., *The Social Democratic Moment: Ideas and Politics in the Making of Interwar Europe*, Cambridge: Harvard University Press, 1998.

Berman, S., "Review: Ideas, Norms, and Culture in Political Analysis," *Comparative Politics* 33 (2), January 2001, pp. 231–250.

Berman, S., *The Primacy of Politics: Social Democracy and the Making of Europe's Twentieth Century*, New York: Cambridge University Press, 2006.

Best, J., "Hollowing out Keynesian norms: how the search for a technical fix undermined the Bretton Woods regime," *Review of International Studies* 30 (3), 2004, pp. 383–404.

Best, J., *The Limits of Transparency: Ambiguity and the History of International Finance*, Ithaca: Cornell University Press, 2005.

Bevan, A., *In Place of Fear*, London: William Heinemann Ltd, 1952.

Beveridge, W.H., *Social Insurance and Allied Services*, London: HMSO, November 1942, Cmd. 6404.

Blair, T., "Socialism," *Fabian Society Pamphlet*, 1994, in P. Richards (ed.), *Tony Blair: In His Own Words*, London: Politico's, 2004, pp. 81–88.

Blair, T., "The Stakeholder Society," *Fabian Review*, London: Fabian Society, February 1996.

Blair, T., *New Britain: My Vision of a Young Country*, London: Harper Collins, 1996.

Blair, T., "Labour Party Conference Speech," Blackpool, 1996. Labour Party archives are available at the British Library on microfilm, via: www.bl.uk/services/document/microrescoll/rescola.html.

Blair, T., "The Third Way," *Fabian Society Pamphlet*, London: Fabian Society, 1998.

Blair, T., interview before the 2005 general election as quoted in P. Riddell, "Impressions of the Election," *Political Quarterly* 76 (3), July 2005, p. 320.

Blanchard, O., G.Dell'Ariccia and P. Mauro, "Rethinking Macroeconomic Policy," IMF Staff Position Note, SPN/10/03, Washington, DC: IMF, February 12, 2010, online, available at: www.imf.org/external/pubs/ft/spn/2010/spn1003.pdf (accessed March 5, 2010)

Blank, S., "Britain: The Politics of Foreign Economic Policy, the Domestic Economy, and the Problem of Pluralistic Stagnation," *International Organization* 31 (4), Autumn 1977, pp. 673–721.

Blyth, M., "'Any More Bright Ideas?' The Ideational Turn of Comparative Political Economy," *Comparative Politics* 29 (2), January 1997, pp. 229–250.

Blyth, M., "The Transformation of the Swedish Model: Economic Ideas, Distributional Conflict, and Institutional Change," *World Politics* 54 (1), October 2001, pp. 1–26.

Blyth, M., *Great Transformations: Economic Ideas and Institutional Change in the Twentieth Century*, Cambridge: Cambridge University Press, 2002.

Blyth, M., "Great Punctuations: Prediction, Randomness, and the Evolution of Comparative Political Science," *American Political Science Review* 100 (4), November 2006, pp. 493–498.

Blyth, M., "One Ring to Bind Them All: American Power and Neoliberal Capitalism," in S. Steinmo and J. Kopstein (eds.), *Growing Apart: America and Europe in the 21st Century*, Cambridge: Cambridge University Press, 2007, pp. 109–135.

Blyth, M., "When Liberalisms Change: Comparing the Politics of Deflations and Inflations," in R. Roy, A. Denzau and T. Willett (eds.), *Neoliberalism: National and Regional Experiments with Global Ideas*, New York: Routledge, 2007, pp. 71–96.

Blyth, M., "Re: tobin tax," email, March 8, 2010.

Blyth, M. and R. Katz, "From Catch-all Politics to Cartelisation: The Political Economy of the Cartel Party," *West European Politics* 28 (1), January 2005, pp. 33–60.

Bogdanor, V. and R. Skidelsky (eds.), *The Age of Affluence, 1951–1964*, London: Macmillan, 1970.

Booth, A., *The British Economy in the Twentieth Century*, Basingstoke: Palgrave, 2001.

Boseley, S., "British children: poor, at greater risk, and more insecure," *The Guardian*, February 14, 2007, online, available at: www.guardian.co.uk/frontpage/story/0,,2012513,00.html (accessed May 10, 2007).

Brewer, M., Goodman, A., Shaw, J. and L. Sibieta, "Poverty and Inequality in Britain: 2006," *Commentary no. 101*, London: Institute for Fiscal Studies, 2006.

Brinkley, D., "Dean Acheson and the 'Special Relationship': The West Point Speech of December 1962," *Historical Journal* 33 (3), September 1990, pp. 599–608.

Brittan, S., *Steering the Economy*, Harmondsworth: Penguin, 1970.

Broadberry, S.N., *The British Economy Between the Wars: A Macroeconomic Survey*, Oxford: Basil Blackwell, 1986.

Broadberry, S.N., "The Emergence of Mass Unemployment: Explaining Macroeconomic Trends in Britain during the Trans-World War I Period," *Economic History Review* 43, 1990, pp. 271–282.

Broadberry, S.N., "Employment and Unemployment," in R. Floud and D. McCloskey (eds.), *The Economic History of Britain since 1700, Volume 3, 1939–1992*, second edition, Cambridge: Cambridge University Press, 1994, pp. 195–220.

Broadberry, S.N. and N.F.R. Crafts (eds.), *Britain in the International Economy 1870–1939*, Cambridge: Cambridge University Press, 1992.

Brown, G., "New Policies for the Global Economy," *Speech to the Labour Party Conference about the Treasury under Labour*, June 25, 1995. Labour Party archives are available at the British Library on microfilm, via: www.bl.uk/ services/document/ microrescoll/rescola.html.

Brown, G., "Speech to the Labour Party Conference," Labour Party, Manchester, 2006, as quoted by BBC News, online, available at: http://news.bbc.co.uk/1/hi/ uk_politics/5378312.stm (accessed May 13, 2010).

Brzezinski, Z., "Terrorized by 'War on Terror': How a Three-Word Mantra Has Undermined America," *The Washington Post*, March 25, 2007, p. B01.

Buller, J., "Britain's Relations with the European Union in Historical Perspective," in D. Marsh et al., *Postwar British Politics in Perspective*, Cambridge: Polity Press, 1999, pp. 107–124.

Büthe, T., "Taking Temporarily Seriously: Modeling History and the Use of Narratives as Evidence," *American Political Science Review* 96 (3), September 2002, pp. 481–493.

Butler, D., *British General Elections since 1945*, second edition, Oxford: Blackwell, 1995.

Butler, D. and G. Butler, *British Political Facts, 1900–1994*, seventh edition, New York: St. Martin's Press, 1994.

Butler, D. and D. Kavanagh, *The British General Election of 1979*, London: Macmillan Press, 1980.

Butler, D. and D. Kavanagh, *The British General Election of 1983*, New York: St. Martin's Press, 1984.

Butler, D. and D. Kavanagh, *The British General Election of 1992*, London: Macmillan, 1992.

Butler, D. and D. Kavanagh, *The British General Election of 1997*, London: Macmillan, 1997.

Butler, D. and D. Kavanagh, *British General Election of 2001*, London: Palgrave Macmillan, 2001.

Cairncross, A., *The British Economy since 1945*, second edition, Oxford: Blackwell Publishers, 1995.

Cairncross, A., "Economic Policy and Performance, 1945–1964," in R. Floud and D. McCloskey (eds.), *The Economic History of Britain Since 1700, Volume 3, 1939–1992*, second edition, Cambridge: Cambridge University Press, 1994, pp. 32–66.

Cairncross, A., "Economic Policy and Performance, 1964–1990," in R. Floud and D. McCloskey (eds.), *The Economic History of Britain since 1700, Volume 3, 1939–1992*, second edition, Cambridge: Cambridge University Press, 1994, pp. 67–94.

Cairncross, A., "The Heath Government and the British Economy," in Ball and Seldon (eds.) *The Heath Government*, pp. 107–138.

Calder, A., *The People's War: Britain 1939–1945*, London: Pimlico, 1969.

Callaghan, J., *Speech at the Labour Party Conference,* Brighton, September 28, 1976. Labour Party archives are available at the British Library on microfilm, via: www.bl. uk/services/document/microrescoll/rescola.html.

Calleo, D., *Britain's Future*, New York: Horizon Press, 1968.

Calleo, D., *The Imperious Economy*, Cambridge: Harvard University Press, 1982.

Calleo, D., *The Bankrupting of America: How the Federal Budget Is Impoverishing the Nation*, New York: Morrow, 1992.

Calleo, D., *Rethinking Europe's Future*, Princeton: Princeton University Press, 2001.

Campbell, J., *Margaret Thatcher, Volume Two: The Iron Lady*, London: Jonathan Cape, 2003.

Campbell, J., *Institutional Change and Globalization*, Princeton: Princeton University Press, 2004.

Castle, B., *In Place of Strife: Policy for Industrial Relations*, Command 3888, London: Stationery Office Books, 1969.

"Cato," *Guilty Men*, London: Penguin Books Ltd., 1990.

Childs, D., *Britain since 1945: A Political History*, sixth edition, London: Routledge, 2006.

Clarke, P., "The Keynesian Consensus and its Enemies," in Marquand and Seldon (eds.), *The Ideas that Shaped Postwar Britain*, 1996, pp. 67–87.

Clarke, P., *A Question of Leadership: From Gladstone to Blair*, second edition, London: Penguin Books, 1999.

Clarke, P., *Hope and Glory: Britain 1900–2000*, second edition, London: Penguin Books, 2004.

Coates, D., "The New Political Economy of Postwar Britain," in C. Hay (ed.), *British Politics Today*, Cambridge: Polity Press, 2002, pp. 157–184.

Combined Committee on Non-Food Consumption, *The Impact of the War on Civilian Consumption in the United Kingdom, the United States and Canada*, London: HMSO, 1945.

Conca, K., *Governing Water: Contentious Transnational Politics and Global Institution Building*, Cambridge: MIT Press, 2005.

Conservative Party, "Mr. Churchill's Declaration of Policy to the Electors," *1945 General Election Manifesto*, London: Conservative Party, 1945.

Conservative Party, "A Better Tomorrow," *1970 General Election Manifesto*, London: Conservative Party, 1970.

Conservative Party, "Firm Action for a Fair Britain," *February 1974 General Election Manifesto*, London: Conservative Party, 1974.

Conservative Party, "Putting Britain First," *October 1974 General Election Manifesto*, London: Conservative Party, 1974.

Conservative Party, "Conservative Manifesto, 1979," *1979 General Election Manifesto*, London: Conservative Party, 1979.

Conservative Party, "The Challenge of Our Times," *1983 General Election Manifesto*. London: Conservative Party, 1983.

Conservative Party, "The Best Future for Britain," *1992 General Election Manifesto*, London: Conservative Party, 1992.

Conservative Party, "You Can Only Be Sure with the Conservatives," *1997 General Election Manifesto*, London: Conservative Party, 1997.

Cox, A., S. Lee, and J. Sanderson, *The Political Economy of Modern Britain*, Cheltenham: Edward Elgar, 1997.

Cox, A. and J. Sanderson, "The Political Economy of Britain since 1939," in Cox, Lee, and Sanderson, *The Political Economy of Modern Britain*, pp. 1–44.

Critchley, J., *Westminster Blues*, London: Future Press, 1986.

Cronin, J., *New Labour's Pasts: The Labour Party and its Discontents*, Harlow: Pearson Education, 2004.

Crouch, C., *The Politics of Industrial Relations*, London: Fontana Press, 1979.

Darling, A., "Chancellor of the Exchequer's Budget Statement," HM Treasury, April 22, 2009, online, available at: www.hm-treasury.gov.uk/bud_bud09_speech.htm (accessed March 5, 2010).

David, P., "Clio and the Economics of QWERTY," *American Economic Review* 75 (2), 1985, pp. 332–337.

Delors, J., "Speech for the Trades Union Congress," September 1988, *Europe and the TUC*, online, formerly available at: www.ukwatch.net/article/europe_and_the_tuc (accessed February 14, 2007). As at May 2010, the gist can be found at http://hansard.millbanksystems.com/lords/1993/jul/22/european-communities-amendment-act-1993.

Economist Intelligence Unit, *UK Country Report: February 2010*, London: EIU, February 2010.

Economist Intelligence Unit, *UK Country Report: July 2009*, London: EIU, July 2009

Eichengreen, B., "Tariffs and Flexible Exchange Rates: The Case of the British General Tariff of 1932," *PhD Dissertation*, New Haven: Yale University, 1979.

Eichengreen, B., "The Blind Men and the Elephant," *Issues in Economic Policy*, The Brookings Institution, January 2006, online, available at: www.brookings.edu/ views/ papers/200601_iiep_eichengreen.pdf (accessed June 3, 2009).

Elbaum, B. and W. Lazonick, "The Decline of the British Economy: An Institutional Perspective," *The Journal of Economic History* 44 (2), June 1984, pp. 567–583.

Esping-Andersen, G., *Politics against Markets: the Social Democratic Road to Power*, Princeton: Princeton University Press, 1985.

Eurostat, *External and Intra-EU Trade*, Brussels: European Commission, 2005.

Eurostat, *Databases*, Brussels: European Commission, 2006, online, available at: www.ec.europa.eu/eurostat (accessed February 6, 2007).

Evans, G. and P. Norris (eds.), *Critical Elections: British Parties and Voters in Long-Term Perspective*, London: Sage Publications, 1999.

Fabian Society, "A History of the Fabian Society," London: Fabian Society, 2009, online, available at: www.fabian-society.org.uk/About/Fabian_History.pdf (accessed January 22, 2009).

Feinstein, C.H., *National Income, Expenditure and Output of the United Kingdom, 1855–1965*, Cambridge: Cambridge University Press, 1972.

Fioretos, K., "The Anatomy of Autonomy: Interdependence, Domestic Balances of Power, and European Integration," *Review of International Studies* 23, 1997, pp. 293–320.

Fioretos, K., "The Domestic Sources of Multilateral Preferences: Varieties of Capitalism in the European Community," in P. Hall and D. Soskice (eds.), *Varieties of Capitalism*, Oxford: Oxford University Press, 2001, pp. 213–244.

Flibbert, A., "The Road to Baghdad: Ideas and Intellectuals in Explanations of the Iraq War," *Security Studies* 15 (2), April–June 2006, pp. 310–552.

Freeden, M., "The Stranger at the Feast: Ideology and Public Policy in Twentieth Century Britain," *Twentieth Century British History* 1 (1), 1990, pp. 9–34.

Frieden, J., "Invested Interests: The Politics of National Economic Policies in a World of Global Finance," *International Organization* 45 (4), Autumn 1991, pp. 425–451.

Frieden, J., *Global Capitalism: Its Fall and Rise in the Twentieth Century*, New York: W.W. Norton and Company, 2006.

Frieden, J. and R. Rogowski, "The Impact of the International Economy on National Policies: An Analytical Overview," in Keohane and Milner (eds.), *Internationalization and Domestic Politics*, 1996, pp. 25–47.

Friedman, M., "The Role of Monetary Policy," *American Economic Review* 58 (1), March 1968, pp. 1–17.

Friedman, M., *Monetary History of the United States, 1867–1960*, Princeton: Princeton University Press, 1967.

Friedman, M., *Capitalism and Freedom*, Chicago: University of Chicago Press, 1982.

Friedman, M., *Capitalism and Freedom*, Chicago: University of Chicago Press, 40th Anniversary Edition, 2002.

Friedman, M., "Inflation and Unemployment: the New Dimensions of Politics," in M. Friedman, *Monetarist Economics*, London: Institute of Economic Affairs, 1991.

Friedman, M., and Friedman R., *Free to Choose: A Personal Statement*, Houghton Mifflin Harcourt Press, 1980.

Friedman, T., *The Lexus and the Olive Tree*, New York: Anchor Books, 2000.

Friedman, T., *The World Is Flat: A Brief History of the Twenty-First Century*, New York: Farrar, Strauss and Giroux, 2005.

Galbraith, James K., "Who Are These Economists, Anyway?" *The NEA Higher Education Journal*, Fall 2009, pp. 85–97.

Galbraith, John K., *The Affluent Society*, 40th anniversary edition (printed in 1998), New York: Mariner Books, 1958.

Gamble, A., *Britain in Decline: Economic Policy, Political Strategy and the British State*, fourth edition, Basingstoke: Macmillan, 1994.

Gamble, A., *The Free Economy and the Strong State: The Politics of Thatcherism*, second edition, London: Macmillan, 1994.

Gamble, A., "Commentary: The Meaning of the Third Way," in Seldon and Kavanagh (eds.), *The Blair Effect: 2001–2005*, 2005, pp. 430–438.

George, A. and A. Bennett, *Case Studies and Theory Development in the Social Sciences*, Cambridge: MIT Press, 2005.

Gerschenkron, A., *Economic Backwardness in Historical Perspective*, Cambridge: Harvard University Press, 1962.

Giddens, A., *Beyond Left and Right: The Future of Radical Politics*, Cambridge: Polity Press, 1994.

Giddens, A., *The Third Way*, Cambridge: Polity Press, 1998.

Giddens, A., "Introduction," in A. Giddens (ed.), *The Global Third Way Debate*, Cambridge: Polity Press, 2001, pp. 1–15.

Giddens, A., "It's Time to Give the Third Way a Second Chance," *The Independent*, June 28, 2007.

Glover, J., "The Five Tests," *The Guardian*, September 29, 2000, online, available at: www.guardian.co.uk/EMU/Story/0,2763,375315,00.html (accessed July 20, 2005).

Goldstein, J. and R. Keohane (eds.), *Ideas and Foreign Policy: Beliefs, Institutions, and Political Change*, Ithaca: Cornell University Press, 1991.

Gould, P., *The Unfinished Revolution: How the Modernisers Saved the Labour Party*, London: Little, Brown, 1998.

Gourevitch, P., *Politics in Hard Times: Comparative Responses to International Economic Crises*, Ithaca: Cornell University Press, 1986.

Grant, C., "Europe's Global Role," *Second Annual CUSE Conference at the Brookings Institution*, Washington, DC, online, available at: www.brookings.edu/fp/cuse/events/2annualconf20050511.pdf, p. 55 (accessed February 1, 2010).

Gray, J., "Blair's Project in Retrospect," *International Affairs* 80 (1), 2004, pp. 39–48.

Gray, J. (2005), "The World is Round," *The New York Review of Books* 52 (13), August 11, 2005, online, available at: www.nybooks.com/articles/18154 (accessed March 2, 2009).

Green, E.H.H., *Ideologies of Conservatism*, Oxford: Oxford University Press, 2004.

Green, E.H.H., *Thatcher*, London: Hodder Arnold, 2006.

Hall, P., "Policy Innovation and the Structure of the State: The Politics-Administration Nexus in France and Britain," *Annals of the American Academy of Political and Social Science* 466, March 1983, pp. 43–60.

Hall, P., *Governing the Economy: The Politics of State Intervention in Britain and France*, Oxford: Oxford University Press, 1986.

Hall, P. (ed.), *The Political Power of Economic Ideas: Keynesianism across Nations*, Princeton: Princeton University Press, 1989.

Hall, P., "Policy Paradigms, Social Learning and the State: The Case of Economic Policymaking in Britain," *Comparative Politics* 25 (3), April 1993, pp. 275–296.

Hall, P. and D. Soskice, *Varieties of Capitalism: the Institutional Foundations of Comparative Advantage*, Oxford: Oxford University Press, 2001.

Hall, R.B., "The Discursive Demolition of the Asian Development Model," *International Studies Quarterly* 47, 2003, pp. 71–99.

Hall, S. and M. Jacques, *The Politics of Thatcherism*, London: Lawrence and Wishart, 1983.

Harrington, W. and P. Young, *The 1945 Revolution*, London: Davis Poynter, 1978.

Hart, D., "Editor's Introduction," in G.B. Shaw and H.G. Wilshire, *Fabian Essays in Socialism*, New York: Humboldt, 2003.

Hartwell, R.M., *A History of the Mont Pelerin Society*, Indianapolis: Liberty Fund, 1995.

Hatton, T., "Unemployment and the Labour Market," in R. Floud and D. McCloskey, *The Economic History of Britain*, Cambridge: Cambridge University Press, 1994, pp. 359–385.

Havighurst, A., *Britain in Transition: The Twentieth Century*, Chicago: University of Chicago Press, 1985.

Hay, C., "Narrating Crisis: The Discursive Construction of the 'Winter of Discontent'," *Sociology* 30 (2), Spring 1996, pp. 253–277.

Hay, C., "Continuity and Discontinuity in British Political Development," in D. Marsh et al., *Postwar British Politics in Perspective*, Cambridge: Polity Press, 1999, pp. 23–42.

Hay, C., "Crisis and the Structural Transformation of the State: Interrogating the Process of Change," *British Journal of Politics and International Relations* 1 (3), October 1999, pp. 317–344.

Hay, C., *The Political Economy of New Labour: Labouring Under False Pretences?* Manchester: Manchester University Press, 1999.

Hay, C., "The 'Crisis' of Keynesianism and the Rise of Neo-Liberalism in Britain: An Ideational Institutionalist Approach," in J. Campbell and O. Pedersen (eds.), *The Rise of Neoliberalism and Institutional Analysis*, Princeton: Princeton University Press, 2001, pp. 193–218.

Hay, C., "British Politics Today: Towards a New Political Science of British Politics?" in C. Hay (ed.), *British Politics Today*, Cambridge: Polity Press, 2002, pp. 1–13.

Hay, C. and D. Wincott, "Structure, Agency and Historical Institutionalism," *Political Studies* XLVI, 1998, pp. 951–957.

Hayek, F.A. von, *The Road to Serfdom*, London: Routledge, 1944.

Hayek, F.A. von, *The Constitution of Liberty*, Chicago: University of Chicago Press, 1960, paperback edition [1978 reprint].

Hayek, F.A. von, *The Road to Serfdom*, fiftieth anniversary edition, London: Routledge, 1994.

Healey, D., *The Time of My Life*, London: Politico's, 2006.

Heath, E., "A Better Tomorrow," *1970 General Election Manifesto*, London: Conservative Party, 1970.

Heath, E., *Speech to the Conservative Party Conference*, Blackpool, October 1970. Conservative Party archives are available at the British Library on microfilm, via: www.bl.uk/services/document/microrescoll/rescola.html.

Heath, E., *The Course of My Life: The Autobiography of Edward Heath*, London: Coronet, 1999.

Heffernan, R., *New Labour and Thatcherism: Political Change in Britain*, New York: Palgrave, 2001.

Heilbroner, R.L., *The Worldly Philosophers: The Lives, Times and Ideas of the Great Economic Thinkers*, revised seventh edition, New York: Simon and Schuster, 1999.

Hennessy, P., "The Attlee Governments 1945–1951," in P. Hennessy and A. Seldon (eds.), *Ruling Performance: British Governments from Attlee to Thatcher*, Oxford: Blackwell, 1987.

Hennessy, P., *Never Again: Britain 1945–1951*, revised second edition London: Penguin Books, 1992 [2006 reprint].

Hennessy, P., *The Prime Minister: The Office and its Holders since 1945*, London: Penguin Books, 2000.

Hennessy, P., *Having It So Good: Britain in the Fifties*, London: Allen Lane, 2006.

Hicks, J.R., "Mr. Keynes and the 'Classics': A Suggested Interpretation," *Econometrica* 5, April 1937, pp. 147–159.

HM Government, *The White Paper on Employment Policy*, London, May 1944, Cmd. 6527.

HM Treasury, *Spending Review 2000*, Cmd. 8074, London, 2000.

Hobsbawm, E., *Industry and Empire: From 1750 to the Present Day*, New York: The New Press, 1999.

Hoffman, J.D., *The Conservative Party in Opposition, 1945–1951*, London: Macgibbon and Kee, 1964.

Hogg, S., "How the Big Bang Made a City Boom," *The Independent*, October 20, 2006.

Holden, R., *The Making of New Labour's European Policy*, New York: Palgrave, 2002.

Howe, G., *Conflict of Loyalty*, London: Pan Books, 1995.

Howlett, P., "The Wartime Economy, 1939–1945," in R. Floud and D. McCloskey (eds.), *The Economic History of Britain since 1700, Volume 3, 1939–1992*, second edition, Cambridge: Cambridge University Press, 1994, pp. 1–31.

Hutchinson, T.W., *Economics and Economic Policy in Britain 1946–1966*, London: George Allen & Unwin, 1968.

Hutton, W., *The State We're In*, London: Jonathan Cape Ltd, 1995.

Hutton, W., "The Stakeholder Society," in Marquand and Seldon (eds.), *The Ideas that Shaped Postwar Britain*, 1996, pp. 290–308.

IMF, *World Economic Outlook – Sustaining the Recovery*, Washington, DC: IMF, October 2009, p. 169.

IMF, *State of Public Finances: Cross Country Fiscal Monitor*, Washington, DC: IMF, November 2009, p. 18.

Institute for Fiscal Studies, "The IFS Green Budget," London: IFS, February 2010, online, available at: www.ifs.org.uk/publications/4732 (accessed March 12, 2010).

Jabko, N., *Playing the Market: A Political Strategy for Uniting Europe, 1985–2005*, Ithaca: Cornell University Press, 2006.

Jefferys, K., *Finest and Darkest Hours: The Decisive Events in British Politics from Churchill to Blair*, London: Atlantic Books, 2002.

Jenkins, P., *Mrs. Thatcher's Revolution: The Ending of the Socialist Era*, Cambridge: Harvard University Press, 1988.

Jennings, J., "Introduction: Raymond Aron and the Fate of French Liberalism," *European Journal of Political Theory* 2 (4), 2003, p. 369.

Johnson, H., "The Keynesian Revolution and the Monetarist Counter-Revolution," in E. Johnson and H. Johnson (eds.), *The Shadow of Keynes*, Chicago: University of Chicago Press, 1978, pp. 183–202.

Jones, B. and D. Kavanagh, *British Politics Today*, seventh edition, Manchester: Manchester University Press, 2003.

Joseph, K., "Inflation is Caused by Governments," Speech at Preston, September 5, 1974, online, available at: www.margaretthatcher.org/archive/displaydocument. asp?docid= 110607 (accessed March 7, 2010).

Joyce, P., *Politico's Guide to UK General Elections 1832–2001*, London: Politico's, 2004.

Judt, T., *Postwar: A History of Europe Since 1945*, New York: Penguin Press, 2005.

Judt, T., "The Future of Decadent Europe," *The Brookings Institution*, US-Europe Analysis Series, February 2006, online, available at: www.brookings.edu/ fp/cuse/analysis/ judt20060210.pdf (accessed June 3, 2007).

Kavanagh, D., "Political Culture," in V. Bogdanor (ed.), *Blackwell Encyclopedia of Political Institutions*, Oxford: Basil Blackwell, 1987, p. 447.

Kavanagh, D., *The Reordering of British Politics: Politics after Thatcher*, Oxford: Oxford University Press, 1997.

Keaten, J., "Blair, Sarkozy Show Unity over Europe," *Washington Post*, May 11, 2007, online, available at: www.washingtonpost.com/wp-dyn/content/article/2007/05/11/ AR2007051101584.html (accessed March 13, 2010).

Keegan, W., *The Prudence of Mr. Gordon Brown*, Chichester: Wiley Publishers, 2004.

Kennedy, P., *The Rise and Fall of the Great Powers*, New York: Random House, 1989.

Kenny, M. and M.J. Smith, "(Mis)understanding Blair," *The Political Quarterly* 68 (3), 1997, pp. 220–230.

Keohane, R. and H. Milner (eds.), *Internationalization and Domestic Politics*, Cambridge: Cambridge University Press, 1996.

Kerr, P., *Postwar British Politics: From Conflict to Consensus*, London: Routledge, 2001.

Keynes, J.M., *Essays in Persuasion*, New York: W.W. Norton, 1963, p. 312 (the essay, "The End of Laissez-faire," was first published by Keynes in 1926).

Keynes, J.M., *The Economic Consequences of Mr. Churchill*, 1925, reprinted in J.M. Keynes, *Collected Writings Volume 9*, second edition, London: Palgrave, 2000.

Keynes, J.M., *The General Theory of Employment, Interest and Money*, London: Macmillan, 1936.

Keynes, J.M., *The General Theory of Employment, Interest and Money*, Amherst, NY: Prometheus Books, 1997.

King, G., Keohane, R., and S. Verba, *Designing Social Inquiry: Scientific Inference in Qualitative Research*, Princeton: Princeton University Press, 1994.

Knight, F., *Risk, Uncertainty and Profit*, Chicago: University of Chicago Press, 1921.

Koselleck, R., *Critique and Crisis: Enlightenment and the Pathogenesis of Modern Society*, Cambridge: MIT Press, 1988.

Kuczynski, J., *A Short History of Labour Conditions in Great Britain, 1750 to the Present Day*, London: Frederick Muller Ltd, 1946.

Kuhn, T., *The Structure of Scientific Revolutions*, Chicago: University of Chicago Press, third edition, 1996.

Labour Party, "Let Us Face the Future: A Declaration of Labour Policy for the Consideration of the Nation," *1945 General Election Manifesto*, London: Labour Party, 1945.

Labour Party, "The New Britain," *1964 General Election Manifesto*, London: Labour Party, 1964.

Labour Party, "Let Us Work Together – Labour's Way Out of the Crisis," *February 1974 General Election Manifesto*, London: Labour Party, 1974

Labour Party, "Britain will Win with Labour," *October 1974 General Election Manifesto*, London: Labour Party, 1974.

Labour Party, "The Labour Way is the Better Way," *1979 General Election Manifesto*, London: Labour Party, 1979.

Labour Party, "The New Hope for Britain," *1983 General Election Manifesto*, London: Labour Party, 1983.

Labour Party, *Report of the Labour Party Annual Conference*, London: Labour Party, 1990.

Labour Party, "It's Time to Get Britain Working Again," *1992 General Election Manifesto*, London: Labour Party, 1992.

Labour Party, "New Labour because Britain Deserves Better," *1997 General Election Manifesto*, London: Labour Party, 1997.

Landes, D., *The Unbound Prometheus*, Cambridge: Cambridge University Press, 1969.

Lawson, N. "The British Experiment," *Mais Lecture*, London: City University Business School, June 18, 1984, online, available at: www.margaretthatcher.org/ commentary/ displaydocument.asp?docid=109504 (accessed June 3, 2009).

Lawson, N., *The View From No. 11: Memoirs of a Tory Radical*, London: Corgi Books, 1993.

Lee, S., "British Culture and Economic Decline," in Cox, Lee, and Sanderson, *The Political Economy of Modern Britain*, pp. 65–107.

Lee, S., "Industrial Policy and British Decline," in Cox, Lee, and Sanderson, *The Political Economy of Modern Britain*, pp. 108–160.

Lee, S., "The City and British Decline," in Cox, Lee, and Sanderson, *The Political Economy of Modern Britain*, pp. 206–256.

Legro, J., *Rethinking the World: Great Power Strategies and International Order*, Ithaca: Cornell University Press, 2005.

Levi, M., "A Model, a Method, and Map: Rational Choice in Comparative and Historical Analysis," in M. Lichbach and A. Zuckerman (eds.), *Comparative Politics: Rationality, Culture, and Structure*, Cambridge: Cambridge University Press, 1997, pp. 19–41.

Liesner, T., *One Hundred Years of Economic Statistics, 1900–1987*, New York: Facts on File, 1989.

Lowe, R., "The Second World War Consensus and the Foundation of the Welfare State," *Twentieth Century British History* 1 (2), 1990, pp. 152–182.

Ludlam, S., "The Gnomes of Washington," *Political Studies* 40 (4), December 1992, pp. 713–727.

McCarthy, P., "Britain: The Melancholy Pleasure of Decline," in P. McCarthy and E. Jones (eds.), *Disintegration or Transformation? The Crisis of the State in Advanced Industrial Societies*, New York: St. Martin's Press, 1995, pp. 179–197.

Macintyre, D., *Mandelson and the Making of New Labour*, London: HarperCollins, 1999.

Macmillan, H., *The Middle Way*, London: Macmillan, 1938.

Macmillan, H., *Speech at Bedford football ground*, July 20, 1957. Conservative Party archives are available at the British Library on microfilm, via: www.bl.uk/services/document/microrescoll/rescola.html.

McNamara, K., *The Currency of Ideas: Monetary Politics in the European Union*, Ithaca: Cornell University Press, 1999.

Major, J., *The Autobiography*, London: HarperCollins, 1999.

Marquand, D. and A. Seldon (eds.) *The Ideas that Shaped Postwar Britain*, London: Fontana Press, 1996.

Marr, A., *A History of Modern Britain*, London: Macmillan, 2007.

Marsh, D., *The New Politics of British Trade Unionism: Union Power and the Thatcher Legacy*, London: Macmillan, 1992.

Marsh, D. and R. Rhodes (eds.), *Implementing Thatcherite Policies: Audit of an Era*, Buckingham: Open University Press, 1992.

Marsh, D. et al., *Postwar British Politics in Perspective*, Cambridge: Polity Press, 1999.

Marwick, A., *Britain in the Century of Total War*, London: Penguin, 1968.

Matthijs, M., "Macroeconomic Imbalances, Neoliberal Ideas, and the Global Financial Crisis: Lessons and Policy Implications," *Johns Hopkins SAIS Bologna Center Lecture Series*, October 15, 2009.

Middleton, R., *Government versus the Market: The Growth of the Public Sector, Economic Management and British Economic Performance, c. 1890–1979*, Cheltenham: Edward Elgar, 1996.

Middleton, R., *The British Economy since 1945: Engaging with the Debate*, Basingstoke: Macmillan, 2000.

Mill, J.S., "Of the Four Methods of Experimental Inquiry," chapter 8 in J.M. Robson (ed.), *A System of Logic*, Toronto: Toronto University Press, 1973, pp. 388–406.

Mitchell, A., *Election '45: Reflections on the Revolution in Britain*, London: Fabian Society, 1995.

Moe, T., "The Politics of Structural Choice: Toward a Theory of Public Bureaucracy," in O. Williamson (ed.), *Organization Theory: From Chester Barnard to the Present and Beyond*, Oxford: Oxford University Press, 1990, pp. 116–153.

Murphy, M.E., "The Role of the Fabian Society in British Affairs," *Southern Economic Journal* 14 (1), July 1947, pp. 14–23.

Myers, W.K., "A Rationale for Appeasement: A Study of British Efforts to Conciliate Germany in the 1930s," *PhD Dissertation*, Baltimore: Johns Hopkins University, 1972.

Newman, A., "Protecting Privacy in Europe: Administrative Feedbacks and Regional Politics," in S. Meunier and K. McNamara (eds.), *The State of the European Union: European Integration and Institutional Change at Fifty*, Volume 8, Oxford: Oxford University Press, 2007, pp. 123–138.

North, D., *Institutions, Institutional Change and Economic Performance*, Cambridge: Cambridge University Press, 1990.

OECD, *Historical Statistics*, Paris: OECD, 1999.

OECD, *Historical Statistics*, Paris: OECD, 2000.

OECD, *Historical Statistics*, Paris: OECD, 2001.

OECD, *Labour Force Statistics*, Paris: OECD, 2005.

OECD, *Economic Outlook*, No. 80, Paris: OECD, 2006, online, available at: www.oecd. org/document/61/0,2340,en_2649_201185_2483901_1_1_1_1,00.html (accessed March 12, 2007).

Offe, C., *Disorganized Capitalism*, Cambridge: Polity Press, 1985.

Olson, M., *The Logic of Collective Action: Public Goods and the Theory of Groups*, Cambridge: Harvard University Press, 1965.

Orwell, G., *The Road to Wigan Pier*, London: Victor Gollancz Ltd, 1937.

Outhwaite, W. (ed.), *The Blackwell Dictionary of Modern Social Thought*, Malden, MA: Blackwell Publishing, 2003.

Owen, G., "Chapter 10: Industry," in A. Seldon (ed.), *The Blair Effect: The Blair Government 1997–2001*, London: Little, Brown, 2001, pp. 209–26.

Pagano, M. and F. Giavazzi, "The Advantage of Tying One's Hands: EMS Discipline and Central Bank Credibility," *European Economic Review* 32 (5), June 1988, pp. 1055–1075.

Page, S.E., "Path Dependence," *Quarterly Journal of Political Science* 1, 2006, pp. 87–115.

Pemberton, H., *Policy Learning and British Governance in the 1960s*, London: Palgrave Macmillan, 2004.

Persson, T. and G. Tabellini (1992), "Economic Policy, Credibility and Politics," *Centre for Economic Policy Research*, Washington, DC: CEPR, online, available at: www. cepr.org/PUBS/Bulletin/meets/GT&TP.htm (accessed July 1, 2008).

Peters, G., Pierre, J., and D. King, "The Politics of Path Dependency: Political Conflict in Historical Institutionalism," *The Journal of Politics* 67 (4), November 2005, pp. 1275–1300.

Phillips, A.W., "The Relations between Unemployment and the Rate of Change of Money Wage Rates in the United Kingdom, 1861–1957," *Economica* 25, 1958, pp. 283–299.

Pierson, P., *Dismantling the Welfare State? Reagan, Thatcher, and the Politics of Retrenchment*, Cambridge: Cambridge University Press, 1994.

Pierson, P., "Increasing Returns, Path Dependence, and the Study of Politics," *The American Political Science Review* 94 (2), June 2000, pp. 251–267.

Pierson, P., "The Limits of Design: Explaining Institutional Origins and Change," *Governance* 13 (4), October 2000, pp. 475–499.

Pierson, P. and T. Skocpol, "Historical Institutionalism in Contemporary Political Science," in I. Katznelson and K. Thelen (eds.), *Political Science: State of the Discipline*, New York: W.W. Norton, 2002, pp. 693–721.

Pierson, P., *Politics in Time: History, Institutions and Social Analysis*, Princeton: Princeton University Press, 2004.

Pierson, P., "The Study of Policy Development," *The Journal of Policy History* 17 (1), January 2005, pp. 34–51.

Pigou, A.C. "Review of *The Road to Serfdom*," *Economic Journal* 54, 1944, pp. 217–219.

Pimlott, B., "The Myth of Consensus," in L.M. Smith (ed.), *The Making of Britain: Echoes of Greatness*, Basingstoke: Macmillan, 1988, pp. 129–141.

Pollard, S., *The Development of the British Economy 1914–1980*, third edition, London: Edward Arnold, 1983.

Posner, E., "Financial Transformation in the European Union," in S. Meunier and K. McNamara (eds.), *The State of the European Union: European Integration and Institutional Change at Fifty, Volume 8*, Oxford: Oxford University Press, 2007, pp. 139–156.

Pratten, C.F., "The Reasons for the Slow Economic Progress of the British Economy," *Oxford Economic Papers* 24 (2), July 1972, pp. 180–196.

Quandt, W., "The Middle East on the Brink: Prospects for Change in the 21st Century," *The Middle East Journal* 50 (4), Winter 1996, pp. 9–17.

Ramsden, J., "The Prime Minister and the making of policy," in Ball and Seldon (eds.) *The Heath Government*, pp. 21–46.

Ranelagh, J., *Thatcher's People: An Insider's Account of the Politics, the Power, and the Personalities*, London: HarperCollins, 1991.

Rentoul, J., *Tony Blair: Prime Minister*, London: Little, Brown, 2001.

Richter, I., *Political Purpose in Trade Unions*, London: George Allen, 1973.

Riddell, P., "Europe," in Seldon and Kavanagh (eds.), *The Blair Effect: 2001–2005*, Cambridge: Cambridge University Press, 2005, pp. 362–383.

Riddell, P., *The Unfulfilled Prime Minister*, London: Politico's, 2005.

Riddell, P., "Impressions of the Election," *Political Quarterly* 76 (3), July 2005.

Ringe, A. and N. Rollings, "Responding to Relative Decline: The Creation of the National Economic Development Council," *Economic History Review* 53 (2), 2000, pp. 331–353.

Rogowski, R., *Commerce and Coalitions: How Trade Affects Domestic Political Alignments*, Princeton: Princeton University Press, 1989.

Rooth, T., *British Protectionism and the International Economy: Overseas Commercial Policy in the 1930s*, Cambridge: Cambridge University Press, 1992 (paperback edition, 2002).

Routledge, P., *Scargill: The Unauthorized Biography*, London: Harper Collins, 1994.

Salant, W., "The Spread of Keynesian Doctrines and Practices in the United States," in P. Hall (ed.), *The Political Power of Economic Ideas*, Princeton: Princeton University Press, 1989, pp. 27–52.

Sanderson, J., "Britain in Decline?," in A. Cox, S. Lee and J. Sanderson, *The Political Economy of Modern Britain*, Cheltenham: Edward Elgar, 1997, pp. 45–62.

SDP-Liberal Alliance, "Working Together for Britain," *1983 General Election Manifesto*, London: SDP-Liberal Alliance, 1983.

Seabrooke, L., "The Everyday Social Sources of Economic Crises: From 'Great Frustrations' to 'Great Revelations' in Interwar Britain," *International Studies Quarterly* 51 (4), 2007, pp. 795–810.

Seager, A., "UK Hailed as the New Goldilocks Economy," *The Guardian*, September 6, 2006, online, available at: www.guardian.co.uk/business/2006/sep/06/politics. economicpolicy (accessed March 12, 2010).

Seldon, A., "The Heath Government in History," in Ball and Seldon (eds.) *The Heath Government*, pp. 1–19.

Seldon, A., "The Second Blair Government: The Verdict," in Seldon and Kavanagh (eds.), *The Blair Effect: 2001–2005*, pp. 410–429.

Seldon, A. (ed.), *The Blair Effect: The Blair Government 1997–2001*, London: Little, Brown, 2001.

Seldon, A. and K. Hickson (eds.), *New Labour, Old Labour: The Wilson and Callaghan Governments*, London: Routledge, 2004.

Seldon, A. and D. Kavanagh (eds.), *The Blair Effect: 2001–2005*, Cambridge: Cambridge University Press, 2005.

Shonfield, A., *Modern Capitalism: The Changing Balance of Public and Private Power*, Oxford: Oxford University Press, 1965.

Sikkink, K., *Ideas and Institutions: Developmentalism in Brazil and Argentina*, Ithaca: Cornell University Press, 1991.

Sills, D. (ed.), *International Encyclopedia of the Social Sciences*, Volume 3, London: Macmillan, 1968.

Skidelsky, R., "Mrs. Thatcher's Revolution," in D. Calleo and C. Morgenstern (eds.), *Recasting Europe's Economies*, Lanham: University Press of America, 1990, pp. 101–129.

Skidelsky, R., "The Fall of Keynesianism," in Marquand and Seldon (eds.), *The Ideas that Shaped Post-war Britain*, 1996, pp. 41–66.

Skidelsky, R., *John Maynard Keynes, Volume 1: Hopes Betrayed (1883–1920); Volume 2: The Economist as Saviour (1920–1937); Volume 3: Fighting for Britain (1937–1945)*, London: Penguin, 2002.

Skidelsky, R., "Keynes' Legacy," *Lecture at Princeton University*, Princeton, November 2006.

Skidelsky, R., *Keynes: The Return of the Master*, London: Allen Lane, 2009.

Skowronek, S., *The Politics Presidents Make: Leadership from John Adams to George Bush*, Cambridge: Harvard University Press, 1993.

Smith, A., *An Inquiry into the Causes and the Nature of the Wealth of Nations*, Amherst, NY: Prometheus Books, 1991 [1776].

Smith, D., "Brown to Break Record," *Sunday Times*, June 6, 2004.

Smith, D. "The Treasury and Economic Policy," in Seldon and Kavanagh (eds.), *The Blair Effect: 2001–2005*, pp. 159–183.

Sparrow, A. and L. Elliott, "Alistair Darling Backs Brown's Tobin Tax Despite Cold Shoulder from the US," *The Guardian*, November 8, 2009, online, available at: www.guardian.co.uk/business/2009/nov/08/darling-brown-tobin-tax-obama (accessed March 5, 2010).

Stephens, P., "Chapter 9: The Treasury under Labour," in A. Seldon (ed.), *The Blair Effect: The Blair Government 1997–2001*, London: Little, Brown, 2001, pp. 185–208.

Strange, S., *Sterling and British Policy*, London: Oxford University Press, 1971.

Supple, B., "British Economic Decline since 1945," in R. Floud and D. McCloskey (eds.), *The Economic History of Britain since 1700, Volume 3, 1939–1992*, second edition, Cambridge: Cambridge University Press, 1994, pp. 318–346.

Taleb, N.N., *The Black Swan: The Impact of the Highly Improbable*, New York: Random House, 2007.

Taylor, A.J.P., *English History 1914–1945*, The Oxford History of England Part XV, New York: Oxford University Press, 1965.

Taylor, R., "The Trade Union 'Problem' in British Politics," in B. Pimlott and C. Cook (eds.), *Trade Unions in British Politics*, London: Longman, 1982, pp. 192–207.

Taylor, R., "The Heath Government, Industrial Policy and the 'New Capitalism'," in Ball and Seldon (eds.) *The Heath Government*, pp. 139–159.

Taylor, R., "The Heath Government and Industrial Relations: Myth and Reality," in Ball and Seldon (eds.) *The Heath Government*, pp. 161–190.

Tebbit, N., *Upwardly Mobile*, London: Weidenfield and Nicolson, 1988.

Tebbit, N., *Upwardly Mobile*, London: Futura, 1991.

Thatcher, M., *Speech to the Conservative Party Conference*, Brighton, October 1980. Conservative Party archives are available at the British Library on microfilm, via: www.bl.uk/services/document/microrescoll/rescola.html.

Thatcher, M., "Interview," *Sunday Times*, May 3, 1981.

Thatcher, M., "Speech to Conservative Rally at Cheltenham," *Margaret Thatcher Foundation*, July 3, 1982, online, available at: www.margaretthatcher.org/ speeches/display-document.asp?docid=104989 (accessed June 4, 2007).

*The Economist*, "Britannia Redux: A Special Report on Britain," London, February 3, 2007.

Theakston, K., "Review of Hugh Pemberton's *Policy Learning*," *Public Administration* 84 (1), 2006, pp. 221–244.

Thelen, K., "Historical Institutionalism and Comparative Politics," *Annual Review of Political Science* (2), 1999, pp. 369–404.

Thomas, B., "Labour Market Structure and the Nature of Unemployment in Interwar Britain," in B. Eichengreen and T. Hatton (eds.), *Interwar Unemployment in International Perspective*, Dordrecht: Kluwer, 1988, pp. 97–148.

Thomas, M., "The Macro-economics of the Inter-war Years," in R. Floud and D. McCloskey (eds.), *The Economic History of Britain since 1700, Volume 2: 1860–1939*, second edition, Cambridge: Cambridge University Press, 1994, pp. 320–358.

Thomson, D., *England in the Twentieth Century: 1914–1963*, Harmondsworth: Penguin Books, 1965.

*Time Magazine*, "Unexpected Triumph," June 29, 1970, online, available at: www.time.com/time/magazine/printout/0,8816,878837,00.html (accessed August 15, 2006).

Tomlinson, J., *Democratic Socialism and Economic Policy: The Attlee Years 1945–1951*, Cambridge: Cambridge University Press, 1997.

Toynbee, P., "We Will Never Abolish Child Poverty in a Society Shaped Like This One," *The Guardian*, July 7, 2006, online, available at: society.guardian.co.uk/ comment/column/0,,1814840,00.html (accessed May 20, 2007).

Turner, A., *Mansion House Speech*, London: Financial Services Authority, September 22, 2009, online, available at: www.fsa.gov.uk/pages/Library/Communication/ Speeches/2009 /0922_at.shtml (accessed March 5, 2010).

Vaitilingham, R., *The UK's productivity gap: What research tells us and what we need to find out*, London: Economic and Social Research Council, September 2004.

Van Evera, S., *Guide to Methods for Students of Political Science*. Ithaca: Cornell University Press, 1997.

Wade, R., "From 'Miracle' to 'Cronyism': Explaining the Great Asian Slump," *Cambridge Journal of Economics* 22, 1998, pp. 693–706.

Wales, *Economic Statistics Monthly*, March 2010, online, available at: www.wales.gov.uk/docs/statistics (accessed May 3, 2010).

Webster, C., "Health, Welfare and Unemployment during the Depression," *Past and Present* 109, November 1985, pp. 204–230.

Weir, M. and T. Skocpol, "State Structures and the Possibilities for 'Keynesian' Responses to the Great Depression in Sweden, Britain and the United States," in P. Evans, D. Rueschemeyer and T. Skocpol (eds.), *Bringing the State Back In*, Cambridge: Cambridge University Press, 1985, pp. 107–163.

Wells, J., "Uneven Development and De-industrialisation in the UK since 1979," in F. Green (ed.), *The Restructuring of the UK Economy*, Hemel Hempstead: Harvester Wheatsheaf, 1989, pp. 25–64.

Wendt, A., *The Social Theory of International Politics*, Cambridge: Cambridge University Press, 1999.

Wheatcroft, G., "The Tragedy of Tony Blair," *The Atlantic Monthly* 294, June 2004, pp. 56–70.

Wheatcroft, G., *The Strange Death of Tory England*, London: Allen Lane, 2005.

Wheatcroft, G., *Yo, Blair!: Tony Blair's Disastrous Premiership*, London: Politico's, 2007.

White, M., "The Gift of Tired Tongues," *The Guardian*, September 30, 1994.

Wickham-Jones, M., *Economic Strategy and the Labour Party: Politics and Policy-Making, 1970–1983*, London: Palgrave Macmillan, 1996.

Wickham-Jones, M., "Right Turn: A Revisionist Account of the 1975 Conservative Party Leadership Election," *Twentieth Century British History* 8 (1), 1997, pp. 74–89.

Wilby, P., "Thatcherism's Final Triumph," *Prospect*, October 2006, pp. 28–29.

Wildavsky, A., "Choosing Preferences by Constructing Institutions: A Cultural Theory of Preference Formation," *American Political Science Review* 81 (1), March 1987, pp. 3–22.

Williamson, J., "What Washington Means by Policy Reform," in J. Williamson (ed.) *Latin American Adjustment: How Much Has Happened?*, Washington, DC: Peterson Institute for International Economics, 1990, chapter 2, online, available at: www.iie.com/publications/papers/print.cfm?doc=pub&ResearchID =486 (accessed June 4, 2009).

Wilson, H., *Speech at the Labour Party Conference,* Scarborough, October 1, 1963. Labour Party archives are available at the British Library on microfilm, via: www.bl.uk/services/document/microrescoll/rescola.html.

Wincott, D., "Review of Mark Blyth's *Great Transformations*," *West European Politics* 26 (4), October 2003, pp. 247–259.

Wolf, M., "Why the Sky may not be Falling," *Financial Times*, London, September 4, 2008.

Wolf, M., "Re: Your two op-eds in the FT this week," email, September 5, 2008.

Wolf, M., "How to Share the Losses: The Dismal Choice Facing Britain," *Financial Times*, December 16, 2009.

Wolf, M., "The British Election that Both Sides Deserve to Lose," *Financial Times*, March 12, 2010.

WTO, *International Trade Statistics*, Geneva: World Trade Organization, 2006.

Yergin, D. and J. Stanislaw, *The Commanding Heights: The Battle for the World Economy*, New York: Touchstone, 2002.

Young, H., *One of Us*, London: Pan Books, 1991.

Young, H., *This Blessed Plot*, London: Macmillan, 1998.

Young, J., "The Heath Government and British Entry into the European Community," in Ball and Seldon (eds.) *The Heath Government*, pp. 259–284.

# Index

For Product Safety Concerns and Information please contact our EU
representative GPSR@taylorandfrancis.com
Taylor & Francis Verlag GmbH, Kaufingerstraße 24, 80331 München, Germany